RWANDA

ENERGY POLICY, LAWS AND REGUILATIONS HANDBOOK

VOLUME 1

STRATEGIC INFORMATION, BASIC REGULATIONS, CONTACTS

International Business Publications, USA
Washington DC, USA - Rwanda

RWANDA

ENERGY POLICY, LAWS AND REGUILATIONS HANDBOOK

VOLUME 1 STRATEGIC INFORMATION, BASIC REGULATIONS, CONTACTS

UPDATED ANNUALLY

We express our sincere appreciation to all government agencies and international organizations which provided information and other materials for this handbook

Cover Design: **International Business Publications, USA**

2017 Edition Updated Reprint International Business Publications, USA
ISBN 1-4330-7252-1
For customer service and information, please contact:

in the USA: **International Business Publications, USA**
For additional analytical, business and investment opportunities information, please contact at (703) 370-8082. Fax: (703) 370-8083. E-mail: ibpusa3@gmail.com
Global Business and Investment Info Databank - www.ibpus.com

Printed in the USA

RWANDA

ENERGY POLICY, LAWS AND REGUILATIONS HANDBOOK

VOLUME 1

STRATEGIC INFORMATION, BASIC REGULATIONS, CONTACTS

TABLE OF CONTENTS

STRATEGIC AND DEVELOPMENT PROFILES

BASIC PROFILE

Capital (and largest city)	Kigali 1°56.633′S 30°3.567′E1.943883°S 30.05945°E
Official language(s)	Kinyarwanda, French, English
Demonym	Rwandan, Rwandese
Government	Unitary parliamentary democracy and Presidential republic
- President	Paul Kagame
- Prime Minister	Pierre Habumuremyi
	Independence
- from Belgium	1 July 1962
	Area
- Total	26,338 km^2 (148th) 10,169 sq mi
- Water (%)	5.3
	Population
- 2011 estimate	11,370,425 (73rd)
- 2002 census	8,162,715[2]
- Density	419.8/km^2 (29th) 1,087.2/sq mi
GDP (PPP)	2011 estimate
- Total	\$13.109 billion[3]
- Per capita	\$1,284[3]
GDP (nominal)	2011 estimate
- Total	\$6.055 billion[3]
- Per capita	\$593[3]
Gini (2003)	41.1 (medium)
HDI (2010)	▲0.385[4] (low) (152nd)
Currency	Rwandan franc (RWF)
Time zone	CAT (UTC+2)
- Summer (DST)	not observed (UTC+2)
Drives on the	right
ISO 3166 code	RW
Internet TLD	.rw
Calling code	250

[1] Estimates for this country explicitly take into account the effects of excess mortality due to AIDS; this can result in lower life expectancy, higher infant mortality and death rates, lower population and growth rates, and changes in the distribution of population by age and sex than would otherwise be expected.

Rwanda is a sovereign state in central and east Africa and one of the smallest countries on the African mainland. Located a few degrees south of the Equator, Rwanda is bordered by Uganda, Tanzania, Burundi and the Democratic Republic of the Congo. Rwanda is in the African Great Lakes region and is highly elevated; its geography dominated by mountains in the west and savanna to the east, with numerous lakes throughout the country. The climate is temperate to subtropical, with two rainy seasons and two dry seasons each year.

The population is young and predominantly rural, with a density among the highest in Africa. Rwandans are drawn from just one cultural and linguistic group, the Banyarwanda, although within this group there are three subgroups: the Hutu, Tutsi and Twa. The Twa are a forest-dwelling pygmy people descended from Rwanda's earliest inhabitants. Scholars disagree on the origins of and differences between the Hutu and Tutsi; some believe differences are derived from former social castes within a single people, while others believe the Hutu and Tutsi arrived in the country separately, and from different locations. Christianity is the largest religion in the country; the principal language is Kinyarwanda, spoken by most Rwandans, with French and English serving as official languages. Rwanda has a presidential system of government. The president is Paul Kagame of the Rwandan Patriotic Front (RPF), who took office in 2000. Rwanda today has low corruption compared with neighbouring countries, although human rights organisations report suppression of opposition groups, intimidation and restrictions on freedom of speech. The country has been governed by a strict administrative hierarchy since precolonial times; there are five provinces delineated by borders drawn in 2006. Rwanda is one of only two countries with a female majority in the national parliament.

Hunter gatherers settled the territory in the stone and iron ages, followed later by Bantu peoples. The population coalesced first into clans and then into kingdoms. The Kingdom of Rwanda dominated from the mid-eighteenth century, with the Tutsi kings conquering others militarily, centralising power, and later enacting anti-Hutu policies. Germany colonised Rwanda in 1884 as part of German East Africa, followed by Belgium, which invaded in 1916 during World War I. Both European nations ruled through the kings and perpetuated a pro-Tutsi policy. The Hutu population revolted in 1959. They massacred numerous Tutsi and ultimately established an independent, Hutu-dominated state in 1962. The Tutsi-led Rwandan Patriotic Front launched a civil war in 1990. Social tensions erupted in the 1994 genocide, in which Hutu extremists killed an estimated 500,000 to 1 million Tutsi and moderate Hutu. The RPF ended the genocide with a military victory.

Rwanda's economy suffered heavily during the 1994 Rwandan Genocide, but has since strengthened. The economy is based mostly on subsistence agriculture. Coffee and tea are the major cash crops for export. Tourism is a fast-growing sector and is now the country's leading foreign exchange earner. Rwanda is one of only two countries in which mountain gorillas can be visited safely, and visitors are prepared to pay high prices for gorilla tracking permits. Music and dance are an integral part of Rwandan culture, particularly drums and the highly choreographed *intore* dance. Traditional arts and crafts are produced throughout the country.

STRATEGIC PROFILE

Background: Throughout their colonial rule, first Germany and then Belgium favored Rwanda's minority Tutsi ethnic group in education and employment. In 1959, the majority ethnic group, the Hutus, overthrew the ruling Tutsi monarch. The Hutus killed hundreds of Tutsis and drove tens of thousands into exile in neighboring countries. The children of these exiles later formed a rebel group, the Rwandan Patriotic Front (RPF), and began a civil war in October 1990. The war, along with several political and economic upheavals, exasperated ethnic tensions culminating in April 1994 in a genocide in which roughly 800,000 Tutsis and moderate Hutus were killed.

The Tutsi rebels defeated the Hutu regime and ended the genocide in July 1994, but approximately 2 million Hutu refugees -many fearing Tutsi retribution - fled to neighboring Burundi, Tanzania, Uganda, and Zaire, now called the Democratic Republic of the Congo (DROC). According to the UN Office of the High Commissioner for Refugees, in 1996 and early 1997 nearly 1.3 million Hutus returned to Rwanda. Even with substantial international aid, these civil dislocations have hindered efforts to foster reconciliation and to boost investment and agricultural output. Although much of the country is now at peace, members of the former regime continue to destabilize the northwest area of the country through a low-intensity insurgency. Rwandan troops are currently involved in a crisis engulfing neighboring DROC.

RWANDA, A COUNTRY OF A THOUSAND HILLS

Rwanda is etended over an exiguous territory of 26,338 square kilometers. It is a small country in the heart of Africa with almost 7,223,255 inhabitants. Rwanda possesses natural ressources of exceptional beauty and variety: its countless lakes and rivers, fauna and flora as well as its magnificient volcanoes and mountains, natural ressources, its expressive folklore and traditional handcraft ...constitute a considerable source of attraction and assets for the country.

Rwanda is located in the Great Lakes region between the Central and Eastern parts of Africa and shares common borders with:

- Uganda in the North
- Burundi in the South
- The Democratic Republic of Congo in the West
- Tanzania in the East

Rwanda is a land-locked country, with no access to the Ocean: The Indian ocean is 1200 km and the Atlantic ocean is 2200 km away from Rwanda. The country is between the 7 400km distance from the Cape to Cairo.

Because of its countless elevations, Rwanda is known as a country of a thousand hills. It is also called "country of perpetual spring". Throughout the year, country has favourable climate: soft, sunny, stable and temperate. The average annual temperature is 18°C. It results from the effect of the trade wind and the coolness from its mountains.

The climate of Rwanda is caracterized by:

- A short rainy season from September to December
- A short dry season from end of January to February
- A long rainy season from March to end of May
- A long dry season from June to August

BASIC INFORMATION

Location: Central Africa, east of Democratic Republic of the Congo
Geographic coordinates: 2 00 S, 30 00 E
Map references: Africa

Area:
total: 26,340 sq km
land: 24,950 sq km
water: 1,390 sq km

Area—comparative: slightly smaller than Maryland

Land boundaries:
total: 893 km

Rwanda and Burundi

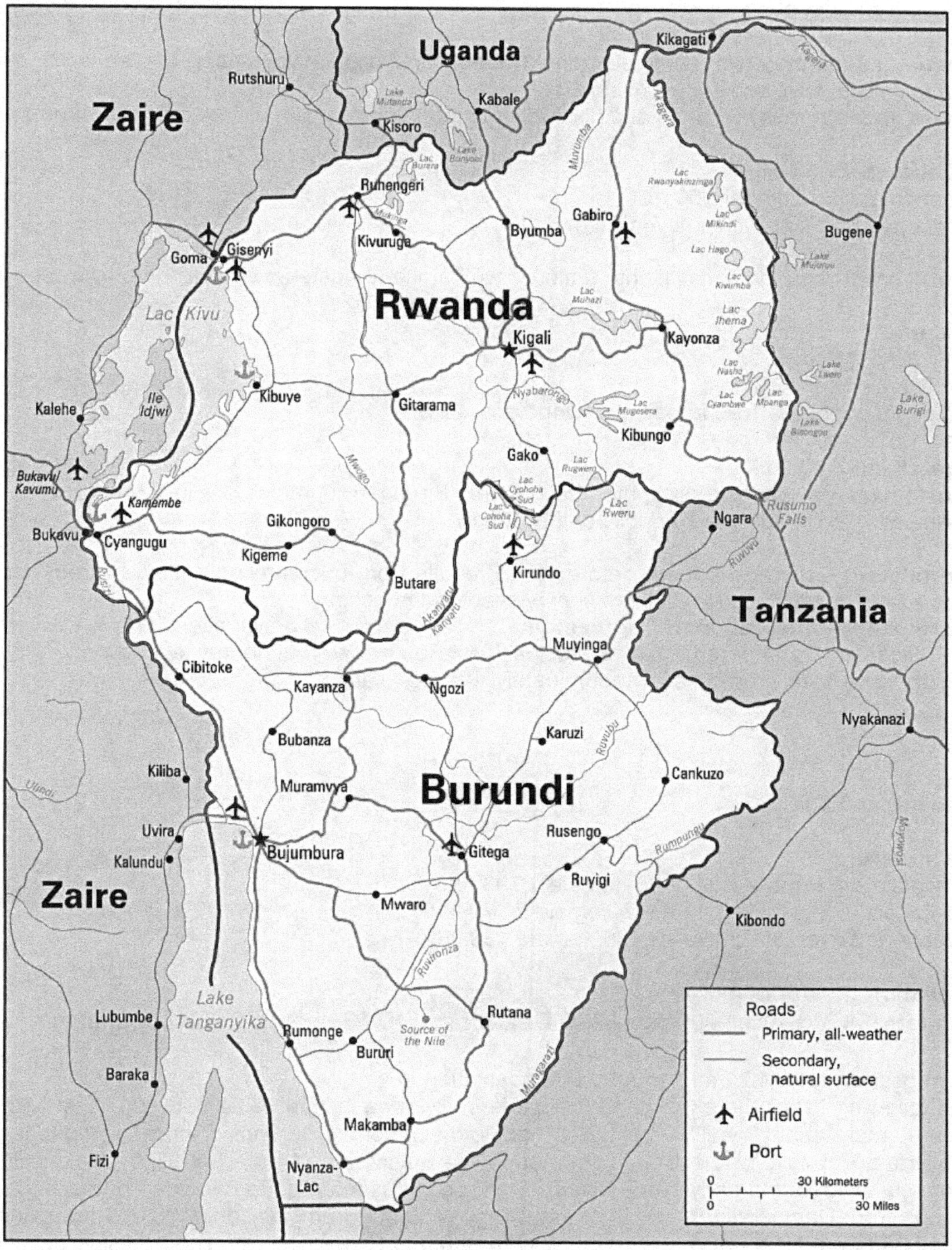

740959 (R01374) 11-96

border countries: Burundi 290 km, Democratic Republic of the Congo 217 km, Tanzania 217 km, Uganda 169 km

Coastline: 0 km (landlocked)
Maritime claims: none (landlocked)

Climate: temperate; two rainy seasons (February to April, November to January); mild in mountains with frost and snow possible
Terrain: mostly grassy uplands and hills; relief is mountainous with altitude declining from west to east
Elevation extremes:
lowest point: Rusizi River 950 m
highest point: Volcan Karisimbi 4,519 m

Natural resources: gold, cassiterite (tin ore), wolframite (tungsten ore), methane, hydropower

Land use:
arable land: 35%
permanent crops: 13%
permanent pastures: 18% forests and woodland: 22%
other: 12%
Irrigated land: 40 sq km
Natural hazards: periodic droughts; the volcanic Birunga mountains are in the northwest along the border with Democratic Republic of the Congo

Environment—current issues: deforestation results from uncontrolled cutting of trees for fuel; overgrazing; soil exhaustion; soil erosion; widespread poaching
Environment—international agreements: party to: Biodiversity, Climate Change, Desertification, Endangered Species, Nuclear Test Ban signed, but not ratified: Law of the Sea
Geography—note: landlocked; predominantly rural population

PEOPLE

Population: 8,154,933

Age structure:
0-14 years: 44% (male 1,807,695; female 1,793,590)
15-64 years: 53% (male 2,148,477; female 2,179,119)
65 years and over: 3% (male 92,490; female 133,562)

Population growth rate: 2.43%
Birth rate: 38.97 births/1,000 population **Death rate**: 19.53 deaths/1,000 population

Net migration rate: 4.91 migrant(s)/1,000 population
note: following the outbreak of genocidal strife in Rwanda in April 1994 between Tutsi and Hutu factions, more than 2 million refugees fled to neighboring Burundi, Tanzania, Uganda, and Democratic Republic of the Congo (formerly Zaire); according to the UN High Commission on Refugees, in 1996 and early 1997 nearly 1.3 million Hutus returned to Rwanda - of these 720,000 returned from Democratic Republic of the Congo, 480,000 from Tanzania, 88,000 from Burundi, and 10,000 from Uganda; probably fewer than 100,000 Rwandans remained outside of Rwanda by the end of 1997
Sex ratio:
at birth: 1.03 male(s)/female

under 15 years: 1.01 male(s)/female
15-64 years: 0.99 male(s)/female
65 years and over: 0.69 male(s)/female
total population: 0.99 male(s)/female

Infant mortality rate: 112.86 deaths/1,000 live births

Life expectancy at birth:
total population: 41.31 years
male: 40.84 years
female: 41.8 years

Total fertility rate: 5.8 children born/woman

NATIONALITY

noun: Rwandan(s)
adjective: Rwandan
Ethnic groups: Hutu 80%, Tutsi 19%, Twa (Pygmoid) 1%
Religions: Roman Catholic 65%, Protestant 9%, Muslim 1%, indigenous beliefs and other 25%
Languages: Kinyarwanda (official) universal Bantu vernacular, French (official), English (official), Kiswahili (Swahili) used in commercial centers
Literacy:
definition: age 15 and over can read and write
total population: 60.5%
male: 69.8%
female: 51.6%

GOVERNMENT

Country name:
conventional long form: Rwandese Republic
conventional short form: Rwanda
local long form: Republika y'u Rwanda
local short form: Rwanda

Data code: RW
Government type: republic; presidential, multiparty system
Capital: Kigali
Administrative divisions: 12 prefectures (in French—prefectures, singular—prefecture; in Kinyarwanda—plural—NA, singular—prefegitura); Butare, Byumba, Cyangugu, Gikongoro, Gisenyi, Gitarama, Kibungo, Kibuye, Kigali, Kigaliville, Umutara, Ruhengeri

Independence: 1 July 1962 (from Belgium-administered UN trusteeship)
National holiday: Independence Day, 1 July (1962)

Constitution: on 5 May 1995, the Transitional National Assembly adopted a new constitution which included elements of the constitution of 18 June 1991 as well as provisions of the 1993 Arusha peace accord and the November 1994 multi-party protocol of understanding

Legal system: based on German and Belgian civil law systems and customary law; judicial review of legislative acts in the Supreme Court; has not accepted compulsory ICJ jurisdiction

Suffrage: NA years of age; universal adult

Executive branch:
chief of state: President Paul KAGAME (since 22 April 2000)

head of government: Prime Minister Pierre Damien HABUMUREMYI (since 7 October 2011)

cabinet: Council of Ministers appointed by the president
elections: President elected by popular vote for a seven-year term (eligible for a second term); elections last held on 9 August 2010 (next to be held in 2017)

election results: Paul KAGAME elected to a second term as president; Paul KAGAME 93.1%, Jean NTAWUKURIRYAYO 5.1%, Prosper HIGIRO 1.4%, Alvera MUKABAR 0.4%

Legislative branch:
description: bicameral Parliament consists of the Senate or Senat (26 seats; 12 members indirectly elected by local councils, 8 appointed by the president, 4 appointed by the Political Organizations Forum - a body of registered political parties, and 2 selected by institutions of higher learning; members serve 8-year terms) and the Chamber of Deputies or Chambre des Deputes (80 seats; 53 members directly elected by proportional representation vote, 24 women elected by special interest groups, and 3 selected by youth and disability organizations; members serve 5-year terms)
elections: Senate - NA; Chamber of Deputies - last held on 16-18 September 2013 (next to be held in 2018)
election results: Chamber of Deputies percent of vote by party - RPF 76.2%, PSD 13%, PL 9.3%, other 1.5%; seats by party - RPF 41, PSD 7, PL 5, 27 members indirectly elected

Judicial branch: Constitutional Court, consists of the Court of Cassation and the Council of State in joint session

Political parties and leaders: significant parties include: Rwandan Patriotic Front or RPF [Charles MULIGANDE, secretary general]; Democratic Republican Movement or MDR [leader NA]; Liberal Party or PL [leader NA]; Democratic and Socialist Party or PSD [leader NA]; Christian Democratic Party or PDC [leader NA]; Islamic Democratic Party or PDI [leader NA]; Rwandan Socialist Party or PSR [leader NA]; National Movement for Democracy and Development or MRND (former ruling party) [leader NA]

Political pressure groups and leaders: Rwanda Patriotic Army or RPA [Maj. Gen. Paul KAGAME, commander]; Rally for the Democracy and Return (RDR)

International organization participation: ACCT, ACP, AfDB, CCC, CEEAC, CEPGL, ECA, FAO, G-77, IBRD, ICAO, ICFTU, ICRM, IDA, IFAD, IFC, IFRCS, ILO, IMF, Intelsat, Interpol, IOC, IOM (observer), ITU, NAM, OAU, OPCW, UN, UNCTAD, UNESCO, UNIDO, UPU, WCL, WHO, WIPO, WMO, WToO, WTrO

DIPLOMATIC REPRESENTATION IN THE US:

chief of mission: Ambassador Theogene N. RUDASINGWA
chancery: 1714 New Hampshire Ave. NW, Washington, DC 20009
telephone: (202) 232-2882
FAX: (202) 232-4544

Diplomatic representation from the US:
chief of mission: Ambassador George M. STAPLES
embassy: Boulevard de la Revolution, Kigali
mailing address: B. P. 28, Kigali
telephone: [250] 756 01 through 03, 721 26, 771 47
FAX: [250] 721 28

Flag description: three equal vertical bands of red (hoist side), yellow, and green with a large black letter R centered in the yellow band; uses the popular pan-African colors of Ethiopia; similar to the flag of Guinea, which has a plain yellow band

ECONOMY

Rwanda is a rural country with about 90% of the population engaged in subsistence agriculture and some mineral and agro-processing. Tourism, minerals, coffee and tea are Rwanda's main sources of foreign exchange. Despite Rwanda's fertile ecosystem, food production often does not keep pace with demand, requiring food imports. Energy shortages, instability in neighboring states, and lack of adequate transportation linkages to other countries continue to handicap private sector growth.

The 1994 genocide decimated Rwanda's fragile economic base, severely impoverished the population, particularly women, and temporarily stalled the country's ability to attract private and external investment. However, Rwanda has made substantial progress in stabilizing and rehabilitating its economy to pre-1994 levels. GDP has rebounded with an average annual growth of 7%-8% since 2003 and inflation has been reduced to single digits. Nonetheless, in 2015, 39% of the population lived below the poverty line, according to government statistics, compared to 57% in 2006.

Africa's most densely populated country is trying to overcome the limitations of its small, landlocked economy by leveraging regional trade; Rwanda joined the East African Community and is aligning its budget, trade, and immigration policies with its regional partners. The government has embraced an expansionary fiscal policy to reduce poverty by improving education, infrastructure, and foreign and domestic investment, and pursuing market-oriented reforms. In recognition of Rwanda's successful management of its macro economy, in 2010, the IMF graduated Rwanda to a Policy Support Instrument.

The Rwandan Government is seeking to become a regional leader in information and communication technologies. In 2012, Rwanda completed the first modern Special Economic Zone (SEZ) in Kigali. The SEZ seeks to attract investment in all sectors, but specifically in agribusiness, information and communications, trade and logistics, mining, and construction.

GDP (purchasing power parity):

$21.97 billion (2016 est.)
$20.73 billion (2015 est.)
$19.39 billion (2014 est.)
note: data are in 2016 dollars
country comparison to the world: 142

GDP (official exchange rate):
$8.341 billion (2015 est.)

GDP - real growth rate:
6% (2016 est.)
6.9% (2015 est.)
7% (2014 est.)
country comparison to the world: 21

GDP - per capita (PPP):
$1,900 (2016 est.)
$1,800 (2015 est.)
$1,800 (2014 est.)
note: data are in 2016 dollars
country comparison to the world: 208

Gross national saving:
12.9% of GDP (2016 est.)
12.8% of GDP (2015 est.)
15.6% of GDP (2014 est.)
country comparison to the world: 134

GDP - composition, by end use:
household consumption: 77.8%
government consumption: 11.4%
investment in fixed capital: 26.4%
investment in inventories: 0.6%
exports of goods and services: 13.6%
imports of goods and services: -29.8% (2016 est.)

GDP - composition, by sector of origin:
agriculture: 34.6%
industry: 15.1%
services: 50.3% (2016 est.)

Agriculture - products:
coffee, tea, pyrethrum (insecticide made from chrysanthemums), bananas, beans, sorghum, potatoes; livestock
Industries:
cement, agricultural products, small-scale beverages, soap, furniture, shoes, plastic goods, textiles, cigarettes

Industrial production growth rate:
6.9% (2016 est.)
country comparison to the world: 18

Labor force:
6.03 million (2016 est.)
country comparison to the world: 70

Labor force - by occupation:
agriculture: 90%
industry and services: 10%

Population below poverty line:
39.1% (2015 est.)

Household income or consumption by percentage share:
lowest 10%: 2.1%
highest 10%: 43.2% (2011 est.)

Distribution of family income - Gini index:
46.8 (2000)
28.9 (1985)
country comparison to the world: 30

Budget:
revenues: $1.865 billion
expenditures: $2.279 billion (2016 est.)

Taxes and other revenues:
22.4% of GDP (2016 est.)
country comparison to the world: 133

Budget surplus (+) or deficit (-):
-5% of GDP (2016 est.)
country comparison to the world: 159

Public debt:
36.6% of GDP (2016 est.)
33.9% of GDP (2015 est.)
country comparison to the world: 127

Fiscal year:
calendar year

Inflation rate (consumer prices):
4.6% (2016 est.)
2.5% (2015 est.)
country comparison to the world: 173

Central bank discount rate:
7.75% (31 December 2010)
11.25% (31 December 2008)
country comparison to the world: 42

Commercial bank prime lending rate:
17.3% (31 December 2016 est.)
17.33% (31 December 2015 est.)
country comparison to the world: 27

Stock of narrow money:
$957.3 million (31 December 2016 est.)
$1.013 billion (31 December 2015 est.)
country comparison to the world: 154
Stock of broad money:
$1.817 billion (31 December 2016 est.)
$1.64 billion (31 December 2015 est.)
country comparison to the world: 159

Stock of domestic credit:
$1.891 billion (31 December 2016 est.)
$1.337 billion (31 December 2015 est.)
country comparison to the world: 141

Current account balance:
-$1.385 billion (2016 est.)
-$1.096 billion (2015 est.)
country comparison to the world: 138

Exports:
$674.9 million (2016 est.)
$683.7 million (2015 est.)
country comparison to the world: 167

Exports - commodities:
coffee, tea, hides, tin ore

Exports - partners:
Democratic Republic of the Congo 19.8%, US 10.8%, China 10.3%, Swaziland 7.9%, Malaysia 7%, Pakistan 6.2%, Germany 5.9%, Thailand 5.5% (2015)
Imports:
$1.961 billion (2016 est.)
$1.917 billion (2015 est.)
country comparison to the world: 161

Imports - commodities:
foodstuffs, machinery and equipment, steel, petroleum products, cement and construction material

Imports - partners:
Uganda 15.7%, Kenya 11.8%, India 8.7%, China 8.7%, UAE 8.6%, Russia 6.6%, Tanzania 5.1% (2015)

Reserves of foreign exchange and gold:
$756.3 million (31 December 2016 est.)
$1.03 billion (31 December 2015 est.)
country comparison to the world: 134

Debt - external:
$2.442 billion (31 December 2016 est.)
$2.178 billion (31 December 2015 est.)
country comparison to the world: 145

Stock of direct foreign investment - at home:
$1.779 billion (31 December 2016 est.)
$1.484 billion (31 December 2015 est.)
country comparison to the world: 110

Stock of direct foreign investment - abroad:
$25.6 million (31 December 2016 est.)
$25.6 million (31 December 2015 est.)

country comparison to the world: 103

Exchange rates:
Rwandan francs (RWF) per US dollar -
787.9 (2016 est.)
720.54 (2015 est.)
720.54 (2014 est.)
680.95 (2013 est.)
616.6 (2012 est.)

ENERGY

Electricity - production:
500 million kWh (2014 est.)
country comparison to the world: 168

Electricity - consumption:
500 million kWh (2014 est.)
country comparison to the world: 173

Electricity - exports:
3 million kWh (2014 est.)
country comparison to the world: 96

Electricity - imports:
95 million kWh (2014 est.)
country comparison to the world: 98

Electricity - installed generating capacity:
100,000 kW (2014 est.)
country comparison to the world: 170

Electricity - from fossil fuels:
34.3% of total installed capacity (2012 est.)
country comparison to the world: 170

Electricity - from nuclear fuels:
0% of total installed capacity (2012 est.)
country comparison to the world: 75

Electricity - from hydroelectric plants:
65.7% of total installed capacity (2012 est.)
country comparison to the world: 32

Electricity - from other renewable sources:
0% of total installed capacity (2012 est.)
country comparison to the world: 174

Crude oil - production:
0 bbl/day (2015 est.)
country comparison to the world: 186

Crude oil - exports:
0 bbl/day (2013 est.)

country comparison to the world: 123

Crude oil - imports:
0 bbl/day (2013 est.)
country comparison to the world: 119

Crude oil - proved reserves:
0 bbl (1 January 2016 es)
country comparison to the world: 133

Refined petroleum products - production:
0 bbl/day (2013 est.)
country comparison to the world: 138

Refined petroleum products - consumption:
6,000 bbl/day (2014 est.)
country comparison to the world: 170

Refined petroleum products - exports:
0 bbl/day (2013 est.)
country comparison to the world: 153

Refined petroleum products - imports:
5,979 bbl/day (2013 est.)
country comparison to the world: 159

Natural gas - production:
0 cu m (2013 est.)
country comparison to the world: 130

Natural gas - consumption:
0 cu m (2013 est.)
country comparison to the world: 188

Natural gas - exports:
0 cu m (2013 est.)
country comparison to the world: 99

Natural gas - imports:
0 cu m (2013 est.)
country comparison to the world: 186

Natural gas - proved reserves:
56.63 billion cu m (1 January 2016 es)
country comparison to the world: 61

Carbon dioxide emissions from consumption of energy:
800,000 Mt (2013 est.)
country comparison to the world: 172

COMMUNICATIONS

Telephones - main 22,000

lines in use:	
Telephones - mobile cellular:	290,000
Telephone system:	*general assessment:* telephone system primarily serves business and government *domestic:* the capital, Kigali, is connected to the centers of the provinces by microwave radio relay and, recently, by cellular telephone service; much of the network depends on wire and HF radiotelephone *international:* country code - 250; international connections employ microwave radio relay to neighboring countries and satellite communications to more distant countries; satellite earth stations - 1 Intelsat (Indian Ocean) in Kigali (includes telex and telefax service)
Radio broadcast stations:	AM 0, FM 8 (two main FM programs are broadcast through a system of repeaters, three international FM programs include the BBC, VOA, and Deutchewelle), shortwave 1 (2005)
Television broadcast stations:	2
Internet country code:	.rw
Internet hosts:	1,592
Internet users:	65,000

TRANSPORTATION

Railways: 0 km
Highways:
total: 12,000 km
paved: 1,000 km
unpaved: 11,000 km

Waterways: Lac Kivu navigable by shallow-draft barges and native craft
Ports and harbors: Cyangugu, Gisenyi, Kibuye
Airports: 7
Airports - with paved runways:
total: 4
over 3,047 m: 1
914 to 1,523 m: 2
under 914 m: 1
Airports - with unpaved runways:
total: 3
914 to 1,523 m: 1
under 914 m: 2

MILITARY

Military branches: Army, Gendarmerie
Military manpower - availability:
males age 15-49: 1,964,118
Military manpower - fit for military service:
males age 15-49: 1,000,204

Military expenditures - dollar figure: $92 million
Military expenditures - percent of GDP: 3.8%

TRANSNATIONAL ISSUES

Burundi and Rwanda dispute two sq km (0.8 sq mi) of Sabanerwa, a farmed area in the Rukurazi Valley where the Akanyaru/Kanyaru River shifted its course southward after heavy rains in 1965; fighting among ethnic groups - loosely associated political rebels, armed gangs, and various government forces in Great Lakes region transcending the boundaries of Burundi, Democratic Republic of the Congo (DROC), Rwanda, and Uganda - abated substantially from a decade ago due largely to UN peacekeeping, international mediation, and efforts by local governments to create civil societies; nonetheless, 57,000 Rwandan refugees still reside in 21 African states, including Zambia, Gabon, and 20,000 who fled to Burundi in 2005 and 2006 to escape drought and recriminations from traditional courts investigating the 1994 massacres; the 2005 DROC and Rwanda border verification mechanism to stem rebel actions on both sides of the border remains in place
Refugees and internally displaced persons:
refugees (country of origin): 77,610 (Burundi); 73,992 (Democratic Republic of the Congo) (2016)
IDPs: undetermined (fighting between government and insurgency in 1998-99; returning refugees) (2012)

IMPORTANT INFORMATION FOR UNDERSTANDING RWANDA[1]

PROFILE

Geography

Area: 26,338 sq. km. (10,169 sq. km.); about the size of Maryland.
Cities: *Capital*--Kigali (est. pop. 800,000). *Other cities*--Muhanga (formerly Gitarama), Huye (formerly Butare), Musanze (formerly Ruhengeri), Rubavu (formerly Gisenyi).
Terrain: Uplands and hills.
Climate: Mild and temperate, with two rainy seasons.

People

Nationality: *Noun and adjective*--Rwandan(s); Rwandese.
Population (est.): approximately 9,997,614.
Annual population growth rate (2008 est.): 2.8%.
Religions (2002 est.): Christian 93.5%, traditional African 0.1%, Muslim 4.6%, 1.7% claim no religious beliefs.
Languages: Kinyarwanda, French, English.
Education: *Years compulsory*--9. *Attendance* (prewar)--75%. *Literacy* (2008)--70%.
Health: *Infant mortality rate* (2008 est., Rwandan Government)--62 deaths/1,000. *Life expectancy* (2008 est.)--49.8 years.
Work force (2000): *Agriculture*--90%; *industry and commerce, services, and government*--10%.

Government

Type: Republic.
Independence: July 1, 1962.
Constitution: May 26, 2003.
Branches: *Executive*--president (chief of state), prime minister (head of government). Broad-based government of national unity formed after the 1994 genocide. *Legislative*--80-seat Chamber of Deputies; 26-member Senate. *Judicial*--Supreme Court; High Courts of the Republic; Provincial Courts; District Courts; mediation committees.
Administrative subdivisions: 4 provinces plus Kigali; 30 districts; 416 sectors; 2,148 cells.
Political parties: There are 10 political parties, including the ruling Rwandan Patriotic Front (RPF), which leads a coalition that includes the Centrist Democratic Party (PDC), the Rwandan Socialist Party (PSR), the Ideal [formerly Islamic] Democratic Party (PDI), the Prosperity and Solidarity Party (PSP), and the Democratic Popular Union (UPDR). Other parties include the Social Democratic Party (PSD), the Liberal Party (PL), the Concord Progressive Party (PPC), and the Social Party Imberakuri (PS-Imberakuri).
Suffrage: Universal for citizens over 18--except refugees, prisoners, and certain categories of convicts.
Central government budget (2009-2010 est.): 900 billion Rwandan francs ($1.5 billion).

Economy

Agriculture: 36% of GDP. *Products*--coffee, tea, pyrethrum (insecticide made from chrysanthemums), bananas, beans, sorghum, potatoes, livestock.
Industry: 14.2% of GDP. *Types*--cement, agricultural products, beer production, soft drinks, soap, furniture, shoes, plastic goods, textiles, cigarettes, pharmaceuticals.
Services: 43.7%.
Trade (est.): *Exports*--$193 million: tea, coffee, coltan, cassiterite, hides, iron ore, and tin. *Major markets*--China, Belgium, and Germany. *Imports*--$963 million f.o.b.: foodstuffs, machinery and

[1] US State Department Profile

equipment, steel, petroleum products, cement, and construction material. *Major suppliers*--Kenya, Germany, Belgium, France, Uganda, and Israel.

GEOGRAPHY

Rwanda's countryside is covered by grasslands and small farms extending over rolling hills, with areas of rugged mountains that extend southeast from a chain of volcanoes in the northwest. The divide between the Congo and Nile drainage systems extends from north to south through western Rwanda at an average elevation of almost 9,000 feet. On the western slopes of this ridgeline, the land slopes abruptly toward Lake Kivu and the Ruzizi River valley, which form the western boundary with the Democratic Republic of the Congo (formerly Zaire) and constitute part of the Great Rift valley. The eastern slopes are more moderate, with rolling hills extending across central uplands at gradually reducing altitudes, to the plains, swamps, and lakes of the eastern border region.

Although located only two degrees south of the Equator, Rwanda's high elevation makes the climate temperate. The average daily temperature near Lake Kivu, at an altitude of 4,800 feet (1,463 meters) is 73° F (23° C). During the two rainy seasons (February-May and September-December), heavy downpours occur almost daily, alternating with sunny weather. Annual rainfall averages 80 centimeters (31 in.) but is generally heavier in the western and northwestern mountains than in the eastern savannas.

PEOPLE

Rwanda's population density is currently the highest in continental sub-Saharan Africa. It is still a very rural society, and many families live in a self-contained compound on a hillside. The urban concentrations are grouped around administrative centers. The indigenous population consists of three groups, or *ubwoko*--Bahutu, Batutsi, and Batwa. Traditionally, the population also is affiliated with one of 18 clans--all with more than one *ubwoko* or group.

Accounts of the respective arrivals of each *ubwoko* centuries ago in the area of modern Rwanda were highly politicized throughout much of the 20th century, and the Belgian colonialists' "racialization" of differences among *ubwoko* was used by the Rwandan Government to fuel the 1994 state-orchestrated genocide. As part of political efforts to overcome divisions that led to the genocide, the Rwandan Government does not collect data on *ubwoko* and banned its inclusion on identity cards. Rwandans share the same language and culture, so *ubwoko* today reflects a family identity that has been passed patrilineally and often a historical narrative. The Rwandan Government does not permit politicization of this identity, any form of discrimination, or "genocide ideology" (hate speech) based on *ubwoko.*

Education

Until 1994, educational opportunities for Rwandans were extremely limited. After the genocide, most primary schools and more than half of prewar secondary schools reopened, though no more than 5% of the adult population received secondary education through 1996. Although educational quality remains an issue, access to education expanded dramatically in recent years and the Government of Rwanda's Nine-Year Basic Education policy, implemented in 2010, contributed to an increase of the primary school completion rate from 52.4% in 2008 to 75.6% in 2010.

The National University (NUR) in Huye (formerly Butare), Rwanda's sole university prior to 1994, reopened in April 1995; enrollment is over 7,000 students. Today, there are about 20 institutions of higher learning in Rwanda. Between 1963-1993, Rwandan university graduates numbered roughly 1,900; today, Rwandan university graduates exceed 44,000. Seventy percent of the adult population is literate (2008). Rebuilding the educational system continues to be a high priority of the Rwandan Government. Rwanda has three official languages--Kinyarwanda, French, and English. The recent transition to English as the language of instruction in schools presents pedagogical challenges even as if offers prospects for increased opportunity within the East African Community and internationally.

HISTORY

Beginning in the 15th century, Rwandans established a monarchy headed by a Tutsi *mwami* (king) with a hierarchy of Tutsi nobles and gentry. In some areas of the country, independent Hutu principalities continued to exist, and in other areas, Tutsi and Hutu lineages lived in interdependent cooperation under the nominal control of the king. Within the monarchy, through a contract known as *ubuhake*, the Hutu farmers pledged their services and those of their descendants to a Tutsi lord in return for the loan of cattle and use of pastures and arable land, creating a relationship somewhat similar to serfdom. However, membership in a *ubwoko* and class were fluid. Affiliation was determined by paternal ancestors. Intermarriage and multiple marriage was common. Some Hutus took Tutsi status and some Tutsis lost their status as Tutsis. Most rural Tutsis enjoyed few advantages over rural Hutus). The first European known to have visited Rwanda was German Count Von Goetzen in 1894. He was followed by missionaries called the "White Fathers." In 1899, the mwami submitted to a German protectorate without resistance. Belgian troops from Zaire chased the small number of Germans out of Rwanda in 1915 and took control of the country.

After World War I, the League of Nations mandated Rwanda and its southern neighbor, Burundi, to Belgium as the territory of Ruanda-Urundi. Following World War II, Ruanda-Urundi became a UN Trust Territory with Belgium as the administrative authority. Reforms instituted by the Belgians in the 1950s encouraged the growth of democratic political institutions but were resisted by the Tutsi traditionalists who saw in them a threat to Tutsi rule. Hutu leaders, encouraged by the Belgian military, sparked a popular revolt in November 1959, resulting in the overthrow of the Tutsi monarchy. Two years later, the Party of the Hutu Emancipation Movement (PARMEHUTU) won an overwhelming victory in a UN-supervised referendum.

During the 1959 revolt and its aftermath, more than 160,000 Tutsis fled to neighboring countries. The PARMEHUTU government, formed as a result of the September 1961 election, was granted internal autonomy by Belgium on January 1, 1962. A June 1962 UN General Assembly resolution terminated the Belgian trusteeship and granted full independence to Rwanda (and Burundi) effective July 1, 1962.

Gregoire Kayibanda, leader of the PARMEHUTU Party, became Rwanda's first elected president, leading a one-party government chosen from the membership of the directly elected unicameral National Assembly. The Kayibanda government promoted a Hutu-supremacist ideology, and a series of anti-Tutsi "pogroms" and other violence gravely affected internal security and provoked the flight of Rwandan Tutsis.

Rwanda established relations with 43 countries, including the United States, during the first 10 years. Despite some progress made, inefficiency and corruption festered in government ministries in the mid-1960s. On July 5, 1973, the military took power by force under the leadership of Maj. Gen. Juvenal Habyarimana, who dissolved the National Assembly and the PARMEHUTU Party and abolished all political activity.

In 1975, President Habyarimana formed the National Revolutionary Movement for Development (MRND) as Rwanda's only legal party. The movement was organized from the "hillside" to the national level and included elected and appointed officials. During his tenure, violence against

Tutsis continued without effective prosecution of wrongdoers, prompting more exoduses.

Under MRND aegis, Rwandans went to the polls in December 1978, overwhelmingly endorsed a new constitution, and confirmed President Habyarimana as president. President Habyarimana was re-elected in 1983 and again in 1988, when he was the sole candidate. Responding to international as well as public pressure for political reform, President Habyarimana announced in July 1990 his intention to transform Rwanda's one-party state into a multi-party democracy. He also indicated that Rwanda "had no room" for its largely Tutsi population living in exile, so they were not welcome to return to Rwanda.

On October 1, 1990, Rwandan exiles banded together as the Rwandan Patriotic Front (RPF) and invaded Rwanda from their base in Uganda. The rebel force, composed primarily of ethnic Tutsis who had not been allowed to return to Rwanda under the Kayibanda or Habyarimana regimes, blamed the government for failing to democratize and resolve the problems of some 500,000 Tutsi refugees living in the diaspora around the world. The war dragged on for almost 2 years until a cease-fire accord was signed July 12, 1992, in Arusha, Tanzania, fixing a timetable for an end to the fighting and political talks, leading to a peace accord and power sharing, and authorizing a neutral military observer group under the auspices of the Organization for African Unity. A cease-fire took effect July 31, 1992, and political talks began August 10, 1992. The talks concluded in a peace accord that was not implemented.

On April 6, 1994, the airplane carrying President Habyarimana and the President of Burundi was shot down as it prepared to land at Kigali. Both presidents were killed. As though the shooting down was a signal, military and militia groups began rounding up and killing all Tutsis and political moderates, regardless of their *ubwoko*.
The Rwandan prime minister and her 10 Belgian bodyguards were among the first victims. The killing swiftly spread from Kigali to all corners of the country; between April 6 and the beginning of July, a genocide of unprecedented swiftness left an estimated 800,000 Tutsis and moderate Hutus dead at the hands of organized bands of militia--*Interahamwe*. Even ordinary citizens were called on to kill their neighbors, friends, and even family members by local officials and government-sponsored radio; many complied. The president's MRND Party was implicated in organizing many aspects of the genocide.

The RPF battalion stationed in Kigali under the Arusha accords came under attack immediately after the shooting down of the president's plane. The battalion fought its way out of Kigali and joined up with RPF units in the north. The RPF then resumed its invasion, and civil war raged concurrently with the genocide for 2 months. French forces landed in Goma, Zaire, in June 1994 on a humanitarian mission. They deployed throughout southwest Rwanda in an area they called "Zone Turquoise," ostensibly to quell the genocide and stop the fighting there, though some Rwandans asserted that they were complicit; many members of the genocidal rump regime established after the genocide began escaped through the French zone to eastern Congo. The RPF defeated the Rwandan Army, which crossed the border to Zaire followed by some 2 million Rwandans who fled to Zaire, Tanzania, and Burundi as refugees. The RPF took Kigali on July 4, 1994, and the war ended on July 16, 1994. The country was decimated, having been ravaged by war and a brutal genocide. Up to 1 million had been murdered, another 2 million or so had fled, and another million or so were displaced internally.

The international community responded to the humanitarian disaster that developed among the refugees in Zaire with one of the largest humanitarian relief efforts ever mounted. The United States was one of the largest contributors. The UN peacekeeping operation, UNAMIR, was drawn down during the fighting but brought back up to strength after the RPF victory. UNAMIR remained in Rwanda until March 8, 1996.

Following the establishment of armed groups and a local rebellion in the camps in eastern Zaire, Rwandan and Ugandan troops invaded in late 1996. This triggered the return of more than 800,000 back to Rwanda in the last 2 weeks of November, followed at the end of December 1996 by the return of another 500,000 from Tanzania, both of which occurred in huge waves. Fewer than 50,000 Rwandans are estimated to remain outside of Rwanda, and they include remnants of the defeated army of the former genocidal government, its allies in the civilian militias known as *Interahamwe*, soldiers recruited in the refugee camps before 1996, as well as children of those groups and opponents of today's government.

In 2001, with over 120,000 Rwandans in prison and virtually no judicial system in existence (most lawyers and judges had been killed or fled during the genocide), the government began implementing a grassroots village-level justice system, known as *gacaca* to address the enormous backlog of genocide cases. Although many convicted were sentenced to public service rather than prison, because of the continuing high numbers of prisoners, the Government of Rwanda periodically arranged prison releases, including the January 2006 release of approximately 7,000 prisoners. By December 2010, *gacaca* officials reported having concluded more than 1.2 million cases. These courts planned to complete their caseload in 2010.

GOVERNMENT AND POLITICAL CONDITIONS

After its military victory in July 1994, the RPF organized a coalition government called "The Broad Based Government of National Unity." Its fundamental law was based on a combination of the June 1991 constitution, the Arusha accords, and political declarations by the parties. The government outlawed the MRND Party. In April 2003, the transitional National Assembly recommended the dissolution of the Democratic Republican Party (MDR), one of eight political parties participating in the Government of National Unity since 1994. Human rights groups noted the subsequent disappearances of political figures associated with the MDR, including at least one parliamentarian serving in the National Assembly. On May 26, 2003, Rwanda adopted a new constitution that eliminated reference to *ubwoko* and set the stage for presidential and legislative elections in August and September 2003. The seven remaining political parties endorsed incumbent Paul Kagame for president, who was elected to a 7-year term on August 25, 2003. Rwanda held its first-ever legislative elections September 29 to October 2, 2003. A ninth political party formed after these 2003 elections.

In the spring of 2006, the government conducted local non-partisan elections for district mayors and for sector and cell executive committees. Elections for the Chamber of Deputies occurred in September 2008; the RPF won an easy victory in coalition with six small parties, taking 42 of 53 directly-elected seats. As provided in the constitution, 24 seats were also accorded to women candidates in indirect elections. Women now hold 45 of the 80 seats in the Chamber. The elections were peaceful and orderly, despite irregularities. A tenth political party formed in 2010.

Presidential elections were held in August 2010; the National Electoral Commission reported that President Kagame won re-election with roughly 93% of the vote. The presidential election was peaceful and orderly, with heavy turnout. However, the pre-election period was marked by events of concern, including waves of terrorist attacks using grenades in populous areas, the murder of a journalist, the unexplained murder of the vice president of the Democratic Green Party, an assassination attempt on a former high-ranking government official accused of fomenting attacks, and the suspension of two local-language newspapers. In addition, two political opposition figures were arrested on criminal charges, and a party that had been seeking to register for many months was unable to do so.

Challenges facing the government include maintaining internal and regional security, promoting further democratization and judicial reform; completion of prosecution of remaining individuals for crimes relating to the 1994 genocide, either by the regular court system or the *gacaca* system; integrating former combatants and prisoners; preventing the recurrence of any insurgency directed by ex-military and *Interahamwe* militia who remain in eastern Congo; and the continuing work on medium- and long-term development.

PRINCIPAL GOVERNMENT OFFICIALS

Cabinet

PRIME MINISTER'S OFFICE

Rt. Hon. Anastase Murekezi Prime Minister

The Prime Minister's Office, PMO in short, under the authority of the Prime Minister, is entrusted with assisting the Prime Minister in the implementation of national policies, leading Government activities along the major guidelines given by the President of the Republic and ensuring law enforcement.

The PMO is also entrusted with the function of formulating the Government programme of action in consultation with Ministerial Departments. In addition to that, PMO provides advice to ministries and supporting agencies in order to speed service delivery.

For more information: www.primature.gov.rw

MINISTRY OF NATURAL RESOURCES

Hon. Dr. Vincent Biruta- Minister of Natural Resources (Land, Forests, Environment and Mining)Hon. Dr. Vincent Biruta - Minister of Natural Resources (Land, Forests, Environment and Mining)

About MINIRENA

The Ministry of Natural Resources (MINIRENA) was established to ensure sustainable management and rational use of natural resources. The imbalance between population and natural resources is the biggest challenge that Rwanda has with regard to the management and protection of the environment and natural resources (land, water resources, forests, minerals, etc.). Degradation has occurred over the decades causing serious ecological and socio-economic problems that, if no adequate recovery measures are undertaken, would lead to an irreversible damage.

For more information: www.minirena.gov.rw

Hon. Evode Imena - Minister of State in the Ministry

For more information: www.minirena.gov.rw

MINISTRY OF FINANCE AND ECONOMIC PLANNING

Hon. Claver Gatete - Minister of Finance and Economic Planning

About MINECOFIN

The Ministry of Finance and Economic planning is responsible for sustainable growth, economic opportunities and living standards of all Rwandans. The ministry is also responsible for establishing and monitoring the highest standards of accountability and transparency in public finance management.

The Ministry of Finance and Economic Planning mobilises internal and external resources and works with public institutions to improve the delivery of public services and accountability through effective financial and fiscal decentralisation.

For more information: www.minecofin.gov.rw

Hon. Uzziel Ndagijimana - Minister of State in the Ministry of Finance and Economic Planning in charge of Economic Planning

For more information: www.minecofin.gov.rw

MINISTRY OF AGRICULTURE AND ANIMAL RESOURCES

Hon. Geraldine Mukeshimana

About MINAGRI

The Ministry of Agriculture's mission is to develop and manage suitable programmes of transformation and modernisation of agriculture and livestock to ensure food security and to contribute to the national economy.

The Ministry's vision is to modernize Agriculture and Livestock to achieve food security. The key pillars of this vision is the transformation of Agriculture from subsistence to a productive high value, market oriented farming that is environmentally friendly and has an impact on other sectors of the economy.

The Ministry also oversees the development and implementation of policy of to increase animal and crop production, modernize farming, reduce poverty, ensure food security and have surplus for the market. This will ultimately result in the increase of the standard of living of the population.

For more information: www.minagri.gov.rw

Hon. Tony Nsanganira - Minister of State in the Ministry of Agriculture and Animal Resources in charge of Agriculture

For more information: www.minagri.gov.rw

MINISTRY OF EDUCATION

Dr. Musafiri Papias Malimba Minister of Education

About MINEDUC

The mission of the Ministry of Education is to transform the Rwandan citizen into skilled human capital for socio-economic development of the country by ensuring equitable access to quality education focusing on combating illiteracy, promotion of science and technology, critical thinking and positive values.

For more information: www.mineduc.gov.rw

Hon. Olivier Rwamukwaya Minister of state in charge of Primary and Secondary Education.

MINISTRY OF HEALTH

Hon. Agnes Binagwaho - Minister of Health

About MOH

The main goal of the Ministry of Health is to provide and continually improve the health services of the Rwandan population through the provision of preventive, curative and rehabilitative health care thereby contributing to the reduction of poverty and enhancing the general well-being of the population.

For more information: www.moh.gov.rw

Hon. Patrick Ndimubanzi - Minister of State in the Ministry of Health in charge of Public Health and Primary Health Care

For more information: www.moh.gov.rw

MINISTRY OF DEFENCE

Hon. James Kabarebe - Minister of Defence

About MINADEF

The Ministry of Defence is responsible for ensuring the sovereignty and defence of the country by protecting Rwanda's interests, territorial integrity, vital resources of the population and of the national values under the ambit of the Constitution and International Law.

The overall goal of the Ministry of Defence is to generate, employ and sustain combat-ready, integrated and rapidly deployable Defence Force, capable of quick assemblage to meet varying contingencies both at home and abroad.

For more information: www.mod.gov.rw

MINISTRY OF JUSTICE

Hon. Johnston Busingye - Minister of Justice / Attorney General

About MINIJUST

The vision of Ministry of Justice is to promote and facilitate the Rule of law in the country by emphasizing equality of all persons before the law and ensuring that judicial institutions are effective and efficient in the provision of legal services to the public.

The Minister of Justice also serves as the Republic of Rwanda's Attorney General.

For more information: www.minijust.gov.rw

MINISTRY OF FOREIGN AFFAIRS AND COOPERATION

Hon. Louise Mushikiwabo - Minister of Foreign Affairs and Cooperation

About MINAFFET

The Ministry of Foreign Affairs is responsible for establishing and maintaining quality relationships with other countries for peace, security and stability of Rwanda, the region and the world while participating in wealth creation through more efficient cooperation for development, promotion of investments and tourism, the transfer of know-how and technologies, and more equitable worldwide trade regional integration.

The Ministry of Foreign Affairs is also responsible for elaborating strategies and programmes, whose objectives are to implement, monitor and evaluate Rwanda's foreign policy as well as to clearly articulate this policy both inside and outside the country.

For more information: www.minaffet.gov.rw

Hon. Amb. Eugène-Richard Gasana - Minister of State at the Ministry of Foreign Affairs and Cooperation

For more information: www.minnaffet.gov.rw

MINISTRY OF GENDER AND FAMILY PROMOTION IN THE PRIME MINISTER'S OFFICE

Dr. Diane Gashumba - Minister of Gender and Family Promotion in the Prime Minister's Office

About MIGEPROF

The Ministry in the Prime Minister's office in charge of Gender and Family Promotion aims at promoting equality and equity for both men and women and ensure empowerment of women through the national development processes of Rwanda. The Ministry further aims at promoting the family, as a natural and cultural basis of the Rwandan society and provide a conducive environment for the overall development of the nation's children according to internationally agreed standards and principles.

For more information: www.migeprof.gov.rw

MINISTRY OF INFRASTRUCTURE

Hon. Musoni James - Minister of Infrastructure

About MININFRA

The mission of the Ministry of infrastructure is to ensure the sustainable development of infrastructure and contribute to economic growth with a view to enhancing the quality of life of the population. To develop institutional and legal frameworks, national policies, strategies and master plans relating to transport, energy, habitat and urbanism, meteorology, and water and sanitation subsectors; To initiate programs to develop, rehabilitate and maintain an efficient and integrated national transport infrastructure network, including roads, bridges, airports, railways, and water transportation which will contribute towards economic development and regional integration.

For more information: www.mininfra.gov.rw

Hon. Germaine Kamayirese - Minister of State in charge of Energy and Water

Hon. Dr Alexis Nzahabwanimana - Minister of State in charge of Transport

For more information: www.mininfra.gov.rw

MINISTRY OF INTERNAL SECURITY

Hon. Sheikh Mussa Harerimana - Minister of Internal Security

About MININTER

The Ministry of Internal Security was formed grouping together, the National Police and Prisons with a perspective of efficiently giving appropriate solutions to requirements of the Rwandan Society in perpetual mutations. The formation of this Ministry is a clear indication that the High Authorities of this country put in issues of security and peace at the centre of governmental priority programmes.

The Ministry of Internal Security's mission is to guarantee the safety and security of Rwandans and their property respecting all relevant international conventions. The Police and Correctional Services work throughout the country, in collaboration where necessary.

For more information: www.mininter.gov.rw

MINISTRY OF EAST AFRICAN COMMUNITY

Hon. Valentine Rugwabiza - Minister of East African Community

About MINEAC

The Ministry of East African Community was established by the Government of Rwanda in 2008 in line with EAC member states' joint commitment to establish national coordinating ministries with primary responsibility for EAC matters. MINEAC serves as an operational link between the Government of Rwanda and other national stakeholders, and the EAC organs and Institutions.

MINEAC's main mission is to lead the widening and deepening of the EAC integration process in order to promote the development goals of Rwanda and the region.

For more information: www.mineac.gov.rw

MINISTRY OF DISASTER MANAGEMENT AND REFUGEE AFFAIRS

Hon Serafine Mukantabana - Minister of Disaster Management and Refugee Affairs

About MIDIMAR

The Ministry of Disaster Management and Refugee Affairs was established to attain a highly proficient mechanism for preventing, mitigating, responding, recovering, securing, monitoring and timely acting positively in order to promote disaster awareness culture within a sector policy framework oriented to management of natural and manmade disasters. The Ministry is tasked with developing a pro- active refugee policy and good mechanism for handling of Rwandan and Foreign Refugees affairs in respect of Rwandan law and international treaties signed for protection of refugees which permit to develop a comprehensive advance response strategy.

For more information: www.midimar.gov.rw

MINISTRY OF CABINET AFFAIRS

Stella Ford MugaboStella Ford Mugabo

Ministry of Cabinet Affairs (MINICAAF)

About MINICAAF

The Ministry of Cabinet Affairs (MINICAAF) is headed by the Minister for Cabinet Affairs, Stella Ford Mugabo, and comprises the Cabinet Secretariat and the Official Gazette of Rwanda.

MINICAAF was established by the Cabinet decision of 28 January 2008 and its mandate is set out in Presidential Order No 03/01 of 02/04/2008 determining the functioning of Cabinet, its membership and procedures for decision making.

The mission of MINICAAF is to ensure that the Cabinet process is run effectively and efficiently and that proper consultations take place before policy decisions are taken. MINICAAF also works to achieve coordination of policy across State institutions in collaboration with the Strategy and Policy Unit in the Office of the President.

For more information: www.minicaaf.gov.rw

MINISTRY OF LOCAL GOVERNMENT

Hon. Francis Kaboneka - Minister of Local Government

About MINALOC

The Ministry of Local Government was established with the main mission of "Promoting the well-being of the population by good governance, community development and social affairs." Among its objectives, the Ministry is tasked with Putting in place democratic, decentralized administrative structures, which are able to mobilize the population in order to implement Government programs and resolve problems.

For more information: www.minaloc.gov.rw

Hon. Dr. Alvera Mukabaramba - Minister of State in the Ministry of Local Government in Charge of Social Affairs.

For more information:www.minaloc.gov.rw

Hon. Judith Uwizeye - Minister of Public Service and Labor

About MIFOTRA

The Ministry of Public Service and Labour was established to Strengthen Institutional and Legal framework to improve conditions of employment in Public and Private sector. The Ministry's mission is to reinforce the national labour standards, promote job creation and institutionalize an efficient and modern public service management framework that will enable private and public sector organizations to perform at their best and effectively contribute to improving the lives of the Rwandan population.

For more information: www.mifotra.gov.rw

MINISTRY OF TRADE AND INDUSTRY

Hon François Kanimba - Minister of Trade and Industry

About MINICOM

The Ministry of Trade and Industry has a vision to achieve accelerated and sustained economic growth led by a dynamic and competitive private sector. The Ministries mission is to facilitate Rwanda's economic transformation through enabling a competitive private sector integrated into regional and global markets, while ensuring a level playing field and the protection of consumers.

For more information: www.minicom.gov.rw

MINISTRY OF SPORTS AND CULTURE

Hon. Julienne Uwacu - Minister of Sports and Culture

About MINISPOC

The Ministry of Sports and Culture was established with a mission to develop, coordinate, monitor, evaluate and support implementation of policies and strategies that promote Sports and Cultural development initiatives that lead to the economic and social transformation as well as to a productive and patriotic generation.

The Ministry's mission is to develop and support implementation of policies and strategies that lead to a winning culture in sports and to make culture foundational to our development agenda.

For more information: www.minispoc.gov.rw

For more information: www.minispoc.gov.rw

MINISTRY OF YOUTH AND ICT

Hon. Jean Philbert Nsengimana - Minister of Youth and ICT

About Ministry of Youth and ICT

The Ministry of Youth and ICT develops, coordinates, monitors, evaluates and supports implementation of policies and strategies that promote youth development aimed at economic and social transformation and a productive and patriotic generation. The ministry is also charged with integrating and disseminating ICT through policy, strategy and action to empower both public and private sectors, in order to accelerate the transformation of Rwanda into a middle-income economy and information society by 2020.

For more information: www.myict.gov.rw

MINISTER IN THE OFFICE OF THE PRESIDENT

Hon. Venantia Tugireyezu - Minister in the Office of the President

About MINIPRESIREP

The Minister in the Office of the President reviews all legislation before promulgation by the President of the Republic. The Minister works closely with the National Unity and Reconciliation Commission, Office of the Ombudsman and National Intelligence Security Service and ensures the establishment and implementation of policies and legislation related to those institutions attached to the Office of the President. The Minister is also charged with resolving the citizen complaints addressed to the President and supervises implementation of Presidential pledges; and serves as liaison between Cabinet and Parliament by briefing both bureaus of the Senate and Chamber of Deputies on Cabinet resolutions or any other issues from the two Chambers concerning government.

RWANDA DEVELOPMENT BOARD

Hon. Francis Gatare - RDB's Chief Executive Officer

About RDB

The Rwanda Development Board was set up by bringing together all the government agencies responsible for the entire investor experience under one roof. This includes key agencies responsible for business registration, investment promotion, environmental clearances, privatization and specialist agencies which support the priority sectors of ICT and tourism as well as SMEs and human capacity development in the private sector.

The RDB is independent and influential. It reports directly to the President and is guided by a Board that includes all the key Ministers (e.g., finance, commerce, infrastructure, agriculture).

For more information: www.rdb.gov.rw

Rwanda maintains an **embassy** in the United States at 1714 New Hampshire Avenue NW, Washington, DC 20009 (tel. 202-232-2882).

ECONOMY

Currency	Rwandan franc (RWF)
Fiscal year	calendar year
Trade organisations	WTO, ECCAS, EAC, COMESA
	Statistics
GDP	$7 billion
GDP rank	144th (nominal) / 136th (PPP)
GDP growth	8.3%
GDP per capita	$644
GDP by sector	agriculture: 33%, industry: 16%, services: 45%
Inflation (CPI)	6.7% (
Population below poverty line	55%
Gini coefficient	24.9
Labour force	5.0 million
Labour force by occupation	agriculture: 90%, industry and services: 10%
Unemployment	no data
Main industries	cement, agricultural products, small-scale beverages, soap, furniture, shoes, plastic goods, textiles, cigarettes
Ease-of-doing-business rank	32nd
	External
Exports	$152.8 million
Export goods	coffee, tea, hides, tin ore
Main export partners	Kenya 32.6% DR Congo 13.1% China 11.7% Malaysia 10.4% United States 5.6% Swaziland 5.2% Pakistan 4.1%
Imports	$365.7 million (
Import goods	foodstuffs, machinery and equipment, steel, petroleum products, cement and construction material
Main import partners	Kenya 18.4% Uganda 16.6% United Arab Emirates 8.3% China 6.9% India 5.4% Tanzania 5.4% Belgium 4.3%

Public finances	
Public debt	$0.7 billion (2010) (external)
Revenues	$560.9 million
Expenses	$654 million
Economic aid	recipient: $285 Million

Rwanda is a rural country with about 90% of the population engaged in (mainly subsistence) agriculture. It is the most densely populated country in Africa; is landlocked; and has few natural resources and minimal industry. Primary exports are coffee and tea. By 1994, farm size, on average, was smaller than one hectare, while population density was more than 450 persons per square kilometer of arable land.

The Rwandan economy is based on the largely rain-fed agricultural production of small, semi-subsistence, and increasingly fragmented farms. It has few natural resources to exploit and a small, noncompetitive industrial sector. While the production of coffee and tea is well-suited to the small farms, steep slopes, and cool climates of Rwanda and has ensured access to foreign exchange over the years, farm size continues to decrease.Prewar population was growing at the high rate of 3% a year.

During the 5 years of civil war that culminated in the 1994 genocide, GDP declined in 3 out of 5 years, posting a dramatic decline at more than 40% in 1994, the year of the genocide. The 9% increase in real GDP for 1995, the first postwar year, signaled the resurgence of economic activity and massive foreign aid inflows.

In the immediate postwar period--mid-1994 through 1995--emergency humanitarian assistance of more than $307.4 million was largely directed to relief efforts in Rwanda and in the refugee camps in neighboring countries where Rwandans fled during the war. In 1996, humanitarian relief aid began to shift to reconstruction and development assistance.

Since 1996, Rwanda has experienced steady economic recovery, thanks to government reforms and foreign aid (now over $500 million per year). Since 2002, the GDP growth rate ranged from 3%-11% per annum, and inflation ranged between 2%-9%. Rwanda depends on significant foreign imports (over $900 million per year). Exports have increased, up to $193 million in 2009. Private investment remains below expectations despite an open trade policy, a favorable investment climate, cheap and abundant labor, tax incentives to businesses, stable internal security, and crime rates that are comparatively low. Investment insurance also is available through the Africa Trade Insurance Agency, the Overseas Private Investment Corporation, and the World Bank's Multilateral Investment Guarantee Agency (MIGA). The weakness of exports and low domestic savings rates are threats to future growth. The global economic crisis has impacted Rwanda. However, while there was a decline in overall exports (28% between 2008 and 2009), remittances, and nongovernmental organization (NGO) transfers in 2009, the agricultural sector performed strongly, propelling Rwanda to a 4% growth in GDP, well above the sub-Saharan average growth for the year. Amidst obstacles, Rwanda appears committed to economic reform and private sector investment. In the World Bank's "Ease of Doing Business" report released in September 2009, Rwanda catapulted from number 143 to number 67; in the 2010 report, Rwanda improved its ranking to number 58.

The Government of Rwanda remains dedicated to a strong and enduring economic climate for the country, focusing on poverty reduction, infrastructure development, privatization of government-owned assets, expansion of the export base, and trade liberalization. The implementation of a value added tax of 18% and improved tax collections are having a positive impact on government revenues and thereby on government services rendered. Banking reform and low corruption also are favorable current trends. Agricultural reforms, improved farming methods, and increased use of fertilizers are improving crop yields and national food supply.

Moreover, the government is pursing educational and healthcare programs that bode well for the long-term quality of Rwanda's human resource skills base.

Many challenges remain for Rwanda. The country is dependent on significant foreign aid. Exports continue to lag far behind imports and will continue to affect the health of the economy. The persistent lack of economic diversification beyond the production of tea, coffee, and minerals keeps the country vulnerable to market fluctuations. Perhaps the largest constraint on private sector development is the cost of electricity, which is currently among the highest in the world at about 24.6 cents per kilowatt hour. Given Rwanda's landlocked geography, strong highway infrastructure maintenance and good transport linkages to neighboring countries, especially Uganda and Tanzania, are critical. Transportation costs remain high and, therefore, burden import and export costs. Rwanda has no railway system for port access to Tanzania or Kenya. The limited availability and high cost of power also continues to impede the growth of manufacturing enterprises. The tourism industry has undeveloped potential for growth given the current political stability, travel infrastructure, and extensive national parks as well as other potential tourist sites. In 2006, Rwanda completed the Multilateral Debt Relief Initiative and the Heavily Indebted Poor Countries (HIPC) debt initiative, significantly lowering its foreign debt load.

American business interests in Rwanda are modest, and the African Growth and Opportunity Act (AGOA) has yet to make a significant impact in Rwanda. In addition to long-standing tea production by an American firm, in 2008 a U.S. corporation concluded an agreement with Rwandan authorities to produce 100 megawatts of electrical power from methane extraction operations in Lake Kivu. In 2009 a U.S.-British consortium signed an agreement with the government to develop a biofuel project based on jatropha, and a U.S. mining company expanded its investment in local mineral production. In 2010, RwandAir signed a contract with Boeing for the purchase of two Boeing 737-800 aircraft, for an estimated $80 million. American exports of aviation, telecommunications, and construction equipment have increased in recent years. Energy needs will stress natural resources in wood and gas, but hydroelectric power development is underway, albeit primarily in the planning stages, as is methane development. Rwanda does not have nuclear power or coal resources. Finally, Rwanda's fertility rate--averaging 5.5 births (2008 est.) per woman--will continue to stress services, and diseases such as HIV/AIDS transmission, malaria, and tuberculosis will have a major impact on human resources.

Rwanda's government-run radio broadcasts 15 hours a day in Kinyarwanda, English, and French, the national languages. News programs include regular re-broadcasts from international radio such as Voice of America, BBC, and Deutsche Welle. There is one government-operated television station. In addition to government-operated Radio Rwanda, there are a number of independent FM radio stations. There are few independent newspapers; most newspapers publish in Kinyarwanda on a weekly, biweekly, or monthly basis. Several Western nations, including the United States, are working to encourage freedom of the press, the free exchange of ideas, and responsible journalism.

The country entered a high period of economic growth in 2006, and the following year managed to register 8% economic growth, a record it has sustained since, turning it into one of the fastest-growing economies in Africa. This sustained economic growth has succeeded in reducing poverty, with growth between 2006 and 2011 reducing the percentage of the country's population living in poverty from 57% to 45%.The country's infrastructure has also grown rapidly, with connections to electricity going from 91,000 in 2006 to 215,000 in 2011.[6]

Existing foreign investment is concentrated in commercial establishments, mining, tea, coffee, and tourism. Minimum wage and social security regulations are in force, and the four prewar independent trade unions are back in operation. The largest union, CESTRAR, was created as an organ of the government but became fully independent with the political reforms introduced by the

1991 constitution. As security in Rwanda improves, the country's nascent tourism sector shows great potential to expand as a source of foreign exchange.

MINING IN RWANDA

Mining in Rwanda consists of extracting such minerals as tin, tantalum, and tungsten. In 2010, Rwanda earned about US$67.8m from mineral exports which constitute 14.9% of total exports, making mining the biggest source of export revenues.

MINERALS EXTRACTED

- Cassiterite (tin ore) had the largest production and export volume at about 3,874 tons valued at US$42.2m in 2010 (down from 4,269 tons in 2009);
- It was followed by coltan with 749 tons in 2010 valued at $18.48m (949 tons in 2009), and wolfram (tungsten ore) with 843 tons in 2010 valued at $7.1m, down from 874 tons in 2009.
- Rwanda produces about 9% of the world's tantalum, used in electronics manufacturing, and about 4% of global tungsten.

In October 2012, Rwanda's Ministry of Natural Resources suspended mining activities in the country's western province on the basis that they were endangering the River Sebeya. The decision was met with negativity due to the affected mining companies' loss of production and the loss of thousands of jobs for workers at the mines

DEFENSE

The military establishment is comprised of a well-trained army and a small, rotary-wing air force. The Rwandan Defense Forces (RDF) is on an aggressive plan to professionalize its military. Following withdrawal of Rwandan Armed Forces from the Democratic Republic of the Congo in October 2009, the government completely restructured the military and launched an ambitious plan to demobilize thousands of soldiers. At end state, Rwanda will have a small, well-equipped army of 20,000 soldiers and a reserve force of more than 100,000. Rwanda has deployed 3,326 peacekeepers to Darfur and Liberia, as well as 21 police officers to Haiti.

FOREIGN RELATIONS

Rwanda is an active member of the international community and has remained in the international spotlight since the genocide. Rwanda is an active member of the UN, having presided over the Security Council during part of 1995. The UN assistance mission in Rwanda (UNAMIR), a UN Chapter Six peacekeeping operation, involved personnel from more than a dozen countries. Most of the UN development and humanitarian agencies have had a large presence in Rwanda. At the height of the humanitarian emergency, more than 200 nongovernmental organizations were carrying out humanitarian operations. In addition to receiving assistance from the international community, Rwanda has also contributed to international peacekeeping missions. Currently, the RDF has four 800-strong battalions deployed in support of the UNAMID Mission in Darfur and one company in UNMIS (Khartoum). As of June 2009, Rwanda was training its 22nd peacekeeping battalion since 2006.

Several nations--including Belgium, Canada, China, Egypt, France, Germany, Japan, the United

Kingdom, Libya, the Netherlands, Russia, Sweden, the Holy See, and all members of the EAC (Kenya, Tanzania, Uganda, Burundi) as well as the Democratic Republic of the Congo (D.R.C.)--maintain diplomatic missions in Kigali, as does the European Union.

In December 2008, after months of bilateral discussions, Rwanda and the D.R.C. announced a joint military operation against a root cause of instability in the Great Lakes Region--the FDLR (Democratic Forces for the Liberation of Rwanda), which took place in January and February 2009. In January 2009 the governments of the D.R.C. and Rwanda accelerated efforts to achieve the rapprochement that they had initiated in late 2008. The two nations' forces also cooperated in reintegrating renegade general Laurent Nkunda's CNDP rebel force into the Congolese armed forces (FARDC); Nkunda was detained by Rwandan authorities.

In the fall of 2006, Rwanda broke diplomatic relations with France, following a French judge's indictment of senior Rwandan officials on charges of having participated in the shooting down of the presidential jet in 1994. Rwanda rejects these charges. In January 2010, Rwanda and France renewed their diplomatic relations after France indicated it had reopened its investigation of the 2006 charges. Rwanda, along with Burundi, joined the EAC in 2007, and it acceded to the Commonwealth in 2009.

U.S.-RWANDAN RELATIONS

U.S. Government interests have shifted significantly since the 1994 genocide from a strictly humanitarian concern focused on stability and security to a strong partnership with the Government of Rwanda focused on sustainable development. The largest U.S. Government programs are the President's Emergency Plan for AIDS Relief (PEPFAR) and the President's Malaria Initiative, which aim to reduce the impact of these debilitating diseases in Rwanda. In partnership with the Government of Rwanda, U.S. Government agencies--Centers for Disease Control and Prevention, Department of Defense, Peace Corps, State Department, and U.S. Agency for International Development (USAID)--work to strengthen the Rwandan health system and build local capacity.

The **USAID** program plays a strong role in helping Rwanda to improve the health and livelihoods of its people and increase economic and political development. To achieve this, USAID activities focus on:

- Prevention, treatment, and care of HIV/AIDS;
- Reducing mortality and morbidity due to malaria;
- Increasing access to, and use of, voluntary family planning methods;
- Improving maternal and child health;
- Promoting rural economic growth through staple crops, specialty coffee, dairy, and eco-tourism;
- Reducing post-harvest losses of agriculture produce;
- Expanding the use of information technology in primary education;
- Encouraging participatory governance and decentralization; and
- Promoting a democratic Rwanda, where the government respects human rights, civil liberties, and the rule of law.

In September 2008, Rwanda signed a Threshold Country Plan (TCP) agreement with the Millennium Challenge Corporation (MCC). USAID implements these programs, which focus on strengthening civil society, the judiciary, police, and media sectors and promoting civic participation and civil society.

The State Department's Public Affairs section (PAS) maintains an Information Resource Center (IRC) in Kigali, which offers public access to English-language publications, an English language lab for those preparing for English language exams, information on the United States, and information on studying in the U.S. PAS also maintains an American Corner at the National University of Rwanda (NUR) in Huye (formerly Butare) and supports an English Language Resource Center at the Catholic Institute of Kabgayi (ICK) in Gitarama.

American business interests have been small; currently, private U.S. investment is limited to the tea industry, franchising (FedEx, Coca-Cola, Western Union, and Moneygram) and small holdings in service and manufacturing concerns. Annual U.S. exports to Rwanda, under $10 million annually from 1990-93, exceeded $40 million in 1994 and 1995. Although exports decreased in the years immediately after the genocide, in 2007 they were estimated at approximately $17 million, a 20% increase over 2006.

Principal U.S. Officials

Ambassador-- Erica J. Barks-Ruggles
Ms. Barks-Ruggles is the United States Ambassador to the Republic of Rwanda. She previously served for three years as U.S. Consul General in Cape Town, South Africa. From January 2009-July 2011, Ms. Barks-Ruggles served as the Deputy to the United States Permanent Representative to the United Nations, leading the Washington office for Ambassador Susan Rice and serving on the Deputies Committee.

Deputy Chief of Mission--Anne Casper
USAID Mission Director--Dennis Weller

The **U.S. Embassy** is located on 2657 Avenue de la Gendarmerie, Kigali (tel. 250-596-400, fax 250-596-591).

TRAVEL AND BUSINESS INFORMATION

Travel Alerts, Travel Warnings, Trip Registration
The U.S. Department of State's Consular Information Program advises Americans traveling and residing abroad through Country Specific Information, Travel Alerts, and Travel Warnings. **Country Specific Information** exists for all countries and includes information on entry and exit requirements, currency regulations, health conditions, safety and security, crime, political disturbances, and the addresses of the U.S. embassies and consulates abroad. **Travel Alerts** are issued to disseminate information quickly about terrorist threats and other relatively short-term conditions overseas that pose significant risks to the security of American travelers. **Travel Warnings** are issued when the State Department recommends that Americans avoid travel to a certain country because the situation is dangerous or unstable.

For the latest security information, Americans living and traveling abroad should regularly monitor the Department's Bureau of Consular Affairs Internet web site at http://travel.state.gov, where current Worldwide Caution, Travel Alerts, and Travel Warnings can be found. The travel.state.gov website also includes information about passports, tips for planning a safe trip abroad and more. More travel-related information also is available at http://www.usa.gov/Citizen/Topics/Travel/International.shtml.

The Department's Smart Traveler app for U.S. travelers going abroad provides easy access to the frequently updated official country information, travel alerts, travel warnings, maps, U.S. embassy locations, and more that appear on the travel.state.gov site. Travelers can also set up e-tineraries to keep track of arrival and departure dates and make notes about upcoming trips. The app is compatible with iPhone, iPod touch, and iPad (requires iOS 4.0 or later).

The Department of State encourages all U.S. citizens traveling or residing abroad to register via the State Department's travel registration website or at the nearest U.S. embassy or consulate abroad (a link to the registration page is also available through the Smart Traveler app). Registration will make your presence and whereabouts known in case it is necessary to contact you in an emergency and will enable you to receive up-to-date information on security conditions.

Emergency information concerning Americans traveling abroad may be obtained by calling 1-888-407-4747 toll free in the U.S. and Canada or the regular toll line 1-202-501-4444 for callers outside the U.S. and Canada.

Passports
The National Passport Information Center (NPIC) is the U.S. Department of State's single, centralized public contact center for U.S. passport information. Telephone: 1-877-4-USA-PPT (1-877-487-2778); TDD/TTY: 1-888-874-7793. Passport information is available 24 hours, 7 days a week. You may speak with a representative Monday-Friday, 8 a.m. to 10 p.m., Eastern Time, excluding federal holidays.

RWANDA LEGAL SYSTEM BASICS

With the promulgation of the Rwandan Constitution, legislative power was vested in an independent bicameral parliament composed of a chamber of deputies, whose members have the title of Deputies, and a senate, whose members have the title of Senators. The Senate has 26 seats of which 12 members are elected by local councils, 8 appointed by the president, 4 by a political organizations forum, and 2 represent institutions of higher learning, to serve eight year terms. The Chamber of Deputies has 80 seats, 53 members elected by popular vote, 24 women elected by local bodies, 3 selected by youth and disability organizations, to serve five year terms.

Parliament deliberates on and passes laws. It legislates and oversees executive action in accordance with the procedure determined by the Constitution.

THE EXECUTIVE

It comprises the Prime Minister, Ministers, Ministers of State and other members who may be determined, if necessary, by the President of the Republic.

THE JUDICIARY

The judicial branch hierarchy is as follows: the Supreme Court, high courts of the Republic, provincial courts, districts courts, and mediation committees. The new Constitution in Rwanda also ushered in reforms in the judiciary such as new legislation, establishing new courts, procedures, structures, standards including academic and professional qualifications as well as regulatory and administrative frameworks. At this point it is also important to note that after the genocide Rwanda faced a very special situation and needed special interventions to try genocide perpetrators. One of the innovations was the establishment of Gacaca Courts to try genocide cases. Gacaaca Courts exact different penalties including compensation, but most importantly emphasize two aspects of confession and forgiveness as a way to heal the wounds.

The Supreme Court

The Supreme Court is the highest court in the country. The decisions of the Supreme Court are not be subject to appeal save in terms of petitions for the exercise of the prerogative of mercy or revision of a judicial decision. Its decisions are binding on all parties concerned whether such are organs of the State, public officials, civilians, military, judicial officers or private individuals.

One can access Rwandan judgments and laws on the website of the Supreme Court of Rwanda. If one clicks on Jurisprudence for cases and texts des *lois* for laws. The Judgments are in Kinyarwanda and the website is in Kinyarwanda and French - the English parts are under construction.

The High Court

The High Court has jurisdiction to try in the first instance certain serious offences committed in Rwanda as well as some offences committed outside Rwanda as specified by the law.

The Provincial Court and Court of the City of Kigali

There are established Provincial Court in each Province of the country and a Court of the City of Kigali.

The District, Municipality and Town Court

There are established District, Town and Municipality Court respectively in each District, Town and Municipality in the country.

Specialized Courts

These include the Gacaca Courts responsible for the trial and judgment of cases against persons accused of the crime of genocide and crimes against humanity which were committed between October 1st 1990 and December 31st 1994 with the exception of cases jurisdiction in respect of which is vested in other courts.

Military Courts

Military courts comprise of the Military Tribunal and the Military High Court. The Military Court tries in the first instance all offences committed by military personnel irrespective of their rank. The Military High Court shall try in the first instance, all offences which constitute a threat to national security and murder committed by soldiers irrespective of rank. The Military High Court is an appellate court in respect of decisions rendered by the Military Tribunal.

Rwandan cases are found in court records, there are no publications where they can be found, mainly because the legal system is based on the French civil law system, not the common law that relies on decided cases/precedence.

APPLICABLE LAW

During colonialism all legislation governing the country was made by Belgian authorities and the mainstay of criminal and civil legislation was the civil and criminal codes of the then Belgian Congo. Though criminal law had universal application, written civil laws was applied only to whites. Customary law continued to apply to the natives. Hence the current Rwanda Civil Law Legal system is based on German and Belgian civil law systems and customary law.

The Constitution is the Supreme law in Rwanda and any law or custom in conflict with it is null and void to the extent of its inconsistency. Rwanda adopted a new Constitution on 26th May 2003.

A number of laws have been revised since Rwanda embarked on legal reform process after the 1994 Genocide and these include, Law modifying and complementing of relating to the code of criminal procedure, organic law determining the organization, powers and functioning of the superior council of the judiciary, law modifying and complementing the law on the statues for judges and other judicial personnel, organic law modifying and complementing the organic law determining the organization, functioning and jurisdiction of the courts and law establishing the organization, functioning and jurisdiction of the Supreme Court. However, the reform of commercial laws is still on-going.

It is important to note that Rwanda is a civil law legal system now undergoing a transformation from purely civil law to a merge between civil law and common law. The evolutionary process has led to the reform of several laws such as the penal code, and the law of evidence among others.

THE MINISTRY OF JUSTICE AND CONSTITUTIONAL AFFAIRS

The ministry of JUSTICE (MINIJUST) bears the political responsibility of ensuring that the Government's programs in the Justice Sector are successful and ensure close coordination among the various sub sectors. The institutions in the sector, though linked by the mission of Justice Delivery, are created by the constitution and are independently responsible for executing their programs, each of which forms an integral part of the common Justice Vision of the Country.

SOURCE OF LEGISLATION

For a publication of legal texts, Presidential Orders, Prime Minister's Orders, Ministerial Orders and official rules and regulations, the source is the Official Gazette of the Republic of Rwanda. It also publishes statutes of commercial companies, cooperatives, non-profit making organizations and others to allow them to operate legally. The Official Gazette of the Republic of Rwanda is a bi-monthly coming out on 1st and 15th of each month.

LEGAL EDUCATION IN RWANDA

In order to study law in Rwanda one requires having completed Advanced Level of Education and passed highly. The Law degree is a four year course taught at the National University of Rwanda. The subjects include criminal law, civil law, constitutional law, comparative law, administrative law, public international law, commercial law, international humanitarian law, environmental law, intellectual property rights and international development law. In order to practice a lawyer is required to work under supervision of a senior lawyer for two years, and thereafter apply to be admitted to the bar. The Bar Association in Rwanda is known as the Kigali Bar Association.

IMPORTANT LAWS AND REGULATIONS AFFECTING BUSINESS

CONSTITUTIONAL LAW

Constitution of the Republic of Rwanda

Act No. 33 bis/2003 of 06/09/2003 against the crime of Genocide, Crimes Against Humanity and War Crimes In

The New Organic Law of Gacaca Jurisdictions

HUMAN RIGHTS

Law Establishing the National Human Rights Commission

Litigation and court procedure

LAW N ° 28/2006 Organic Law of 06.27.2006-modifying and complementing Organic Law No. 16/2004 of 19/06/2004 Establishing the organization and competence of Gacaca Courts charged fonctionnement with Prosecuting and Trying the Perpetrators of the Crime of Genocide and Other Crimes Against Humanity

LAW N ° 22/2006 establishing the Higher Institute Of Practice And Development Of Law

ORGANIC LAW No. 02/2004 On Organisation, powers and functioning of the Higher Judicial Council

ORGANIC LAW No. 16/2004 On Organisation, Competence and Functioning of Gacaca Courts charged with prosecuting and trying the perpetrators of the crime of genocide and other crimes against humanity committed between October 1, 1990 And December 31, 1994, as amended and completed to day (OJ N ° Special of 19/06/2004)

ORGANIC LAW No. 31/2006 On Organisation, Spring, competence and functioning of the Mediation Committee

ORGANIC LAW No. 31/2006 On Organisation, Spring, powers and functioning of the Committee Of conciliators

ORGANIC LAW No. 51/2008 OF 09/09/2008 On organization, functioning and jurisdiction

ORGANIC LAW No. 59/2007 of 16/12/2007, Establishing Organization, functioning and jurisdiction of courts of Commerce

ACT ORGANIC No. 01/2004 On Organisation, Operation and juridiction of the Supreme Court (OJ N ° 3 From 01/02/2004)

LAW No. 08/2004 creation, organization, Operation And Allocation Of National Service in charge of monitoring the supervision And the coordination of activities of Gacaca Courts

LAW No. 09/2004 of 27/04/2004 Carrying Code of Judicial Ethics

LAW No. 09/2004 of 27/04/2004 establishing the Code of Judicial Ethics

LAW No. 15 / 99 amending and supplementing Law No. 03/97 From 03.19.1997 establishing a Bar in Rwanda.

LAW No. 17/2005 OF 18/08/2005 amending and supplementing Law No. 25/2003 From 15/08 / 2003 on organization and functioning of the office of Ombudsman.

LAW No. 22/2006 28.4.2006 establishing the Higher Institute Practice and Development of Law

LAW No. 3/97 establishing the Bar in Rwanda.

LAW No. 31/2001 establishing and organizing Du Corps of Judicial Professionals.

LAW # 6 From 04.14.2004 Bis/2004 Wearing Status of Judges and Officers of the judicial

LAW No. 6 From 14/04/2004 Bis/2004 Wearing Status of Judges and Officers of the judicial

LAW No. 08/2004, Establishing Organization, Assignment And Operation Of National Service Manager for monitoring, Supervision and Coordination of activities Gacaca Courts

Law Determining the Organisation, Functioning and Jurisdiction of Courts

Law Determining the organization, Powers and Functioning of the Prosecution Service

Law Determining the organization, Powers and Functioning of the Superior Council of the Judiciary

Law Establishing the organization, and jurisdiction of the fonctionnement Supreme court

Law Relating to the code of ethics for the Judiciary

Ministerial Order on Legal Fees for Criminal Matters

Ministerial Order on Legal Fees in Civil, Commercial, Social and Administrative Matters

Modifying law n0 06 bis / 2004 of 14/04/2004 on the statutes for judges and judicial staff Other

Organic Law No. 40/2000 of 26.1.2001 setting up "Gacaca Jurisdictions" and Organizing Prosecutions for Offences Constituting the Crime of Genocide or Crimes Against Humanity-committed Octoberr Between 1 and 1990 december 31, 1994 and Organic Law No. 33/2001 of 06/22/2001 Modifying and Completing Organic Law No. 40/2000 of january 26, 2001

ELECTORAL LAW

ORGANIC LAW No. 16/2003 governing political Politicians And The

ORGANIC LAW No. 17/2003 of 07/07/2003 Presidential and Legislative Elections

ACT No. 02/2006 25/01/2006 On Organisation Of The Elections Local Administrative Authorities

ADMINISTRATIVE / PUBLIC LAW

DECREE LAW N ° 4/81. Urban Planning and Territory.

DECREE-LAW No. 11/79. Creation and delineation of Urban Districts.

DECREE-LAW No. 2/81 On Organisation Of Higher Education In Rwanda And Establishing The National University of Rwanda

DECREE LAW. Organization Of Social Security

DECREE LAW. Organization Of Social Security.

DECREE-LAW No. 6/81 to reorganize the National Bank of Rwanda

Immigration Law 1999 (No. 17/99)

LAW No. 17/99 One Of Immigration And Emigration 16/08/1999

LAW N ° 20 / 2002 21/05/2002 Establishing Of The Organization And Functioning Of The Common Development Fund For Districts, Towns And The City Of Kigali

LAW No. 45/2001 of 08/12/2001 Determining The National Anthem Of The Republic of Rwanda

ACT, NO 03/2002 establishing the Rwanda Bureau of Standards

LAW N ° 14/98 establishing the Rwandan Office For The Promotion Of Investments

ORGANIC LAW No. 29/2005 Covering the administrative entities of the Republic of Rwanda

ORGANIC LAW No. 01/2005 on organization of statistical activities in Rwanda

ORGANIC LAW No. 02/2005 on rules for the procedure of the Senate.

ORGANIC LAW No. 03/2004 on organization, powers and functioning of the prosecution

ORGANIC LAW No. 03/2005 Relative the Means of Communication And Control Of Parliament In respect of the Governmental Action Action

ORGANIC LAW No. 06/2006 on rules for the internal order of the Chamber of Deputies

ORGANIC LAW No. 14/2004 laying down general provisions applicable to public institutions

ORGANIC LAW No. 20/2003 on the organization of education

ORGANIC LAW No. 22/2004 on the Statute of the Public Ministry and Personnel of the Prosecution

ORGANIC LAW No. 29/2004 Carrying Code of Rwandan nationality

LAW ORGANIC No. 34/2003 determining allowances and other benefits accorded to top political appointees State

ORGANIC LAW No. 37/2006 of 12/09/2006 on Finance and the State Assets

LAW No. 30/90 From 28 May 1990 amending the Act concerning the determination of the Capital of Rwanda

LAW No. 01/2006 on organization and functioning of the Province

LAW No. 03/99 Establishing the Commission for Unity and National Reconciliation The

ACT n ° 05/1987. Sports and recreation organization in Rwanda.

LAW No. 05/98 Wearing Of The Office Of The Auditor General of Finance of the State

LAW No. 08/2006 on organization and functioning Du District

LAW No. 12/2007 From 27/03/2007 on Public Procurement

LAW No. 17/2002 Wearing Of Finance And Districts Cities and its management.

LAW No. 19/2001 establishing the National Examinations Council Of Primary And Secondary Level.

LAW No. 20 / 2005 on organization and functioning of Higher Education

ACT No. 21/1982. Restructuring of the Institute of Agricultural Sciences Rwanda

LAW No. 22/2002 on General Statutes for Rwanda Public Service The

ACT No. 241 2001 Wearing Institution, Organization and Operation of a system of Health Insurance Agents In The State

LAW No. 25/2003 on organization and functioning of the Office of The Ombudsman

LAW No. 25/2007 of 27/06/2007 establishing the Office of Geology and Mines in Rwanda (OGMR) and determining its responsibilities His organization and operation

LAW No. 27/2003 determining the organization, attributions and 'Operation Of The National Council of Women

ACT No. 29/2003 on organization and functioning of preschool and primary education and Secondary

LAW No. 34/2001 of 05/07/2001 relating to Refugees

LAW No. 43/2007 of 10/09/2007 establishing the Inspectorate General of Education and determining its responsibilities, Organization And Operation

LAW No. 44/2004, Establishing Organization And Operation Of Development Agency institutional capacities and human resources

LAW No. 44/2004, Establishing Organization And Operation Of Development Agency institutional capacities and human resources

LAW No. 51/2001 on Labour Code

LAW No. 52/10 of 04/10/2007 establishing the Centre National De Developpement educational programs (NCDC)

LAW No. 57/2001 Features Wearing Ceremonial And Respect The Flag National

ACT No. 57/2007 OF 15/12/2007 to repeal Act No. 06/98 22/06/1998 From creation, organization and management of the leased housing finance

LAW No. 10/2006 on organization and functioning from From Kigali City

ACT No. 24/2003 determining the functioning and the National Council Of The Organization Of Youth

LAW No. 01/2007 of 20/01/2007 on the protection of disabled people generally

LAW No. 07/2002 establishing and organizing of The Higher Institute Of Health From Kigali

LAW No. 09/2005 establishing the National Institute of Statistics of Rwanda

LAW No. 15/97 establishing the Rwanda Revenue

LAW No. 17/99 on immigration and Emigration

LAW No. 18/99 amending Decree-Law N º 18/76 From 20 April 1976 establishing the Public Establishment for Generation, Transmission and Electric Utility, Water & Gas (Electrogaz)

LAW No. 19 / 2001 establishing the National Examinations Council

LAW No. 21/2002, Establishing And Organization Of The School Of Advanced Studies of Finance and Banking

LAW No. 21/2004 establishing and organizing of the Rwanda Civil Aviation From The

LAW No. 23/2005, Establishing Organization And Operation Of MILITARY MEDICAL INSURANCE

LAW No. 25/2001 establishing the Institution Rwandan Management Administration

LAW No. 26/2003, Establishing And Organization Of The Higher Institute Of Agriculture and Livestock

LAW No. 32/2002 establishing the Rwandan Information Office and Technology (RITA)

LAW No. 35/1987, Organization Of Attorney.

LAW No. 39/2001 establishing the Agency Regulatory Utilities

LAW No. 48/2001 establishing and organizing the Institute of Science, Technology and Management, Kigali

LAW No. 49/2001, Establishing And Organization Of Higher Pedagogical isntitut From Kigali

LAW No. 51/2007 of 20/09/2007 determining the responsibilities, Organization And Operation Of The Gender Observatory in Rwanda

LAW No. LAW N ° 16/2006 On Organisation, Functions And Operation Of The Office Of Management In The Rwandan environment

Law Modifying and Complementing Law n0 03/99 of 12/03/1999 Setting Up the National Unity and Reconciliation Commission.

Law Establishing Independent National Commission responsible annually for collection of evidence indicating indication the role of the French State in the genocide perpetrated in Rwanda That Was in 1994

Law No. 39/2001 09.13.2001 Of Establishing An Agency For The Regulation Of Certain Public Utilities.

Law Establishing the Rwanda Defence Forces

Law Establishing the organization and Functioning of the Office of the Ombudsman

Law on Rwandan Nationality Code,

Law on the Establishment, Organization, Duties and Functioning of the National Service in Charge of the Follow-Up, Supervision and Coordination of the Activities of Gacaca Jurisdictions

Act No. 2 Wearing Privatization And Public Investment

Organic Law No. 29/2004 of 03/12/2004 on Rwandan Nationality Code

Act. In determining the capital of Rwanda.

Nationality Law 2004

ORGANIC LAW No. 29/2004 OF 03/12/2004 One Rwandan Nationality Code

Organic Law No. 08/2005 07.14.2005 Of Determining The Use And Management Of Land In Rwanda

Organic law setting up "Gacaca Jurisdictions"

Land Tenure

CRIMINAL LAW

DECREE-LAW No. 21/77 Penal Code

DECREE-LAW No. 12/79. Regime Firearms and ammunition.

ORGANIC LAW No. 05/2005 From 14/04/2005 Establishing the Independent National Commission to gather evidence of the involvement of the French State in the genocide in Rwanda In 1994

ORGANIC LAW No. 11/2007 of 16/03/2007 concerning referral of cases to Rwanda By The Republic Of The International Criminal Tribunal for Rwanda and from Other States

ORGANIC LAW No. 31/2007 From 25 / 07/2007 to abolish the Death Penalty

Law n 34/1987 on Police And From Rolling Road Traffic

Law n 47/2001 Wearing Crimes Discrimination and Sectarianism

LAW No. 09/2000 16 / 06/2000, Establishing Organisation Generale and juridiction of the National Police

LAW No. 09/2007 of 16/02/2007 on the Responsibilities, Organization And Operation Of The National Commission for the Fight Against Genocide

LAW No. 15/2004 And Wearing Fashion Administration Of Proof

LAW No. 23/2003 on the prevention and suppression Of Corruption and related offenses

LAW No. 25/2004, Establishing Organization And Operation Of Local Service to assist the maintenance of security " Local Defence

LAW No. 27/2001 on the Rights and Protection Of A Child Against Violence The

ACT No. 33 bis/2003 against the crime of Genocide, Crimes Against The imanite And Crimes Of War

ACT No. 38 / 2006 of 25/09/2006 establishing and organizing the National Prison Service

LAW No. 13/2004 of 17/5/2004 concerning the Code Of Criminal Procedure

LAW No. 13/2004 Carrying Code of Criminal Procedure (OJ No Special From 30 / 07/2004)

Act No. 23/2003 of 07/08/2003 on the prevention and suppression Of Corruption and Related Offences

Act No. 13/2004 From 17/5/22004 Carrying Code of Criminal Procedure

Act No. 13 / 2004 From 17/5/22004 Carrying Code of Criminal Procedure,

Ministerial Order on Legal Fees for Criminal Matters

Regulations of leasing activities and conditions for the exercise of these activities

CIVIL LAW

DECREE-LAW No. 09/76 Purchase And Sale Photography customary land or rights of land use.

DECREE. And Authentic Acts Notary. - Land Titles

DECREE. Regime Foncier

ORDER. Civil Code - [Book 1:] Of Contracts or Conventional Obligations.

ORGANIC LAW No. 08/2005 Land Wearing Rigime In Rwanda

LAW No. 18/2004 From 20/06/2004 on the Code of Civil Procedure, Commercial, Social and Administrative

LAW No. 18/2004 on the Code of Civil Procedure, Commercial, Social and Administrative

LAW No. 18/2007 OF 19/04/2007 Wearing Expropriation for Public Utility

LAW No. 22/99 supplementing the first book From Civil Code and INSTITUTE PART FIVE REGARDING MATRIMONIAL REGIMES, liberalities and Estates

LAW No. 42/1988. Preliminary Title and First Book Of Civil Code.

Law Relating to the Management of Abandoned Property

ORGANIC LAW No. 08/2005 OF 14/07/2005 Determining The Use And Management Of Land In Rwanda

Organic Law No. 08/2005 Of 14/07 / 2005 Determining The Use And Management Of Land In Rwanda

COMMERCIAL LAW

Investment code

DECREE LAW N º 18/76. Public Establishment Production, Transport and Distribution of electricity, water and gas (Electrogaz).

DECREE-LAW No. 09/78. Of The Office Of Pyrethrum From Rwanda (OPYRWA).

DECREE-LAW No. 10/76. Transfer of commercial activities.

DECREE-LAW No. 19/78. Creation Of National Accounting

DECREE-LAW No. 26/78. Of The Office Of Tea.

DECREE-LAW No. 27/78. Office Of The Coffees (RISO-coffee).

DECREE. Sedentary capitas Of Commerce.

DECREE. Trade of cattle - Patent.

DECREE. Livestock control skins for export.

DECREE. Matrimonial agreements merchants.

DECREE. Culture, Industry And Commerce Of Cotton.

DECREE. The Letter of Exchange, promissory note and protests.

DECREE. Traders And The Proof Of Commercial Commitments.

DECREE. Warrants.

DECREE. Gage's goodwill, discount and Gage From the commercial invoice.

DECREE. Drinking places - Acquisition And Transfer Of Credit In Free Or Alcoholic Beverages - Prohibition. .

DECREE. Export Products From Plants Picking Or Culture.

DECREE. Manufacturing and trade in food.

DECREE. Books Of Commerce.

DECREE. Sale Cafes in Rwanda.

LEGISLATIVE DECREE No. 3/82. CHAMBER OF COMMERCE AND INDUSTRY OF RWANDA.

LAW No. 03/2002 establishing the Rwanda Bureau of Standards (RBS).

LAW No. 18/2004 From 20/06/2004 on the Code of Civil Procedure, Commercial, Social Administrative and

LAW No. 18/2004 on the Code of Civil Procedure, Commercial, Social and Administrative

LAW No. 31/1982. Ambulant reorganization Du Commerce.

LAW No. 35/91 On Organisation of Internal Trade (OJ, 1991, P.1138). Amended and supplemented by Law No. 15/2001

LAW No. 36/91. From the Trade Registry.

LAW No. 43/90. Promotion Of Exports.

LAW. The Skin Trade.

LAW. The price control.

Act No. 36/91 From 5 August 1991 on the register of Trade

Act to establish an excise tax on some imported and locally manufactured

order of the Governor General. Edible rice trade.

LEGISLATIVE ORDER No. 57/AERéglementation Du Commerce, possession and consumption of Foodstuffs.

LEGISLATIVE ORDER No. 186/Agri. Prohibition pounded rice trade.

LEGISLATIVE ORDER No. 92/AE Price Paid At To The Native Café Du Rwanda.Stocks Unsold.

ORDER No. 41/412. Edible oils trade.

ORDER No. 41/424. And Trade Preparing Eggs In Shell.

ORDER No. 441/71. Conditions of Purchase From Coffee Producers To Glory - Repeal Of Ordinance No. 41/35 From 28 April 1950.

ORDER No. 109/AE Export - Conditions of packaging, presentation and quality.

ORDER No. 22/AE The Export Shelled peanuts.

ORDER No. 40/4. Preparation Of Commerce And Flour, Bread And Other foods derived from flour.

ORDER No. 41/162. Conditions for exporting fibers.

ORDER No. 41/539. Flowers And Export Of Pyrethrum powders.

ORDER No. 41/98. From the Corn Trade.

ORDER No. 51/28. Decree Cotton - Measures of Application.

ORDER No. 51/418. Importation of plants, seeds, powders and all derived from the pyrethrum kenya, uganda and the Tanganyika.

ORDER No. 51/431. Importing From Corn.

ORDER No. 53/260. From the Tea Trade.

ORDER No. 53/389. Export Essential Oils From Geranium Rosat, ¬ OF euca lyptus, vetiver, Lemongrass and Mint.

ORDER No. 53/390. Export Leaves Digital De Belladonna And Flowers Camomile.

ORDER No. 95/AGRI. Coffee seeds or seedlings - Import - Prohibition.

ORDER. Packaging, preparation and production of foodstuffs.

COMPANY LAW

LAW No. 20/2000 relating to non-profit.

LAW No. 50/2007 OF 18/09/2007 establishment, organization and functioning of cooperative in Rwanda

LAW No. 06/1988. Organization Of Trading Companies.

LAW No. 39/1988 Supplementing Act No. 06/1988 From 12 February 1988 concerning the organization of Trade. OJ No. 23 Bis From December 1, 1988

Law Relating to Non-profit making organisms.

LABOR LAW

Code of Labour

Law No. 51/2001 30.12.2001 Of Establishing The Labour Code.

Law Establishing the Labour Code

HEALTH LAW

DECREE. Red Cross or Geneva Cross - Protection.

DECREE. Hygiene and Public Safety.

LAW No. 10/98 Bearing Exercise In The Art Of Healing

LAW No. 12/99 relating to art Pharmaceutical

LAW No. 30/2001 On Organisation, functioning and jurisdiction of the Association Of Doctors

LAW No. 62/2007 of 30/12/2007 establishing, Organization, Operation And Management of mutual health

MINING LAW

DECREE. In Search Of Ban Uranium, thorium and Any Substance, Containing radioactive minerals.

DECREE. Ordinary legislation powders, explosive substances and gear Murderers Acting For Explosion.

INSURANCE LAW

DECREE-LAW No. 32/75. Compulsory insurance against civil liability in respect of Motor Vehicles

DECREE-LAW No. 20/75. Insurance

LAW No. 24/2001 Wearing Institution, Organization and Operation of a system of Health Insurance Agents In The State

LAW No. 18/1982. Terms exploit Casualty Insurance Companies.

LAW No. 23/2005, Establishing Organization And Operation Of Military Medical Insurance

TAX LAW

Customs Law

DECREE LAW N ° 16/79 Laying Down The duties on The Café.

LAW No. 06/2001 Wearing Introduction Of Tax On Value Added.

LAW No. 02/2000 on the sale by public auction goods seized or confiscated by the Customs.

LAW No. 03/2001 amending Law No. 18/98 of 31/12/1998 on the rates of consumption tax to be levied on some imported and locally manufactured.

LAW No. 04/2004 determining the Applicable Tariff on imported cement in Rwanda

LAW No. 04/2004 determining the Applicable Tariff on imported cement in Rwanda

LAW No. 04/97 on the consumption tax to be levied on The Beer manufactured locally or imported.

LAW No. 05/2000 amending Decree-Law No. 013/01 From 15 February 1995 fixing the scale of import duties on imported products, as confirmed by Law No. 06 / 95 On August 24, 1995

ACT No. 05/97 on the consumption tax to be levied on Lemonade, Water And Drinks Mineral Water manufactured locally or Imported

LAW No. 05/97 on the consumption tax to be levied on The Lemonade, Water And Drinks Mineral Water manufactured locally or Imported

LAW No. 06/97 on the consumption tax to be levied on cigarettes manufactured locally or imported.

LAW No. 07/97 on the consumption tax On perceiving Liquors And Wines

LAW No. 10/95 amending the Act Of March 5, 1968 as amended on This Day, A Relative consumption tax to be levied on locally produced beers

LAW No. 10/97 Relative At the consumption tax to be levied on petroleum products

LAW No. 17/2001 amending Law No. 18/98, 31/12/1998 On The Rate Of The consumption tax collected upon some imported and locally manufactured Local.

LAW No. 22/2001 amending Act No. 7/98 From 08.08.1998 laying down the duties on imported products.

LAW No. 25/2002 determining the Fees Tariff ' The entry on Imported Products

LAW No. 25/2005 on Establishment of Tax Procedures

LAW No. 26/2006 of 27/05/2006 determining and establishing the excise duty on some imported and locally manufactured

LAW No. 46 / 2001 amending Law No. 08/2001 01/20/2001 Modifying the Applicable Tariff on Cement Imports (OJ N ° Special Ter From 31/12/2001)

LAW No. 52/2001 determining the Applicable Tariff Products originating in Member States of the Common Market States Of Africa In Eastern And Southern Africa (Comesa)

LAW No. 52/2001 determining the Tariff Applicable On Products originating from Member States Du Marche The common African States Vest And Southern Africa (Comesa) (OJ N ° Special Ter From 31/12/2001)

LAW No. 54/2001 amending Law No. 18/98 From 31 / 12/1998 amending the rates from the consumption tax to be levied on some imported and locally manufactured

ACT No. 7/98 determining the rate of import duties on Imported Products

LAW No. 8/97 on the Code of Taxes direct on different profits and professional income

LAW No. 9/95 amending Decree-Law From 31 December 1974 concerning the tax on the consumption of Lemonade, carbonated waters and other soft drinks manufactured locally

LAW No. 16/2005 Relative to Direct Taxes On Income, OJ N ° 1 From 1 January 2006

LAW No. 18/98 Modifying the rates of the consumption tax to be levied on some imported and locally manufactured

LAW No. 21/2006 Covering Customs system

LAW No. 38 / 91 Fixing the Rate of import duties.

LAW No. 45/90 From price of export duties.

Law Establishing the customs system 2005

Law No. 26/2006 Determining and Establishing Consumption Tax on Some importé and Manufactured products available locally.

Law on Direct Taxes on Income and

Law on Direct Taxes on Income and

Law on Tax Procedures

Law on Tax Procedures

Act to establish tax procedures

law on direct taxes on income

104/AGRI ORDER NO. Cotton Tax.

ORDER No. 53/233. The compensatory tax on essential oils of geranium Rosat, Eucalyptus, Vetiver, And Of Lemongrass Mint.

Customs Regime

Value Added Tax Law 2005

BANKING LAW

DECREE-LAW No. 04/78. Creating a special guarantee fund.

DECREE-LAW No. 6/81. Reorganization Of The National Bank of Rwanda.

DECREE. Cheque - Introduction The Uniform Act.

DECREE. Of Bankruptcy.

DECREE. The Concordat of Preventive In Bankruptcy.

DECREE. Mortgage Plan.

DECREE-LAW No. 25/79. Regulations in savings bonds.

Foreign exchange regulation

LAW No. 007/2008 08.04.2008 Of Organization Of Banking Regarding

LAW No. 55-2007 30-11-2007 OF CENTRAL BANK OF Governing the RWANDA

LAW No. 05/98 Wearing Of The Office Of The Auditor General Of The State Finance

Law n ° 08/99 on the regulation of banks and other financial institutions. (OJ No. 13 From 07.01.1999)

LAW No. 55/2007 of 30/11/2007 governing the National Bank of Rwanda

LAW No. 28/90. Exchange controls.

Act No. 08/99 From 18.06.1999 on the regulation of banks and other financial institutions.

REGULATION No. 04/2008 We Insider Lending

REGULATION No. 05/2008 And One Large Credit Exposure Concentration

REGULATION No. 06 / 2008 is Corporate Governance

Exchange Regulation

Regulation No. 03/2008 One Of Licensing Banks

COMMUNICATIONS AND MEDIA LAW

DECREE. Control film showings.

LEGISLATIVE DECREE No. 43/76. Postal Plan Of Organization.

LAW No. 44/2001 of 30/11/2001 governing telecommunications

LAW No. 44/2001 Relative To The Telecommunications.

LAW No. 2/92. Of The National Office of Post.

LAW No. 31/1987 on the approval and ratification of the Acts From The Universal Postal Union.

LAW No. 32/2002 establishing the Office Of Technology In Information And Communication .

LAW No. 18/2002 governing the Press

Law No. 44/2001 30.11.2001 Of Governing Telecommunications

Law governing the Press

Act governing telecommunications

Ministerial order of 07/06/2004 No. 2/DC/04 instructions are for the publication in the official gazette of modifications made to telecommunications licenses

Ministerial order of 07/06/2004 No. 3/DC/04 telecommunications networks and services are not requiring a telecommunications license

Ministerial order No. 4/DC/04 of 07/06 / 2004 Annual fees are payable by public utilities

Ministerial order No. 5/DC/04 of 07/06/2004 on the general terms and Pricing Principles To Be RespectED in interconnection agreements

Ministerial order No. 6/DC/04 of 07/06 / 2004 Requests for Installation of one telecommunications terminal equipment and facilities on public and private property

Ministerial order of 07/06/2004 No. 7/DC/04 Specifying the content of the Regulatory Board's register of telecommunications activities

Ministerial order No. 8/DC / 04 of 07.06.2004 is additional and Specific kinds of agreements, decisions, practices and codes of conduct regarded To Be Anti-competitive or abuse of a dominant year position

Ministerial order No. 9/DC/04 of 07/06 / 2004 on conditions to Be Incorporated Into telecommunications and radio communications licenses

Presidential order No. 04/01 of 15/03/2004 Determining Specific Duties of the Regulatory Board in telecommunications Matters

Presidential order No. 05/01 of 15/03/2004 Determining the fonctionnement of the universal access fund operations and public contributions

TRANSPORT AND MARITIME LAW

DECREE. Of carrier liability.

DECREE. False Statements In transport.

LAW No. 44/2006 of 05/10/2006 Determining The Responsibilities, Organization And Functioning Of Rwanda Civil Aviation Authority (RCAA)

LAW No. 21/2004, Establishing And Organization Of The Office Of The Rwandans' Civil Aviation

LEGISLATIVE ORDER No. 71/241. Sick And Wounded - Priority Of Transportation.

ORDER No. 176/AGRI. Protection Of Meat Carried.

ORDER No. 74/241. Transport and trade of meat in urban ridings.

ENVIRONMENTAL LAW

Biosafety Law 2005

DECREE On The easements for groundwater, to the waters of Lakes And Rivers, and their use.

DECREE LAW. Rwandan Office of Tourism and National Parks.

DECREE. Hunting And Fishing

DECREE. And concessions Administration of lake water and river water.

DECREE. Institute of National Parks of Belgian Congo - Albert National Park boundary.

DECREE. Institute of National Parks of Belgian Congo. Creation Of The Kagera National Park.

DECREE. The Sanitary Police Pets.

DECREE. Protection Of Animals.

DECREE. The Fishing Licences Regulations.

ORGANIC LAW No. 04/2005 the modalities of protection, conservation and promotion of environment in Rwanda, OG

LAW No. 11/82. Protection, Conservation and Land Use.

LAW No. 16/2006 On Organisation, Functions And Operation Of The Office Of Rwandans Protection Of The Environment

ACT No. 22/2005 establishing the Nyungwe National Park, OJ N ° 2 / From 2006 2006 15 Jnavier

LAW No. 47/1988. Organization of the forestry regime.

Protecting, safeguarding and promoting the environment

INTELLECTUAL PROPERTY LAW

LAW No. 03/98 concerning Right of Patente

LAW No. 27/1983. Copyright.

LAW. Patents.

LAW. Industrial Designs.

LAW. From brand and trademarks.

Act No. 03/98 From 02.14.1998 concerning Right of Patente

ARBITRATION LAW

ACT No. 005/2008 of 14/02/2008 on arbitration and conciliation in commercial matters

ENERGY LAW

DECREE. Import of petroleum products and mineral oils from lubrication.

LAW NO [XX/2007] Of [Date] Governing Gas (Draft)

LAW [NO XX/2007] Of [Date] Governing Electricity (Draft)

LAW No. 39/2001 Wearing Creation Of The Regulatory Agency Utilities

TREATIES

Bamako Convention of 30 January 1991 On Prohibition Of Import Of Hazardous Waste In Africa, the Control of Transboundary Movement And Management Of Those Products in Africa, ratified by Law No. 21/2005 From 21/10/2005 , OJ 4/2006 From 15 February 2006

Brussels Convention on the Establishment of an International Union for the Publication of Customs Tariffs.

cooperation agreement signed between the Republic of Rwanda and Zaire To The Republic Of Exploitation, Transport And The Marketing of methane gas from Lake Kivu.

From Geneva Convention Creating A Union Internationale de Secours. Approved by Act of April 5, 1929.

Convention Of The Conference of Postal and Telecommunications In Central Africa (CAPTAC), Signed at Brazzaville.

From Geneva International Convention on the Simplification of Customs Formalities. Approved by Act of September 6, 1924

From Kyoto International Convention for the Simplification and Harmonization of Customs Procedures.

Universal Postal Convention And Various Arrangements for mail, Signed at Stockholm.

Universal Postal Convention, Final Protocol and Annexes, Regulations and Appendices Provisions Concerning The Airmail correspondence, Final Protocol and Annexes signed in Brussels.

Convention on the creation of offices and the collaboration of the Excise, Signed With Zaire in Kinshasa.

Convention Relative To The Creation Of The African Institute and Mauritian Statistical and Applied Economics (IAMSEA).

Regional Convention on the Recognition of Studies, Certificates, Diplomas, and Degrees of Higher Education in the States of Africa, Adopted at Arusha.

Convention On The Protection Plant Between The States Members Of The Economic Community of Great Lakes Countries, Signed In Bukavu.

LAW No. 31/1987 on the approval and ratification of the Acts From The Universal Postal Union

Tax treaty with Belgium

treaty with Mauritius Tax

Treaty Between Belgium and Great Britain. Use of river water, Water Courses And Being Part Of The Section Of The Border Between Rwanda [-urundi] And [From Territory] Tanganyika.

AGRICULTURE LAW

DECREE. Prohibition to export and slaughter livestock.

DECREE. Limitation of banana plantations used in the preparation of fermented beverages Natives.

DECREE-LAW No. 08/79. Excise tax to be levied on locally manufactured cigarettes.

LEGISLATIVE ORDER No. 166/Vét. And marking livestock markets.

LEGISLATIVE ORDER No. 41/222. Production, sale, possession and processing of plant products, livestock, Hunting And Fishing.

ORDER No. 41/414. Reporting of quantities of meat or debited by The Butchers Meat Sellers.

Organic Law No. 08/2005 14.07.2005 Of Determining The Use And Management Of Land In Rwanda

RWANDA ENERGY SECTOR - STRATEGIC INFORMATION AND DEVELOPMENTS

ENERGY SECTOR BASICS

Total installed electricity capacity:	**72.5 MW**	
Hydroelectric:		**59.1 %**
Thermal:		**40.5%**
Solar:		**0.4%**
Total primary energy supply:	**1,610 ktoe**	
Wood:		**57%**
Wood for Charcoal:		**23%**
Petroleum Products:		**11%**
Agricultural Peat:		**6%**
Electricity:		**3%**

The main energy sources for cooking are: electricity, gas, oil, firewood, charcoal and agricultural residues. Charcoal is the source most used in urban areas and is among the causes of environmental degradation. Available capacity as of 2009 was 54.6 MW, 11.5 MW of which was provided by hydropower imports from the Democratic Republic of Congo, and 15 MW of which was provided by rented thermal generators. Rwanda holds joint ownership of the Ruzizi II 12 MW hydroelectric plant with Burundi and the DRC, with SINELAC, a company created and owned by the three involved governments, operating the plant. Total domestic electricity generation in 2010 was 344.7 GWh, with a further 65.8 GWh supplied to the system through imports.

Diesel remains the primary fuel for self-generation in rural areas, and for emergency supply in urban areas. Kerosene is the main fuel used for lighting. In rural areas, biomass accounts for the vast majority of energy supply. A 2007 study indicated that approximately 80% of fuelwood used in the country was foraged, and therefore did not pass through the market economy of the country.

Diesel fuel is imported and transported by truck from the Tanzanian port of Dar es Salaam. Petroleum products account for 25 percent of total imports, estimated at 5,623 bbl/day in 2007. Electricity imports in 2010 accounted for approximately 16% of the total electricity supply, with the majority coming from the Ruzizi II project. Electricity imports to the country have remained static since 2008 at 65.8 GWh, indicating limited scope for further increases in import volume, with current infrastructure arrangements.

About 7% of the population had access to electricity, in total. Of the 90% of the population who live in rural areas, only 1% had access to electricity.

Grid extension has been extremely limited, and economically justified only to meet rural industrial loads and emerging population clusters. The electricity grid consists of 3,300 km of 110 kV, 70 kV, 30 kV and 15 kV lines, with the primary concentration of grid connections running from the West to the North of the country.

Rwanda is currently experiencing a net deficit of power. Domestic demand in 2010 was 438 GWh, with final supply being 410.5 GWh, and billed consumption merely 365.3 GWh, a shortfall of 17%. The government plans to double the electrification rate, increasing connections to 16% of the population (200,000 connections) up from the current 100,000 customers by 2012 at a cost of US$400 million.

In recent years, the combination of strong demand growth with unexpectedly low lake-water levels exacerbated by high technical losses (upwards of 20%) and unreliability of the system, led to extensive power cuts. Transmission and distribution losses have fallen in recent years, but still amounted to 13% in 2010, predominantly from the low-voltage distribution network. If climate change affects biomass resources, this could exacerbate the problem. The lack of sufficient electricity is increasing deforestation, as people seek other ways to produce light and heat.

HYDRO POWER IN RWANDA

Hydropower potential in the country is estimated to be 500 MW, with only 72 MW having been exploited. The country has substantial hydroelectric resources, as well as natural gas deposits under Lake Kivu, which could make Rwanda self-sufficient in electricity, or even a net exporter. But the development of natural gas power plants, or new dam construction, requires both time and investment. Nevertheless, the Ministry of Infrastructure is financing 11 hydropower plants with installed capacities from 100 kW to 9.5 MW. GIZ (Deutsche Gesellschaft für Internationale Zusammenarbeit, formerly GTZ) are also providing support to MININFRA for the promotion of SMEs in the small-hydro sector. Three companies have currently commissioned small-hydro projects, with a combined capacity of 755 kW, with a further 3.6 MW under consideration from 10 other projects. By 2015, the Government hopes to have promoted an additional 45 MW of small-hydro capacity in the country.

Rwanda's major Rivers have proven 333 potential sites for Micro-hydropower countrywide. Opportunities exist in Micro and Small Hydropower projects and shared regional hydropower projects with East Africa (EAC) Partners.

A couple of micro, mini and small Hydropower Projects are currently under construction. The largest domestic hydropower project under construction is Nyabarongo I, with an installed capacity of 28 MW. Some shared hydropower projects with neighboring countries are also underway, including 145MW project shared by Burundi, DRC and Rwanda and a 90 MW project to be jointly developed by Tanzania, Burundi and Rwanda.

MINI AND SMALL HYDROPOWER

There are 20 projects totaling 9MW bid as 4"bundles"with an expected investment of approximately 25-30 million. The planned completion date is 2014-2015 and 3 bundled bids for 10MW of projects bid every year from 2015-17.

MEDIUM HYDROPOWER

12-17 MW Nyabarongo II is being evaluated, with an expected investment amount of approximately $80 million. This is a multipurpose project envisaged to cater for water supply, irrigation as well as electrical power generation. The project may develop either under Public or PPP arrangement and is planned to generate 12-17 MW and the power will be fed into Rwanda National Grid. The project consists of 48m high concrete gravity dam with crest of 228m and a surface power station with 2*8.5MW Keplan turbines just situated at the dam toe.

REGIONAL HYDROPOWER

Ruzizi III (145MW) supported by EU, AfDB, among others with an expected investment capital of $450 million and completion date in 2016.The project is being developed under CEPGL umbrella for Rwanda, Burundi and DRC.

Ruzizi III hydropower project is planned to generate 145MW and the power output is shared equally by three countries. The project consist of 105m long dam crest whose height is 20.5m, 2.28km Headrace Tunnel and a surface power station with 3*50 MW Francis Units.

Rusumo (90MW) falls supported by World Bank and others. Its expected investment amount is $300 million and planned completion date is 2017.The project is being developed under NELSAP umbrella for Rwanda, Burundi and Tanzania.

Rusumo falls Hydropower Project is planned to generate 81 MW and the power output will be shared equally by three countries. The project consists of concrete dam with crest length of 150m,Headrace Tunnel of 460m and a surface power station with 3*30MW Kaplan turbines.

PEAT ENERGY

A first Peat master plan was developed in 1993 and indicates the potential to develop around 700MW of generation from Rwanda's Peat resources. The master plan indicates that Rwanda has estimated reserves of 155 million tons of dry peat spread over an area of about 50,000 hectares. About 77% of peat reserves are near Akanyaru and Nyabarongo rivers and the Rwabusoro Plains.

However, the study was not detailed enough to allow the full understanding of the entire country's peat resources. Thus, the detailed study to provide the detailed picture of peat reserves in Rwanda is underway.

POTENTIAL FOR PEAT-TO POWER GENERATION

The theoretical potential (assuming all peat bogs are exploited) for electricity energy generation from peat is estimated to about 1,200MW. Peat reserves in Rwabusoro marshland and around Akanyaru River can fuel 450MW of electricity generation for 25years.

The Rwabusoro marshland and Rucahabi in Nyanza and Bugesera districts present significant opportunity for large scale peat harvesting for power generation. Rwanda plans to develop its peat resources to generate about 200MW of power by 2017.

PEAT-TO-POWER PROJECTS IN RWANDA

The Government of Rwanda is developing a15MW peat-to-Power in Rusizi District in Bugarama Sector. The government is negotiating with a strategic partner to develop a 100 MW peat fired power plant in South Akanyaru prospect and the project is to be developed as Public Private Partnership (PPP) .The government of Rwanda has advertised tenders for EPC Contractor and an Owner's engineer for 100MW peat-to-power project in Rwabusoro prospect and which is to be structured either as public or private.

Currently, The Government of Rwanda is preparing a Peat Policy to sustainably and safely harvest peat resources for power generation.

INVESTMENT OPPORTUNITIES IN PEAT PROJECTS (GREENFIELD 100MW PROJECT)

Rwanda is also keen to develop its peat resources as part of its short-term strategy to sustainably increase power capacity. The Government of Rwanda is open to discussions with any potential investor for the development of the 100MW plant. The government is also open for a long term concession with a strategic investor as long as the off-take price and project structure makes sense.

The project is planned to be developed as a Public Private Partnership (PPP) and the government may consider a PPP or Joint Venture (JV) structure to lower the cost of capital and the cost of power generation projects.

PEAT PROJECTS ALONG EDPRS II

Along the EDPRS II period (2013-2018), Rwanda envisages to implement the following peat projects to deliver the energy demand driven roadmap:

- Hakan Peat Project (100MW) expected to deliver in 2017; the project is under implementation.
- Gishoma Peat to Power (15MW) expected to deliver in June 2014; the construction is underway.
- Three Small Peat projects (expected to generate 15 MW each); the projects are planned to deliver at the end of 2015, mid 2016 and the end of 2016 respectively.
- 100 MW of additional Peat generation expected to be delivered through a Power Purchase Agreement (PPA) in 2017; the detailed feasibility study is underway.

For the Three Small Peat projects; the pre-feasibility studies on seven such sites was completed early 2013. It is anticipated that at least three of these sites are suitable for developing small scale peat energy generation (15 MW).

As for the 100 MW of additional peat generation, following the conclusion of the Power Purchase Agreement with Hakan, there is considerable private sector interest in developing generation from peat reserves. Building from this interest, the competitive tender will be launched for a private developer to operate mining and generation infrastructure to provide an additional 100 MW to the national grid. The potential sites were identified, including the Akanyaru and the site around Akagera.

METHANE GAS IN RWANDA

Methane Gas in Rwanda is found in Lake Kivu in the Eastern African Rift Zone and the DRC. The 2,400 sq.km lake contains high concentrations of naturally occurring methane gas (CH_4) and carbon dioxide (CO_2), with the highest concentrations at depths ranging from 270m to 500m. The oxygenated upper layer of the lake from the surface to a depth of 60m supports the lake's biology. The resource is shared equally between Rwanda and the DRC.

The PMP (Peat, Methane, and Petroleum) Unit, at EWSA is developing methane projects potential for Methane-to-Power Generation. Lake Kivu contains about 300 billion cubic carbon dioxide and 60 billion cubic meters of CH_4.An estimated 120 to 250 million cubic meters of CH_4 is generated annually in the Lake.

Rwanda wishes to utilize this resource to develop methane-to-power projects and other uses such as fertilizer and gas-to liquids projects.

The Methane in Lake Kivu is estimated to be sufficient to generate 700 MW of electricity over a period of 55 years. Rwanda's share of the total generation potential is about 350 MW, with the rest being DRC's share.

It has the capacity to generate 120 million to 150 million m^3 of CH_4 per annum, representing a power potential of 90 to 130 MW.

USE OF LAKE KIVU METHANE IN RWANDA

Lake Kivu methane was first taped by Union chimique de Belge with a gas pilot plant at cape Rubona in 1963 to supply the Bralirwa brewery. Bralirwa brewery converted one of its boilers to use gas in place of fuel oil, and was supplied with 5,000 cubic meters/day of methane gas purified to 80%.The pilot plant was recently shut down after operating for over 40 years.

EXISTING METHANE-TO-POWER PROJECTS IN RWANDA

· KivuWatt,a subsidiary of Contour Global(USA),is developing a 100 MW plant,KP I, a 45 MW pilot plant developed by GoR,is operating about 1.5 MW since late 2007 with plan to scale-up capacity to 50MW.
· REC (Rwanda Energy Company) is subsidiary of RIG (Rwanda Investment Group) undertaking a 3.6 MW plant project, is seeking new partners and investors to revive and scale up the project.
Numerous reports on Lake Kivu going to 1937 are available. Recent studies by LAHMEYEROSAE and K.Tietze, and Lake Management Prescriptions are also available.

INVESTMENT OPPORTUNITIES

Opportunities in Existing Concessions:
· Kivuwatt's 25 MW phase I(Estimation cost $140m) is under construction with GoR Sovereign Guarantee and MIGA guarantee. The 75 MW second phase will need financing. The estimated cost is $260m and completion is planned for 2014.
· REC is seeking partners and financing to revive the plant and scale it up to scale to 50 MW. The estimated cost is $ 106m and completion is planned for 2015.
· Ongoing negotiations with private partners for 100 MW may be an opportunity once they are not concluded.

POLICY, LAW & REGULATION

· Draft Gas Law and Regulations for methane projects is under review by Parliament.
· A draft concession Agreement and draft PPA is under development for new projects(existing projects have PPAs with utility).
· Management Prescriptions for the safe extraction of Lake Kivu gas resources are to be adopted.

SOLAR ENERGY

Average horizontal irradiation is 5.5 kWh/ m2/day. Rwanda is also home to the largest single solar installation in Africa - the Kigali Solair plant- which generates 250 kW and feeds into the national electricity grid. The plant was funded by the German municipal power company Stadtwerke Mainz, and installed by Juwi in 2008.

Wind energy

The Ministry of Energy recently commissioned a feasibility study to determine the wind power capacity of Rwanda. This National Wind Atlas is being developed with the help of the Belgian government. Wind energy is currently exploited only in decentralised off-grid applications.

Biomass energy

An estimated 2.3 million tons of wood fuel are consumed in the country annually. The Rwanda Energy Management Authority (REMA) estimates that Rwanda has a deficit of 4 million cubic metres of wood fuel, due to extensive deforestation, and over-reliance on biomass for heating and light in rural areas. Also, as the majority of rural biomass is foraged, market mechanisms to improve the quality of fuel will be slow to take effect. Fuel-wood caps are to be imposed in several districts of the country to combat this. Aforestation measures, accompanied by a concurrent reduction in biomass consumption, aim to increase the forested area of the country to 23.5% by 2012. The country also has significant peat reserves, estimated at 155 million tonnes in 2008.

GIZ are supporting the development of the National Biogas Development Program, which aims to install upwards of 15,000 biogas digesters for schools and farming households, to provide biogas for cooking and lighting, and reduce dependence on fuel-wood. Plans have also been put in place to increase national annual biodiesel production to 16 million litres, and install an additional 1 MW of biogas-fired power capacity.

GEOTHERMAL ENERGY

Potential exists for between 170 – 320 MW of geothermal power generation, due to the country's proximity to the geothermal resource of the Great Rift Valley. Studies have indicated thermal waters with temperatures of up to 150ºC.

Geothermal energy is a clean and reliable source of energy, which is not affected by short-term fluctuations in the weather or world producer prices of oil. Most of the geothermal plants when installed have relatively very low maintenance costs and high availability. Geothermal energy is not dependent on whether it is day or night as solar energy is, or whether the wind blows strongly or not.

In Rwanda, two zones with geothermal potentials are found in the western region associated with volcanoes and the southern region (Bugarama) associated with faults in the East African Rift. Based on reconnaissance surface studies, the western region has been divided into three areas of Gisenyi, Karisimbi and Kinigi prospects that can be developed as separate geothermal prospects.

According to surface studies, the most promising of which are Karisimbi and Kinigi where it is likely GoR will discover a commercially viable geothermal resource for power generation using either binary or condensing steam turbines.

With extensive exploration and appraisal drilling geothermal can contribute more than 20 MW in short term and over 300 MW in the long term. The exact size of the resource is not yet proven. This will only be determined once exploratory drilling completed and once established the low costs of Geothermal and its high availability makes it the cheapest form of generation available.

It is evident from available information that Rwanda has areas that have low-temperature geothermal resources that can also be utilized for both power generation and direct industrial uses.

The development of Geothermal Resources is the highest priority over EDPRS II period and among envisaged developments we will have:

- 10 MW from Test Generation site at Kinigi
- 10 MW from Test Generation site at Karisimbi
- 50 MW of production scale generation at Kinigi / Karisimbi

BIOGAS

The National Domestic Biogas Program (NDBP) was started way back in 2007(Phase I) with financial and technical support provided by SNV and GIZ. The program objective was to develop a commercial and sustainable domestic biogas sector, substituting firewood with biogas for cooking and increasing agricultural production through provision of bio-slurry as a fertilizer.

CURRENT STATUS

To date (End Aug. 2013) close to 3,365 biogas digesters have been disseminated in households by about 41 local companies. The installations costs are borne by the consumers (on their own revenues or credit from lenders) and the government (subsidy) on a 50/50 cost sharing principal. The subsidy is disbursed through the districts which have signed MoUs with local Credit giving institutions (SACCOS) to extend credit to the biogas project owners on request.
Initially, the Government has a memorandum of understanding with BPR to lend to biogas project owners at an interest rate of 13.5% per anum, slightly lower than market rates. However, the MoU was expired last year and is yet to be renewed.
To ensure the continued access to credit, 24 out of 30 districts have signed MoUs with SACCOs to extend credit to biogas projects. There is currently no uniform lending terms for biogas projects as previous required to protect consumers from rates higher than rate of return on investment. The terms of lending are negotiated on a case-by-case basis depending on the negotiating position of each district. Some form of collateral security is required before accessing a loan from SACCOs.
Biogas technologies: The dominant biogas plant technologies available are code named "Rwanda I" (foundation made of stones, round wall, dome, inlet and outlets made of bricks) and "Rwanda II" (foundation and round wall made of stones with dome, inlet and outlet made of bricks). The cost of each technology varies mainly depending on the size and the material inputs used in construction. The available plant sizes range between 4m3, 6m3 and 10m3 especially for domestic users.

EMERGING TECHNOLOGIES

Some new technologies have emerged including the flexi-biogas technology (from Kenya) and Fibre Glass Reinforced Biogas Technology (From china). The two technologies have only been used on a small scale (testing phase) and are not readily available on the Rwandan market. However, they present another potential option in the scaling up the use of biogas for cooking.

ENERGY SECTOR DEVELOPMENT

GOVERNMETN AGENCIES

The overall energy planning process is driven by the government, yet with strong participation by international donors organisations (NGOs, World Bank), which are key to environmental and poverty issues. Institutionalising planning is the core responsibility of the Ministry of Infrastructure. Under the guidance of the Ministry for Environment and Lands (MINELA) the Rwanda Environment Management Authority (http://www.rema.gov.rw/) is responsible for the co-ordination and implementation of national energy and environmental policies, and formulating the subsequent required legislation.
RURA is mandated to control and regulate an efficient, sustainable and reliable energy sector. The Agency is responsible for promoting effective competition, advising government during formulation of energy policy, protecting consumers, educating stakeholders, approving contractual undertakings with regard to distribution and transmission of electricity and gas and assessing the tariff structure.

MINIFRA

The Ministry of Infrastructure (www.mininfra.gov.rw/) is responsible for national energy infrastructure, and is the primary government ministry in the energy sector. Rural energy is part of this mandate. The MINIFRA views its role in the off-grid energy sector to include training, strategy, development of technical specifications for energy equipment, recommendation of strategies for the development of the private sector.

MINIRENA

The Ministry of Natural Resources (http://www.minirena.gov.rw/) is responsible for the management of the forest and water resources of the country, as well as environmental protection and management. The aforestation and wood consumption targets set out in the EDPRS fall under the remit of the MINIRENA.
The National Energy Policy has an objective of ensuring energy audits are carried out in industries, particularly the energy intensive ones, in order to enhance energy efficiency. The Energy Development and Poverty Reduction Strategy (EDPRS) aims at reducing technical losses from 23% to 15%, and to increase the share of energy efficient appliances to roughly 30 MW by 2012. The National Energy Policy has also identified the need for improved demand-side management measures, especially in fuel-wood consumption, and the necessity for improved efficiency in the transport sector to reduce petroleum imports (approximately 75 per cent of all imported petroleum is consumed within the transport sector). To this end, a project for the distribution of 800,000 compact fluorescent lights (CFLs) was included in the most recent strategic energy plan.

Electricity use per capita in Rwanda is extremely low, due to the small percentage of the population who have access to electricity services, standing at 22 kWh per capita
In order for the energy sector to contribute in a substantial manner to accelerated economic growth, and in order to meet basic energy needs, the Government of Rwanda has set clear objectives and targets for the energy sector to be fulfilled by 2012, under the Economic Development and Poverty Reduction Strategy (EDPRS), such as increasing the electricity access rate from the current 6% to 16% by the year 2012; increasing electricity supply to 130MW, reducing the costs of electricity service and the introduction of cost-reflective tariffs, energy diversification and security. To achieve these targets, many projects are under-way. The Belgian Development Agency, for example, is aiding grid extension, as well as capacity development in energy institutions. The current Sector-Wide Approach (SWAP) for the power sector in the country includes procedures for improving energy security, as well as promoting national and regional conventional and renewable energy projects.
The Regulatory Agency is defined by law as a national institution with legal powers, and autonomous administrative and financial management. The board of directors of the regulator are appointed by the Prime Minister, with a term of three years, renewable once. Financing for the Agency is derived from fees levied on the application for, and granting of licenses, a percentage of the turnover of public utilities (determined by the Minister responsible for each utility sector), and other grants and donations.
Whilst regulations are established in law, the current crisis facing the Rwandan energy market is hampering implementation and development. The regulatory framework for sustainable energy in particular is in its infancy, but programs put in place under the EDPRS will serve to promote the need for improved regulatory frameworks. Tariff-setting for electricity is still the responsibility of the national utility, which can lead to an imbalanced tariff structure, particularly if the structure of tariffs is hoped to be used to promote end-user energy efficiency. The assumption of further responsibilities by the RURA, as well as the promotion of competition in the energy sector, for example through unbundling and increased private-sector participation, would further improve fairness and accountability in the energy sector.

ECONOMIC DEVELOPMENT AND POVERTY REDUCTION STRATEGY (EDPRS)

The EDPRS covers the period 2008-2012, and is the medium-term framework for achieving the country's long term development aspirations as embodied in the Rwanda Vision 2020, and the intermediate targets of the 2015 Millennium Development Goals (MDGs). The Energy Sector Strategy has been developed to support sustained growth in the economy, and raise the standard of living for the Rwandan people by improving access to modern forms of energy at the household level. Objectives include the grid-electrification of 16% of the populace, as well as the provision of reliable electricity supply, through either on- or off-grid measures, to 100% of health centres and 50% of schools. Other objectives include a revision of the currently-outdated tariff structure to better reflect costs, and the establishment of a favourable legal and institutional framework for increased private sector participation. New laws for the electricity and gas sectors are currently being discussed in Parliament.

NATIONAL ENERGY POLICY

The Energy Policy for Rwanda which was updated in November 2008 laid down the Government's commitment to the development and utilisation of renewable energy resources and technologies and energy efficiency promotion.

NATIONAL ENERGY STRATEGY (2008-2020)

The principal objective of the energy sector is to contribute to accelerated sustainable socio-economic development. A number of objectives for the development of renewable energy and energy efficiency are included in the strategy. These include; the further diversification of energy sources, including exploitation of the country's geothermal potential and the increased use of solar water heaters; the increased use of CFLs in households and businesses to reduce energy consumption, energy auditing for industries, and information campaigns on good energy management practices.

Government policy to promote rural electricity access is primarily based on the extension of the transmission and distribution network, operated by the EWSA. However, where customers are not centralised enough for economic grid extension, solar PV, generators or hydropower may be offered through private suppliers. The Electricity Access Roll-out Program (EARP), jointly-operated by the EWSA and MININFRA (and supported by a number of development partners, including the ADB, the Belgian Government, the JICA and the World Bank), is the implementing program for grid and off-grid electricity access improvements, as set out in the EDPRS.

ENERGY MARKET

The priority for Rwanda is to implement projects now, to tackle electricity capacity constraints now and in the future, begin to tackle pro-actively the wood crisis, begin to provide greater access to modern energy, and to reduce reliance on petroleum products.

2011 has seen some key developments in the energy sector of Rwanda. The African Development Bank and other lenders have committed US$ 91.25 million to the development of the Kivuwatt power project, in conjunction with ContourGlobal, an American project developer. The loan agreements were finalised in August 2011, and will finance phase 1 of the project, an integrated methane gas extraction and generation facility on Lake Kivu, near the city of Kibuye. Drilling for the exploration of geothermal energy has commenced near the volcanic Mt. Karisimbi, and is set to commence at three other potential sites (Gisenyi, Kinigi and Bugarama). Finally, the EWSA has begun a solar water heater dissemination program, with customers able to pay either Rwf 210,000 for a 200 litre system, or Rwf 231,250 for a 300 litre system, supplied and installed by the EWSA.

ELECTRICITY MARKET

1976- REGIDESO Rwanda became ELECTROGAZ by Decree n° 18/76 of April 1976, and t was granted a monopoly for the production and distribution of water and electricity for 99 years.

1999- Law n° 18/99 removed the monopoly and liberalized the two sectors.

2003- ELECTROGAZ was placed under a management contract with Lahmayer International to manage and restructure ELECTROGAZ in collaboration with Hamburg Water Works for 5 years.

2006- 31 March, management contract was terminated, and reverted to the Government of Rwanda through the Board of Directors and the Management of the company.

2008- ELECTROGAZ was split into the Rwanda Energy Corporation (RECO) and the Rwanda Water and Sewerage Corporation (RWASCO). RECO is in charge of electricity generation, transmission and distribution while RWASCO runs water supply and sanitation services provision.

2009- December, the Lower Chamber of Parliament passed a law abolishing RECO/RWASCO, replacing them with the Energy, Water and Sanitation Authority (EWSA, http://www.ewsa.rw/). The EWSA is a wholly-owned subsidiary of the Government of Rwanda, and holds a de facto monopoly on most activities within the energy and water sectors of the country, being the only market actor in the transmission and distribution sectors. Private-sector power generation is in it's infancy in Rwanda, and the Government is keen to increase the market share of independent power producers. Currently, the EWSA is the dominant market player in the energy sector. EWSA is a vertically-integrated company in both its energy and water sector operations.

In the liquid fuels sector, the prices of diesel and gasoline are fixed by the government. Other petroleum products prices are not controlled. ERP, SGP and Rwanda Petrolgaz are privately owned companies. PetroRwanda, the former parastatal petroleum product company, was purchased by Shell in 1999.

LIQUID FUELS MARKET

The petroleum sector is controlled by the Ministry of Commerce and Consumption, which is responsible for setting the pricing policy of petroleum products. Rwanda has no upstream oil industry or refinery activities. In the downstream sector, all of the country's oil imports come through Kenya and Tanzania. Distribution and marketing of fuels products is carried out by ERP (Enterprise Rwandaise de Petrole), SGP (Societe Generale de Petrole), Rwanda Petrolgaz, Engen (www.engen.rw) and Shell.

ENERGY SECTOR OPPORTUNITIES

Electricity accounts for only about 5% of primary energy use in Rwanda. Biomass is the primary source of energy accounting for some 84% of primary energy use, and petroleum products account for the rest. Rwanda has one of the lowest electricity consumption per capita compared to other countries in the region, and generation capacity is low – the country currently has about 100. MW of installed capacity and only about 11% of households are connected to the grid.

Existing Generation Capacity

The existing installed generation capacity and available capacity is show in Table 1.

Of the installed generation capacity, hydropower accounts for about 59%, thermal generation, primarily hired diesel and heavy oil fuel based generation units, for 40%, and methane gas for about 1%. The high reliance on thermal generation

comes at a significant cost to Rwanda,

especially given the present high prices for oil products.

ENERGY LAWS, POLICIES, AND ENABLING ENVIRONMENT

ELECTRICITY LAW

Rwanda's draft Electricity Law was enacted into law in june 2011 and gazetted in july 2011.

The law on electricity governs the activities of electric power production, transmission, distribution and trading both within and outside the national territory of Rwanda. The primary objectives of the law are:

Liberalization and Regulation of electricity sector;

Harmonious development of power supply for all population categories and for all the country's economic and social development sectors in the framework of laws in force;

Setting up economic conditions enabling electric power sector investments;

Respect for the conditions of fair

and loyal competition and for

rights of users and operators.

Category	Name
In house Hydro Power	Ntaruka
	Mukungwa
	Gihira
	Gisengy
	Rukarara
Imported Hydro Power	Rusizi (SNEL)
	Rusizi (SINELAC)
Micro Hydro Power	Nya,yotsi I
	Mutobo
	Agatobwe
	Nyamyotsi II
	Murunda (REPRO)
	Rushaki
In house Thermal Power	Jabana (Diesel)
	Jabana (Heavy Fuel Oil)
Rental Thermal Power	Aggreko (Gikondo)
Methane to Power	KP1
Solar Power	Kigali Solar

Source: Electricity Development Strategy 2011-2017, MININFRA, March 2011

The Electricity Law gives the Ministry in-charge of electricity the rights to provide concession

Agreements to firms, and provides

the legal basis for the Rwanda Utilities Regulatory Agency (RURA) to approve and grant licenses for the production, transmission, distribution and sale of electricity, the conditions for licensing, and addresses the rights and obligations of the license holders.

The Law specifies that the

electricity market of Rwanda shall be a single market based on free and open third party access to the transmission and distribution networks based upon the principles of regulated access to ensure a transparent and non-discriminatory marketplace.

The Electricity Law authorizes the issuance of an International Trade

License for the import and export of electric power across the borders of Rwanda, and for the supply and sale to eligible customers in conformance with sector policies and other laws in force.

The Law also provides for a “Universal Access fund” to provide greater access to rural and other un-served areas.

ENERGY POLICY

the Ministry of Infrastructure (MININfRA) developed a draft National Energy Policy whose principle objectives are to;

a. Harmonize the National Energy Policy with Rwanda’s long-term development plans and strategies;

b. Give particular attention to requirements for the progressive development of the electricity sector to support economic development and the National Access Roll Out Program

c. Have greater focus on household energy requirements and gender dimensions;

d. Bring down the average cost of electricity supply

e. Bring the (policy) statement upto-date by reflecting the latest

developments in methane and renewable energy and their environmental implications;

f. State more clearly Rwanda’s commitment to private sector participation and to regional cooperation in energy.

g. clarify the roles and responsibilities of public sector agencies and develop public sector skills in planning, procurement, and transactions’ negotiation

h. Develop the legal, institutional and financial framework for rapid development of the electricity sector

The Energy Policy is a comprehensive document, which addresses the principal issues in developing the energy sector in Rwanda. Some of the key issues include:

Integrated approach to energy planning: The need to develop energy plans within the framework of the broader national economic plan and strategic developmental objectives of the country.

Use of indigenous energy resources: Given the high cost of imported oil products, there is a need to fully develop available indigenous energy resources to the extent that they are financially, economically and socially beneficial.

Energy efficiency and conservation:

use efficient technologies to make the best use of available energy supplies and reduce environmental impacts.

Energy pricing and subsidy policies: develop cost-reflective

energy prices to ensure that energy suppliers can operate on a sustainable basis and make the necessary investments to expand power supply. Direct subsidies to one-time capital expenditures rather than to recurrent costs, and provide all subsidies in a transparent manner.

Regulatory framework:

Empower RURA and build its capacity to ensure independence in energy price regulation and licensing of energy providers. Energy sector governance: Management of the energy sector, including decision-making about PROJECTS, must be open and transparent and in the best interests of the country. Procurement should be rooted in the principles of transparency, equal treatment and non-discrimination between competing bidders.

Institutional framework and capacity building: Strong energy sector institutions with adequate capacity are essential to meet ambitious growth targets. An effective energy information system is to be established and capacity building is to be provided to all sector institutions to undertake implement their roles and responsibilities.

Private sector participation in energy:

Private sector participation should be promoted at all segments of the energy supply industry. Where Public-Private Partnerships (PPPs) are desirable, government will work with private sector entities to ensure the speedy structuring and financing of PPP PROJECTS in the energy sector.

Financing energy sector investments:

GoR to leverage private sector financing with public financing, where appropriate. Reduce the need for government guarantees and contingent liabilities. New and renewable energies: Promote the use of renewable energy technologies that are financially, economically and socially beneficial.

Develop feed-in tariffs or other mechanisms to provide incentives and reduce risks for electricity production from renewable sources. Establish norms, codes of practice, guidelines and standards for new and renewable energy technologies.

ELECTRICITY REGULATION

Some of the key functions of Regulator, RURA, are to:

i. conduct all technical regulatory activities for the power production, transmission and distribution

sectors

ii. Issue permits and licenses to firms that satisfy licensing requirements

iii. Monitor, evaluate and ensure the quality of the technical services provided by the electric utility

iv. Ensure both compliance to the adopted standards and a fair competition between electricity operators

v. Study and recommend tariffs and review and approve licensee tariffs

vi. Promote sustainable provision of quality and safe services

vii. Promote the utilization of renewable electrical energy resources in rural areas,

viii.Promote energy efficiency and conservation measures.

The Electricity Law empowers RURA to set and approve electricity tariffs, in consultation with the Ministry and pursuant to laws and regulations in force. The Law also allows for cost-based tariffs to ensure adequate return on investments made by license holders. The Law also allows for performance based pricing and benchmarking

ELECTRICITY TARIFFS

Rwanda has some of the highest electricity tariff in the region. The current electricity tariff is fRW 112/kWh (+vAT) for small Lv (low voltage) consumers, and fRW 105/kWh (+vAT) for large commercial and industrial Mv (medium voltage) consumers. A consultant study estimates that the tariff for residential and smaller non-residential customers is below the marginal cost of supply to residential customers, whereas the current industrial tariff is above the marginal cost of supply. The cost of supply is expected to reduce by 2012-13 when electricity production shifts from expensive diesel fuelled plants to cheaper hydropower and other generation options.

The GoR has been supporting the power sector through:

Direct operating cost support by paying for fuel imports/ equipment rental or exempting import-tax

capital Expenditure support by seeking external funds as well as funds allocation from budget

Other indirect subsidies

feed-in tariffs (fIT) for eligible generation technologies is being considered and consultant studies are being reviewed to determine appropriate feed-in tariffs, especially for small hydro and other renewable energy sources. fIT for select generation technologies to be adopted by RURA by early 2012.

THE ELECTRICITY DEVELOPMENT STRATEGY

The objective of Rwanda's electricity strategy is to increase access to modern energy and to meet the ever increasing power demand for economic development of the country. To attain these objectives, the accelerated electricity generation mix proposed in the "Electricity Development Strategy 2011-2017", is to generate 1,000 MW from both the indigenous energy resources and from shared energy resources with neighboring countries. The following specific targets have been set in the

Electricity Development Strategy:

Hydropower generation to be increased to about 333 MW

Geothermal power plants with capacity of 310 MW to be developed

Methane gas to power PROJECTS will deliver 300 MW to the national grid

20 MW of additional diesel generation required for immediate power needs and serve as a back-up

5 MW to be generated from renewable energy sources (solar Pv, micro hydro power or wind) and distributed to local communities beyond the national electricity grid

Electricity connections to increase from 200,000 to a total of 1,200,000 by 2017, which will be equivalent to 50% of access

• Electrify 100% of schools, 100% of health facilities and 100% of sector offices by 2017, either through connection to the grid or through reliable off-grid systems

Explore the possibility of developing all relevant PROJECTS as cDM PROJECTS right from the planning phase in order to sell emission reductions.

• Emphasize energy efficiency measures such as reduction of technical and commercial losses on the national grid, distribution of energy efficient lamps (CFL's) and the establishment of a Solar Water Heater subsidy scheme in order to decrease electricity costs and save energy (potential to save around 50 MW per year)

The Rwanda Energy, Water and Sanitation Authority (EWSA) was established in 2011 as a 100 percent publicly owned utility. EWSA is responsible for the planning and implementation of power PROJECTS in the country, while policy formulation and sector oversight functions remain within MININfRA.

POWER MARKET

EWSA is presently the sole off-taker for all power generated in Rwanda. Rwanda is also a member of the Eastern Africa Power Pool and plans to strengthen transmission interconnections with neighboring countries of Burundi, DR congo, Tanzania and Uganda.

EWSA provides long-term power purchase agreement (PPA) to project developers.

Once the interconnection with neighboring countries is strengthened and the Eastern Africa Power Pool becomes operational, power can be exported through bilateral trades or to the power pool.

DEMAND FORECAST

An Electricity Master Plan (EMP) has developed a revised demand

forecast reflecting the goals of a

new Electricity Strategy for the country, which envisages the development of 1,000 MW of generation capacity by 2017.

Domestic demand is expected to account for 60% of peak demand, while cross border mining PROJECTS are expected to account for 20% and sub regional electricity markets for the remaining 20%.

TRANSMISSION NETWORK IN RWANDA

Rwanda has about 383.6 km of 70 kv and 110 kv high-voltage (Hv) transmission lines, and about 4,900 km of and medium-voltage (Mv, 30 kv, 15 kv and 6.6 kv) lines and low-voltage (Lv, 380 v and 220 v) lines. Rwanda's electric network is interconnected with the networks of Burundi, the DRc and Uganda (there presently is no inter-linkage with Tanzania).

Power flows between Rwanda, Burundi and the DRc are managed by the Societe Internationale d'Electricite des Pays des Grands Lacs (SINELAc).

According to the Electricity Development Strategy for 2011-2017, Rwanda intends to extend its grid by 2,100 km (700 km of Hv lines and 1,400 km of Mv lines).

In addition to 110 kv lines, 220 kv interconnection lines are planned to evacuate power from planned generation plants and meet the expected demand in the future.

construction of 400 kv lines is also under consideration within the framework of the interstate network development.

feasibility studies have been prepared, or are under preparation, for a number of transmission inter-linkages including the 220 kv Kibuye- Kigali line, the 220 kv Kigoma–Rwegura (Burundi) and Birembo–Mbarara (Uganda) lines, and the 220 kv Rusomo– Kigali line.

POLICIES, LAWS AND REGULATIONS TO PROMOTE POWER GENERATION PROJECTS

INCENTIVES TO POWER PROJECT DEVELOPERS

Infrastructure support and transmission access: The GoR provides transmission access to all power PROJECTS at its cost, and also provides road access, water supply and other basic infrastructure needed to develop PROJECTS.

The GoR has also acquired at its cost land for power PROJECTS or compensated private developers for land acquisition. The GoR provides a variety of tax and fiscal incentives to promote private sector investment in the country, which is applicable also to power project developers.

Public-Private Partnership (PPP): The GoR has a draft PPP policy, which is designed to promote PPP investments in infrastructure development including in the power sector.

HYDROPOWER SUBSECTOR

The GoR is in the process of developing a Hydropower Policy. The country also plans on developing a Hydropower Master Plan to develop water resources in the country, and has shortlisted consultants to conduct the study. fIT are to be adopted to promote development of micro and small hydropower PROJECTS.

GEOTHERMAL SUBSECTOR

The GoR is in the process of developing a Geothermal Policy and Geothermal Resources Exploration, Development and Management Act to guide the development geothermal resources in the country.

METHANE SUBSECTOR

The GoR has developed a draft Gas Law and Regulations to develop methane based PROJECTS. The draft is currently under review by Parliament and is expected to be gazetted soon. Management Prescriptions for the development of Lake Kivu gas resources have been prepared and the GoR is expected to endorse and adopt the prescription.

PEAT SUBSECTOR

The GoR is in the process of developing a Peat Policy to sustainably and safely harvest peat resources for power generation.

Standardized Legal Document

The GoR is developing standardized legal documents and contract templates for the following:

Memorandum of Understanding

Letter of Intent

Non-Disclosure Agreements

Power Purchase agreements for different generation technologies

such as hydropower, geothermal,

peat and methane gas

concession agreements for energy PROJECTS: Peat concession Agreement, Gas concession Agreement, Geothermal concession Agreement

fuel supply agreements (for example steam supply agreements in order to allow IPPs to buy steam from a developer, or equivalent gas or peat supply

Management contracts for power plants (for example for the Government owned hydropower plants)

Engineering, Procurement and construction contracts

GoR Agencies/Institutions involved in Power Generation

Rwanda Utilities Regulatory Authority (RURA): The regulator is empowered to issue licenses to power generators, and provides licenses to private power developers following a transparent process.

The Rwanda Environmental Management Authority (REMA): provides environmental clearances to power PROJECTS.

The Rwanda Development Board (RDB): is the nodal agency for all private sector investment and foreign Direct Investment in the country. The RDB negotiates all concession agreements with private project developers.

Business Process for Power Sector Project Development

The flowcharts below broadly map

the general business process for development of power sector PROJECTS

in Rwanda. The flow charts also

indicate the principal GoR agencies and institutions involved in the development and approval of power PROJECTS in Rwanda.

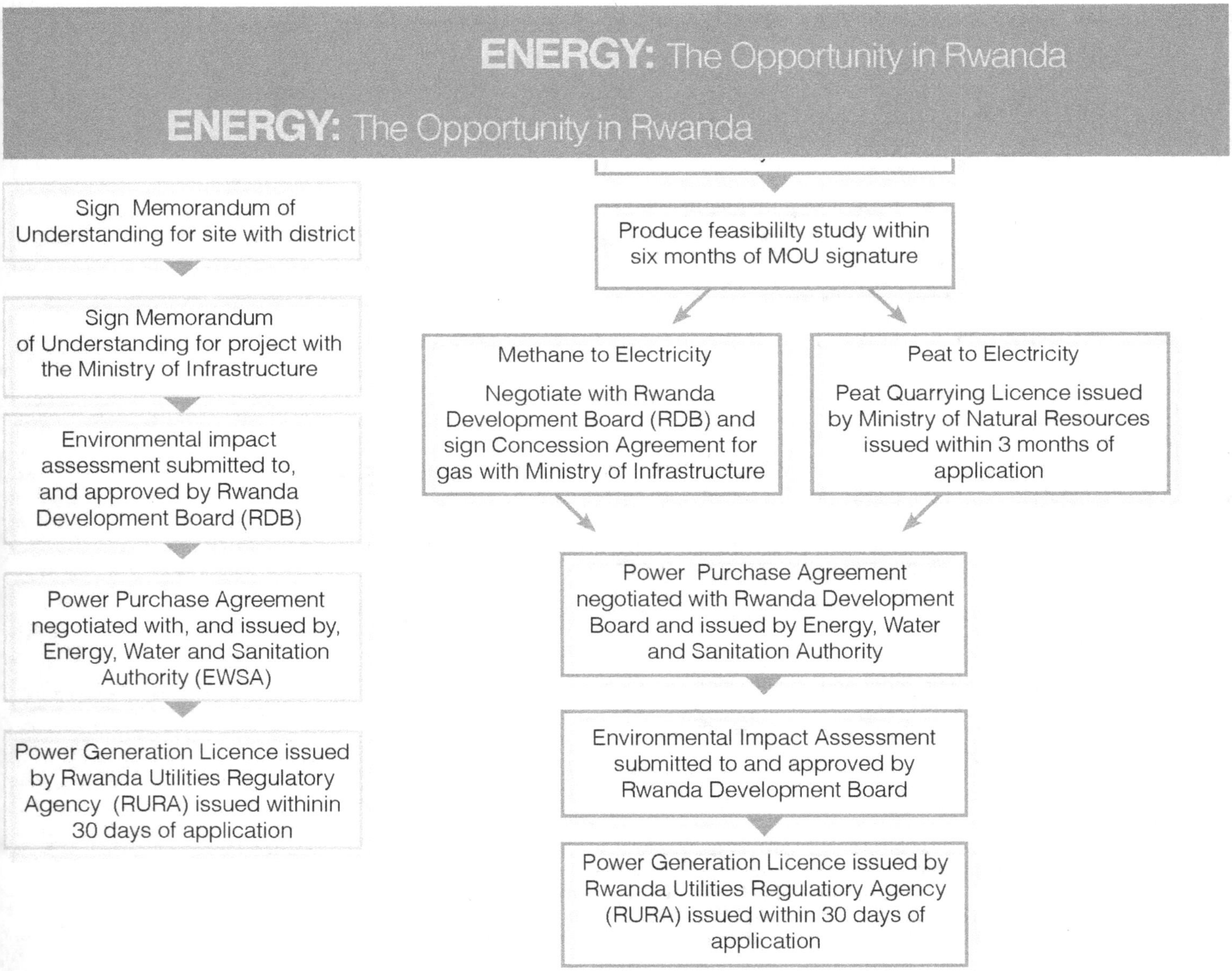

Rwanda's major rivers have proven potential to support run-of-the-river hydropower plants in a total of 333 sites across Rwanda.

Micro/Mini/Small Hydropower PROJECTS

Small hydropower PROJECTS totaling 20.9 MW are currently under construction and will be operational between 2011 and 2013.

Domestic Medium/Large Hydropower PROJECTS

The largest domestic hydropower project is Nyabarongo I, with an installed capacity of 28 MW. The project is under construction and will be commissioned by 2014.

Regional Hydropower PROJECTS

Some shared hydropower PROJECTS with neighboring countries include;

Rusizi III (145 MW)- shared by Burundi, DRc and Rwanda with an estimated 48 MW Rwandan share

Rusizi IV (287 MW) - With ≈96 MW,

estimated as Rwanda's share.

Rusumo falls (90 MW) -Planned to be jointly developed by Tanzania, Burundi and Rwanda. Rwanda's share would be 30 MW.

The Akanyaru project- Between

Burundi and Rwanda with ≈ 4 MW

potential.

Existing Potential

There is an estimated potential

of ≈83 MW to be exploited with further sites with a potential of ≈ 22

MW. feasibility studies to develop these PROJECTS are planned with the support of World Bank.

KEY INVESTMENT OPPORTUNITIES

Mini & Small hydropower: 20 PROJECTS totaling 9 MW bid as 4 "bundles" with an expected investment of $25-30 million. Planned completion date is 201415 and 3 bundled bids for 10 MW of PROJECTS bid every year from 201517

Medium hydropower: 12-17 MW

Nyaborongo II is being evaluated, with an expected investment

amount of ≈ $80Mn

Regional hydropower: Ruzizi III (145 MW) supported by EU, AfDB, among others with an expected investment capital of $450Mn and completion date in 2016. There is also a 90 MW Rusumo falls supported by WB and others. Its expected investment amount is $300Mn and planned completion date is 2017

PROjEcT: RUSIZI III HYDROPOWER PROjEcT

HYDROPOWER

Rusizi River, DRc/Rwanda Border in the Great Lakes Region

Ministry of Infrastructure/EWSA; EGL/cEPGL

The project is being developed under cEPGL umbrella for Rwanda, Burundi and DRc. Ruzizi III hydropower project is planned to generate 145MW and the power output is shared equally by three countries. The project consist of 105 m long dam crest whose height is 20.5 m, 2.82 km Headrace Tunnel and a surface power station with 3x50 MW francis Units. Objectives: • Improving the electricity system security, reliability and economic power supply by switching to the cheap and renewable sources. • Increase electricity access rates. • Improve on cross-boundary energy trade among CEPL member Countries

145 MW

The Project is structured as a Public Private Partnership

2013

feasibility Study Report 2010; ESIA Report 2011

• A Transaction Advisor is in place and preparing Tender document for recruitment of a preferred Investor • Three Investor candidates have been prequalified • Team of national negotiators have appointed in order to conduct negotiations with the would be selected Investor

US$ 565 Million, Private Public Partnership

Director General Energy Water & Sanitation Authority (EWSA) P.O. Box 537 Kigali. Rwanda Email: ymuyange@ewsa.rw or yuwamahoro@ewsa.rw

PROJECT: RUSIZI IV HYDROPOWER PROJECT

HYDROPOWER

Rusizi River, DRc/Rwanda Border in the Great Lakes Region, Africa

Ministry of Infrastructure/EWSA; EGL/cEPGL

The project is being developed under cEPGL umbrella for Rwanda, Burundi and DRc. Ruzizi Iv hydropower project is planned to generate 287 MW utilizing 224 m natural head and the power output will be shared equally by three countries of Burundi, DRc and Rwanda. The project is envisaged to consist of 80 m feed channel, 4.5 km long low pressure tunnel, surge shaft and a surface power station with 4x72 MW francis units. Objectives: • Improving the system security, reliability and economic power supply by switching to the cheap and renewable sources • Increase electricity access rates • Improve on cross-boundary energy trade among CEPL member Countries

287 MW

The Project may be structured as a Public Private Partnership

2016/17

Pre-feasibility Study Report 2009 by fitchner GmbH;

Only Prefeasibility Study completed

US$ 432 Million as per Prefeasibility Study Report 2009, Private Public Partnership

Director General Energy Water & Sanitation Authority, P.O. Box 537 Kigali, Rwanda. Email: ymuyange@ewsa.rw or yuwamahoro@ewsa.rw

PROJECT: RUSUMO FALLS HYDROPOWER PROJECT

HYDROPOWER

Kagera River, Tanzania/Rwanda Border in East Africa, At Rusumo falls, on the Kagera River about 2 km downstream of its confluence with the Ruvubu River

Ministry of Infrastructure/EWSA; NELSAP

The project is being developed under NELSAP umbrella for Rwanda, Burundi and Tanzania. Rusumo falls Hydropower Project is planned to generate 90 MW and the power output will be shared equally by three countries. The project consists of concrete dam with crest length of 150 m whose height is 14.5 m, Headrace Tunnel of 460 m and a surface power station with 3x30 MW Kaplan turbines. Objective: • Improving the system security, reliability and economic power supply by switching to the cheap and renewable sources • Increase electricty access rates • Improve on cross-boundary energy trade among EAc member countries

90 MW

The Project is structured as a Publicly financed but privately managed

2013

feasibility Study Report 2012 by SNc Lavalin

• Draft feasibility Study Report and Institutional framework complete with support from WB • Tripartite Agreement signed between the three Governments in feb 2012 • Procurement process of Owners Engineer commenced

US$ $400m Million, Public financed but Privately Managed

Director General Energy Water & Sanitation Authority, P.O. Box 537 Kigali, Rwanda. Email: ymuyange@ewsa.rw or yuwamahoro@ewsa.rw

PROjEcT: NTARUKA A

HYDROPOWER

On Ntaruka River, Busanze Sector in Nyaruguru District, Sothern Province, Rwanda

Ministry of Infrastructure/EWSA

The project is to be developed under IPP arrangement and is planned to generate 2 MW and the power fed into the Rwanda National Grid. The project consists of diversion weir with crest length of 14 m, Headrace canal 258, Penstock 30 m long and a surface power station with 1.125 x2 MW francis turbines. Objectives: • Increasing national generation installed capacity hence meeting increasing power demand • Improving the national energysecurity, reliability and economic power supply by switching to the cheap and renewable sources • Increase electricty access

2 MW

The Project is structured as IPP

2013/14

feasibility Study Report 2010 by SHER Engineers

• feasibility Study completed in june 2010

Euro 10.4 Million as per SHER Engineers june 2010 Report, IPP

Director General Energy Water & Sanitation Authority, P.O. Box 537 Kigali, Rwanda. Email: ymuyange@ewsa.rw or yuwamahoro@ewsa.rw

PROJECT: AKANYARU HYDROPOWER PROJECT

HYDROPOWER

On Akanyaru River, in Nyaruguru District, Sothern Province, Rwanda

Ministry of Infrastructure/EWSA

The project will be developed under IPP arrangement and is planned to generate 4 MW and the power be fed into the Rwanda National Grid. The project consists of 35 m high dam with crest length of 125 m, Headrace Tunnel of 383 m long, Surge chamber, Penstock 110 m long and a surface power station with 2 x2 MW francis turbines. Objectives: • Increasing national generation installed capacity to meet increasing power demand • Improving the national energysecurity, reliability and economic power supply by switching to the cheap and renewable sources • Increase electricty access

4 MW

The Project is structured as IPP

2014/15

feasibility Study Report 1992 by SOGREAH Engineers

feasibility Study completed in 1992

USD 13 Million as per SOGREAH Engineers 1992 Report, IPP

Director General Energy Water & Sanitation Authority, P.O. Box 537 Kigali, Rwanda. Email: ymuyange@ewsa.rw or yuwamahoro@ewsa.rw

PROJECT: NYABARONGO II HYDROPOWER PROJECT

HYDROPOWER

Along Nyabarongo River, Bwenda Sector in Gakenke District, Northen Province, Rwanda

Ministry of Infrastructure/EWSA

This is a multipurpose project envisaged to cater for water supply, irrigation as well as electrical power generation. The project may be developed either under Public or PPP arrangement and is planned to generate 12- 17 MW and the power will be fed into the Rwanda National Grid. The project consists of 48 m high concrete gravity dam with crest length of 228 m, and a surface power station with 2x8.5 MW Kaplan turbines just situated at the dam toe. Objectives: • Increase the country's hydropower potential. • Improve the availability of municipal and industrial water for Kigali; • Enhance agricultural water supply for Bugesera; • Provide better flood control

12-17 MW

The project may be structured either as Publicly financed or PPP

2013/14

feasibility Study Report 2008 by KOIcA

feasibility Study completed in 2008

USD 150 Million as per KOIcA2008 Report, Public/PPP

Director General Energy Water & Sanitation Authority, P.O. Box 537 Kigali, Rwanda. Email: ymuyange@ewsa.rw or yuwamahoro@ewsa.rw

HYDROPOWER

The sites are situated in Northern, Western and Southern Provinces of Rwanda

Ministry of Infrastructure/EWSA

These are mini hydropower potential sites that so far have their Pre-Assessment Studies and costing reports prepared. Planned completion: 2014-15. Objectives: • Increase the country's energy generation sufficiency by utilizing hydropower resources hence reducing costly fossil fuel dependence.

9 MW

The PROJECTS are structured as PPP

2013/14

HydroAtlas Report by SHER Engineers 2008 and Pre Assessment Report by Ifc 2011

Identified in HydroAtlas 2007 and Pre-Assed by IFC in December 2012

Expected investment: US$25-30 Million. Envisaged to be developed as IPPs

Director General Energy Water & Sanitation Authority, P.O. Box 537 Kigali, Rwanda. Email: ymuyange@ewsa.rw or yuwamahoro@ewsa.rw

HYDROPOWER

The plants/PROJECTS are situated in Northern, Western and Southern Provinces of Rwanda

Ministry of Infrastructure/EWSA

GoR intends to privatize some of its existing small hydropower assets (totaling 15.6 MW) by placing them under private sector management. Objectives: • To ensure efficiency and operational sustainability of the country's power systems. • To encourage wide participation of players in the Energy/Power Sector hence build confidence to the private investors and business community from both local and foreign circles.

18.8 MW

The plants/PROJECTS may be leased and/or private operated and maintained.

2012

feasibility Studies and Design as well as final As built documentations

Rukarara 9 MW, Keya (2.2 MW), Nkora(680 kW), cyimbiri (300kW) and Rugezi 2.2 are in operation since 2011 while Mutobo 200 Kw; Nyamyotsi I & II 200 kW and Agatobwe 100kW became operational in 2010 while Mukungwa (II) 2.5 MW; Gashashi 200 kW; Nyabahanga 200 kW; Nyirabuhombohombo 500 kW; Nshili I 400 kW; janja 200 kW are still under construction and earmarked to be completed end of 2012

Expected investment: Negotiable Planned to be placed under Private Management contract

Director General Energy Water & Sanitation Authority, P.O. Box 537 Kigali, Rwanda. Email: ymuyange@ewsa.rw or yuwamahoro@ewsa.rw

METHANE GAS

LAKE KIVU METHANE IN RWANDA

Background

• Lake Kivu is located in the East African Rift Zone between Rwanda and the DRc

The 2,400 sq.km. lake contains high concentrations of naturally occurring cH4 and cO2, with the highest concentrations at depths ranging from 270m to 500m

The oxygenated upper layer of the lake from the surface to a depth of

60m supports the lake's biology

The resource is shared equally between Rwanda and the DRc

The PMP (Peat, Methane and Petroleum) Unit, at EWSA is developing methane PROJECTS

Potential for Methane-to-Power Generation

• Lake Kivu contains about 300 billion cu.m of cO2and 60 billion cu.m of cH4 gas. An estimated 120 to 250 million cu.m of cH4 is

generated annually in the lake

• Rwanda wishes to utilize this resource to develop methane-topower PROJECTS and other uses such as fertilizer and gas-toliquids PROJECTS

• The methane in Lake Kivu is estimated to be sufficient to generate 700 MW of electricity over a period of 55 years; Rwanda's share of the total generation potential is about 350 MW, with the rest being DRc's share

Characteristics of Methane in Lake Kivu	
Methane	24.9% vol
Carbon Dioxide	73.5% vol
Hydrogen Sulphide	0.05% vol
Other gases	1.5% vol

Characteristics of Scrubbed Gas After Extraction	
Methane	80%
Carbon dioxide	18%
Nitrogen	2%

Historic Use of Lake Kivu Methane in Rwanda

• Lake Kivu methane was first tapped by Union chimique de Belge with a gas pilot plant at cape Rubona in 1963 to supply the Bralirwa brewery

• Bralirwa brewery converted one of its boilers to use gas in place of fuel oil, and was supplied with 5,000 cu.m/day of methane gas purified to 80%

• The pilot plant was recently shut down after operating for over 40 years

Existing Methane-to-Power PROJECTS in Rwanda

KivuWatt, a subsidiary of contour Global (USA), is developing a 100 MW plant: 25 MW 1st Phase by end 2012, and 75 MW 2nd Phase by 2015. Phase I is currently under construction

KP1, a 4.5 MW pilot plant developed by GoR, is operating at about 1.5 MW since late 2007. GoR is in negotiations with a strategic partner to scale-up capacity to 50 MW in phases

• REc, a subsidiary of RIG (Rwanda), is a 3.6 MW plant. The plant is presently not operational and REc is seeking new partners and investors to revive and scale up the project

Opportunities in Existing Concessions

• KivuWatt's 25 MW Phase I (est. cost $140m), is under construction with GoR Sovereign Guarantee and MIGA guarantee. The 75 MW 2nd Phase will need financing. Estimated cost: $260m. completion: 2014

• REc is seeking partners and financing to revive the plant and scale it up to 50 MW. Estimated cost: $106m. completion: 2015

• Ongoing negotiations with private partners for 100 MW may be an opportunity once they are not concluded

PROJECT STRUCTURING AND FINANCING

Methane-to-Power Financing Opportunities

• 25 MW KivuWatt Phase I financed

by a lending syndicate - Emerging Africa Infrastructure fund, fMO, AfDB, etc. 75 MW Phase 2 needs financing. Project is an IPP

• The 4.5 MW REc pilot plant was developed as an IPP. Project may be restructured depending on the new partners and investors

Financing Support for Investors financing institutions such as AfDB, WBG (WB, Ifc, MIGA), EU and other bilateral donors and development partners will support eligible PROJECTS GoR will consider providing other incentives

Risk mitigation instruments including PRI, PRG, PcG, from the AfDB, the WB, and MIGA will be available to eligible PROJECTS and developers

Policy, Law & Regulation

Draft Gas Law and Regulations for methane PROJECTS is under review by Parliament, and is to be gazetted

A draft concession Agreement and draft PPA is under development for new PROJECTS (existing PROJECTS have PPAs with the utility)

Management Prescriptions for the safe extraction of Lake Kivu gas resources are to be adopted

Numerous reports on Lake Kivu going back to 1937 are available. Recent studies by LAHMEYEROSAE and K. Tietze, and Lake Management Prescriptions are also available Project specific documents may be available subject to confidentiality agreements

Why invest in methane gas to power?

Methane demonstration plants prove that the gas extraction technology is feasible.

Rwanda is keen to develop its methane resources as part of its strategy to substantially increase the power capacity

GEOTHERMAL RESERVES IN RWANDA

There are 4 geothermal prospects 3 in the Nothern Region(Gisenyi, Karisimbi and Kinigi) associated with volcanoes and one in the Southern region (Bugarama) associated with faults along the East Africa Rift

Potential for Geothermal Energy Generation

The potential for power generation from geothermal energy in the country is estimated to be more than 700 MW out of which 310MW is planned to be developed by 2017.

Surface exploration and reconnaissance studies have been carried out in the Western region (no studies have been conducted in the Southern region)

Rwanda has conducted detailed surface studies and plans to drill three exploratory wells in August 2012 to confirm the commercial viability of geothermal-to-power PROJECTS

• 10MW well head generation units are expected to be operational in 2014.

Scientific Exploration Studies

Reconnaissance surface studies by BRGM in 1982 reported estimated temperatures above 100°c

Reconnaissance surface studies by chevron in 2006 estimated reservoir temperatures in excess of 150°c

Detailed geo-scientific data (geochemistry, MT and TEM) by the BGR, KenGen, ISOR and the ITER in 2008 indicated the possibility of high temperature geothermal system

Uniservices of AU-IESE has conducted geophysical and MT & TEM studies, micro-seismic and micro-earthquake monitoring, heat flow measurements, geological

mapping, and analysis of geochemistry data to prepare 3-D geological and physical models. Preliminary interpretation and analysis confirms previous findings and provides higher potential for one of the sites (Kinigi) GoR will organize a peer review meeting to discuss the study results and validate the findings and help locate optimum sites for test drilling

Present Status of Development

• To reduce drilling and exploration risk, GoR is financing three exploratory wells in Karisimbi starting August '12.

• Infrastructure development (water supply, access road) to the geothermal site is ongoing

• feasibility studies and SEIA studies planned to assess commercial viability of developing geothermal energy in Rwanda

Greenfield Investment Opportunities

10 MW wellhead pilot plant to be installed if test wells are productive. Estimated cost: $30m. Planned completion: 2014

GoR plans to develop 300 MW (4 x 75 MW) of geo-thermal power by 2017. Estimated cost: $900m. completion: 2014-17

Greenfield 10 MW Wellhead and

Additional PROJECTS

The initial 10MW will be publicly financed, and the scale up will be structured as PPP

Financing Support for Investors

financing institutions such as AfDB, WBG (WB, Ifc, MIGA), EU and other bilateral donors and development partners will support eligible PROJECTS GoR will consider providing other incentives

• Risk mitigation instruments including PRI, PRG, PcG, from the AfDB, the WB, and MIGA will be available to eligible PROJECTS and developers

Policy, Law & Regulation

GoR has drafted a geothermal policy, a geothermal resources exploration, development and management act and regulations

Available Documents

Studies by BRGM, chevron, BGR, ISOR, ITER, KenGen, and Uniservices available for review International experts to peer review the Uniservices study feasibility and SEIA studies to be completed after exploration drilling in 2013

Why Invest in Geothermal?

GoR is committed to cover the upstream risks

Rwanda is keen to develop its geothermal resources as part of its strategy to substantially increase power capacity Geothermal energy is base load

PEAT-TO-POWER PROJECTS IN RWANDA

A Peat Master Plan prepared by EKONO indicated that Rwanda has an estimated reserves of 155 million tons of dry peat spread over an area of about 50,000 hectares

About 77% of peat reserves are near Akanyaru and Nyabarongo rivers and the Rwabusoro plains

Potential for Peat-to-Power Generation

The theoretical potential (assuming all peat bogs are exploited) for electricity energy generation from peat is estimated to be about 1,200 MW Peat in the Rwabusoro marsh land and around the Akanyaru river can fuel 450MW of electricity generation for 25 years

The Rwabusoro marshland and Rucahabi in the districts of Nyanza and Bugesera present significant opportunity for large-scale peat harvesting for power generation Rwanda plans to develop its peat resources to generate about 200 MW of power by 2017

Present use of peat in Rwanda

• Two firms are mechanically harvesting peat in Rwanda PEc(Peat Energy company) supplies 2,000 tons per month to a cement plant RAS (Rwanda Auto Service) supplies peat prisons for cooking *Peat-to-Power PROJECTS in Rwanda*

• GoR is developing a 15 MW peat-to-power in Bugarama Rusizi district.

• GoR is negotiating with a strategic partner to develop a 100 MW peat fired power plant in South Akanyaru prospect. Project to be developed as a PPP.

• GoR has advertised tenders for EPc contractor and an Owner's engineer for 100 MW peat-to-power project in Rwabusoro prospect. Project to be structured either as public or private.

Greenfield 100 MW Project

The GoR is open to discussions with investors for the development of the 100 MW plant

GoR is open to a long term concession with a strategic investor as long as the off-take price and project structure makes sense

The project is planned to be developed as a PPP. GoR may consider a PPP or jv structure to lower the cost of capital and the cost of power generation financing institutions such as AfDB, Ifc, MIGA and other bilateral donors and development partners will support eligible PROJECTS

GoR will consider providing other incentives

Risk mitigation instruments including PRI from the AfDB and MIGA will be available to eligible PROJECTS and developers

Policy, Law & Regulation

The GoR is preparing a Peat Policy to sustainably and safely harvest peat resources for power generation

Available Documents

The Peat Master Plan (1992/93) study prepared by EKONO energy

An updated Peat Master Plan is under review

Peat to power Pre-feasibility studies on 8 sites are under preparation

Why invest in peat to power?

Peat-to-power technology is a proven commercial technology and the risks are low and peat mining PROJECTS are in operation

Rwanda is keen to develop its peat resources as part of its short-term strategy to substantially increase power capacity

ENERGY SEcTOR PROjEcT PROfILES

Sector

ENERGY : Greenfield 15MW peat fired power plant

Location

Bugarama, Rusizi Dstrict, Rwanda

Responsible Agent(s)

EWSA/ Ministry of Infrastructure

Project Description & Rationale / Objectives

Description This is a Government of Rwanda project intended to increase the installed capacity up to 1000MW by 2017 to support the national economic development, favor regional energy trade. The rationale of the project is to increase access to energy as enshrined in EPDRS and vision 2020. The objectives are; 1. Improve access to energy for the Rwandan population 2. To boost economic activities 3. To support regional integration inter alia with energy trade.

Project Size

approx – 35 Million USD
Proposed Procurement Process
• Open tender for EPc contractor and supervising company
Planned project start Date
Mid 2012
Project Documentation
• Peat Master Plan • feasibility study prepared
current Status
GoR is looking for an EPc contractor financing amount & structure Required

• Public financing. The project is planned to be developed as Public. GoR may consider a PPP or JV structure to lower the cost of capital and the cost of power generation

contact Person

Charles NYIRAHUKU Manager, Peat, Methane & Petroleum / Energy, Water and Sanitation Authority (EWSA). P. O. Box: 537 KIGALI Email: charles_nyir@yahoo.fr or cnyirahuku@ewsa.rw

ENERGY SECTOR PROJECT PROFILES

Project
Greenfield 100MW peat fired power plant
Location
Akanyaru, Bugesera district ,Rwanda
Responsible Agent(s)
EWSA/ Ministry of Infrastructure
Project Description & Rationale / Objectives

Description This is a Government of Rwanda project intended to increase the installed capacity up to 1000MW by 2017 to support the national economic development, favor regional energy trade. The rationale of the project is to increase access to energy as enshrined in EPDRS and vision 2020. The objectives are; 1. Improve access to energy for the Rwandan population 2. To boost economic activities 3. To support regional integration inter alia with energy trade.

Project Size
100 MW
Proposed Procurement Process

• The GoR intends to procure the services of private developers and investors to develop the 100 MW • The project is planned to be structured as PPP.

Planned project start Date
End 2012
Project Documentation
• Peat Master Plan • Tender document with technical specifications
current Status
Request for proposals
financing amount & structure Required
approx – USD 400 Millions, to be structured as PPP.
contact Person
charles NYIRAHUKU Manager, Peat, Methane & Petroleum / Energy, Water and Sanitation Authority (EWSA). P. O Box: 537 KIGALI Email: charles_nyir@yahoo.fr or cnyirahuku@ewsa.rw

SOLAR ENERGY

Rwanda is located in East Africa at approximately 2 degrees below the equator. It boarders with Burundi in the south, Democratic Republic of congo in the west, Tanzania in the East and Uganda in the North.

It is generally characterised by Savannah climate and its geographical location endows it with sufficient solar radiation intensity approximately equal to 5kWh/m2/day and peak sun hours of approximately 5 hours per day.

Existing PROJECTS

In 2006, the Government of Rwanda signed an MoU with the German state Rhineland-Palatinate to construct, own and operate a 250 kWp grid connected solar plant.

The plant was constructed on the top of mount jali in Kigali city. Since its commissioning date, the plant has been operating successfully.

Greenfield 10MW grid connected Solar PV plant

• following the successful operation of the 250 kWp solar plant and good potential for solar energy in Rwanda as highlighted above, the Government of Rwanda has identified and reserved 25 hectors of land for the construction of 10 MW solar plant.

This site is located in Eastern province of Rwanda in Nyagatare District , approximately 190 km from Kigali. Access is made from main road by a secondary road that cuts through the land plot, 2.4 km long. Within the site there is a 30 Kv transmission line and a 50KvA transformer that will be up graded to evacuate the power generated from the 10 MW plant.

The plant (10MW solar plant) will be constructed on IPP (Independent Power Producer) basis. The PPA (Power Purchase Agreement) and a 25years Land Lease Agreement will be signed between the investor and theGovernment of Rwanda.

consquently, interested investors are invited to construct, own and operate the above mentioned solar plant.

	ENERGY SEcTOR PROjEcT PROfILES
Project	construction of a 10 MW grid connected solar Pv plant
Location	Nyagatare District, Rwanda
Responsible Agent(s)	EWSA/ Ministry of Infrastructure
Project Description & Rationale / Objectives	Description This is a project of the Government of Rwanda (GoR) to reduce diesel consumption used in thermal plants. The rationale is to reduce expense on diesel and save the environment from pollution. Project objectives The objectives are; 1. To reduce the quantity of fuel (diesel) used for thermal generators 2. To save the environment by using clean energy 3. To save money spent in buying fuel (diesel) for thermal plants
Project Size	$29M

Proposed Procurement Process	The project will be conducted as a Private Public Partnership
Planned project start Date	October 2012
Project Documentation (available proj. documents)	Site survey and data collection completed
current Status	Preparations for feasibility studies are ongoing
financing amount & structure Required	Private Public Partnership
contact Person(to be provided later)	Director General of EWSA ymuyange@ewsa.rw or yuwamahoro@ewsa.rw

WASTE-TO-POWER

from households, restaurants, hotels and markets.

Other types of waste solid waste available in the country include: agricultural waste, livestock waste, water hyacinth.

The waste is transported to Nyanza landfill where it is dumped and covered with soil by using bulldozers. Kigali city council and MININfRA are in charge of waste to power PROJECTS.

Opportunities in Waste to Power PROJECTS

It is estimated that 100 tons per day of raw municipal solid can produce 1MW, using traditional thermal technologies.

The population in Kigali is expected to reach about 1.5 million by 2020. It is believed that the waste collected will reach about 1000 t per day.

This represents about opportunity of 10 MW plant.

Key parameters for a biogas to power project (5 MW) Policy, Law & Regulation

Amount of Gas Extractable	6 million m3/yr
Electricity Generation	4,000,000 kWh/yr
Capital Expenditure	2.5 million Euros
Operation Period	10 years

Regulations regarding solid waste management (collection and disposal waste) have been developed by RURA and REMA.

Kigali city has developed also the rules and directives on sanitation and hygiene promotion.

GoR is developing the strategic plans of integrated solid waste management.

Strategies and Solutions developed

Renovation and eventual closure of Nyanza landfill

construction of a new engineered landfill

Recovery of all recoverable material from the waste stream

Proper and sustainable waste management through 3R (Reduce, Reuse and Recycle) principles.

Available Documents

Numerous reports on Waste to Power PROJECTS are available

Waste-to-Power Opportunities

Waste to power PROJECTS are eligible for climate change funds (eg. cDM), this means that additional revenues for emission reduction can be generated by the project.

An integrated waste to power project will not only generate the much needed power for the grid, but also contribute to addressing issues related to sanitation, health and environment.

RWANDA ENERGY POLICY

LIST OF ACRONYMS AND ABBREVIATIONS

BEST	Biomass Energy Strategy
BTC	Belgian Technical Cooperation
CDM	Clean Development Mechanism
CFL	Compact Fluorescent Lamp
DRC	Democratic Republic of Congo
DSM	Demand-Side Management
EAC	East African Community
EDCL	Electricity Development Company Limited
EDPRS	Economic Development and Poverty Reduction Strategy
REP	Rwanda Energy Policy
ESSP	Energy Sector Strategic Plan
EUCL	Electricity Utility Company Limited
EWSA	Energy Water and Sanitation Authority Ltd.
FONERWA	Rwanda National Climate Fund
GDP	Gross Domestic Product
GHG	Green House Gases
GoR	Government of Rwanda
GiZ	German Technical Cooperation Agency
HFO	Heavy Fuel Oil
IPP	Independent Power Producer
JADF	Joint Action Development Forums
KWh	Kilowatt-hour (Unit of energy)
LPG	Liquefied Petroleum Gas
MIGA	Multilateral Investment Guarantee Association
MIGEPROF	Ministry of Gender and Family Promotion
MINAGRI	Ministry of Agriculture and Animal Resources
MINALOC	Ministry of Local Government
MINECOFIN	Ministry of Finance and Economic Planning
MINEDUC	Ministry of Education
MINICOM	Ministry of Trade and Industry
MININFRA	Ministry of Infrastructure
MINIRENA	Ministry of Natural Resources
MoU	Memorandum of Understanding
MT	Metric tones
MTEF	Medium Term Expenditure Framework
NAMA	Nationally Appropriate Mitigation Action
NCST	National Commission of Science and Technology
NDBP	National Domestic Biogas Programme
NICA	National Standards Inspectorate, Competition and Consumer Protection Authority
NIRDA	National Industrial Research and Development Agency
PMO	Prime Minister's Office
PPA	Power Purchase Agreement

PPP	Public-Private Partnership
PSF	Private Sector Federation
PV	Photovoltaic
RSB	Rwanda Standards Board
RDB	Rwanda Development Board
RECO	Rwanda Electricity Corporation
REG Ltd	Rwanda Energy Group Limited
REFIT	Renewable Feed-in Tariff
REMA	Rwanda Environment Management Authority
RET	Renewable Energy Technology
RURA	Rwanda Utilities Regulatory Authority
RWASCO	Rwanda Water and Sanitation Corporation
RT&D	Research Technology & Development
SACCos	Savings and Credit Cooperatives
SEZs	Special Economic Zones
SPDs	Small-Scale Power Distributors
SWAp /eSWAp	Sector Wide Approach / Energy Sector Wide Approach
SWG	Sector Working Group
TVETs	Technical and Vocational Education Training Centers
UNECA	United Nations Economic Commission for Africa
UNEP	United Nations Environment Program
UNFCCC	United Nations Framework Convention on Climate Change
VAT	Value Added Tax

Energy is pivotal to most of the challenges and opportunities the world faces today. Whether one speaks of maintaining national stability, economic growth, protecting ecosystems or promoting social equity, they all hinge at least to some degree on access to secure and sustainable energy. In Rwanda, energy is a critical productive sector that can catalyze broader economic growth and contribute significantly to facilitating the achievement of the country's socio-economic transformation agenda.

This Energy Policy has been elaborated to guide and influence decisions on the extraction, development and use of Rwanda's energy resources in a transparent and sustainable manner. The policy framework outlined herein comprises a set of governing laws and regulations, strategic directions and guiding principles that Rwandan institutions and partners shall adopt and adhere to, in subsequent implementation of actions. The vision of the energy sector is to become one of Rwanda's most dynamic sectors and investment destinations. In addressing both demand and supply side issues across all key sub-sectors, this policy will contribute to realizing that vision. The energy policy is founded upon three essential government principles:

i. A resolve for transparent and effective sector governance
ii. Easing doing business and reducing barriers to private investment
iii. Enhancing institutional, organizational, and human capacities as well as the legal and regulatory framework.

The Energy Policy and the Energy Sector Strategic Plan (ESSP) are mutually reinforcing. Whereas the policy outlines a long-term vision, provides high-level goals, and recommends clear and coordinated approaches for achieving that vision, the ESSP outlines targets and an implementation framework against which to measure progress towards the realization of the policy. In this way, the policy can guide the actualization of aligned implementation strategies, while the ESSP outlines the priority strategies and actions that give practical thrust to the policy.

The Ministry of Infrastructure is grateful to all stakeholders who provided very useful inputs into enriching this Policy document and the Technical Team both at the Ministry of Infrastructure and other sister Ministries, who worked really hard to complete the development of this document.

EXECUTIVE SUMMARY

Energy is the life-blood of development. The energy sector plays a pivotal role in supporting socio-economic transformation and has an inherently systemic link to the growth of other sectors of the economy. Since energy is a critical input to other key economic sectors, such as manufacturing, construction, mining and quarrying, agro-processing, transport, and tourism, a sound and comprehensive Rwanda energy policy is critical for economic growth.[1]Investments in the energy sector generate fiscal revenues through taxes, levies, and other duties imposed on various sector activities such as petroleum products imports (fuel oils and LPG) as well as tariffs on electrical consumption (18% VAT), supporting the country's resource envelope. In order to achieve sustainable economic growth, an enabling environment and policy framework is needed to facilitate new energy investments that meet the needs of Rwandan consumers.

Ensuring access to modern, sustainable, and affordable energy services is integral to Rwanda's economic development, poverty eradication and socioeconomic transformation agenda.[2] Lack of modern energy services stifles income-generating activities and hampers the provision of basic services such as health care and education. In addition, smoke from polluting and inefficient cooking, lighting, and heating devices is a leading contributor to respiratory diseases and death in Rwanda.[3] Where provision of cost effective, appropriate solutions to the poor is enabled, particularly in rural areas where energy services are scarce or expensive, poverty reduction can occur. Additionally, shifting consumption from biomass-based energies to clean energies like electricity and LPG reduces pressure on forest resources, protecting land arability and mitigating climate change through sustainable environmental conservation.

Increased, broadly shared prosperity also hinges upon developing the energy sector as key pillar or engine of economic growth. In the household sector, energy services for cooking, lighting, heating, brewing, firing, boiling, ironing, and operating electric appliances are important to maintaining human security, good health and quality of life. A modern, more service-industry based, industrialized economy requires predictable, sufficiently available, competitively priced energy commodities (e.g., electricity and petroleum products). This drives agricultural mechanization, increasing returns per hectare and people's disposable

[1]According to the Ministry of Trade and Industry, Rwanda's 2013 industrial production expanded by 11% compared to 4.6% for the economy as a whole. This growth was primarily driven by the construction sector and mining activities. [2]According to the UN Foundation almost 3 billion people rely on traditional biomass for cooking and heating, and about 1.5 billion have no access to electricity, with 1 billion more having access only to unreliable electricity networks. [3]Smoke from polluting and inefficient cooking, lighting, and heating devices kills over four million people globally a year.

Global Burden of Disease Issue, *The Lancet*, December 2012.

income. Petroleum products drive the transport sector and petroleum price movements impact on macroeconomic balances. Distributed energy solutions support business creation, productivity, and entrepreneurship in rural areas, widening the tax base and supporting the socioeconomic transformation agenda. The manner in which energy investments and access programs are designed can also strongly support government policies on boosting youth productivity and employment.[4]

In order for the energy sector to leverage a most positive impact on the other sectors in a way that supports Rwanda's development and socioeconomic transformation agenda, the Rwanda Energy Policy has been elaborated. This policy is well aligned to the country's overall long-term economic policies and calls upon various institutions to undertake measures that support private sector growth and socio-economic transformation as reflected in the Medium Term Economic Development and Poverty Reduction Strategy for 2013-2018 (EDPRS-II). This policy offers high level guidance on the development of Rwanda's energy sector in a manner that fulfills the sector commitments. The energy sector and industry is complex, encompassing multiple subsectors, including electricity, biomass and petroleum. The wide-ranging objectives and planning frameworks contained herein cut across all sub-sectors of the energy, and likewise address issues related to upstream exploration, production, transportation, pricing, distribution and consumption.

While the ESSP and Rwanda Energy Policy are mutually reinforcing, the latter provides high-level direction on the longer-term goals, priorities, and approaches needed in the sector. In this way, the energy policy directives support the development of harmonized implementation strategies and action plans that are clear, well-coordinated, and aligned to EDPRS-II. Closely linked to the policy, the laws and regulations of the sector act as a solid foundation upon which to base actions; these are principally concerned with the conduct, rights and operational constraints affecting the market-place and policy delivery.

The ESSP is a more focused action plan that measures short-term progress toward long-term goals and objectives. It also takes into account anticipated resource constraints and risk/uncertainties in the implementation strategies. The ESSP shall be updated at minimum on an annual basis. Falling underneath the ESSP, and in parallel to the ongoing least cost power development plan, sub-sector implementation Action Plans owned by the relevant ministries (and generally not subject to Cabinet approval) shall be elaborated. These shall be developed for seven priority areas in the electricity sub-sector, including: hydropower, methane gas, geothermal, bioenergy, solar power, peat and efficiency and demand-side management. The action plans shall be aligned to the overall policy objectives.

[4]These are key thematic areas of EDPRS II which targets the creation of 200,000 off-farm jobs per annum.

CHAPTER ONE: POLICY CONTEXT

1.1. COUNTRY OVERVIEW

Rwanda is a small land-locked country of 26,338 km^2 in area with a population of 11,689,696 people *(national census, 2012)*. It is a densely populated country in comparison to other African countries. In 2014, GDP was 643 USD/capita. Rwanda's economy has been growing at an annual average rate of 8.3% and government is targeting to achieve an annual average growth rate of 11.5% over the EDPRS II period (2013-2018). Ensuring access to affordable and modern sources of energy is essential to achieve the EDPRS II objectives.

1.2. NEED FOR AN ENERGY POLICY FRAMEWORK AND SECTOR CHALLENGES

There are several reasons why a Rwanda National Energy policy is required. Firstly, the lack of a modern, long-term approved energy policy is widely recognized by stakeholders as contributing to coordination failures and institutional underperformance. The current document reflects a revision to a national policy that was drafted in 2011. Although used as a guiding framework, this policy was never formally approved by Cabinet. Prior energy policies include a 2004 Energy Policy that largely responded to emergency energy security considerations, rather than addressing a broad range of issues, as well as a proposed policy elaborated in 2008, following EDPRS I, that was rejected by the Cabinet.

Secondly, a general policy shift is required due to underlying changes in the country. The economy has experienced stable growth for some time, and power supply crises have stabilized. Rwanda's population is growing quickly and is projected to reach 14 million by 2020 and 16.4 million people by 2030.[5] In the household sector, essential energy services for cooking, lighting, heating, brewing, firing, boiling, ironing, and operating electric appliances is thus expected to grow significantly. At the same time, Rwanda currently has low levels of access to modern energy carriers such as electricity and LPG. This marked energy poverty constrains efforts to achieve medium-term thematic and macroeconomic objectives of the EDPRS II, including attaining middle income status by 2020.

The current electricity tariff is relatively high compared to other countries in the region and heavily subsidized.[6] High relative energy costs and unreliable power supply dis-incentivize stronger industrial growth and business expansion. This particular challenge is perceived as most critical in the manufacturing, mining, and agro-processing sectors. Power cuts,

[5]These represent base-case population growth scenarios according to the Rwandan National Institute of Statistics. [6] *Review of Current Electricity End User Tariffs*: Final Report to RURA by Energy & Economics Consulting, 30 April 2014.

8 unstable power supply conditions, and uneven power quality are additional constraints to industrial sector growth.

Thirdly, EDPRS-II calls for an unprecedented degree of investment in Rwanda's emerging energy systems and markets to come from the private sector. This major shift requires new policies and strategies to leverage private capital and facilitate private sector engagement and partnership. A transparent and stable policy framework will be critical.

The policy needs to address the following critical sector challenges:

i. Energy security and a sound demand-supply balance;

ii. Dramatic increase in access to modern energy services;

iii. Improvement and streamlining of stakeholder coordination to ensure effective partnership and delivery on set targets;

iv. Need for a robust legal and regulatory framework required;

v. Necessity for an institutional, organizational, and human capacity development;

vi. Inadequate infrastructure requiring huge investment;

vii. High cost of fuel for electricity generation;

viii. Vulnerability to climate change.

In addition, the development of relevant policies for the energy sector mandates that, the key issues that affect the supply and demand of energy in Rwanda be delineated. Broad issues of the energy sector in Rwanda include the following:

i. Inadequate co-ordination and information sharing between/or among the various projects, government bodies, the private sector and civil society organizations;

ii. Lack of investment;

iii. Inadequate energy planning information system (energy supply and demand analysis);

iv. Lower rate of access to modern energy;

v. Inadequate financial resources to plan for and monitor the energy sector and carry out appropriate research and development (R&D);

vi. Lack for appropriate curricula in energy studies at many institutions of higher learning;

vii. Inadequate human resource and institutional capacity.

For each of the energy-sub sectors there are specific issues to consider, which are given below. The various energy sub-sectors include the following:

Electricity;

Petroleum;

Biomass;

Energy Efficiency and Demand Side Management.

1.3.1 Electricity

The electric power sub-sector issues in Rwanda include the following:

i. Insufficient investment to develop electricity generation, transmission and distribution projects including the interconnection projects that can facilitate and enhance the energy trade;
ii. Large technical and non-technical electricity losses;
iii. Inadequate maintenance;
iv. High costs of supply due to the past insufficient investment in power generation, transmission and distribution and sometimes coupled with a very low operational efficiency and lack of financial planning;
v. Lack of cost reflective tariffs;
vi. Lower electricity access;
vii. Low quality of electricity supply and customer service;
viii. Inefficient commercial operations in terms of lack of an accurate customer database, inadequate systems and controls for meter reading and high accounts receivable.

PETROLEUM

The petroleum sub-sector issues include the following:

i. The evolution of prices, in particular, oil prices on the international market impacts negatively on the balance of payments of oil-importing and renders the cost of energy supply unbearable;

ii. High transport costs due to insufficient transport facilities and being landlocked;

iii. Inadequate quality control of the fossil fuels products, posing an increasing hazard to public health and the environment.

Biomass and other Renewable Energy Sources

Issues of Biomass and other renewable energy sources include the following:

i. Inefficient production and use of wood-fuels resulting in the depletion of forest resources, which, in turn, has an adverse environmental impact in terms of accelerating climate change, threatening biodiversity and increasing erosion. It also has an adverse impact on the health of wood-fuels users, especially in rural households;

ii. Low public awareness about the efficacy and potency of renewable energy technologies (RETs);

iii. Little production of equipment and components and underdeveloped markets in RETs equipment and services because of high initial investment cost and lack of financial capacity to cover the initial investment;

iv. Lack of mechanisms to monitor standards and ensure quality control of RETs: the poor quality of some technologies available on the market reduces their lifetime and damages the image of RETs;

v. Inadequate financing mechanisms;

vi. Inadequate data available on the potential of indigenous renewable energy sources (geothermal, solar, wind, peat, methane gas, mini and micro hydro);

vii. Shortage of local actors capable of carrying projects financially, technically, and in terms of management; and

viii. Institutional, policy, fiscal and regulatory barriers.

Energy Efficiency and Demand Side Management

Energy efficiency and demand side management issues include those generic issues for the major sectors which include transport, industry, households and agriculture. Accordingly, energy efficiency and demand side management issues include the following:

(i) Low level of awareness among energy end users about energy conservation practices, options and benefits and insufficient information about improved energy technologies;

(ii) Insufficient incentives, including financing mechanisms to invest in modern efficient technologies and practices and to introduce fuel / technology substitution, e.g., LPG, kerosene, solar, more efficient fuel technology, for wood-fuels;

(iii) Dominance of energy-inefficient technologies, including traditional stoves; lights and other appliances.

These critical sector challenges and sub-sector issues can only be addressed through a clear energy policy framework.

SECTOR OVERVIEW

The energy sector in Rwanda consists of four components: Electricity, Biomass, Gas and Petroleum, with each playing a key role in Rwanda's transition to a middle income country by the end of the decade.

Although Rwanda has had considerable success over recent years in addressing issues related to environment to the extent that it's one of only a few countries in Africa where there is not a major link between biomass and the negative environmental effects of deforestation, social and health problems emanating from the use of biomass need to be solved. The government is promoting the use of alternative fuels such as biogas from animal and plant waste. This will not only save lives but also free up the time spent by women and children in collecting firewood, giving them more time to study and undertake more productive commercial activities.

The use of electricity is required for both low consumption devices and large consumers. Our priority is to extend the network to allow productive and heavy users of electricity across the country to connect to the grid. For lighter users of electricity, grid connections are unlikely to make economic sense in the short term and as such, off-grid will be preferred. The government intends to provide 70% of the population with access to electricity both on-grid and off-grid by the end of EDPRS II which is now at 23%.

To keep pace with the increased demand for electricity, the government will ensure increased electricity generation capacity above the current capacity of 160 MW (March 2015). Diversifying away from diesel generation will enable the government to maintain a regionally competitive tariff whilst eradicating subsidies to the electricity tariff. There is considerable private sector interest in electricity generation from Rwanda's indigenous resources.

Petroleum subsector's objective is to ensure safe, sufficient, reliable, sustainable and affordable supply of petroleum and LPG. Currently, Rwanda depends entirely on imported fuel products, because its petroleum resources are yet to be commercially proven and developed. Rwanda plans to expand domestic exploration and production, boosting investment in supply and storage infrastructure, and promoting sound management of downstream resources.

ELECTRICITY

Total installed electricity generation capacity is currently 160 MW, of which roughly more than 60% comes from hydrological resources and less than 40% from diesel-powered generators and other sources.[7] Rwanda has a very pronounced peak demand load and hence supply is occasionally unable to match demand in these peak hours. The current on-grid access to electricity is estimated at 23% of households.

National Electricity Consumption: The cost of electricity is currently not cost reflective and heavily subsidized. The diesel fuel and heavy fuel oil required to run petroleum-based power plants represents a large share of the total national import burden, and is one factor driving the high cost of electricity and currency depreciation. The loss estimate of 2014 in the power system (both technical and non-technical) was 23%.

[7] EWSA, Grid Audit Report, 2013.

Petroleum

Currently, Rwanda depends entirely on imported fuel products, because its petroleum resources are yet to be commercially proven and developed. Petroleum consumption increased in absolute terms by over 16% between 2000 and 2012, yet the oil import bill grew by more than 700% in the same period. As a share of GDP, oil imports increased from about 2.5% in 2000 to above 5.5% by 2012. Still, this level of growth has been relatively more modest compared to Rwanda's neighbours. The demand for petroleum products will continue to rise on account of increased transport vehicles and expansion of the fleet for the National airline. The reduction of imported diesel for electricity production will be more than off-set by the increased need for petroleum products in transportation, particularly aviation and heavy industry.

Biomass

In Rwanda, biomass energy subsector covers mainly wood, charcoal, biogas and biofuels. Biomass resources are exploited in form of firewood, charcoal or agricultural residues mainly for cooking purposes by households and also in some industries[8]. Country-wide, biomass meets up to 85% of energy needs; with the balance being met by other options such as kerosene, diesel, dry cells, grid and non-grid electricity, biogas, solar, wind and other renewable energies. Biomass is already in short supply with the country facing a biomass deficit of over 4 million m^3 per year[9]. Although fuel wood consumption is expected to increase in the short-term, the long-term strategy of the EDPRS II is to reduce fuel wood consumption from 85% to 50% by 2018.

Rwandan households will not eliminate the use of wood fuels in the short run. Instead, as the economy develops wood fuels will be phased out where it makes sense. This will be supported with the introduction of enabling frameworks for use of LPG and other alternatives including solar and thermal applications, particularly in urban and semi-urban areas.

[8] MININFRA, 2008 [9] BEST Strategy, 2009

CHAPTER TWO: ENERGY POLICY VISION, MISSION, GOALS, KEY PRINCIPLES AND OBJECTIVES

1 VISION

The vision of the energy sector is to contribute effectively to the growth of the national economy and thereby improve the standard of living for the entire nation in a sustainable and environmentally sound manner.

2 MISSION

The mission of the Rwanda energy sector is to create conditions for the provision of sufficient, safe, reliable, efficient, cost-effective and environmentally appropriate energy services to households and to all economic sectors on a sustainable basis.

3 OVERARCHING POLICY GOALS

The overall goal of the policy is to ensure that all residents and industries can access energy products and services that are sufficient, reliable, affordable, and sustainable.[10] Specific core global objectives of the energy policy include:

Ensuring the availability of sufficient, reliable and affordable energy supplies for all Rwandans;

Creating an enabling environment for increased private sector participation in energy supply and service provision;

Encouraging and incentivizing more rational, efficient use of energy in public institutions, and amongst industrial and household end-users;

Ensuring the sustainability of energy exploration, extraction, supply, and consumption so as to prevent damage to the environment and habitats;

Promoting safe, efficient, and competitive production, procurement, transportation, and distribution of energy;

Developing the requisite institutional, organizational, and human capacity to increase accountability, transparency, national ownership and decentralized implementation capacity for sustainable energy service delivery.

Collaborating with the private sector, the Government will also work towards meeting national, regional, and global targets to enhance access to modern energy services. Rwanda is a signatory to the United Nations Sustainable Energy for All Initiative (SE4ALL), and is in

[10]Sustainable energy use is the practice of providing energy solutions in a manner that meets the needs of the present without compromising the ability of future generations to meet their needs (Renewable Energy and Efficiency Partnership, August 2004). Not all energy resources are renewable in human lifetimes. For this reason, wasteful or inefficient use of resources could well lead to reduced security and affordability for future generations of Rwandans.

the process of preparing a detailed road map, Action Agenda, and investment prospectus. Rwanda is also a signatory to the Regional Strategy on Scaling up Access to Modern Energy Services adopted by the EAC Council of Ministers. In order to increase access, electricity and clean fuels must be available and affordable. For this reason, policies herein aim to create a sound enabling environment for;

- off-grid energy service provision including the development of distributed, small-scale renewable energy solutions and business models; and

- Lean fuels energy service provision, including the development of infrastructure and distribution for LPG and biogas.

4 KEY POLICY PRINCIPLES AND PRIORITIES

The following principles summarize Government's guiding approach to energy development. They reflect a need to balance and protect the interest of citizens and energy consumers, private investors, and other stakeholders. They give high-level policy prescriptions on how Rwanda's energy resources should best be exploited, distributed, and utilized. These foundational principles promote an enabling environment for successful achievement of commitments reflected in the

ESSP and future sub-sector action plans in the development of specific policy directives and guidelines.

1) Building decentralized energy policy implementation capacity

A strong principle underlying the development and implementation of the energy policy is the need to ensure strong national ownership over decision-making and to undertake measures to empower local companies and Rwandan experts in fulfilling the vision of the sector. This entails having a much stronger focus on building domestic human, organizational, and institutional capacity. Local authorities are encouraged to include and monitor obligations for providing improved energy services and access to clean energy technologies. Moreover, energy issues should be regularly addressed in relevant integrated development Steering Committees and Joint Action Development Forums (JADF).

2) Promote value-for-money and increased market competition in energy development

Government shall establish transparent processes and guidelines for all energy project procurement. Given the increased role of the private sector in the delivery of energy projects and services, it is important to ensure that more competitive and transparent practices are put into place. Under the policy, competitive bidding of all energy-related projects, including independent power production (IPP) generation activities, shall henceforth be the *default* procurement option. This is vital to realize more market transparency and to ensure value-for-money in the use of public funds.[11] Provided a project still conforms to value-for-money principles, exceptions may be warranted in cases of:

i. *Urgent need.* Ensuring continuity of supply or providing services rapidly due to emergency situations;
ii. *Public security.* Where the project may directly pose a risk to public security or involves matters pertaining to state security;
iii. *Technological uniqueness.* For example, when provision of the service necessitates technology for which unique intellectual property, trade secrets, or other exclusive rights are owned or possessed by a single firm or entity;
iv. Other compelling reasons in the national or public interest.

Projects in these categories may be procured through unsolicited proposals through the signing of a MoU between a private party and the contracting authority.

3) “Smart” subsidies aligned to social protection principles. In line with existing principles under EDPRS-II for improving the effectiveness of social protection interventions, a gradual shift away from indiscriminate subsidies toward “smart subsidies” shall be pursued for all energy related interventions. The latter term refers to direct mechanisms that targets specific groups including the poorest, most vulnerable end-users. Targeted “smart” energy subsidies and welfare support measures to ensure affordability of energy services should be primarily targeted to vulnerable groups within the limits of the state’s capacity.

4) Private operation of government owned power plants In order to increase efficiency and create market opportunities for local business, where it is deemed appropriate, government owned power plants shall be considered for lease to the private sector for operation and management. Private operation of such projects tends to always deliver advantages in terms of value for money and more reliable power supply.

5) Promoting private sector participation

Meeting the goals under EDPRS II entails both significant absolute levels of investment in the sector and a much greater relative share projects being privately financed than ever before. Government shall encourage and facilitate private sector participation in the development of

Rwanda's energy resources and in all phases of energy project delivery, including development, construction, financing, installation, maintenance and operations. Increased participation by the local and foreign private sector is particularly encouraged in the electricity supply and clean cooking fuels industry. Government shall pursue a variety of

[11]It should be noted in this context that the application of a REFIT tariff for power procurement through IPPs would comply with this principle, as there would be little room for negotiation of the set and transparent terms and conditions.

actions to enable marked growth in private sector as outlined in detail below.

I. Streamline investment promotion processes for IPPs.

IPP processes shall be streamlined by clarifying the exact steps, prerequisites, and outcome milestones for each major stage of the investment process, (i.e., obtaining an energy project concession). Resources shall be mobilized for establishing integrated IT systems for tracking project development progress across key energy sector players.

II. De-risk investments through upstream resource assessments and pre-feasibility studies

Commercial investment in Rwandan energy projects is constrained by high up-front risk before energy resources are confirmed. Government will thus increase investments in better energy resource assessments and resource mapping to de-risk transactions and investments in the sector. Unless already taken into account under mechanisms, such as the feed-in tariff for specific renewable energy resources, Government may also invest in pre-feasibility or "proof of concept" studies as well as feasibility studies and demonstration projects for technologies not yet commercially "proven" or bankable.

III. Accelerate and facilitate energy sector Public-Private Partnerships (PPPs)

PPP structures are particularly relevant for the energy sector, especially for complex activities where risks are high and innovation can be harnessed from private sector actors. Areas particularly suitable for PPP structures include: rural energy service provision such as off-grid and mini-grid systems.

IV. Empower local enterprises to engage in energy sector

Government shall strive to create more favorable conditions for local enterprises to do energy business in Rwanda including ensuring transparency and equity. For example, the legal and regulatory framework for developing off-grid solutions will be streamlined to attract more local private investors and operators. While provisions to ensure that local content is a feature of new energy investments is already incorporated into concession agreements, new policy measures include standardizing "local content" guidelines suitable for different categories of projects, incorporating clear language on requirements into PPAs, and systematically monitoring compliance for local content participation.

Rwanda's energy sector can be viewed as encompassing: electricity, energy efficiency and demand-side management, electricity access, biomass, and petroleum. For each of these, the following policy objectives define how it shall be sustainably developed in a manner that can achieve the overall energy sector goals and objectives. The policy objectives have also been elaborated to be consistent with the overall key principles of the energy policy.

2.5 ELECTRICITY

The main policy objective for the electricity sub-sector is to ensure sufficient, reliable, sustainable and more affordable power supply. This will be achieved through the following measures:

i. Revise and upgrade the existing policy, legal, regulatory, institutional, and financial frameworks to support the rapid development of the electricity industry;

ii. Diversify power generation resources over time and increase the share of clean power in the total mix over time;

iii. Ensure supply is closely aligned to projected demand[12], and better align investment planning and funding mobilization more closely to a power generation road map and master plan, a least-cost power development plan, and an electricity sub-sector action plan;

iv. Enhance regional cooperation and trade in electricity, including investment in transmission network development, to further improve security of supply;

v. Streamline IPP processes and fast track project delivery by securing long-term funding for planned projects through a medium-term budget expenditure framework, revising and expanding the existing Renewable Energy Feed-In Tariff regime, developing new information management systems to streamline procedures, and building greater capacity in planning, procurement, and negotiating power transactions.

Additional, related policy objectives are outlined below.

ENSURE COST-REFLECTIVE ELECTRICITY TARIFF

The policy aims to achieve a sustainable transition to a cost-reflective, yet affordable electricity tariff. Addressing this challenge shall be met through a four-pronged approach:

i. Disaggregating tariffs by end-user categories in order to ensure that they fairly reflect the relative contributions to the cost base;

ii. Increasing operational efficiencies and savings on the required revenues of the utility;

iii. Reducing the long-run marginal cost of power generation through increased imports and exploitation of alternative technologies; and

[12]Peak demand is expected to exceed 400 MW by 2018 according to the latest estimations.

iv. Implementing loss reduction and demand-side management programs to shave peak demand load and grid reserve margin requirements.

STRENGTHEN NATIONAL ELECTRIC POWER SYSTEM

In order to improve the quality and security of electricity supply and to drive down long-term costs, the GoR shall:

i. Increase investments in generation capacity, transmission and distribution systems and rehabilitation;

ii. Reduce technical and commercial losses in the power system;

iii. Increase reserve margin between demand and supply to a necessary level;

iv. Develop transmission lines connecting Rwanda to neighboring countries.

OPTIMIZE THE POWER MIX

The policy aims to:

i. Increase the share of renewable energy in the power mix by exploiting indigenous resources (i.e. hydropower, geothermal, solar, and methane gas);

ii. Refocus petroleum-based power generation to serve peak load and back-up power demands;

iii. Manage the share between domestic production and imports in the total mix;

iv. Revise and update periodically power generation road map and investment plan guided by a Least Cost Power Development Plan (LCPDP).

ENHANCE ATTRACTIVENESS OF EXPLOITING DOMESTIC ENERGY RESOURCES FOR POWER GENERATION.

Government will increase the attractiveness of domestic power generation to the private sector by:

i. Initiating public-funded exploration and risk mitigation mechanisms;

ii. Funding energy resource mapping, pre-feasibility studies, upstream exploration, and piloting of projects to gain a clearer picture of the extent to which domestic hydropower, peat, solar and wind resources can generate power on commercially viable, competitive terms;

FACILITATE AUTONOMOUS POWER GENERATION

While autonomous generation investments are explicitly allowed for under the law, uptake has nevertheless been slow. The establishment of private or self-generation power plants for industrial or household purposes is explicitly allowed for under the Electricity law, with generation under 50 kW installed capacity currently exempted from all licensing requirements. Policy guidelines and regulations to more explicitly facilitate autonomous generation shall be adopted, particularly those geared toward mining and agro-industries.

For example, the current Mining Sector Strategy intends to pilot "green" energy solutions based on solar PV, micro-hydro, and bio-energy resources that could be developed by mining companies as self-generation investments. In order to further streamline and encourage such activities, measures to simplify licensing regulations for mini-grids or small-scale power distributors (SPDs) shall also be extended to appropriate autonomous generation activities. Guidelines and new regulations concerning autonomous generation shall, however, continue to ensure the respect for existing laws on right of way and expropriation in the event that any distribution infrastructure falls on public lands.

ELECTRICITY ACCESS

The main policy objective for the sub-sector is to enhance access to sustainable, modern energy services for all Rwandans. This policy priority is reflected in political commitments and targets that Rwanda has made at the global, regional, and national level. To a large degree, making electricity services more affordable and extending consumer credit for grid connection fees is pivotal to reaching this objective. Policies and a supportive regulatory framework shall also be enacted to expand investment and private sector engagement in off-grid electricity service provision, including through partnerships and innovative business models.

Attaining energy access commitments will not only entail increased political will, but also the development of a robust monitoring and evaluation framework that takes into account a variety of criteria. The policy objectives in the sub-sector focus on:

i. Greater clarity on, and harmonization of, preferential approaches between grid and off-grid energy access efforts for different target population groups;
ii. Piloting new approaches and scaling up innovative partnerships to increase energy access through distributed renewable technologies;
iii. Introducing more flexibility and competition through measures to simplify licensing and increase the attractiveness for private operators to service the off-grid electricity market;
iv. Ensure 100% access to electricity in all schools, health centers and administrative offices by 2018;
v. Scale-up innovative partnerships to increase rural access to appropriate off-grid solutions;
vi.
Introduce greater competition and flexibility in off-grid service provision.
vii. Develop financial support mechanisms for off-grid service provision and consumption.

7 ENERGY EFFICIENCY AND DEMAND-SIDE MANAGEMENT

The policy objective of the energy efficiency and demand-side management is to constrain uncontrolled future energy consumption growth and to support realizing Rwanda's Green Economy vision. Given growing demand for electricity at household and industrial levels, and the fact that Rwanda's natural resources are more limited compared to other countries in the region, actions to manage demand for electricity is an important and more prominent thrust of the current policy. An increased focus on energy efficiency[13], energy conservation, and demand-side management activities is sensible. Fundamentally, it is also cheaper to use energy more intelligently and efficiently than to meet demand by expanding energy production unnecessarily.

Rwanda has a pronounced peak demand load, which is both a key factor for power disruptions, because the existing power reserve margin is low, and a key driver for new generation capacity investment. Measures that encourage efficient end-use technologies, sound and optimally timed energy consumption practices, and other demand-side management activities will play a critical role in shaving peak demand and maintaining the affordability and reliability of energy services.

Energy efficiency will be promoted through a combination of approaches, including:

i. Incentivizing demand side management through changes in the electricity tariff methodology;

ii. Mandatory regulations, such as new codes and standards;

iii. The introduction of economic incentives, such as subsidies for installation of solar water heaters and for industrial end-users to undertake energy efficiency audits;

iv. Barrier removal programs, for example, examining systemic disincentives or reducing split incentives for energy-efficient technologies in buildings;

v. Pursuit of bulk procurement strategies, for example, importation of LED and CFL lamps; and

vi. Other measures to promote alternative sources of energy for cooking, water heating and purification, heating, cooling, and lighting.

Priority measures to be pursued in this area include:

ADOPT NEW LAWS, REGULATIONS AND CODES THAT MANDATE ENERGY EFFICIENCY MEASURES

New laws and regulations will be developed to ensure that public institutions, households, and commercial businesses support the energy efficiency objectives. Among these shall

[13]Improving energy efficiency means using less energy to produce the same desired output.

include an Energy Efficiency Law as an umbrella framework to upgrade existing technical guidelines. Responsible institutions shall introduce new building codes, reflecting provisions for introducing of energy-smart and energy-efficient technologies and practices, including passive solar design and rain water tank storage.

RESTRUCTURE ELECTRICITY TARIFF METHODOLOGY TO INCENTIVIZE EFFICIENCY

A free-standing "demand charge" tariff component for all customers served through medium-voltage lines will be initiated. This methodological change provides a stable, continuous incentive for industries to conserve power and to shift consumption away from peak periods.

ESTABLISH A DEMAND-SIDE MANAGEMENT PROGRAM WITHIN THE UTILITY

A demand-side management (DSM) program or dedicated corporate unit shall be formed to undertake planning and monitoring of all activities designed to modify consumer demand patterns. The program will also implement load management programs that reduce demand spikes and encourage end-users to shift consumption away from peak times. This program shall also implement priority policies for reducing demand load under the direct control of the Utility itself. Other measures to intensify the provision of consumer information, education and technical advice towards the use and conservation of energy shall be implemented and overseen by the DSM program.

ENCOURAGE AND INCENTIVIZE ENERGY AUDITS AMONG COMMERCIAL AND INDUSTRIAL END-USERS

Major users of energy, particularly industries, shall be encouraged and incentivized to carry out regular energy audits. The Rwanda Resource Efficient and Cleaner Production Centre has already supported local industry with the successful implementation of a number of audits that delivered bankable returns linked to savings on energy and other resource inputs. The scope of such audits will include the feasibility of fuel switching from thermal power to off-grid solar PV for agro-industries as well as measures to reduce leaks and inefficiencies associated with petroleum consumption for mechanical and pumping activities in industrial processes. MININFRA shall investigate the feasibility of developing an energy efficiency facility that would provide matching grants to large energy end-users for the purpose of undertaking energy efficiency audits and to provide incentives for investing in the implementation of the audit recommendations. The savings from such investments would be used to recapitalize the facility. In addition, advanced, high-efficiency power generation technologies which could include shifting to cogeneration facilities shall be investigated as part of the audits or whenever new feasibility studies are commissioned by the utility.

DEVELOP A REGIONAL STANDARDS AND LABELING SCHEME FOR COMMON APPLIANCES

Appliance rating or labeling schemes are a very cost-effective policy measure for achieving energy consumption savings. Providing information about the energy performance of an appliance, particularly in comparison against a minimum and maximum benchmark, incentivizes consumers to purchase more energy efficient products. It is critical that consumers are better informed of the energy performance of appliances that they are considering to purchase. RSB in collaboration with RURA and MININFRA shall establish an ongoing working group to harmonize energy efficient labeling practices and standards for appliances sold and imported in Rwanda and the EAC.

PROMOTE AND REMOVE BARRIERS TO THE IMPLEMENTATION OF PRIORITY EFFICIENT LIGHTING INITIATIVES

Lighting is by far the most important use of electrical energy. Energy efficient lighting programs' impact will be enhanced through better program design, marketing plans, and leveraging market-based incentives and private sector participation to maximum advantage. An expansion of efficient lighting for public services, including street lighting in public institutions and administrative buildings, shall be supported through the new strategy and implementation programs.

DEVISE AND IMPLEMENT "GREEN" PUBLIC PROCUREMENT GUIDELINES AND STRATEGIES.

As a large energy consumer, government agencies and other public sector institutions play an important role in implementing national energy efficiency targets. RPPA, REMA, and MININFRA shall collaborate to develop clear energy efficiency criteria and guidelines that can be incorporated into sustainable procurement policies and processes. These shall focus on equipment with a high-energy footprint.

BIOMASS ENERGY

The main policy objective for the biomass sub-sector is to facilitate fuel-switching from traditional biomass energy carriers toward modern biomass energy technologies and cleaner fuel alternatives in order to achieve a more sustainable wood fuel balance and reduce consumption of non-renewable biomass, and to deliver related social, health, and environmental benefits. In addition to measures to promote switching to more sustainable biomass energy technologies at household level, such as biogas, LPG, and peat briquettes, among others, small-scale, commercially viable biogas projects including gasification of crop residues will be promoted through inclusion under an expanded REFIT regime. Existing biomass resources should be exploited in a manner that promotes greater sustainability of supply, while reducing the negative impacts of harvesting to the environment and Rwandan habitats.

MININFRA will develop strategies and action plans including capacity building and enhancing market transformation.

The implementation of sustainable biomass energy programs focused on cleaner cooking technologies shall be decentralized in order to accelerate delivery and improve impact. MININFRA will continue to provide technical assistance through REG Ltd to the districts.

With support and guidance of MINALOC, district authorities will be required to incorporate delivery of sustainable biomass energy technologies into their annual performance contracts. This will promote more ownership. Districts will play a pivotal role in education and awareness-raising, and the extension of government subsidy mechanisms and micro-finance schemes. MINALOC shall monitor district development plans more closely for meeting clean cooking targets and strategies. RSB shall elaborate updated national ICS standards with the support of REMA, MININFRA, and the private sector and other stakeholders.

Increase access to cleaner cooking technologies

In the medium-term, the policy vision foresees extensive fuel switching among households to modern energy technologies and carriers including biogas, LPG, "green charcoal", and biomass pyrolysis stoves.

Measures to be adopted in biomass energy strategies include the following:

Social marketing/behavioural change models and partnerships with financial institutions

Since the economic rationale for some households to switch to cleaner cooking technologies is limited by the fact that are able to collect wood fuel and biomass residues at no cost, a much stronger emphasis will be placed on social and behavioural change campaigns in implementation approaches.

Updated technology standards

In cooperation with other stakeholders, technology standard for biogas digesters and installations shall be formulated and adopted building upon existing technical guidance. Through new technology standards and regulations, alternative options to increase consumer choice and affordability shall be promoted.

Subsidy reform

In cooperation with MININFRA, MINECOFIN shall reform the design, targeting and administration of subsidies for biogas and other clean cooking technologies in order to improve the impact and scale-up potential of existing programs.

Develop new policy and regionally-integrated market for sustainable liquid bio-fuels

A new bio-fuels policy shall be developed that harmonizes agricultural and land-use approaches and that takes into account a much stronger regional integration dimension to market development. A preliminary bio-fuel policy drafted by the former Institute of Scientific and Technological Research (IRST) in 2008 to promote bio-diesel exploration, production and use shall be updated and integrated into this policy in line with regional policy approaches. Increasing the share of bio-fuels in Rwanda's energy mix will increase energy security by reducing dependency on imported petroleum products. Markets particularly suitable for bio-fuels include public and agricultural transport vehicles and agroprocessing machinery by replacing petroleum fuels entirely with fuel produced from biocrops.

PETROLEUM

Rwanda's petroleum sub-sector covers both upstream (petroleum exploration, development and commercial production) and downstream (transportation-for crude and refined products, refining, storage, distribution and marketing) activities. The sub-sector is characterized by three main challenges: unreliable supplies and uneven product quality, insufficient storage and distribution capacity, and high exposure or vulnerability to global price volatility. In a global perspective, petroleum exploration and development activities have become progressively more capital intensive, technologically complex, and environmentally sensitive. Thus, it is essential that national policies are aligned to international realities and best practice and sophisticated enough to ensure that international companies and investment partners with the right mix of expertise and technological know-how are enticed to operate in Rwanda in a manner that ensures environmental sustainability and mutually beneficial cooperation from the extraction of non-renewable, mineral rents.

The main policy objective for the sub-sector is to ensure safe, sufficient, reliable, sustainable and affordable supply of petroleum and LPG. This entails expanding domestic exploration and production, boosting investments in supply and storage infrastructure, and promoting sound management of downstream resources and markets. Existing policies on upstream development and downstream use have been developed by MINIRENA and MINICOM, respectively. Investments shall be facilitated by: proving Rwanda's national resources using public funds; developing streamlining procedures for resource exploration and joint ventures; increasing the transparency of the legal, regulatory and licensing framework; developing technical standards and environmental management protocols; and opening up the market to greater competition. A Downstream Petroleum Policy was adopted by Cabinet in late 2012. It gives guidance on the transportation (of both crude and refined products), refining, storage, distribution and marketing of petroleum products in Rwanda. In order to address current sub-sector challenges, the Rwanda Energy Policy complements these and reinforces the implementation of existing sub-sector policies through the following objectives:

i. Accelerate regional cooperation and strategic infrastructure development;
ii. Ensure adequate storage infrastructure to maintain appropriate strategic reserve levels;
iii. Enhance the effectiveness of price stabilization mechanisms;
iv. Improve data collection and enforcement of fuel quality standards;
v. Improving Liquefied Petroleum Gas (LPG) market and distribution infrastructure.

CHAPTER THREE: POLICY PRINCIPLES ON CROSS CUTTING ISSUES

1 CAPACITY BUILDING

Vision 2020 calls for the creation of a Knowledge Based Economy built upon continuous upgrading of skills. Lack of capacity in both an institutional and technical sense is a genuine bottleneck to economic growth and achieving the sector vision under the EP. Building sustainable national capacity throughout the entire energy sector in both the private sector and across the government agencies is thus a critical cross-cutting theme.

Clear strategies and operational guidelines on skills development, transfer, utilization, and retention shall be adopted to better align curricula development in higher learning institutions and TVETs to the sector strategy and workforce gaps.

Based on previous assessments and the results of the stakeholder consultations, priority capacity building needs include strengthening and retaining staff resources and capacity in energy sector to formulate and oversee policies, programs, and projects.

2 REGIONAL INTEGRATION

Rwanda energy policy and strategies need to better understand how regional energy integration brings new energy security, challenges as well as opportunities. These issues shall be formulated in subsequent policies and guidelines concerning energy security. For example, regional power trading is expected to materially reduce the average cost of power and the carbon intensity of the grid. On the other hand, supply guarantees and third country guarantees on allocated power shares may, however, need to be put into place in order to achieve energy security in a scenario with dramatically increased power trading. In addition, while grid interconnections can mitigate the risk associated with excess supply in the event of inaccurate demand forecasts, exporting power will only make economic sense if Rwanda's tariff becomes more regionally competitive.

3 ENERGY DATA COLLECTION AND STATISTICS

Good data is required for energy policy formulation and integrated energy planning. Although proper data systems are costly, the lack of information and cross-cutting challenges that arise from a lack of data are widely seen as a major capacity constraint in the energy sector. MININFRA shall establish an energy sector information system or depository that can serve as a central mechanism for integrated energy data collection, management and dissemination. This system can be used as a key input to energy sector planning and models that take into account all available energy resources and primary consumption patterns to match investments with future demand.

Through this portal, government shall inform research and investment decisions by giving easy online access to data and information to the public. The portal shall include all available resource assessments and upstream feasibility studies that have been undertaken to date.

4 ENERGY STANDARDS

Stronger public awareness-raising to inform target audiences of existing technology standards and ensuring adequate enforcement of existing laws and regulations in a cost-effective manner is absolutely fundamental to creating an enabling environment for cleaner energy technologies and development pathways.

5 RESEARCH, DEVELOPMENT & TECHNOLOGICAL INNOVATION

In Rwanda, investments in energy-related research and development have been at very low levels, both by the private and public sector. As most energy technology is imported (e.g., up to 80% of all power related equipment, such as turbines for hydro projects) average total investment costs remain high. Investments in developing scientific and technological infrastructure, manpower build long-term capacity and ownership, and contribute to socioeconomic transformation by reducing the cost of energy. Rwandan research institutions need support to develop appropriate energy technologies, efficiency measures, and locally appropriate guidelines for sustainable resource extraction and development.

The following policies will be adopted to advance research, development, technological transfer and innovation in the energy sector:

i. MININFRA shall work with MINEDUC through NCST to drive this process. The institutions shall also collaborate with Rwandan Universities to organize Energy Research Symposium with private sector participation to enhance dialogue and cooperation on practical energy research and technological innovation matters;

ii. To encourage private sector and academic institutions to undertake research in developing and adopting new energy technologies to inform future investment decisions, especially related to cleaner energy resources;

iii. Industrial training and practical skills related to energy shall be promoted through technical and vocational colleges as well as through practical pupilage programs;

iv. To develop specific mechanisms to encourage more academics and researchers, particularly in the higher education sector, to focus their research on topics aligned with national energy priorities.

6 ENERGY SECURITY AND DISASTER MITIGATION

Fuel supply shocks can result not only in economic, but also in political and social instability. In the Rwandan context, "energy security" encompasses the following policy imperatives:

Promoting self-reliance through the development of domestic energy resources to the greatest extent feasible from an economic and technical perspective;

Diversifying the energy mix (including power generation portfolio) to decrease reliance on any one single resource;

Limiting the degree of power imports to within a reasonable threshold to mitigate supply risk linked to political insecurity or technical system failures beyond Rwanda's control;

Having a sufficient level of energy commodity reserve stocks or capacity;

Improving the preparedness for, and resiliency to, exogenous market shocks, including price spikes;

Ensuring a consistent availability of public funds committed to co-finance major energy infrastructure projects with the private sector, as part of financing plans and strategies;

Gradually reducing reliance on external development partner contributions to be more self-reliant;

Preventing catastrophic failure and mitigating the impact of a severe natural disaster that could cripple the economy.

In order to enhance energy security, the following actions shall be taken:

i. A clear disaster prevention and management plan including specific anticipatory risk mitigation measures shall be developed for each sub-sector by the respective competent Ministry or Agency. While ensuring security over energy supplies falls under the mandate of MININFRA, all Ministries and agencies engaged in the delivery of energy services have a responsibility to undertake measures that uphold this principle. MININFRA shall ensure mainstreaming of disaster prevention guidelines into operational policies as well as guidelines to be followed by its implementation agencies;

ii. A hydropower climate-related risk assessment shall be conducted to highlight major vulnerabilities to climate change, natural disasters, and other extreme weather events;

iii. Promoting a mix of energy supply and power generation options by increasing investment in domestic resources, even if not at the lowest financial cost of production, and by expanding regional trade in all energy commodities to ensure sufficient supplies and reliable reserves.

7 INTEGRATED PLANNING AND SECTOR GOVERNANCE

As a complex sector encompassing diverse forms and carriers, it is important that clear linkages and investment strategies are made through integrated planning processes, both within the energy sector and other sectors. The benefits of more integrated planning processes include creating positive synergies and economies of scale between new infrastructure investments and minimizing unnecessary cost. The agricultural sector strategic plan, for example, implies a dramatic increase in the land under irrigation; this needs to be effectively coordinated with power system expansion, otherwise it could lead to grid instability. Thus, it is important that arrangements between energy and other sectors such as agriculture and mining be put into place in the long-term in order to ensure sustainable exploitation of scarce resources.

New investments in the electric power sector shall be in line with demand, based on: a sound forecast, taking into account complex factors such as demographic trends and industrial growth strategies; reserve margin requirements set in the Grid Code; the flexibility to meet sudden changes in demand and exogenous shocks; and the robust findings of a least cost power project development plan. Electrification plans shall be in greater alignment with industrialization, agro-processing, and urbanization strategies.

8 GENDER-BASED EQUITY, ENVIRONMENTAL SUSTAINABILITY AND CLIMATE CONCERNS

Exploitation of energy resources can lead to severe impacts on the environment and may result in greenhouse gas (GHG) emissions known to contribute to climate change. Likewise, climate change can have a severe impact on energy projects. The dominant modern energy source in the country, hydropower, is likely to be the most directly affected by climate change, because it is sensitive to the amount, timing, and geographical patterns of precipitation and temperature.[14]

Achieving the policy objectives related to environmentally sustainability will entail elaborating clear planning criteria that influence the prioritization of new energy investments toward environmentally friendly and climate resilient energy infrastructure, promoting technological innovation and transfer, developing stronger national technology standards for energy products and services, and outlining clear environmental guidelines to be used for major energy investments and programs. Guidance toward harmonizing approaches to climate technology transfer and adoption shall be further taken from the EAC Climate Change Policy.

[14]During 2004 and 2005, Rwanda suffered from a prolonged drought, drying up the seasonal rivers that were its primary source of electric power. The immediate impact of the situation was a doubling of electricity prices in the country.

Among the priority actions to achieve this objective include:

i. Introducing controls and systems in energy infrastructure planning and design processes to robustly address climate change and disaster risk management;

ii. Progressively reducing the carbon intensity of the electricity grid[15] through increased investment in and use of renewable energy resources such as micro-hydro, solar, and possibly geothermal power;

iii. Promoting cleaner fuels and technologies for heating and cooking such as LPG, biogas, and modern biomass technology solutions in both households and institutions as well as more sustainable biomass energy consumption through promoting more efficient charcoal production practices, market transformation activities, fiscal reforms, and smart subsidies;

iv.

Aligning energy strategies to the green growth strategies and integrated infrastructure solutions, especially in secondary cities;

v.

Pursuing bilateral research and technology development cooperation with other governments and research centers.

More proactive efforts to increase the flow of climate finance into low-carbon energy projects ranging from renewable power generation projects to dissemination of improved cook stoves. This includes registration of projects and activities the UN Clean Development Mechanism (CDM) and Nationally Appropriate Mitigation Actions (NAMAs) falling under the United Nations Framework on Climate Change (UNFCCC) as well as voluntary carbon market channels.

The Rwandan Constitution assures equal rights between women and men, especially as it relates to national development policies. Gender concerns shall be mainstreamed across energy planning processes.

Guidelines for gender mainstreaming formulated by MIGEPROF shall be adopted in energy planning strategies. In practice, this means fundamentally recognizing that men and women can have different roles, responsibilities, and decision-making powers over energy usage. A more market-oriented approach to energy sector development and policy interventions shall also take gender differences into account in relation to end-user needs, preferences, and behaviors.

Measures to mainstream gender in national energy planning and policies include following:

i. Considering gender issues at every stage of the energy project cycle and in all major sub-sector strategies and action plans developed;

[15]The current carbon intensity of the grid is roughly 0.52 tons of CO_2 equivalent emissions per Megawatt Hour.

ii. Addressing energy concerns in a gender-sensitive manner shall be undertaken in the process of identifying and evaluating *appropriate* technologies for any given service;
iii. Proactively targeting female-headed households in awareness-raising and behavioral change programs focused on sustainable energy and clean cooking technologies;
iv. Undertaking education, outreach, and awareness-raising activities focused on identifying and altering cultural norms, behaviors, structures and practices that can lead, whether intentional or not, to inequitable energy access;
v. Addressing knowledge gaps in gender and energy, through research and advocacy programs and providing information support to improve women's access to energy services in Rwanda;
vi. Developing credit enhancement and micro-finance programs specifically targeting women for driving investments in clean energy technologies, such as solar powered lamps, and promoting women as energy entrepreneurs;
vii. Incorporating meaningful roles to women in the planning, design and execution of energy programs, including those relating to energy efficiency and conservation;
viii. Encouraging girls to study sciences and mathematics and courses related to building knowledge of energy technologies and basic engineering.

CHAPTER FOUR: LEGAL, REGULATORY, AND INSTITUTIONAL FRAMEWORK

1 LEGAL AND REGULATORY FRAMEWORK AND IMPLICATIONS OF REVISED POLICY

The main laws and regulations connected to the exploitation and use of Rwanda's energy resources comprise the Investment Code (2008, pending revision, 2014), Electricity Act (2011), the Law Establishing EWSA (2010) and the Law Repealing EWSA (2013), the Law Establishing and Determining the Mandate of the Rwanda Utilities Regulatory Authority (2001) and as revised (2013), the Law on Mining and Quarry Exploitation (2008),[16] and the Petroleum Law (2013). A set of other proposed laws, including the Gas Law and Law on Public-Private Partnerships are still in final draft, pending approval by Cabinet. The mandate to regulate business operations across all energy subsectors falls under the Rwanda Utilities Regulatory Authority (RURA). As an independent regulatory agency, RURA is obliged to regulate in an accountable, transparent and fair manner for the benefit of all stakeholders.

Ultimately, the existence of a clear legal and regulatory framework for the sector plays a fundamental role in boosting investors' confidence in Rwanda and attracting more private sector operators. The action agenda for strengthening the legal and regulatory framework to align with the policy includes revising current legislation and putting in place new laws, regulations, and technical guidelines and standards. This includes potential new laws specific to promoting renewable energy and energy efficiency. A legal study is currently being implemented to examine the consistency of the legal framework and its adequacy to attract more investment in cleaner energy investments. In the longer-term, consolidation and integration of various laws and regulations into a unified national energy law shall be pursued. New legislation shall be benchmarked with other East African countries, and attempts made to harmonize regional frameworks wherever possible.

2 INSTITUTIONAL FRAMEWORK

Given the complexity of the sector and its diverse resource base, the mandate of developing the sector is shared across multiple institutions. There is continuous need and efforts to streamline the sector institutional framework to enable integrated resource planning and support improved inter and intra institutional decision-making, avoiding duplication of efforts. The following section outlines some of the key actors in the energy sector and their respective roles, while making recommendations on institutional reform.

[16] Under the national Mining Law, and Ministerial Order N°003/Minifom/2010 on Requirements for Granting the License for Purchasing and Selling Mineral Substances in Rwanda, peat is classified as a mineral substance. Furthermore, a quarry extraction license is required for commercial development and use in the context of an energy project.

• Ministry of Infrastructure (MININFRA) The Ministry of Infrastructure (MININFRA) is the lead Ministry responsible for developing energy policies and strategies, and for monitoring and evaluating projects and program implementation. It is in charge of setting an enabling policy and legal framework for the sector, including a suggested general approach to the optimal use of state subsidies in the sector, budget preparation, resource mobilization (together with MINECOFIN), and political oversight over government programs designed to expand energy access and service provision. With regards to petroleum, it is in charge of developing and managing petroleum related infrastructure.

• Ministry of Trade and Industry (MINICOM) MINICOM is responsible for the development and oversight of the downstream[17] petroleum subsector, including implementation of the downstream petroleum policy, establishing and developing petroleum-related legislation, setting the strategic reserve requirement, and creating an enabling environment for petroleum products trade in line with the national energy policy objectives.

• Ministry of Finance and Economic Planning (MINECOFIN) The Ministry of Finance and Economic Planning leads on resource mobilization to support energy investment and related financing requirements. MINECOFIN ensures the fiduciary framework to manage grants, loans, and other concessional finance from development partners into the sector.

• Ministry of Natural Resources (MINIRENA) The Ministry of Natural resources is responsible for ensuring the sustainability of natural resources exploitation, including water extraction, and for developing and managing compliance to the national environment policy and law. MINIRENA is in charge of developing and implementing policies on petroleum exploration and development until the point of resource extraction.

• Ministry of Education (MINEDUC) The Ministry of Education and its affiliated research agencies (NIRDA and NCST), plays a role in the energy sector by building the competency and human resources base for sector development and by helping to link sector policies and strategies to research, technology development, and innovation. MINEDUC ensures that TVETs address skill shortages in the sector, including jobs related to electrical engineering and renewable energy technology installation and maintenance.

[17] In Rwanda's case, this refers to the marketing and distribution of petroleum products and natural gas.

• Ministry of Local Government (MINALOC) Local governments have the authority and mandate to coordinate the implementation of discrete enabling policies to drive local economic transformation. Districts are responsible for maintaining the District's infrastructure. Specifically, they have direct responsibility for all decentralized service delivery, including those that may be related to energy at the grassroots (such as ICS, Biogas and many more). This includes national programs to scale up sustainable energy consumption currently being implemented by the electricity utility targeting communities.

• Ministry of East African Community (MINEAC) The Ministry for East African Community Affairs is a coordinating body for EAC and Rwandan priorities within EAC Protocols, Treaties and Strategies. MINEAC follows commitments signed by Rwanda on energy projects and ensures Rwanda and Partner States deliver on them. The Ministry advocates on energy-related government positions and interests in regional meetings and forums.

• Rwanda Energy Group Ltd (REG Ltd) The legal mandate of Rwanda Energy Group Ltd is to translate energy sector policies and programs into the implementation of tangible projects to achieve government's vision in the sector and to efficiently operate and maintain the country's power transmission system.

• Rwanda Development Board (RDB) Rwanda Development Board plays the lead role in investment mobilization and promotion for the energy sector, acting as a gateway and facilitator. It actively promotes private investor participation in the energy sector, including local financial institutions. It leads on facilitation of foreign direct investment (FDI) into strategic energy generation projects, as well as other programs and activities involving cleaner, more energy-efficient technologies. RDB also issues Environmental Impact Assessments for all energy projects for which one is required. It is expect to also host a centralized authority or advisory agency for PPPs across government.

• Rwanda Utilities Regulatory Authority (RURA) The scope of its mandate extends to public utilities involved in renewable and nonrenewable energy, electricity, industrial gases, pipelines and storage facilities, and conventional gas extraction and distribution. As the regulator, RURA's principal mandate is to ensure consumer protection from uncompetitive practices while ensuring that such utilities operate in an efficient, sustainable, and reliable manner. RURA also has the important role of updating the electric grid code, ensuring quality of service standards for power, assessing and reviewing energy tariff structures, licensing all power generation, transmission, and distribution companies as well as retail petroleum filling stations and related storage facilities.

• National Industrial Research Development Authority (NIRDA) Its scope will evolve around continuous research on energy mix to feed the growing industries and will also provide the necessary information after thorough research on which industries employ clean efficient energy needs.

• Rwanda Environment Management Authority (REMA) REMA has the mandate to coordinate, oversee and implement environmental policy. Generally speaking, all infrastructure development is subject to environmental impact assessment. REMA is mandated to enforce environmental compliance in the development of energy resources.

• Rwanda Standards Board (RSB) As an agency under the Ministry of Trade and Industry, RSB develops national technical regulations including national technology and performance standards. RSB plays an increasingly important role in establishing, publishing, and disseminating national standards for energy technologies such as biogas digesters and solar appliances.

• National Commission of Science and Technology (NCST)

NCST with aid from higher institutions of learning, will continue to oversee the scientific tools and provide modern necessary technology to be employed in the energy sector.

CHAPTER FIVE: POLICY MONITORING AND IMPLEMENTATION PLAN

The National Energy Policy will ensure high-level ownership and institutional co-ordination to achieve the EDPRS II and ESSP targets. An overview of the institutional division of responsibility is set out in the Policy Implementation Matrix. This demarcates clear lines of institutional accountability and demonstrates the political will behind the process of energy sector development and increasing private sector participation.

MININFRA and the eSWAP Secretariat shall regularly monitor and evaluate the implementation of the policy so as to ensure its benefits reach all Rwandans. They will oversee government-wide policy implementation and enforcement, while helping to continually refine guidelines and processes to promote integrated energy planning. In this regard, they will regularly monitor and engage with other Ministries and their agencies according to Institutional Responsibility/Policy Implementation Matrix provided in the Annex. High level oversight of policy implementation will be the mandate of the Economic Cluster under the Chairmanship of MINECOFIN, and if necessary, the PS Forums shall be used to raise awareness of areas where policy implementation is lagging. In addition, additional technical-level working groups and subsector coordination mechanisms to be established under the Energy Sector Working Group will ensure continual dialogue and awareness of the key policy objectives among key stakeholders such as MINECOFIN, REG Ltd, RDB, RURA, MINIRENA, RSB, and representatives of private sector chambers or associations. The SWG will support MININFRA in policy monitoring, evaluating progress against sector performance and intended policy outcomes. This may include, but is not limiting to, initiating and/or endorsing impact evaluations and interim policy reviews in conjunction with regular performance assessments against sector delivery targets.

The financial implications of this policy are complex, since it involves an array of institutions and a number of measures that are both already budgeted, as well as new measures. The ESSP estimates that roughly US$ 4 billion is required to finance Rwanda's energy goals over five years. MININFRA has elaborated an extensive draft MTEF for negotiation with MINECOFIN which full incorporates all of the different elements envisioned in the policy and strategy, clearly articulated and disaggregated by energy sub-sector.

An appropriate mix of financing resources will be used to implement the policy and strategy. In order to reach sector targets, significant levels of new private sector investment are required. This will be leveraged through strategic public investments in upstream resource and project development activities, as well as through risk reduction tools. Among intended investment risk mitigation strategies include the provision of sovereign guarantees for those projects as deemed absolutely necessary to support strategic infrastructure by MININFRA and the RDB Strategic Investment Unit.

In addition, as outlined in the Investment Code, a number of new measures shall be instituted to enhance the attractiveness of investors to fund energy projects, and energy is treated as a strategic sector. It is assumed that many energy projects in Rwanda will require a minimum amount of 30% equity, with the balance raised between commercial and concessional debt as well as grant funding, whether up front or paid upon delivery of predetermined output results. Wherever possible, climate finance mechanisms will be drawn upon to co-finance appropriate financing structures for specific investment projects and major government programs in the sector. Increased engagement between policy makers and domestic banks, pension funds, and insurance companies will be pursued in order to identify promising areas for domestic capital investment growth.

A more detailed financing strategy for the implementation of the policy is elaborated in the energy sector strategic plan.

LIST OF ANNEXES

PREVAILING LEGAL AND REGULATORY FRAMEWORK

No one single law or set of regulations governs the entire energy sector. Activities and investments are governed by a set of stand-alone laws and regulations specific to each individual subsector. Most but not all of the above references sub-sectors have their own law covering the exploitation, utilization, and sales of energy resource. The general legal framework or hierarchy includes several national laws that are indirectly applicable to activities in the energy sector, laws specific to a particular energy sub-sector, regulations in force for a particular sub-sector, as well as technical guidelines, codes, and standards in place that may or may not be legally binding. A high-level overview of the key laws and regulations applicable to each of these sub-sectors is provided below. It is not intended to be an exhaustive inventory, but rather a tool to inform decision-makers, investors, and researchers on the key legal and regulatory frameworks that shape governmental policy, program implementation, and investment incentives.

The principle laws and related regulations connected to the exploitation and use of Rwanda's energy resources comprise the Investment Code (2014), PPP Law (2014), Electricity Act (2011), the Law Establishing EWSA (2010) and the Law Repealing EWSA (2013), the Law Establishing and Determining the Mandate of the Rwanda Utilities Regulatory Authority (2001) and (2013) respectively, Organic Law on Environment (2005) and the Petroleum Law (2013). A set of other proposed laws, including the Gas Law, are still under development.

The mandate to regulate business operations across all energy subsectors falls under the mandate of the Rwanda Utilities Regulatory Authority (RURA). As an independent agency RURA is obliged to regulate in an accountable, transparent and fair manner for the benefit of all stakeholders.

MAIN CROSS-CUTTING LAWS AND REGULATIONS APPLICABLE TO SECTOR

01) Investment Code (2014). The RDB has been in the process of updating the investment code applying to all strategic and foreign investors in 2014. Energy is treated as a strategic sector and a number of specific fiscal and other incentives are outlined in the code to promote greater investment and private sector engagement in the energy sector.

02) Public Private Partnerships Law (anticipated 2014). Providing the legal framework for the implementation and management of PPPs, this law clarifies the rules governing Public-Private engagement and procurement. It provides a streamlined framework for PPP approvals and procurement as an alternative to public procurement methods. Ministries will need to undertake feasibility studies to show the viability and advantages of using a PPP procurement approach versus public procurement methods. The law

II - 1 provides for sector-specific rules for the procurement of PPP projects to be developed by relevant line ministries.

03) Organic Law on Environment (2005). Rwanda's National Environment Policy is legally codified in the Organic law n° 04/2005 of which was adopted in August 2005, determining the modalities of protection, conservation and promotion of environment originating in the Ministry of Natural Resources and with guidelines to be implemented by the Rwanda Environment Management Authority (REMA). Article 73 of the Environmental Law notes that industries that import equipment and which assist in eliminating or reducing atmospheric carbon dioxide and chlorofluorocarbons and those which manufacture equipment that reduce the pollution of the environment are subject to reduction of customs duty on the equipment, which shall be administered under the law concerning taxes and revenues. It should also be noted that the Environment Law affords an opportunity for the Treasury to establish regulations to reduce income taxes for individuals and persons undertaking activities that promote the environment. Ministerial Order N° 003/2008 lays out the procedures and requirements for undertaking EIA while Ministerial Order N° 004/2008 outlines the list of works, activities, and project types that are subject to completing an EIA.

04) Law Establishing RURA (2013): The Rwanda Utilities Regulatory Authority (RURA) is an autonomous public entity that was initially created by the Law N° 39/2001 of 13 September 2001 with the mission to regulate specified public Utilities including electricity and the extraction and distribution of gas from Lake Kivu. This law was replaced by Law Nº 09/2013 of 01/03/2013 establishing and determining RURA's mission, powers, organization and functioning. The revised law gives RURA the mandate to regulate, among others, electronic technologies, renewable and non-renewable energy, industrial gases, pipelines, and storage facilities. The law gives the regulator the legal authority to contribute to energy policy making, licensing of energy service providers, and the protection of energy consumers. Chapter II article 7 gives the regulator the legal mandate to regulate tariffs and other charges related to electricity among other regulated utilities. RURA shall carry out regular reviews of tariffs and charges required by providers of regulated services, taking into consideration the costs of production and supply, the return on assets, the consumer's and the investor's interests and the desire to promote competitive tariffs.

Under Ministerial Order 4/DC/04 OF 07/06/2004, RURA is allowed to collect 1% of the previous year's annual turnover of the electric power utility for its operations.

ELECTRIC POWER LAWS AND REGULATIONS

Electricity Law (2011): The main legal instrument for the power sector is Law N°21/2011 of 23/06/2011 governing electricity activities in Rwanda, which is progressive and forward looking. The law aims to create an enabling environment for the development and distribution of electric power for the entire population and for all sectors. It covers the general market set-up, as well as the licensing regime for the production, transmission, distribution and trading of power within and outside of the national territory.

Market structure. The electricity market shall be a market-based one based on free and equal access to the activities of electricity production, transmission and distribution. Electricity transmission and distribution activities shall be nondiscriminatory, and based on tariffs approved and published by RURA; however, transmission or distribution through the grid may be denied where such grid is of a low capacity or where granting it would cause prejudice to existing grid users (Article 27 and 28).

Tariff setting. Principles relating to determining electricity tariffs shall be prepared by the regulatory agency and approved by the Minister in charge of electricity (Article 29). After consultation with the Minister concerning the amount of the State subsidy, RURA sets tariffs in accordance with the regulations (Article 30). These must ensure that the investor has a normal return on his/her investments. The capital investment shall be determined on the basis of infrastructure and equipment value used for the project implementation (Article 32).

Power concession agreements. MININFRA, through the Minister in charge of electricity, has the power to issue concession agreements related to electric power generation.

Licensing. A license is required by all market participants undertaking generation, transmission, distribution, purchasing, or trading operations both within and outside the national territory. This shall be issued by RURA and payable against a fee as determined by the agency. (Articles 4 to 7). Licenses shall be granted within sixty (60) days after a concession has been obtained. Depending on the content of the license, the holder of a license for electricity production shall have the rights and responsibilities to construct, operate, maintain and manage his or her electricity production facilities, contract for delivery and sale of electric power generated in his or her production unit, and connect to the transmission and distribution grid.

Autonomous generation and wheeling. The Law provides for the operation of a project meant for autonomous electricity production. Projects with an installed

II - 3 capacity of less than fifty kilowatts (50 kW) are exempted from a license altogether and not subject to any prior notification to the regulator. Under the Law Establishing RURA, activities of production, transmission and distribution of electricity through transmission and distribution power plants and grids established by a company or a household for their own consumption, or for consumption by other companies thereto, shall be authorized (article 36). Where such power plants are established within private properties, there must be no violation of public and State private domain.

02) Law repealing EWSA: The law establishing EWSA (N°43/2000 of December 2010) merged RECO& RWASCO, the former national parastatal companies in charge of energy and water distribution, giving rise EWSA. A new policy vision to "corporatize" the utility, however, gave rise to the adoption of the Law Repealing EWSA (Law N°97/2013), which repealed the 2010 law and

essentially reversed its intent. The new law mandates a separation between the electric power utility and the water and sanitation utility. All legal and financial responsibilities and obligations from EWSA have been fully transferred to the newly registered companies (REG Ltd and WASAC Ltd).

03) Regulations for electric power resources exploitation: With specific reference to the electric power sub-sector, RURA has as its core role to regulate electric power production, transmission, supply and distribution, as well as sales. In reviewing electricity tariffs and ensuring compliance to the adopted standards, RURA works to enforce fair competition between operators.

04) Rural Electrification licenses: A rural electrification license is not precisely defined in the Electricity Law. RURA has drafted a regulation for simplified licensing procedures in order to expedite off-grid and mini-grid based rural electrification.

05) Electricity licensing regulations: RURA is responsible for issuing permits and certificates

to all electrical operators that satisfy the licensing requirements outlined in the (NO

Electricity Law (2011). The regulations on electricity licensing 002/energy/el/rura/2013), which came into effect on 25 July 2013, establish a framework for undertaking electricity activities with a view to an efficient, effective, sustainable and orderly development of electricity supply operations. Chapter III of the regulations outlines the different categories of licenses required in this context, including production, transmission, domestic and international trade. These regulations do *not* govern concession licenses or agreements.

Production (generation) license: A license holder shall have the right to generate electrical power and sell it to other licensees or large scale customers inside the

country and to access transmission or distribution networks, however, prior to the approval by RURA of the contractual agreement between the license-holder and the relevant transmission or distribution company is required by law.

Transmission license: License-holders for the transmission of electricity must comply with Article 17 and shall have the right to buy/transmit/sell electrical energy on their network to other Licensees or consumers connected to the transmission network inside the country. The license-holder shall also have the right to access the transmission network in accordance with any contractual agreement subject to prior approval by RURA. This transmission network can also be used for communication purposes as long as it does not negatively affect the performance of the transmission network. Articles 11 and 12 of these regulations stipulate the rights and obligations for license holders to undertake domestic and international trade (Regulation No. 002/energy/el/rura/2013, July 2013)

Distribution license: In addition to needing to comply with Article 18 of the Law governing electricity in Rwanda, license holders for the distribution of electricity shall have the right to purchase electrical power from the transmission company or any other Licensee and to sell it to other Licensees or consumers inside Rwanda, consistent with license conditions set by RURA.

06) Regulations for electric power quality: In August 2013, RURA published the Rwandan Grid Code which establishes the rules and procedures that allow all participants to use the interconnected power system in a safe, reliable, efficient and economical manner. In connection with ensuring reliability, RURA is responsible for the compilation, approval, implementation, of the Grid Code which encompasses a set of technical guidelines for guaranteeing the principles above. RURA monitors and evaluates the quality of services provided by electricity service providers, assuring conformity to the Grid Code and licensing requirements. A Grid Code

Advisory Committee shall be regularly constituted to recommend appropriate updates and revisions to the Code. Individual generation plants which do or potentially could threaten the stability of the grid and the power quality standards under the Grid Code would therefore be subject to rejection, revocation, or suspension of their licenses.

07) Regulations on Renewable Energy Feed-in Tariffs (REFIT): Law 09/2013 of 01/03/2013 establishing RURA gives it the legal mandate to establish and regulate electricity tariffs in consultation with the Minister in charge of energy and REG. Following the recommendations of a study conducted in 2012, a set of regulations determining feed-in tariffs for micro-hydro projects ranging from 50 kW to 10 MW were developed (Annex 1 of regulations 01/energy/rura/2012 of 09/02/2012). Tariff levels reflected a cost recovery plus return basis to encourage mobilization of private investors. RURA undertook a review of the existing regime in 2013 to better align tariffs to market

II - 5 realities, and drafted an updated regulation. This is reflected in, and has been incorporated into the EP objectives.

08) Draft regulations on solar water heaters installation: RURA drafted regulations on mandatory installation of solar water heaters and guidelines on installation, as well as rules for the accreditation of installers and the issuing of permits for conducting this trade. This builds upon technical guidelines that were published in November 2012 describing how solar collectors especially those larger than $4m^2$ can be safely installed on roofs: *Guidelines for Solar Water Heaters Installation*. The guidelines target suppliers, installers and building consent authorities to improve the quality of installation of solar water heater systems, providing a range of options and performance-based solutions to end-users.

09) Electrical installations regulations: Regulation N° 002/el/energy/rura/2012 adopted by RURA in October 2012 covers requirements for undertaking electrical installations, aiming to protect people, properties, and the environment from hazards that can arise under both normal and faulty conditions. It applies to installations in all premises, whether residential, commercial, public or industrial and outlines the corresponding required permits, depending on the complexity of the installations.

TECHNICAL GUIDELINES ON UTILIZATION OF ENERGY SOLUTIONS

01) Energy Efficiency Promotion: RURA adopted *Guidelines Promoting Energy Efficiency Measures* in May 2013, outlining specific measures to enhance efficient use of electricity. Technical guidance and a number of useful tips for saving electricity on common uses and appliances are provided to different targeted end-users such as business/industry, large public institutions, and residential consumers. All energy facilities are encouraged to meet Minimum Energy Performance Standards (MEPS) that effectively limit the maximum amount of energy that may be consumed by a single product per specified task. The guidelines stipulate that all energy consuming appliances and equipment bear labels and meet MEPS for efficient energy use and conservation.

02) Electrical power standards: Related to regulations on electrical installations, RSB has enacted over a dozen different power quality standards concerning electric and optical fiber cables, wiring, plugs and outlets, lamps and luminaries, etc. Any person or company involved in electrical installations works who fails to comply with the above regulations is subject to revocation or suspension of permits and operating licenses. All electrical installations should comply with the provisions contained in the following standards; RS 565-1: 2011 (Electrical Wiring of Premises-Part 1: Low-voltage

Installations), RS 474-1: 2011(Power Installations exceeding 1kV a.c.–Part 1: Common rules) and any other relevant standards issued by RSB which may include the following:

	Electrical engineering standard	Rwandan National Standard and Year of Adoption
41	Electric and optical fiber cables-Test methods for non-metallic materials-Part 201:General tests-Measurement of insulation thickness	IEC 60811-201:2012
42	Electric and optical fiber cables-Test methods for non-metallic materials-Part 202:General tests-Measurement of non-metallic sheath	IEC 60811-202:2012
43	Electric and optical fiber cables-Test methods for non-metallic materials-Part 203:General tests-Measurement of overall dimensions	IEC 60811-203:2012
44	Electric and optical fiber cables-Test methods for non-metallic materials-Part 401:Miscellaneous tests-Thermal ageing methods-Ageing in an air oven	IEC 60811-401:2012
45	Electric and optical fiber cables-Test methods for non-metallic materials-Part 412:Miscellaneous tests-Thermal ageing methods-Ageing in an air bomb	IEC 60811-412:2012
46	Electric and optical fiber cables-Test methods for non-metallic materials-Part 501:Mechanical tests-Test for determining the mechanical properties of insulating and sheathing compounds	IEC 60811-501:2012
47	Polyvinyl chloride insulated cables of rated voltages up to and including 450/750V – Part 5: Flexible cables (cords).	IEC 60227 - 5:2011 Ed2
48	Polyvinyl chloride insulated cables of rated voltages up to and including 450/750V - Part 7: Flexible cables screened and unscreened with two or more	IEC 60227 - 7:2012 Ed2

No.	Title	Standard
	conductors.	
49	Power cables with extruded insulation and their accessories for rated voltages from 1 kV(Um = 1,2 kV) up to 30 kV(Um= 36kV) Part 1:Cables for rated voltages of 1 kV(Um=1,2kV) and 3 kV(Um=3,6kV)	IEC 60502 -1:2009 Ed2
50	Electric toys - Safety	IEC 62115 :2011 Ed2
51	Safety requirement for electrical equipment for measurement, control, and laboratory use - Part 1:General requirements	IEC 61010-2:2010 Ed2
52	Uninterruptible power supplies(UPS) - Part 3:Method of specifying the performance and test requirements	IEC 62040 - 3:2011 Ed2
53	Electrical installations of buildings -Selection and erection of electrical equipment - Earthling arrangement and protective conductors	IEC 60364-5-54:2011 Ed2
54	Incandescent lamps -Safety specifications - Tungsten filament lamps for domestic and similar general lighting purposes	IEC 60432-2:2012 Ed2
55	Household and similar electrical appliances - Safety -Part2 - 7: Particular requirements for washing machines	IEC 60335 -2 -7:2012 Ed2
56	Electrical installations of buildings - Part 4-42: Protection for safety - Protection against thermal effects	IEC 60364 – 4 – 42:2010 Ed2
57	Luminaires -Part 2 - 2: Particular requirements. Section two: Recessed luminaires	IEC 60598 – 2 – 2: 2011 Ed2
58	Plugs, socket-outlets, and socket-outlets and couplers for industrial purposes -part1: General requirements	IEC 60309-1:2012 Ed2
59	Luminaires - Part 2-3: Particular requirements - Luminaires for road and street lighting	IEC 60598 -2 -3:2011 Ed2
60	Incandescent lamps - Safety	IEC

specifications - Part 3: Tungsten halogen lamps (non-vehicle)	60432-3:2012 Ed2

LAWS AND REGULATIONS FOR PETROLEUM SUB-SECTOR ACTIVITIES

The petroleum industry is typically divided into three major components i.e. upstream, midstream and downstream ends. In Rwanda, upstream regulations are not yet developed since petroleum exploration and exploitation activities are yet to be commercially developed.

01) Law Regulating Petroleum and Petroleum Products Trade: Law N°85/2013 OF 11/9/2013 applies to the import, export, transportation, processing, storage, distribution, wholesale and retail sale of petroleum and petroleum products in Rwanda, including LPG. The law provides clarity on licensing categories, requirements, procedures to be followed. Any person or company may free participate in the trade of petroleum products as long as they are licensed. Licensees must meet quality standards set out by relevant regulatory authorities. Various requirements for maintaining a strategic reserve of stocks are outlined.

02) Petroleum (Exploration and Production) Law: The law provides provisions for licensing, divided between exploration licensing and production licensing. Upon discovery of a resource, the holder of an exploration license may apply for a production license. The law further obliges companies to prioritize the employment of Rwandan citizens for managerial positions and provides other conditions for capacity development. The main regulatory tool for the management of petroleum resources is a system of licensing companies to carry out petroleum exploration

II - 8 operations in return for the performance of explicit and enforceable obligations. The objective of the licensing system is to allocate petroleum exploration rights to those best able to conduct exploration activities and, to carry out commercial exploration and production of petroleum resources in an efficient and responsible manner.

03) Law Establishing the National Standards Inspectorate, Competition, and Consumer Protection Authority (NICA).Under Law No. 61/2013 of 23 August 2013, a new competent authority shall be established to ensure adherence to quality standards and pro-competition measures. It is envisioned under the downstream petroleum policy that NICA shall be at the core of efforts to enforce technical standards for the sub-sector.

A number of regulations have been passed to manage the importation and storage of petroleum liquid fuels, petroleum depots, use of LPG, as well as oil pipelines. RURA, in collaboration with Kigali City Council (KCC), RSB, MININFRA and MINICOM developed guidelines for the construction of petrol stations and these are currently being enforced by KCC. The following are some guidelines regulating petroleum business in Rwanda:

01) Regulations on above-ground Petroleum Storage Facilities (N°006/Energy/RURA/2012) adopted by RURA on 8 June 2012 determine the modalities of constructing and managing petroleum storage facilities in Rwanda. Any person intending to construct an above-ground petroleum storage facility (e.g., bulk storage, filling plant, and pipeline) must first obtain a permit subject to fulfilling certain prerequisites. All tanks, pipes, valves and pipe fittings shall be designed and built in accordance with approved national standards (i.e. API STD 650) and have a safety factor adequate for the conditions of service. Guidelines are also given on the design and construction of facilities used to store petroleum products of over 150 m^3 in capacity. Preference is given to vertical tanks consisting of not more than one compartment and use of elevated tanks for petroleum storage are discouraged.[18] Owners or operators of above-ground storage facilities or tanks shall prepare a spill prevention control and mitigation plan prepared in accordance with applicable national Environment, Health and Safety (EHS) guidelines and relevant national

standards. Other regulations promulgated by agencies such as the Rwanda Revenue Authority and the APSF concerning the taxation, labeling, safe storage and disposal of hazardous substances are also material to such facilities.

02) Regulations for fluid transportation pipelines have been prepared by RURA.

[18]Where deemed necessary, a special permit must be issued.

03) Regulations on LPG: On 7 May 2012, RURA adopted Liquefied Petroleum Gas Regulation (No.005/RURA/2012) which covers the importation, transportation, construction, storage and distribution, wholesale and retail trade of LPG. Licensing started in June 2013, initially mainly targeting big LPG dealers, with a plan to apply this to LPG retailers as well. According to the regulations, no person shall conduct a business of importation, transportation, supply, storage, distribution, wholesale and retail supply and sale to industrial consumers of LPG and related activities except under and in accordance with the terms and conditions of a license granted by RURA.

Importation: Section III stipulates that importation of LPG into Rwanda shall only be carried out by entities holding a valid license from RURA. Furthermore, the vehicle used for importation must meet the requirements of RS 573 and RS 579. Where no national standard exists, the relevant international standards approved by RSB shall apply.

Filling: LPG may only be filled into cylinders by a valid license holder issued by RURA. A licensee shall at all times ensure that LPG is contained in a secure cylinder that conforms to RS 569, RS 570, RS 571, RS 572, RS 574 and RS 576.The standard capacities of LPG cylinders shall be as specified in RS 569 & RS 570 and cylinders shall be fitted with unified valves. Cylinders not falling in the categories specified above are not allowed to be filled with LPG.

Distribution: A "special license" may be granted to operators involved in multiple aspects of the LPG supply chain (e.g.., importation, bulk storage, transportation, distribution, wholesale and retail). Any person intending to construct an LPG facility (bulk storage, filling plant, and pipeline) shall, before commencing such construction, apply in writing to RURA for a permit.

Technical guidelines for petroleum sub-sector activities

01) Technical guidelines on petrol stations: RURA issued technical guidelines for the construction of new petrol filling stations in 2011. To ensure public safety and worker health and safety compliance, RURA provides ongoing technical advice during construction. The guidance is based on a national standard established by RSB on "Installations, modification and decommissioning of underground storage tanks, pumps/dispensers, pipe work at service stations and consumer installation." The guidelines provide minimum standards for the construction and operation of filling stations, specifications for underground storage tanks, environmental protection measures, fire preventions and fighting, calibration of equipment, waste water management, among others. A filling station should have at least the following minimum specifications:

One underground storage tank for each petroleum product sold at the station with a minimum capacity of 5 m^3

One digital dispensing pump (two-way) for each petroleum product sold at the station. All dispensing pumps should be covered.

One service bay, wash bay

Office premises

One wastewater drainage system and firefighting equipment

LAWS AND REGULATIONS UNDER THE BIOMASS SUBSECTOR

There are no general guidelines on the exploitation of biomass energy resources in Rwanda save for a few regulations on charcoal harvesting and technical guidelines on construction of biogas digesters issued by RURA. Details are discussed below.

01) Technical Guidelines on construction of fixed domestic biogas digesters: In September 2012, RURA issued technical guidelines for the construction of domestic fixed dome biogas digesters to be used by local construction companies as well as public enterprises. The guidelines aim to ensure for the quality and required productivity of digesters as well as the safety of end-users. Specifically, they cover responsibilities of a biogas plant constructor, plant design and gas production optimization, plant siting, feedstock requirements, and construction methods including appropriate materials to be used. The guidelines should be used by all those constructing fixed-dome biogas digesters for the main fixed dome plant models in Rwanda plant of 4, 6, 8 and 10 cubic meters capacity respectively. Any deviation from this should be after approval by a skilled technical supervisor with appropriate accreditation and licensing.

02) Regulations on Charcoal Harvesting. A permit is needed to cut mature trees; however, such a permit is not needed for own use. At national level, cutting young trees is prohibited. While carbonization is most efficient during the dry season, as dry wood gives a higher output per unit input, some districts prohibit charcoal production in this period to prevent fire outbreaks. A wood transport permit is needed from district authorities to bring products to market. For charcoal, the permit is limited to a particular Sector.

TECHNICAL GUIDELINES UNDER THE BIOMASS SUBSECTOR

01) Technology standards for ICS. RSB has developed a technology standard for ICS.

02) Technical Guidelines on Construction of Cook Stoves. The former EWSA prepared informal technical guidelines on the construction of ICS, but compliance is not mandatory.

POLICY ROAD MAP & STAKEHOLDER CONSULTATIONS

Perceiving a need to revise the existing energy policy (2011) to better align with new priorities and meet sector challenges, MININFRA initiated a process to update the policy in 2013. There was felt to be a strong need for the revised policy to reflect EDPRS-II targets, a new 5-year Energy Sector Strategic Plan (ESSP) drafted in 2012, as well as other major policy and regulatory shifts in the dynamic energy landscape. The policy was developed under a highly consultative approach involving all key stakeholders who were made aware of the road map and process for policy development. This road map, circulated in early 2014, indicated the main phases, activities, and timelines to be followed. The key stages were divided into: i) drafting; ii) refining; iii) validating; iv) adopting; and v) enforcing the policy. A high level-timeline for the road map is depicted below. Whilst the dates are no longer accurate due delays in the finalization of the policy, it is presented here for illustrative purposes.

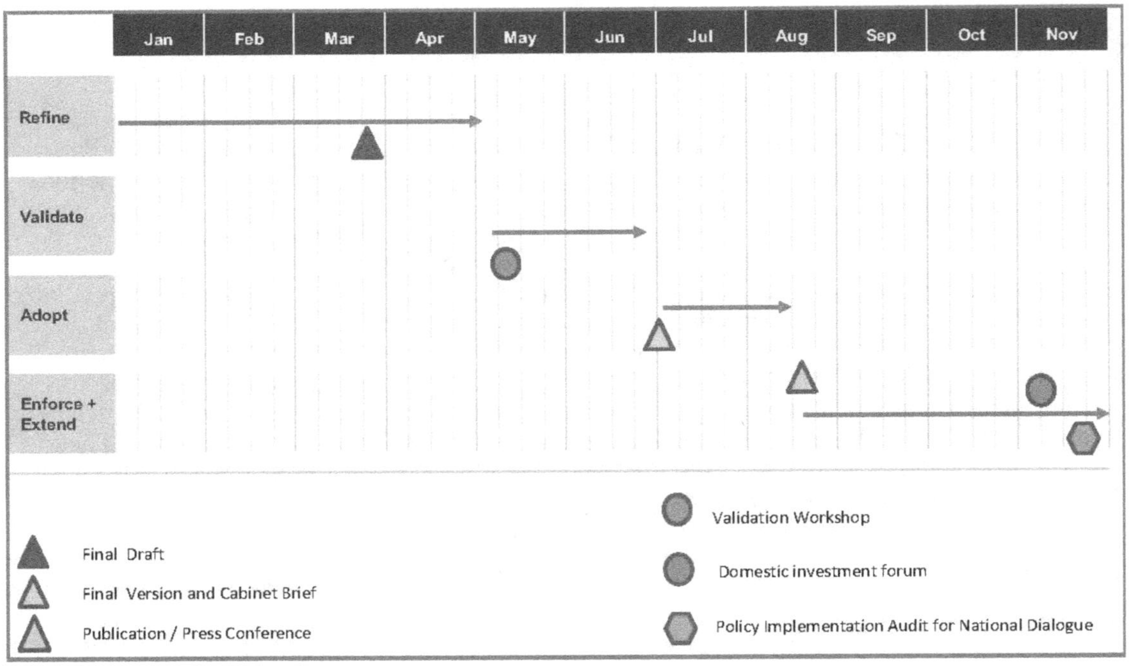

An initial policy "refining" retreat was held on 7 and 8 March 2014, in Musanze, where an initial draft was discussed among over twenty participants representing a core group of institutions involved in the sector. Policy priorities, challenges, and opportunities were discussed in small working groups. Following the retreat, a series of formal stakeholder consultation meetings were held over the course of April and May 2014. Approximately 50 different organizations from both within and outside of government were bilaterally consulted. These allowed for an exchange of views and receipt of critical inputs on the draft principles, goals, objectives, and strategic prioritization. The consultations were also a key instrument for gaining stakeholders' clear appreciation for the new energy sector policy vision.

A national validation workshop was held on 12 June 2014 in Kigali at Lemigo Hotel, which was attended by roughly 75 participants from across government, civil society, development partners and the private sector. The meeting reached its objectives: (i) to give all stakeholders a clear understanding of the main policy objectives and vision for Rwanda's energy sector; furthering institutional consensus on the proposed key policy principles and objectives for each sub-sector; (iii) to harmonize inconsistencies, contradictions, and overlaps; and (iv) to identify any remaining gaps or critical views omitted from the final draft. On the basis of the validation workshop, a summary matrix of the policy was developed highlighting areas for further development and updating of the ESSP prior. A finalized version of this matrix is included in Annex IV.

Finally, an inter-ministerial consultation meeting was held in Kigali at MININFRA on 25 September at which time the final draft document was circulated for review and feedback, together with the updated ESSP. The purpose of the meeting was to ensure broad awareness of the final contents and to get final feedback prior to Cabinet submission and deliberations. A table summarizing the stakeholders and institutions consulted in the policy development process is below.

Consolidated List of Stakeholders Consulted

Private Sector Federation	Private-General
Energy Private Developers	Private-Energy

Rwanda Chamber of Industry	Private-General
Rwanda Renewable Energy Association	Private-Energy
Rwanda Mining Association-RMA	Private-Mining
Rwanda Mining Investment Forum-RMIF	Private-Mining
Petroleum Importers	Private-Energy
World Bank	DP
African Development Bank	DP
Belgian Technical Cooperation	DP
Japan International Cooperation Agency	DP
GIZ	DP
KfW	DP
European Union	DP
World Vision	NGO
Action Aid	NGO
Care International	NGO
CIMERWA	Private-General
UTEXRWA	Private-General
RIG (PEC, REC, etc.)	Private-General
Ngali Energy	Private-Energy
BRALIRWA	Private-Manufacturing
Kabuye Sugar works	Private-Manufacturing
Ministry of Agricultural and Animal Resources	GoR-Ministry
Ministry of Finance	GoR-Ministry
Ministry of Foreign Affairs and Cooperation	GoR-Ministry
Ministry of Natural Resources	GoR-Ministry
REMA	GoR-Agency
Ministry of Gender and Family Protection /Gender Monitoring Office	GoR-Ministry
Ministry of Education	GoR-Ministry
Ministry of Commerce	GoR-Ministry
Ministry of Health	GoR-Ministry
Ministry of East African Community Affairs	GoR-Ministry
Ministry of Justice	GoR-Ministry
Rwanda Revenue Authority	GoR-Agency
Ministry of Local government	GoR-Ministry
Prime Minister's office	GoR-Other
Rwanda Utilities Regulatory Authority (RURA)	GoR-Other/Regulator
Rwanda Energy Group	GoR-Company
Rwanda Standards Board	GoR-Agency
Rwanda Development Board	GoR-Agency
National Women Council	GoR-Agency
Environmental and Natural Resources Authority	GoR-Agency
Nile Basin Initiative	Regional Org
CEPGL	Regional Org
NELSAP	Regional Org
SINELAC	Regional Org

City of Kigali	Local Government
University of Rwanda College of Science & Technology	Academia
IPRCs	Academia

The following methods will be used to continue to inform and engage the public on the policy:

Presentation of the policy document at the Energy Sector Working Group meeting and at a special meeting of the Private Sector Forum with energy investors.

Posting of the document to the MININFRA website for easy download

Distributing of the document at future energy seminars and workshops to be held with stakeholders

Distribution of the document at investment promotion forums such as the Rwanda Power & Infrastructure Investment Forum

Organize a series of sensitization workshops on the policy after its approval.

Collaborate with MINAFET to distribute the policy to Embassies and consulates.

Presentation to local districts via quarterly meetings organized by MINALOC.

SUMMARY OF ENERGY POLICY OBJECTIVES & PRINCIPLES AND LINKS TO EDPRS & ESSP

In following summary table, a comprehensive overview of all National Energy Policy objectives and principles is provided. The table also highlights linkages between the energy policy and the EDPRS-II goals and cross-cutting thematic issues. Finally in the last column, it is shown how the policy directives are expected to be translated into headline implementation strategies under the Energy Sector Strategic Plan (ESSP). The legend further indicates how the policy actions and measures to be undertaken in support of the sub-sector objectives and global principles can be categorized.

LEGEND:

(P) A pure policy instrument, signifying a shift in approach, philosophy, or principle underlying strategic direction or implementation
(E) An economic instrument to affect desired policy outcome, including fiscal reform, public funding of a target investment program, investment incentives
(R) A regulatory instrument, including the adoption or amendment of a law or regulation to drive policy compliance, as well as the development of any related standards, codes, and technical guidelines.

(I)An institutional reform, such as a consolidation or re-organization of government agency mandates to implement the policy.

ENERGY SECTORSTRATEGIC PLAN (ESSP)

High-Level Target Objectives(to be achieved by end ofFY2018)

The electric power system equivalent installed capacity(domestic generation + imports) to 563 MWIncrease household access to grid electricity to 48% and off-grid electricity to22%. Achieve savings from energy efficiencymeasures of up to50,000 MWh Reduce carbon intensityof the grid by 10% by2018 and 25% by 2025(from 2013 baseline).Ensure 80% of all households employclean cooking energy technologies. Realize all EAC Regional Integration Policypriorities for energy sector.

NATIONAL ENERGY POLICY (EP)

Overarching Goal Core Objectives

Policy Vision: "To contributeeffectively to the growth of the national economyand thereby improve thestandard of living for the entire nation in a sustainable and environmentally sound manner."Overall Goal:"To ensure all residents and industries can access energy productsand services that are sufficient, reliable,affordable, and sustainable." Enhance access to modern,sustainable energy services for allRwandans;Optimize the power generation mix in order to reduce long-run costs,promote energy security, and reduce the carbon-intensity of thegrid over time. Create an enabling environment forincreased private sectorparticipation in energy supply and service provision; Encourage and incentivize morerational, efficient use of energy; Achieve cost-reflective provision of energy services, a gradual transition toward "smart subsidies," greater market competition, and more transparent tariff-setting. Ensure the sustainability of energyexploration, extraction, supply, and consumption.

EDPRS II Overarching Goal EDPRS II goals stronglylinked to the energy sector

"Accelerate progress to middle income status and better quality of life for all Rwandans through sustained growth of 11.5% and accelerated reduction of poverty to less than 30% of population." Increased economic competitiveness, taking intoaccount the role of energy as a productive input/catalyst.Pursuit of a 'green economy' approach to economic transformation.Youth empowered and rural communities connected toeconomic opportunity through jobs and better infrastructure. An enabling environment for private-sector driven growth and socioeconomic transformation.Improved service delivery through accountable governance

General (all Sub-Sectors)

High-Level Target Objectives(to be achieved by end ofFY2018)

1. Promote integrated planning and streamline sector governance. 2. Boost national ownership of Rwanda's energy vision and build more decentralized implementation capacity (including through enhanced human, organizational and institutional capacity. 3. Mainstream gender-based equity, environmental sustainability, and climate concerns into energy planning and sector strategies.4. Promote value-for-money and increased market competition in energy development. 5. Transition from indiscriminate to "smart subsidies" aligned to social protection principles.

EDPRS II Overarching Goal EDPRS II goals stronglylinked to the energy sector

• Inclusive engagement and strong ownership by all stakeholders. • Innovative approaches and home-grown initiativesfostered to address development challenges.• Empower community and district-driven development and coordinate mutually reinforcing linkages between sectorpolicy goals and decentralization strategies. • Focus on emerging priorities, including "green growth" and overall sustainability.

KEY GUIDING PRINCIPLES

High-Level Target Objectives(to be achieved by end ofFY2018)

1. Regional integration 2. Energy technology standards, and related compliance and enforcement 3. Energy data collection and statistics4. Energy research, development, and technological innovation 5. Energy security and disaster mitigation

1. Streamline investment promotion processes for IPPs.2. Accelerate energy sector Public-Private Partnerships (PPPs), taking advantage of new national guidelines and procurement procedures 3. Extend and expand investment incentives to private investors. 4. De-risk investments through financing risky upstream resource assessments and pre-feasibility studies. 5. Empower local enterprises to engage in energy sector deals and introduce more competitive, transparent approaches to service provision where appropriate.

• Capacity Building • Environment and climate change• Family and Gender • Regional Integration • HIV/AIDS and NCDs • Disaster Management

• Private sector participation central to delivery strategy, particularly in energy sector. • Job creation and skills development through private-sector expansion and opportunity.

CROSS -C UTTING THEMES

Private Sector Participation/Engagement

High-Level Target Objectives(to be achieved by end ofFY2018)

1. The shall convene and coordinate regular cross-sector planning meetings with regards to the National Energy Policy and Integrated Planning.2. Improve stakeholder communication, education, and public outreach mechanisms3. Revamp energy sub-sector coordination mechanisms and technical working groups.

EDPRS II verarching Goal EDPRS II goals stronglylinked to the energy sector Governance

Reduce coordination failures through integrated planning and joint solutions to infrastructure development and service delivery. • Strengthen citizen participation and demand for accountability.

ain policy objective: Ensure sufficient, reliable, sustainable and affordable power supply to all Rwandans

1. Reform the power sector in long-term to increase institutional accountability and operational efficiencies. Restructure EWSA into electricity utility, energy development, and water utility companies. (P)

1.1. EWSA restructuring and corporatization - a three phase process.

2. Transition to a cost-reflective yet affordable electricity tariff. (P), (E)

2.1. Establish a "glide-path" to cost-reflectivity that reflects the principle of moving toward "smart subsidies" targeting strategic industries and vulnerable social groups vs. the indiscriminate subsidization of power. 2.2. Achieve operational efficiencies in EUCL and implement energy efficiency and demand-side management programs to shave peak load and reduce required generation capacity.

3. Optimize the power mix so as to reduce long-run cost of service, diversify energy generation technologies, and gradually reduce the carbon-intensity of grid over time. Vision to reduce

petroleum-based power generation over time so as to be used only for peaking and back-up power by 2020.

IV -3.1. Ensure future energy demand is realistically forecasted and contribute to lowering the cost of electric power supply through improvements in analysis and planning effectively translated into National Power Master Plan and EAPP Power Master Plan. 3.2. Power Master Plan and generation road map to achieve strategic balancing act between increasing net imports of expected demand, optimizing exploitation of domestic energy resources, and 5 accelerating progress toward a regionally-integrated power market. 3.3. Conclude economically advantageous trading agreements with regional power houses (net exporters) in line with technical constraints and energy security guidelines (i.e. import cap of up to a maximum of 20%.19 3.4. Develop and enhance regulations facilitating regional trading arrangements.20 3.5. Gradually phase out expensive, petroleum-based generational capacity on a rental operational basis. Instead, build a utility-owned peaker power plant to cover peak demand and/or maintain a reserve margin to hedge against short-term power supply unavailability or import shocks. 3.6. Short-term priority to be given to domestic methane gas for base load applications over hydro-based imports and petroleum-based generation sources. Develop other indigenous energy resources such as biomass and solar power subject to being as sustainable, affordable, and reliable compared to imports. 3.7. Integrate findings of Strategic Environmental Assessment for the Energy Sector and other macro-level climate risk and sustainability assessments

[19] Additional analysis by energy planning team is necessary to come up with justifiable target. A 30% target represents a big increase from status quo, while still maintaining a high level of energy security. Moreover, it is well in line with average import-export ratios of other countries in the region. [20] Revised power tariff already paves way through unique transmission-related component. IV - 6

into future power Master Plans and ESIA guidelines to be elaborated by REMA specifically tailed to power generation projects. 3.8. Develop a strategy to access climate financing and incorporate into planning and budgeting processes to incentivise cleaner technologies and practices.

4. DEVELOP NATIONAL ELECTRICAL POWER SYSTEM TO SERVE GROWING DEMAND IN AN ECONOMICALLY EFFICIENT WAY AND REDUCE TECHNICAL AND NON-TECHNICAL LOSSES. (P), (E)

4.1. Utility to increase long-term investments in new generation capacity as well as transmission and distribution systems extension and rehabilitation. 4.2. Accelerate implementation of system loss-reduction investment activities (technical and nontechnical). 4.3. Implement quick win supply-side energy efficiency measures, i.e. grid loss-reduction programs. 4.4. Implement regional grid integration strategies and actions, taking into account required institutional, regulatory, technical, and investment reforms. Champion solutions associated with optimization of interconnected grids at regional level (e.g., EAC/EAPP technical meetings).

5. Enhance the attractiveness of exploiting domestic resources for power generation and increase local private sector participation through government-funded risk mitigation mechanisms and IPP investment streamlining. Revise and expand renewable energy feed-in tariff

General 5.1. Adjust REFIT tariff schedule subject to a set fixed price cap, 3 year review to see the impact on the utility and determine whether the REFIT tariff schedule should remain the same or be revised downwards, incorporate standardized PPA into the regulation, and add more clean energy resource (REFIT) mechanism. Government to prioritize funding of resource mapping, pre-feasibility studies, upstream exploration, and piloting to gain a clearer picture of the extent to which domestic hydropower, peat, solar and wind resources can generate electricity on commercially viable and competitive terms. (P), (E), (R), (I) types to be covered beyond hydropower such as grid-connected solar, biogas and landfill gas under an "avoided cost approach. 5.2. Relevant technology standards to be developed by RSB. REMA to develop relevant environmental guidelines. REMA, RURA, and NICA, as appropriate to enforce compliance. 5.3. Review investment procedures relevant to the energy sector, including the investment code and modalities of engagement. Peat 5.4. MININFRA to undertake peat energy strategy and action plan including socio-economic impact assessment to ascertain optimal use for: power generation, direct industrial heat steam applications, or use as domestic charcoal substitute 5.5. REG to undertake detailed national resource assessment (inventory) of existing bogs. Methane 5.6. Consider splitting extraction and power generation components in IPP procurement. 5.7. Prioritize technologies that allow for maximum sustainable extraction subject to value for money. Geothermal energy 5.8. Upgrade existing legal and regulatory framework to unique needs of geothermal energy activities 5.9. Government to de-risk by exploring the prospective geothermal areas until proven resources available, including carrying out stepwise exploration and ranking of all prospects. 5.10. Operationalize a Geothermal Development Program to act as umbrella structure for coordinating all exploration and public-led investment activities. 5.11. Manage tendering of PPP for development of up- and downstream facilities and for commercial exploitation of proven resources. Closely coordinate mining and energy concessions between relevant ministries. Conduct a feasibility study to evaluate viable direct applications of geothermal energy beyond power.

6. FACILITATE AUTONOMOUS POWER GENERATION THROUGH UPDATED POLICY GUIDELINES, STREAMLINED LICENSING, AND REGULATORY REFORMS. (P),(R)

6.1. Regulatory changes to encourage uptake of dedicated power plants for industry, geared toward mining and agro-industries. 6.2. Scope of simplified licensing regulations targeting rural electrification activities to be extended to autonomous generation. 6.3. Research optimal systems integration of solar energy in grid and undertake planning measures to increase transmission efficiency and stability in intermittent power supply.

ELECTRICITY ACCESS

Main policy objective: Enhance access to sustainable, modern energy for all Rwandans

1. Introduce short and long-term institutional reforms to increase sector coordination, accountability, and delivery effectiveness.

1.1. Increase household access to grid electricity to 48% and off-grid electricity to 22% based on analysis by REG Ltd and MININFRA. 1.2. Prioritize connections to productive uses: either large users or small and medium enterprises. In the short term, all major off-grid energy access and rural electrification programs implemented by the Utility on behalf of MININFRA should be consolidated under the umbrella of the EARP.

2. Ensure 100% access to electricity in all schools, Sector offices and health centres by 2018. (P) MINEDUC, MINALOC & MINISANTE to elaborate guidelines for budgeting responsibility for operations and maintenance and ongoing electricity services. (I)

2.1. EARP to examine feasibility of reaching target for each remaining unelectrified institution through on-or off-grid connection, whichever more economical. 2.2. EARP to analyze costs and benefits of expanding access to other public services (e.g., administrative, community centers).

3. Scale up innovative partnerships to increase rural access to appropriate off-grid technology solutions. (P), (E)

3.1. MININFRA shall develop, pilot, and scale-up innovative PPPs for off-grid energy delivery, following new process and project cycle under PPP Policy. Government shall support programs through in-kind assistance and other measures, including provision of new investment and fiscal incentives. 3.2. Initiate grassroots awareness-raising campaign to

IV FISCAL REFORMS

4. Fiscal reforms to inject market-based incentives targeting urban and periurban citizens to switch from kerosene and wood fuels to solar lighting and clean cooking technologies, such as phasing out a tax exemption on kerosene, extending a VAT exemption for LPG. (E)

4.1. Study the market, fiscal and socio-economic impacts of phasing out subsidies on kerosene. Determine degree to which market demand for solar-home-systems and solar-powered lamps would be benefited from such fiscal reforms. 4.2. Incorporate social protection principles into design of any fiscal reforms.

5. Introduce greater competition and flexibility in off-grid service provision through measures to simplify licensing and stimulate Small-scale Power Distributors (SPDs). (R)

5.1. Adopt and enforce new secondary regulations under the Electricity Act to simplify licensing frameworks and processes for SPDs. 5.2. Utility to publish National Electrification Plan put in the public domain and remaining valid for at least three years. This will encourage private investment in off-grid electricity businesses.

6. Allow cross border electrification. (P), (R)

6.1. Facilitate regulatory frameworks for low-voltage cross-border electrification interconnection lines and service delivery.

ENERGY EFFICIENCY AND DEMAND-SIDE MANAGEMENT

Main policy objective: Constrain unbridled future energy consumption growth and support realizing Rwanda's Green Economy vision.

1. Adopt new laws, regulations and codes that mandate energy efficiency measures in public institutions, households, and commercial businesses. (R)

1.1. MININFRA to introduce an Energy Efficiency Strategy and Law as framework to support series of new regulations by RURA. 1.2. Integrate promotion of energy smart building technologies into monitoring and implementation of new government asset management policy. 1.3. Introduce energy-smart and energy-efficient technologies and practices into Rwandan building codes, including mandatory installation of solar water heaters for large water consumers (e.g., hotels, integrated developments) in parallel to extending subsidy to end-users to incentivize switching. RHA to elaborate codes. RURA to ensure enforcement. Rwanda Housing Authority to oversee training, skills development.

2. Restructure electricity tariff methodology to incentivize efficiency (R)

2.1. RURA to regulate a "demand charge" tariff component along with a time-of-use based scheme.

3. REG Ltd to establish a dedicated demand-side management/energy efficiency unit to oversee implementation of relevant programs aligned to the policy. (I)

3.1. Develop a staffing and business plan as part of EWSA restructuring/institutional reform. 3.2. Develop and outsource a comprehensive behavioral change marketing campaign targeting common sense energy management among high-consumption commercial and household end-users. Translate existing RURA guidelines into educational curriculae and public awareness programs. 3.3. Water Utility Company shall retrofit existing water pumping systems with variable speed drives to reduce energy demand load and operational costs. 3.4. Assess viability of other incentives for LV customers on pre-paid-meters (e.g., rebates) to shift demand patterns to smooth demand load during the day.

4. Promote and remove barriers to the implementation of priority efficient lighting initiatives through bulk procurement, social marketing campaigns, and targeted subsidies for retrofits. (P), (E)

4.1. REG Ltd EE/DSM Unit to manage bulk procurement and distribution of CFLs for residential customers (based on current consumption and end-user affordability)

4.2. REG Ltd EE/DSM Unit to manage energy-efficient lighting retrofits in public institutions in collaboration with MININFRA. 4.3. Districts empowered to take responsibility for the ongoing maintenance and running costs of street lighting through regulatory reforms. Technical support to be provided by REG Ltd EE/DSM Unit to conduct cost-effective street lighting retrofitting.

5. Develop and adopt an EAC-wide energy standards and labeling scheme for common household appliances. (R)

5.1. RSB to establish a working group. Align regional standards to EAC under existing regional integration processes.

6. Encourage and incentivize regular energy audits in industry and commerce. (P), (E)

6.1. Major end-users, such as industries, encouraged and incentivized to carry out regular energy audits. 6.6. MININFRA to develop a strategy and business model for an energy efficiency finance facility to bankroll audits (50/50 cost split) and retrofits. Facility would be initially capitalized by MINECOFIN through a reallocation of power tariff subsidy and DP contributions. Capital would be replenished on the basis of savings achieved. It would also establish energy performance benchmarks for industry.

7. Institutionalize "green" public procurement guidelines and strategies focused on equipment with a high energy footprint. (P)

7.1. RPPA and REMA to develop clear criteria, guidelines for integrating energy and resource efficiency into existing procurement policy and processes.

BIOMASS SECTOR

Main policy objective:

1. Consolidate institutional mandates and

1.1. MINALOC to promote improved charcoal

IV - 13

Facilitate fuel-switching from traditional biomass energy carriers toward modern biomass energy technologies and cleaner fuel alternatives in order to reduce non-renewable fuel wood consumption and related social, health, and environmental costs.

initiate stronger involvement of local districts (I)

production and improved cook stoves. 1.2. Local districts to take more ownership of biomass program implementation, with the support and guidance of MINALOC. 1.3. Better coordination and monitoring of local district development plans with respect to clean cooking targets and implementation strategies.

2. Formalize charcoal production and supply to facilitate more effective regulatory control as well as mainstreaming improved harvesting and carbonization techniques. (P), (R)

2.1. Efforts to increase more formalization of sector including better-organized and consolidated charcoal producer cooperatives and associations. 2.2. Better enforcement by RNRA of current regulations, including licensing regime, to stop illegal wood harvesting at the district level. 2.3. MININFRA and MINALOC to ramp up support for capacity development of local charcoal producers in improved harvesting and carbonization methods. Ensure the delivery of ongoing technical assistance under a "train-the-trainers" model in every district. 2.4. Carry out supply chain analysis to ensure more reliable, affordable, sustainable product on market. 2.5. REMA shall continue to promote agro-forestry on local shumbas to reduce fuel wood pressure.

3. Increase access to cleaner cooking energy carriers (e.g., biogas, LPG, green charcoal, and biomass pyrolysis stoves) by promoting technology standards, introducing fiscal reforms where appropriate, and piloting new market transformation activities. (E), (R)

3.1. Rebalance budget to address clean cooking priorities as heavily skewed toward power sub-sector. 3.2.Strategy to identify appropriate technologies for household cooking and ICS at different income levels/geographies. 3.3. RSB shall elaborate updated national ICS standards with the support of REMA, MININFRA, and the private sector. 3.4. Implementation strategy shall place more emphasis on social marketing/behavioural change campaigns and awareness raising through, inter alia, public demonstrations at "Umuganda" meetings. 3.5. Promote more market-based PPP approaches to scaling up clean cooking programs. Evaluate feasibility of piloting similar PPP models program under concession agreements that can offer turnkey modern biomass cooking solutions. 3.6. Implement green fiscal reforms − enhance local skills development programs − expand partnership agreements with financial institutions in order to expand credit access to households in order to facilitate fuel switching. 3.7. Promote LPG by: − Continuing VAT exemption − Providing incentives to retailers to improve LPG distribution infrastructure − Undertake a social marketing campaign. 3.8. Promote green charcoal through REG Ltd targeting peat and agriculture waste. 3.9. Support biogas utilization by: − Restructuring approach to the NDBP. More focus on institutions vs. households.

− Reforming subsidies for biogas to be more means-tested and in line with system capacity, market demand. MINALOC to ensure more consistency of concessional financing terms across local districts. − RSB to define and adopt new national technology standard for biogas digesters.

4. Develop a harmonized, regionally integrated market for sustainable liquid biofuels. (P)

4.1. MINICOM and MININFRA shall promote and harmonize policies and market opportunities for regional biofuel industry development. Explore feasibility for regional biorefineries whereby feed stocks imported into Rwanda duty free from EAC.

Petroleum

Main policy objective: Ensure safe, sufficient, reliable, sustainable and affordable supply of petroleum and LPG.

1. Enhance attractiveness of Rwanda as investment destination for upstream oil and gas exploration and development. (P), (R)

1.1. Implement National Petroleum Exploration and Production Policy adopted by Cabinet in 2013

2. Institute an effective public-private hybrid model for maintaining strategic petroleum products. Recommend MINICOM review strategic reserve requirements to balance cost/security imperatives. (P), (R)

2.1. MINICOM to consider updating reserve requirement levels to reflect current market situation. 2.2. Introduce incentives to incentivize retailers and wholesale fuel distributers to increase investments in gas (LPG) storage facilities.

3. Accelerate regional cooperation and strategic infrastructure development including new refining, pipeline transportation, and railway infrastructure. (P), (E)

3.1. Strategic joint investment in Hoima regional refinery and target participation in other multinational investments, including bio-diesel blending facilities. 3.2. Develop transportation infrastructure interconnections for faster, more reliable supplies of petroleum and LPG. Study extension of refined petroleum pipeline to Kigali.

4. Enhance effectiveness of petroleum price stabilization mechanisms, such as introducing new price control methodologies, expanding bulk procurement, and introducing hedging requirements for large public consumers (R)

4.1. Conclude bulk purchasing agreements for petroleum products with Tanzania, Uganda, and Kenya. 4.2. Encourage and incentivize private investors to undertake bulk purchasing arrangements 4.3. Adopt, enforce appropriate fuel pricing methodology. 4.4. Encourage or mandated large fuel consumers to enter into fuel hedging arrangements.

5. Introduce mandatory petroleum statistics (R)

5.1. Adopt regulation for mandatory submission to regulator of data related to petroleum products' trade, sales, and strategic stores. 5.2. Closley track market growth and penetration rates for LPG through surveys, etc.

6. Determine and enforce petroleum standards to ensure even product quality (R)

6.1. RURA shall set and enforce standards for all downstream petroleum products.

7. Implement market transformation activities, including possible revision of fiscal incentives to strengthen incentivize for LPG fuel-switching, targeting urban areas. (P), (E)

7.1. Implement a social marketing and behavioral change campaign to increase market uptake of LPG targeting middle-class households in urban areas. 7.2. Assist local importers with storage and distribution infrastructure investment and bulk purchasing arrangements in order to reduce LPG price. 7.3. TVETs to provide training in the production and /or assembling of LPG low cost stoves to match increased demand.

ENERGY SECTOR STRATEGIC PLAN[2]

The main objective of the Rwandan Energy Sector Strategic Plan (ESSP) is to ensure effective delivery of the set targets in the energy sector as set out under the EDPRS-II and to guide in the implementation of the National Energy Policy (EP). The ESSP thus functions as a detailed plan that serves to translate the policy directives and principles into concrete measures necessary to reach medium-term targets, reflecting current resource constraints and risk/uncertainties. The ESSP also contains high-level target objectives, and a monitoring framework with key performance indicators and interim milestones.

The ESSP addresses the challenges facing the sector and outlines strategies to meet critical needs. Principal among these needs are:

i. To enhance energy security and to better align demand and supply balances;

ii. To ensure that tariffs and prices for energy services are cost-reflective;

iii. To reduce coordination failures and the cost of financing infrastructure;

iv. To meet energy access targets without raising the average cost of electricity services, increasing subsidies, compromising service quality, or compromising environmental sustainability;

v. To develop the requisite institutional, organizational, and human capacity to increase accountability, transparency, national ownership and decentralized implementation of energy service delivery;

vi. To dramatically scale-up energy investments through more effective private sector engagement.

An earlier version of the ESSP was drafted in 2012 in conjunction with the national EDPRS-II formulation process. This updated ESSP outlines several new high-level target objectives (HLTOs) that have been determined on the basis of political ambitions and rigorous technical analyses. These cut across all key energy sub-sectors. The HLTOs serve to translate the policy goals laid out in the EP and EDPRS-II into tangible outcome indicators achievable by the end of the EDPRS-II period (2013 to 2018).

ESSP high-level target objectives

* Increase the electric power system equivalent installed capacity (domestic generation + imports) to 563 MW.

* Increase household access to grid electricity to 48% and access to off-grid electricity to 22%.

* Achieve savings from energy efficiency measures of 10% through demand-side management measures and grid-loss reductions (from a 2013 baseline).

* Reduce the carbon intensity of the grid by 10% by 2018, and 25% by 2025 (from a 2013 baseline).

---

[2] 2013/14 - 2017/18 REPUBLIC OF RWANDA MINISTRY OF INFRASTRUCTURE

* Ensure 80% of all households employ clean cooking energy technologies.

* Realize all EAC Regional Integration Policy priorities for energy sector.

* Ensure the necessary infrastructure is in place to meet current petroleum strategic reserve requirements (currently 3 months' supply)

The government intends to provide 70% of the population with access to electricity both on-grid and off-grid by the end of EDPRS II. The priority is to extend the grid network to allow heavy users of electricity across the country to connect to the grid. For lighter users of electricity, grid connections are unlikely to make economic sense in the short term and as such, off-grid solutions will be preferred.

To keep pace with increased demand for electricity and to facilitate achievement of EDPRS-II targets for economic growth, the government will ensure increased electricity generation capacity to a level of up to 563 MW by the end of 2017/2018. Diversifying power generation sources and reducing diesel generation over time will enable the government to lower the long-term cost of service and gradually phase out indiscriminate subsidies to the tariff.

The total estimated cost of all programs is around $4.1 billion, with around $2 billion selected to come from public funds. The anticipated power generation road map, a large contributor to the future sector budget, is detailed in Table 20, in Annex I.

Table 2 Summary of sector strategies and HLTOs by Sub-Sector (FY 2012 to 2017)

ELECTRICITY

On-Grid Electricity Supply	□ Electric power system installed capacity (domestic generation + imports) to reach 563 MW by 2018. * Demand: Current projections at roughly 470 MW by 2018. A 15% reserve margin shall be factored into plans to improve power quality and reliability. * Supply: The generation portfolio will be optimized to reduce long-term costs, increase energy security, and achieve environmental sustainability objectives. Government will increase investment in resource assessments and feasibility studies to reduce perceived investment risks and attract greater private sector participation.
Electricity Access	□ Reach 70% electricity access based on differentiated grid and off-grid strategies and targets. * Grid access (48%): Priority to be given to productive end-users and households consuming sufficient electricity to make connections financially sustainable. Off-grid access (22%): Implement market transformation initiatives and PPPs to increase household access to off-grid solutions such as solar PV. These will target households where grid connection financially unviable. Regulatory changes to encourage mini-grids and SPDs. □ All schools and hospitals to have 100% access to electricity by 2018 through on/off-grid mix.
Environmental Sustainability	□ Reduce the carbon intensity of the grid by 10% by 2018 (from a 2013 baseline). * Measures to promote renewable energy and low-carbon power supply, including expanding REFIT scope. * Gradual reduction in petroleum-based power generation over time. * Mainstreaming climate vulnerability into hydropower planning.

Electricity tariff	□ Make power increasingly affordable and phase out indiscriminate subsidies to the electricity tariff by 2017/2018. * Specific strategic industries and vulnerable population groups will be targeted for "smart" subsidies as matter of policy and to achieve cost transparency.
	* The power generation mix will be diversified to gradually reduce petroleum-based power generation. * Revised tariff methodology to disaggregate tariffs based on end-user categories, and to reduce barriers to new customers by removing fixed meter charges. * Increased regional imports from EAPP countries at cheaper tariff levels expected. * EWSA restructuring to yield operational efficiencies and reduced non-technical losses that contribute to high cost of power.
Energy Efficiency	□ Save up to 10% of 2013 power output by implementing priority energy efficiency programs including demand-side management and grid-loss reduction measures. * New Energy Efficiency Strategy developed to shave peak-demand and avoid unnecessary investment in new power generation. * Consolidation of institutional responsibilities to execute priority demand-side energy conservation and management programs (such as industry audits, lighting retrofits, and solar water heater subsidies). * Implement a grid-loss reduction program and improve plant maintenance. * Develop new regulations and a regionally appropriate appliance standards and labelling program.
BIOMASS	
Sustainable biomass solutions	□ Ensure 80% of all households employ clean cooking energy technologies * Further decentralise and streamline the implementation of programmes, including promotion of improved cook stoves (ICS) and biogas digesters. Reform subsidy program for household biogas digesters. * Implement market transformation activities that incentivize fuel switching to cleaner, more sustainable fuels and cooking technologies such as biogas, biomass pyrolysis, LPG, and vetted improved cook-stoves models. Strategies will vary depending on end-user appropriateness and economic viability. * Promote efficient charcoal production, including wood-harvesting and carbonisation techniques.
PETROLEUM	
Security of supply	□ Ensure adequate storage infrastructure (equivalent to 3 months' supply), and implementation of regional projects. * Strategic Stocks: New storage facilities to be built in Kigali based on strategic reserve levels set by MINICOM. This has been decided upon as 3 months strategic supply split between government and private sector, but may be revised based on future analyses. * Decrease import costs: Regional oil pipeline and refining projects will be developed. Bulk purchasing and hedging strategies will be pursued. LPG market assessment to be undertaken.
Upstream Exploration	* Streamlined new licensing procedures to be implemented

Affordability	* MINICOM to enact new fuel pricing methodology and regulatory mechanisms.
Quality	* Streamline and consolidate approach to regulation of sector. * Strengthen enforcement of quality standards through increased tests and checks.

ENERGY SECTOR OVERVIEW

The energy sector is pivotal to the Rwandan economy, given its systemic link to almost all other sectors of the economy such as transportation, housing and urbanization, manufacturing, agro-processing, mining and IT services. A core focus continues to be on electric power supply and transmission. Electricity can be generated from a variety of technologies and natural resources in Rwanda, such as petroleum-based fuels, hydro, solar, methane gas, peat, geothermal, biomass, waste, and wind. An increasing focus is also given to energy efficiency and conservation measures, which includes both demand-side and supply-side elements. The ESSP scope goes beyond electricity, however, to include the bioenergy sub-sector, including bio-products1, such as wood fuel, charcoal, and biogas, as well as petroleum products, such as diesel, kerosene, LPG and natural gas.

Considering energy use broadly, the main consumers are households (91%), which mainly use energy in the form of traditional fuels such as wood, followed by the transport sector (4%), industry (3%), and public services (2%)2. Households are also the dominant consumers of electricity (51%), the bulk of which demand is primarily used for lighting. The industrial sector (42%) is the second largest consumer of energy, which mainly comes from motor-drivers and lighting. Major industrial consumers include companies in the cement, mining, textile, and agricultural sector (including tea estates). Public sector consumption of electricity (6%) is mainly for powering public buildings, street lighting and water pumping3.

Figure 1. Total Energy (2009) & Electricity Consumption (2012) by Sector

Biomass energy resources represent 85% of the energy balance. In fact, the primary source of energy in Rwanda continues to be biomass, principally used in cooking. The most basic forms of biomass are firewood, which represents 57% of all energy use, and charcoal, which represents 23%. Crop waste and other fuels (6%) are used to a limited extent, but new technologies are increasing their commercial appeal4. In urban areas, electric stoves and microwaves are used only to a limited extent. Commercial establishments and wealthier households in urban areas are also increasingly using Liquefied Petroleum Gas (LPG).

Table 3 below illustrates projected usage trends by energy carrier and across the main different demand end-uses. It summarises the anticipated demand shifts and transitions across the main energy carriers as a result of current policies and strategies.

Table 3 Illustrative view of energy use patterns and transitions from different sources by 2018

Note: A red arrow indicates where a significant rise in use of a particular energy source for a given activity is anticipated

The following sections summarize expected trends and transitions across the sub-sectors.

ELECTRICITY SUB-SECTOR

Electricity is an essential driver of modern technology and socio-economic development. Its use is required at low levels for devices such as lights and mobile phones, as well as at high levels for industrial processing activities that contribute to economic value-added products and job creation.

At the end of 2012, electricity represented only about 4% of primary energy consumed in Rwanda.5 Total installed electricity generation capacity is currently 160 MW of which roughly 60% comes from hydrological resources and 40% from diesel-powered generators.6 Since 2008, power supply has increased by 10% to a total of 502,053 MWh. In July 2014, the utility had about 450,775 household customers and 170 customers in the industrial category. Total consumption has been growing on an annual basis, following a logarithmic trajectory. Rwanda has a very pronounced peak demand load, which was registered at 87.9 MW on average annually in 2013. Supply is occasionally unable to match demand in these peak hours. Future demand for electricity by 2017/2018 is projected to reach 470 MW. Power demand does not fluctuate seasonally.

Figure 2 Energy Demand and Supply Situation (2001-2013)

The electricity tariff is currently not cost reflective and heavily subsidized. A reliance on costly petroleum-based power generation, which was brought in temporarily to respond to an extended drought over a decade ago, has led to high costs; the cost of supplying electricity is around 50% higher than the average tariff in East Africa, and over 20% higher than the regional average in sub-Saharan Africa. Approximately US$ 56,000 is spent per day

as operational expenditure on diesel imports. A combination of high-cost generation from diesel and Heavy Fuel Oils and low demand for electricity has also impeded the financial sustainability of the Utility.

ON-GRID ELECTRICITY

Currently, Rwanda has one of the lowest per capita electricity consumption rates in the world, at 42kWh per annum compared to an average of 478 kWh for sub-Saharan Africa and 1,200 kWh for developing countries as a whole.7 Presently around 20% of Rwanda's households are connected to the grid. This partially reflects a situation of "supressed demand," which can be partly attributed to the fact that the tariff of $0.24/kWh is relatively high for the region, and the geo-spatial realities and dispersed settlement patterns in Rwanda render the infrastructure costs of grid extension projects expensive.

While network connections require significant capital costs, they provide stable, high-voltage electricity required to power large domestic and industrial equipment for commercial and large residential users. Thus, expanding on-grid access will facilitate a shift from the current agriculture based economy towards industrialisation. In recent years, there has been an aggressive program to increase access to the electricity services by all sectors of the economy, especially industry and small and medium enterprises (SMEs). Grid connections do however require significant capital investment which needs to be financed and repaid. Calculations indicate that consumption would have to reach around 130 kWh/month to recover these financing costs.

Several challenges and complexities are associated with power generation and supply, more general, and in Rwanda, in particular: First, it cannot be stored on a large scale,8 unlike other energy sources. Careful planning and network operations are required to allow power to travel instantaneously from the source of generation to the end user. During this journey, a significant amount of energy is lost as heat. Proper network planning and operation is essential to minimise these losses. The current average estimate of losses in the power system (both technical and non-technical) is around 23%. Secondly, generation output must continuously flex with end user demand, which is not constant throughout the day. As a result, different generation technologies can fulfil different roles. Third, electricity is capital intensive. Unlike petroleum, where the majority of costs are variable and associated with the commodity cost, electricity production costs are mainly associated with infrastructure investment costs. These are typically paid off over multiple years over the useful (depreciated) life of the asset. Therefore, a decision to invest or enter into an agreement with the private sector must make sense not just for the next few years but for the entire

life of the asset. A small change in the financing costs will result in a large change in the total cost and long-term return, which brings with it inherent risks. As a result, careful consideration must be given to ways to mitigate investor risk.

OFF-GRID ELECTRICITY

Lighting in rural areas is in most cases provided by kerosene. Use of other energy sources such as solar, biogas and LPG is limited. At current tariff levels, on-grid electricity access is unaffordable to most rural customers and their consumption is insufficient to recover up-front costs. These users would mainly use electricity to charge their phones, radios and for a few hours of lighting per day.

Government has already had some degree of success with various initiatives. For instance: donor supported programs have connected over 150 remote rural schools with 1.7kW solar energy solutions and 300 schools, and 46 health centres are now being connected. Solar lantern kits of 5W have been distributed to 15 rural settlements (approximately 1500 households) and lastly, 400 solar kits of 300W have been installed in 4 rural settlements. This is in addition to private sector initiatives with several, now well established, companies operating in Rwanda.

GENERATION RESOURCES

Rwanda has a range of indigenous resources that complement each other in the energy mix. Table 9 illustrates how this can be split across the different generation technologies:

Table 4 Overview of Rwanda's indigenous energy resources

Resource potential	Characteristics and Considerations
Hydropower 313-400 MW9	Hydropower has generated the bulk of electricity in Rwanda since 1960s. Its overall potential is estimated at about 400 MW but the current installed hydro capacity is 98.5 MW. As a result of extremely low operational costs however, hydro is still one of the cheapest forms of generation in the long run.
Methane 350 MW10	Pilot projects have demonstrated the commercial and technical viability of extracting methane from Lake Kivu. Following completion of KivuWatt 1, this will be further proven, and increased interest from private investors can be expected.
Peat 700 MW11	A Peat master plan was first developed in 1993. It indicated the potential to develop around 700MW of peat generation based on estimated reserves of 155 million tons of dry peat spread over 50,000 hectares. About 77% of peat reserves are near Akanyaru and Nyabarongo rivers and the Rwabusoro Plains. The cost of electricity produced from peat will be slightly higher than from methane gas, due to the cost of

	peat mining. Peat is considered less risky for power generation compared to methane or geothermal, and can therefore deliver increased capacity sooner.
Geothermal (TBD)	Rwanda's geothermal resource is yet to be proven. Geo-scientific studies are on-going which will lead to the development of the necessary drilling strategy to confirm the resource. A quantitative estimation of Rwanda's geothermal potential would thus be premature at this point in time.
Solar Energy	There is a high interest from private sector in on-grid solar power development. However the penetration level of solar power to the grid is limited by technical capacity of the grid. Solar Power will be added according to the increase of generation capacity from non-intermittent sources and reinforcement of the grid.
Biomass (TBD)	Small-scale power generation using agricultural residues (either directly, in the case of bagasse or rice husks) or biomass briquettes from compacted waste residues or charcoal dust is feasible at low levels of capacity. In addition, there is a small potential for generating power from landfill gas, waste water effluent, and municipal solid waste. A more detailed resource assessment for the purpose of power generation needs to be conducted.
Wind Energy	Commercialy wind power resources are not expected to be significant based on past resource assessments and modeling work. However, MININFRA is proceeding with more detailed assessments of national wind energy potential to verify niche contributions to the country's energy needs.

HYDRO POWER GENERATION

Studies suggest that Rwanda's topography is most suitable for medium- to high-head pico- and micro-hydro run-of-river schemes. Rwanda's overall technical hydropower potential has been estimated at 400 MW, although this varies according to different studies made at different times. The most significant resource assessment conducted to date—the Rwandan Hydropower Atlas conducted roughly five years ago—found that the majority of potentially feasible sites would be rated between 50 kW and 1 MW in capacity. This study estimated a potential of 96 MW for the category of micro-hydro projects. Although fairly comprehensive, with some 333 potential sites identified across a large number of locations, additional viable sites have already been, and are likely to continue to be identified.12 An assessment of the energy sector undertaken by the African Development Bank in 2013 estimated Rwanda's domestic hydropower potential at 313 MW, broken down into 130 MW of domestic and 183 MW of regional hydro resources. Feasibility studies have been completed or are under way for a number of sites, representing at least 32 MW of technically viable new capacity. In addition, over 192 sites have been identified for pico-hydro with a capacity below 50 kW.

Evidently, a more detailed resource mapping for the hydropower sector would be valuable, particularly taking a spatial river basin approach before prioritizing specific sites for

development. An on-going comprehensive assessment of hydro resources on the Akanyaru River basin, located on the border between Rwanda and Burundi, adopts this approach. These resources can be developed in cascade form, with 11 domestic sites and 3 shared sites recommended for further feasibility analysis. Based on preliminary estimates, these projects could potentially augment Rwanda's total installed capacity by over 25 MW.13

PEAT TO POWER

Currently peat is used as an input in cottage industries, cement production, and as a cooking fuel in a small number of decentralized institutions. Rwanda has estimated reserves of 155 million tons of dry peat14 spread over about 50,000 hectares in Akanyaru, Nyabarongo, Rwabusoro and other areas. Approximately one-third of this resource is currently commercially extractable for industrial heat or electric power production. These estimates are largely based upon a 'high level' master plan undertaken in 1993, with only a small number of samples having been taken and the majority of work being carried out as desk research. In late 2013 and early 2014, REG undertook more detailed resource assessments in order to complement and refine the existing peat master plan. Parallel to this, several projects have independently developed feasibility studies based on resource potentials identified in specific locations. However, it is important that at the national level Rwanda has an accurate assessment of its resources in order to determine how to use them most efficiently and sustainably, as peat energy is not generally considered to be renewable. In addition, some peat resources are located in environmentally sensitive habitats.

GEOTHERMAL ENERGY RESOURCES

Rwanda may have geothermal potential which is manifest in the form of hot springs. Three main prospect areas have been demarcated for further exploration: Kinigi, Gisenyi and Bugarama. The potential of geothermal energy is still uncertain. Given the complexity involved in determining the commercial viability of geothermal power, however, much more detailed exploration studies and sub-surface drilling are required.

SOLAR ENERGY

Rwanda's solar radiation and solar resources were assessed by the U.S. National Air and Space Agency (NASA) as well as the University of Rwanda. Rwanda's Eastern Province has the greatest potential for generating energy from solar resources, as shown in solar energy resource map that was created from this study. Another academic assessment, undertaken in partnership with the MININFRA Department of Meteorology in 2007, used a

meteorological data set to estimate monthly averaged global solar radiation. This was found to vary between 4.3 and 5.2 kWh per m2 per day over all regions of Rwanda.15

Source: NASA 'Rwanda Agriculture & Energy' (2013)

WIND

Being located close to the equator, Rwanda's inherent resource potential for wind energy is low. A rapid wind energy resource assessment was carried out in Rwanda in five locations over the course of 2011. Preliminary indications from the analysis of recorded field measurements of wind speeds and climate data were that most of Rwanda is not highly suitable for wind energy. The Eastern province was identified as the location with the most promising potential, and a simple analysis comparing wind and solar energy feasibility suggested that wind energy could be competitive in this region. Another academic study using modelling analyses based on recorded wind measurements at selected Rwandan meteorological stations noted that electricity production in the area of the Gisenyi station could be possible with a good mean value of both wind speed and power density, whereas in areas such as Kigali, Butare and Kamembe, wind energy potential is only sufficient for windmills or water pumping for agricultural and intuitional needs.16 More detailed resource assessments and feasibility studies are required to determine commercially viable wind energy potential in Rwanda.

METHANE GAS

The majority of the country's methane gas resources stem from the globally unique geology of Lake Kivu and the naturally regenerating methane gas that is found there. Some 1000 studies have been carried out, the consensus of which is that Lake Kivu is estimated to

contain around 55 billion cubic metres of methane gas, with a further 150 to 250 million cubic metres of methane being generated annually. In recent years, Government has put great efforts on proving the technical and commercial viability of safely extracting methane from Lake Kivu to produce power. Indeed, the more methane gas that is extracted, the safer are riparian communities, as there will be less methane gas that could potentially explode in case of a sub-surface volcanic eruption. According to feasibility studies undertaken [by EWSA], it is possible to sustainably extract sufficient gas to generate around 700MW of power. This would put the national potential at 350MW, as the resources are shared equally by Rwanda and DRC through an international agreement. A small pilot plant, owned and operated by Kibuye Power (KP I), and having an installed capacity of 3.6MW, has been operational for some time. The expected commissioning of the 25MW KivuWatt power plant in late 2014 will go a long way, however, toward corroborating the commercial feasibility of Lake Kivu methane gas as resource for large-scale power generation. In addition to Lake Kivu, Rwanda also possesses inherent methane resources that can be extracted from underground mining seams.

Methane gas has a variety of commercial and industrial uses, beyond the production of electricity, although it is currently anticipated that the primary end-use of the resource will be for electricity. Feasibility studies for direct use of methane gas in heating applications, fertilizer, and petrochemical production have already been conducted and more are to be expected with a lower risk of extraction of the resource.

BIOGAS

Biogas can be generated from a variety of biomass resources, including agricultural, human, and municipal waste. The national resource potential for these alternative sources of methane or biogas has never been systematically estimated through surveys or extensive resource assessments. Pre-feasibility studies have been conducted for a landfill gas-to-electricity project in Kigali, however, which suggested that commercial plant could be feasible in the near-term future given higher population growth and volumes of waste collected and more systematic separation of waste streams.

ENERGY EFFICIENCY AND DEMAND-SIDE MANAGEMENT

Government is undertaking various *ad hoc* energy efficiency programs, although these are not streamlined in an energy efficiency and demand-side management strategy. Current programs include:

Compact Fluorescent Lights (CFL): Lighting is the main use of electricity in Rwanda. A CFL distribution program took place in 2007, and targeted residential customers: 400,000 CFLs were sold to the existing 95,000 beneficiaries over several phases, and 400,000 CFLs were provided to 80,000 new customers as part of a 'welcome pack'. It was estimated that 54 GWh per year were saved, along with 260,000 tCO2e.

'SolaRwanda' Solar Water Heaters (SWH): Initiated in 2012, the project aims to establish a SWH market through promotion and financial incentives to suppliers. The target is to distribute 12,000 units by 2015 with an estimated saving of 23,000MWh per year. However, currently only 800 units have been distributed, mainly due to supply and incentives issues.

Street Lighting: A pilot project was implemented by the City of Kigali to replace high-pressure sodium (HPS) lamps with LEDs in street lights. This led to a 60% reduction of power consumption from the baseline level. The financial savings or payback of the program requires further analysis in order to justify scale-up and replication.

BIOMASS ENERGY SUBSECTOR

In Rwanda, the biomass energy subsector covers mainly cooking energy and boiler fuels, but it also concerns power generation and transport fuels to a lesser extent. Biomass resources are exploited in form of firewood, charcoal or agricultural residues mainly for cooking purposes by households and also in some industries.17 Country-wide, biomass meets up to 85% of energy needs; the balance being met by other options such as kerosene, diesel, dry cells, grid and non-grid electricity, biogas, solar, wind and other renewable energies.

Rwandans have traditionally used biomass as their main source of energy, currently meeting 84% of the primary energy needs. It is estimated that Rwanda's sustainable supply potential of wood fuel was 3.2 million tonnes in 2009, and this can be increased further with forestry programs. Currently over 80% of the country's firewood and charcoal comes from privately operated plantations of eucalyptus trees and other small-scale agro forestry programs. Many farmers dedicate a small portion of their plots to eucalyptus for self-consumption; however, much of this wood is either used for construction, rather than energy.

Charcoal is the preferred cooking fuel for urban households. Experience across Africa suggests that demand for charcoal will increase rapidly with urbanization trends. Households will first use it as a complementary fuel to firewood but gradually shift entirely as it is more convenient, and alternatives such as LPG and electricity are currently expensive.

Biomass consumption is putting pressure on existing resources, with an estimated 870,00018 tonne woody biomass deficit in 2009. Along with this the use of biomass for fuel is having harmful effects through health impacts and emissions. To rectify this, the Government is further developing the public sector forestry programs, has licensing for tree harvesting and is diversifying away from traditional wood fuel to look at other forms of biomass such as papyrus and rice and coffee husks, as well as biogas which benefits from the 'One cow per

poor family' scheme. The Government has put in place strict tree harvesting regulations; only licensed persons with permits are allowed to cut trees, including those from private lands. These measures have helped to reduce deforestation and Rwanda is one of only a handful of countries in Africa where the relationship between charcoal consumption and deforestation no longer exists. Government is to focus on increased wood production

IMPROVED COOKING TECHNOLOGIES

According to a recent study, traditional wood fuel is the energy used by the vast majority of rural households (i.e. over 90%) for cooking.19 The average household uses around 1.8 tonnes of firewood each year to satisfy its cooking needs with a traditional stove. The average monthly consumption per household on fuel wood is RWF 1,930.

The government program has been running since the 1980s with 60% household penetration. Private sector led efforts are also distributing cook stoves that are up to three times more efficient than the traditional 3-stone stove, and can reduce biomass consumption by anywhere between 68-94%20 This will free up the time spent by women and children in collecting firewood, giving them more time to study and undertake more productive commercial activities

Whilst it must be noted that there are significant health and social benefits of transitioning to charcoal, it is likely to increase the pressure on the limited wood supplies. This issue is likely to be accelerated as more and more people move from rural to urban and peri-urban settlements where charcoal is more common and convenient.

BIOGAS

The potential biogas market in Rwanda is estimated at 150,000 households, among predominantly rural customers. Government has put in place an elaborate program for disseminating bio digesters in households, schools and prisons to reduce demand for wood and charcoal and improve people's health since 2007—the National Domestic Biogas Programme (NDBP). The NDBP's initial focus was on capacity development, training technicians and entrepreneurs, and social marketing. The institutional Biogas Program began at KIST as a pilot in 1999. In 2008, Government announced a policy to introduce biogas digesters in all schools (estimated at around 600), large health centers and institutions with canteens. Through this Institutional biogas program, 11 out of the 14 prisons in Rwanda are currently using biogas for cooking. Since the beginning of the program, 3,687 domestic biogas digesters have been installed in households and 68 institutional digesters have been installed mainly in schools and prisons. Government continues to subsidize biogas technologies, with a 50% government subsidy and the use of local microfinance institutions, even after the termination of financial support by DPs to the

program. The biogas systems installed in the schools and prisons have reduced firewood consumption by close to 60% and 40% respectively, along with significantly improved hygienic conditions and cost savings.

BIO-FUELS

Bio-fuels could significantly reduce Rwanda's dependency on imported petroleum products by replacing fuels (especially transport fuels), with fuel produced from domestically harvested crops. Bio-crops generally require significant areas of land in order to produce any significant level of output. Given the current challenges of land shortages, the trade-off between bio-crops for fuel and food production is likely to be too great to be attractive.

The Institute of Scientific and Technological Research (IRST) drafted a policy in 2008 to promote bio-diesel exploration, production and use in Rwanda. This came following a country-wide study conducted by IRST on bio-diesel production that revealed its viability in Rwanda. NIRDA currently carries out research and piloting activities on biofuels, including running a small dedicated fleet on biodiesel.

PETROLEUM SUBSECTOR

Currently, Rwanda depends entirely on imported fuel products, because its petroleum resources are yet to be commercially proven and developed. Petroleum consumption increased in absolute terms by over 16% between 2000 and 2012, yet the oil import bill grew by more than 700% in the same period. As a share of GDP, oil imports increased from about 2.5% in 2000 to above 5.5% by 2012. The cost of procurement has an important macro-economic impact. At present, oil products account for 25% of import costs and the proportion of export revenues spent on oil products is even higher at around 55%21. Still, this level of growth has been relatively more modest compared to Rwanda's neighbours.

The reduction of imported diesel for electricity production will be more than off-set by the increased need for petroleum products in transportation, particularly aviation and heavy industry.

For example, more transport vehicles on the road and expansion of air traffic at Kigali International airport will contribute to rising demand for petroleum products.

As illustrated in the table below, diesel and petrol are the dominant petroleum product imports, where diesel is being mainly used in the generation of Electricity whilst petroleum products are used in transport.

Table 5 Petroleum products importation (Litres) – 2011/12

Product	Annual consumptions (litres)
Petrol	82,263,817
Diesel	121,937,405
ILLUMINATING KEROSENE	15,222,724
HEAVY FUEL OILS	33,666,910
JET A-1	12,454,649
TOTAL	265,545,505

Source: MINICOM (Downstream Petroleum Policy, 2012)

The petroleum subsector is vital if government is to achieve required levels of growth over the coming 5-years. Due to Rwanda's geographical location, and lack of commercially developed resources, the economy depends entirely on imports to satisfy the country's need for petroleum products such as diesel, petrol, oil, kerosene and natural gas. Currently around 84% of all petroleum imports come to Rwanda from Tanzania, and 16% of all petroleum imports come to Rwanda from Kenya. Automotive gas oil (i.e., diesel fuel used in road vehicles) represents the largest share of these imports, followed by premium gasoline, and kerosene products, which represent less than 5.5% of all total petroleum imports. The figure below illustrates the current demand22, and expectation of demand growth for all petroleum products over the coming years:

The demand for petroleum products is forecast to grow at rates commensurate with GDP growth each year23 between now and 2020, but will not be evenly distributed:

1) Diesel imports will gradually decline, following plans to transition away from diesel to other lower cost, indigenous forms of power generation.

2) Aviation fuel demand is expected to grow at a significantly higher rate, as Rwanda is positioned to be a preferred hub for air transportation in the region.24

UPSTREAM PETROLEUM SUB-SECTOR

* Preliminary Exploration work: The Government of Rwanda signed a Technical Evaluation Agreement to conduct preliminary exploration on Lake Kivu and a management prescription developed outlining best practice for sustainable extraction of Rwanda's petroleum resources if found.

* Development of the Legal and Regulatory Framework: A draft policy and strategy have been developed for the upstream petroleum sector with the intention to *"Promote and accelerate petroleum exploration in Rwanda to achieve commercial discovery of*

petroleum resources". Details for the developments under the upstream side of petroleum subsector are highlighted in detail in the Environment and natural resources (ENRA) Sector strategic plan. An upstream petroleum strategy, policy and gas law were approved by cabinet in 2013. A draft Gas Law should be adopted at the end of 2014, outlining the main requirements and regulatory structures for developing methane gas projects.

* Petroleum sharing agreement on Lake Kivu: The sharing of methane gas resources in Lake Kivu has been spelled out in a MOU between the governments of Rwanda and the DRC; however, this could be upgraded and extended into the form of an International Agreement or Treaty subject to Cabinet approval.

* Upstream petroleum policy issues and recommendations: To mitigate energy insecurity that emanates from excessive energy import dependence in the oil and gas sub-sector, it is clear that Rwanda would have to accelerate exploration of domestic oil and gas resources. The degree to which exploration and potential discovery can be accelerated depends on upstream exploration and development policies, their inherent investor incentives and the expediency of the licensing and regulatory process.

DOWNSTREAM PETROLEUM SUBSECTOR

Regulations: In line with their role to regulate infrastructure within the Petroleum sector, RURA has recently approved regulations relating to the storage and transit of LPG and petrol station facilities.

Downstream petroleum policy developed: In July 2012, a downstream petroleum policy was presented to Cabinet. The purpose of the policy was to lay the policy framework through which Rwanda can *"achieve cost-effective, affordable and high-quality petroleum*

products". The policy was approved and currently a draft strategy is in the process of adoption.

Rwanda has no domestic production of natural gas. The country relies on imported gas especially LPG from other countries. The LPG market in Rwanda is dominated by six importers and marketers including Société Pétrolière-SP (37%), Kobil (34%), Sulfo (15%), Rwanda Oxygène (6%), Merez (5%) and Hashi energy that takes about 3% of the LPG market. All LPG is imported by road tankers of 10-20 metric tons through either Kenya or Tanzania. Retail distribution is done through service stations, independent distributors, and supermarkets in an assortment of cylinder sizes ranging from 3 kg to 35 kg. The country has a storage facility of 186 tons corresponding to a reserve equivalent to 1.7 month's consumption.

LPG consumption has increased exponentially since 2002, as inferred by importation records, rising by 25% annually between 2009 and 2012. All LPG sold on the Rwandan market is imported from Kenya and Tanzania, independently stored in tanks by each importer, and either filled in cylinders for distribution or imported in filled cylinders directly distributed to retailers. Import cargos vary from 1 to 3 times a month per importer. In November 2012, LPG imports amounted to 1,300 metric tons (equivalent to 2,756 m3) and an annual per capita consumption of 0.12 kg per year.25 The evolution of LPG imports over time is highlighted in the chart below.

Figure 5 Progress of LPG imports and other gases between 2001 and 2012

Source: MINICOM (Downstream Petroleum Policy, 2012)

Strategic Reserves: Transported oil and gas imports require domestic storage capacity. Rwanda maintains a 30 million litres storage capacity, with an upgrade plan to 150 million litres by 2017.

Oil companies are required to keep 10,000 cubic meters of stock as well. These are important steps in strengthening domestic petroleum supply stability..

Table 6 Location and storage capacity of existing fuel depots26

Location	Petrol (M3)	Diesel (M3)	Kerosene (M3)	Fuel oil (M3)	Jet fuel (M3)	Total (M3)
Gatsata	7200	5100	1500	1900	0	15700
Kabuye	3000	2100	0	600	0	5700
Bigogwe	3000	2000	0	0	0	5000
Rwabuye	1900	1900	0	0	0	3800
Kanombe	0	0	0	0	1500	1500
Total	15100	11100	1500	2500	1500	31700

Source: RURA

Product quality standardization: One key element of energy security in the region is the degree of petroleum products adulteration and deterioration of quality. RURA is entrusted with such regulatory oversight and inspection. Proper regulation and maintaining statistics on incidence of product adulteration are useful in managing product quality challenges.

Implement energy diversification and domestication strategies to mitigate oil dependence including viable regional bio-fuels. It is therefore recommended that the case of Ethiopia is reviewed: the only mandated bio-fuels program in Eastern Africa. From there it will be possible to consider the long term viability of integrated fuel mix standards and mandates that will open market for bio-fuels in Rwanda.

STRATEGIC FRAMEWORK

The chapter provides an overview of the key measures and instruments that will be deployed to implement the National Energy Policy. Each sub-sector is structured as follows:

(i) The policy objective and HLTOs; (ii) Analysis of the main challenges; (iii) corresponding actions to address those challenges; and (iv) a summary action plan. In order to more effectively mainstream them, cross-cutting themes discussed in the EP and EDPRS-II are integrated into these strategic implementation frameworks.

ELECTRICITY

POLICY OBJECTIVES

The main policy objectives for the electricity sub-sector are to ensure sufficient, reliable, sustainable and more affordable power supply through the following measures:

* Revise and upgrade existing policy, legal, regulatory, institutional, and financial frameworks to support the rapid development of the electricity industry;

* Meet projected demand expected to exceed 400 MW by the end of 2018 with generation of 563 MW, to account for a reserve margin and system losses, by diversifying resources and increasing the share of clean power generation in the total generation mix over time;

* Align investment planning and funding mobilization more closely to a power sector master plan informed by the ESSP, a least-cost power development plan, and electricity sub-sector action plans;

* Enhance regional cooperation and trade in electricity, including investment in transmission network development, to further improve security of supply;

* Streamline IPP processes and fast track project delivery by securing long-term funding for planned electricity projects through a medium-term budget expenditure framework, revising and expanding the existing Renewable Energy Feed-In Tariff regime, developing new information management systems to streamline project development steps and procedures, and building greater capacity in planning, procurement, and negotiating power transactions.

CHALLENGES WITHIN THE ELECTRICITY SUB-SECTOR

Challenge 1: Ensuring financial sustainability of network investments: Rwanda has a relatively high cost of electricity compared to other countries in the region, and at the same time, extremely low average volumes of consumption. The average annual cost of each connected customer is around $50. Currently this would require a consumer to use approximately 130KWh per month to fund her new connection, whilst in reality roughly half of consumers are using less than 20KWh per month. This challenge and the corresponding solutions are discussed further in chapter 2.2 Electricity Access.

Challenge 2: Ensuring financial sustainability of the generation investment: Approximately 80% of the tariff amount goes toward recovering the cost of generating electricity. Of this, the majority of the costs are fixed. If generation capacity and demand are kept aligned, an efficient tariff can be maintained. If demand fails to keep pace with increased generation capacity, then the tariff will increase. Investment decisions taken today, particularly in generation, will have an impact on future prices and competitiveness. Every MW of generation capacity installed must be paid for whether consumed or not. This should inform decision-makers to ensure that investment in generation is in line with demand.

Challenge 3: Insufficient reserve margin to meet power quality standards: Generation cannot run all of the time. At any moment, it is likely that some of our generation capacity will be unavailable, either through a planned outage for maintenance or for other reasons (shortage of fuel, technical error). Thus, there must always be a reserve margin (i.e., a surplus of generation capacity above maximum demand). The reserve margin mitigates or counteracts against any reduction in generation capacity experienced through planned or unplanned outages of generation plants or the loss of network connectivity. Current reserve margins are not adequate to maintain quality of supply standards according to the Grid Code. The exact reserve margin will depend on the level of uncertainty over demand and the nature of generation plan (more reliable plants would require a lower reserve margin).

Challenge 3: Capacity to deliver the electricity infrastructure: Project development, monitoring, and implementation require skilled and experienced managers and efficient coordination. There is strong need to hire and retain enough qualified staff to monitor energy projects and engage in strategic investment negotiations.

Challenge 4: Minimising system losses: A loss in energy between generation and consumption is an inherent feature of electricity networks. Current network distribution losses stand at 23%, which is above average for the region and is a serious issue that requires more attention.27 Whilst these losses cannot be eradicated completely, they can be materially reduced cost-effectively. This challenge is discussed further in chapter 2.3.

Challenge 5: Lack of timely maintenance and servicing of electric power infrastructure: Power plants require regular maintenance to ensure optimum productivity; otherwise, capacity is threatened by regular breakdowns that can impact electricity generation and contribute to technical losses. High losses in electricity distribution (≈23%)

The proposed solutions to the above challenges are described in the following sections.

EWSA Restructuring and Corporatization

The electricity sector has undergone significant changes in the last 12 years. ELECTROGAZ, which had a monopoly over the production and distribution of water and electricity until late 1990s, lost its monopoly power by a law enacted in 1999. After extensive deliberations, ELECROGAZ was placed under a management contract with Lahmayer International in 2003. This ended in 2006, when the company management reverted to the Government. In 2008, ELECTROGAZ was split into the Rwanda Energy Corporation (RECO) and the Rwanda Water and Sewerage Corporation (RWASCO). These were integrated in 2011 within the Energy and Water and Sanitation Authority (EWSA).

EWSA institutional reforms address historical and chronic problems such as lack of focus on planning and investment, low operational performance and transparency, and lack of autonomy over delivery. The strategic thrust of the reform measures is to restructure the company organization by 'corporatizing' its governance structures to inject more autonomy and accountability in management decision-making and to streamline its processes with the support of state-of-the-art modern management information systems. Law n°97/2013 of 30th/12/2014 prescribed the split of the Energy and Water Sanitation Authority (EWSA) in two corporations Rwanda Energy Group Ltd (REG Ltd) and Water and Sanitation Corporation Ltd (WASAC Ltd), focused on service delivery of energy and power and water and sanitation, respectively. Two companies have subsequently been created. The resulting Power and Energy Holding Company is organized in two subsidiaries:

Energy Utility Corporation Limited (EUCL): The EUCL is in charge of day-to-day operations of power generation, transmission, distribution and sales to final customers. Refocusing EUCL on customer service and improving service delivery in line with quality of service parameters lies at the heart of EWSA reform. The EUCL will take charge of planning the transmission and distribution grid in areas already reached by electrification and promoting energy efficiency and demand side management programmes. New management contracts will strengthen incentives for the company to achieve aims such as cost reductions, technical and non-technical loss reductions, and improving customer satisfaction.

Energy Development Corporation Limited (EDCL): The EDCL is responsible for developing both generation and transmission projects, exploiting new energy resources, and executing a least cost power development plant. Its core objective is to facilitate the development and exploitation of domestic energy resources and investments. In pursuing this objective, it will have autonomy in managing its affairs, but will regularly report to MININFRA on progress towards set targets. Specifically, the EDCL will:

* Collaborate with MININFRA in conducting all activities necessary to explore and assess the country's indigenous resource base;

* Collaborate with MININFRA and RDB to reduce the risk profile of energy projects to a level acceptable to the private sector;

* Execute generation and transmission and distribution projects necessary to expand on-grid assets to new areas. These will be handed over to EUCL once commissioned;

* Define and update the overall power system master plan, and a least cost power development plan;

* Negotiate along with MININFRA long-term electricity import agreements with neighbouring countries.

Transition to a Cost Reflective Tariff

The EP aims for realizing a cost-reflective, yet still affordable electricity tariff to be reached through a transition period by 2018/19. The strategy to achieve this involves reducing the cost of generation, reducing losses and promoting more demand-side management28, increasing operational efficiencies through the restructuring of EWSA, and adjusting the tariff structure or methodology.

To ensure the financial sustainability of the EUCL, and to make it an attractive partner for international investors, RURA shall define a clear pathway to a cost reflective tariff structure following the tariff reform conducted in 2013/14. As part of these annual reviews, RURA will assesses the cost structure of the EUCL and set new tariff levels to enable the company to be financially sustainable. The methodology adopts a commonly used "required revenue" approach and takes into account regional benchmarks for utility regulation. Throughout this transitional process, MININFRA and RURA will collaborate with MINECOFIN to agree on incrementally eliminating indiscriminate subsidies to all consumer categories and defining a new "smart subsidies" approach. Under this approach, specific social groups will be protected from any necessary unit price increases, including through systems that target strategic industries and particularly vulnerable social groups.

Some other key features that will be implemented through tariff restructuring are:

* Tariffs will reflect a potential combination of four different categories of charges, but not all of these would be borne by all end-user groups. These are: standing charges, demand charges, energy charges, reactive power charges, and transmission charges. While published, transmission charges are not likely in the short-term to be used by other parties besides REG. With policy and regulatory changes adopted to encourage wheeling through international imports and autonomous generation investment activities, however, this will become more relevant.

* Instead of differentiated tariff structures between households and industry, tariffs will be primarily based on an end-users' voltage requirements (i.e. medium voltage vs. low voltage customers). This is more efficient, as voltage is the main underlying determinant of the economic cost of service provision. While the tariff structure

presents only one category of low voltage customers, covering all residential and small business users, within fiscal year 2014/15 RURA will review this approach and differentiate residential from non-residential users and provide support to low income customers, following an "ability to pay" impact assessment.

* "Metering" charges previously collected monthly to recoup capital investment costs for installing pre-paid meters shall be permanently removed. Instead, "standing fees" will be

applied to all medium-voltage customers in the short-term, and eventually to multiple meters installed in commercially oriented low-voltage customers.

* Replacing the current "time of use" tariff regime, characterized by having set time parameters for differentiated tariffs, with "demand" charges applied on a continuous, non-time bound basis as a function per kW consumed. In this way, the charge reflects total peak load demand (i.e. the level largely depends on the capacity needed to accommodate peak demand and to build and maintain assets to meet this) and has proven in other countries to be more effective. Demand charges would also apply only to medium voltage customers (an almost complete overlap to industries formerly able to benefit from the time-of use regime). RURA shall ensure that customers have the required information to adjust their consumption patterns and that demand charges are clearly and separately indicated in their bills through its regulation of EUCL. This will encourage end-users to implement demand-side management programs to shave peak load. This will have a positive effect on the tariff as it will reduce the generation capacity necessary to cover the peak demand and reduce overall service delivery costs.

Under the proposed new tariff methodology, unit tariffs for industry are lower relative to that for households. To ensure the transition to a cost-reflective tariff does not negatively impact on industry and large-users, strategic industries will be considered for further targeted subsidies, as required and as mutually agreed by MININFRA and MINECOFIN. Reductions in non-technical losses will also contribute to lowering required tariff levels.

Balancing Demand/Supply and Achieving Security of Supply

In order to strike the right balance between increasing access to grid connectivity, ensuring the long term financial sustainability of the utility, maintaining a reliable supply of electricity, and making electricity more affordable, investments in new power generation and transmission infrastructure need to be tightly aligned to projected power demand. Ensuring an efficient balance between demand and supply in the power system is one of the core functions of the REG. Its Planning Units shall be responsible for projecting electricity demand over a 20-year horizon, and updating this figure annually. REG will also focus on managing key risks and uncertainties, including future demand, availability of financial resources, fuel commodity prices, and project development timelines, etc.

Demand can be measured in absolute terms (i.e. the total volume of energy consumed in a given year) as well as on a "peak demand" basis (i.e. the maximum consumption at any

point in time during a given period). Peak demand will dictate how much generation capacity needs to be developed. The shape of the demand curve (as illustrated in the figure) dictates what type of generation should be installed and how much of it will be used.

Figure 6 Peak vs Absolute Demand

In deriving peak demand, the Planning Unit shall consider four main components:

* Residential remand: This is a function of the number of households connected to the grid and their typical level of consumption. As households tend to consume most of their energy at peak times (18:00 – 19:00), residential demand is a key driver of peak demand.

* Industrial and commercial demand: This covers all non-residential demand. Significant contributors will be in the mining, manufacturing and agricultural sectors, along with commercial premises. The coincidence with peak is less than with residential demand.

* Export demand: Rwanda's attractiveness to export power in any significant volume is unlikely in the short-term. On the contrary, Rwanda will most likely increase imports.

* Losses - Reducing power losses from current levels of at around 23% will be prioritized.

In addition to meeting peak demand, there is need for a sufficient reserve margin of power to be available in the system. Following international best practice, the plan is to gradually reach around a 15% reserve margin by 2018. The EUCL as custodians of the Grid Code shall reflect this new guideline into subsequent Grid Code updates. In addition to this policy, the EUCL shall strive for better communication of power outages with an internal tracking system developed to monitor timely responses to outages.

(1) BASELINE DEMAND AND SUPPLY FORECAST

Summing up demand from each of the above four categories, and factoring in the reserve margin, four generation requirement scenarios have been derived and presented in Table 7.

These scenarios include conservative assumptions29 that may tend to overestimate demand.

Table 7 Demand and supply projections under different scenarios

Demand scenarios	On-Grid Electricity Access Target
	48% Target
Likely Demand	Supply: 444 MW Total Demand: 377 MW
Optimistic Demand	Supply: 563 MW Total Demand: 473 MW

Source: REG (2014)

Table 8 Assumptions common to both scenarios to 2018

Demand End-User Category	Scenario Dependant Assumptions to 2018	
	Likely Scenario	Optimistic Scenario
Residential and SMEs	Demand by customers increases 5-fold in 6 years.	Demand by customers increases 5-fold in 6 years.
Commercial and Industrial	50 % of large user projects will materialize	100 % of large user projects will materialize

Source: REG (2014)

The current sub-sector HLTO aims for power capacity to increase from a current level of 160 MW installed to up to 563 MW of electric power installed capacity equivalent by the end of the ESSP period, taking into account an increased reserve margin and imports. It is important to stress that these figures are preliminary, and will be updated once a Power Master Plan and Least Cost Power Development Plan (LCPDP) are finalized (see below). The LCPDP is a key planning tool and input to the Master Plan, wherein a rigorous demand forecast, a "bottom-up" inventory of potential generation and import projects, and planning of future transmission infrastructures are combined. As connecting new generation projects to users will require the expansion of the existing transmission network, the contribution of grid expansion plans to the overall system costs has to be factored in to identify the most cost effective solutions. The output of the LCPDP would be a recommended sequence of supply investments to ensure long term balance at least cost.

The LCPDP will be developed for the first time in 2014, and updated every year thereafter. Existing project development plans and the LCPDP will be effectively integrated into a single National Power Master Plan, which will contribute to an East African Power Pool (EAPP) Master Plan.

The chart below illustrates how the proposed generation investment plan aligns to differing peak demand forecasts. The dotted lines indicate generation requirements under various scenarios, inclusive of reserve margin requirements.

Figure 7 Generation and Load Forecast

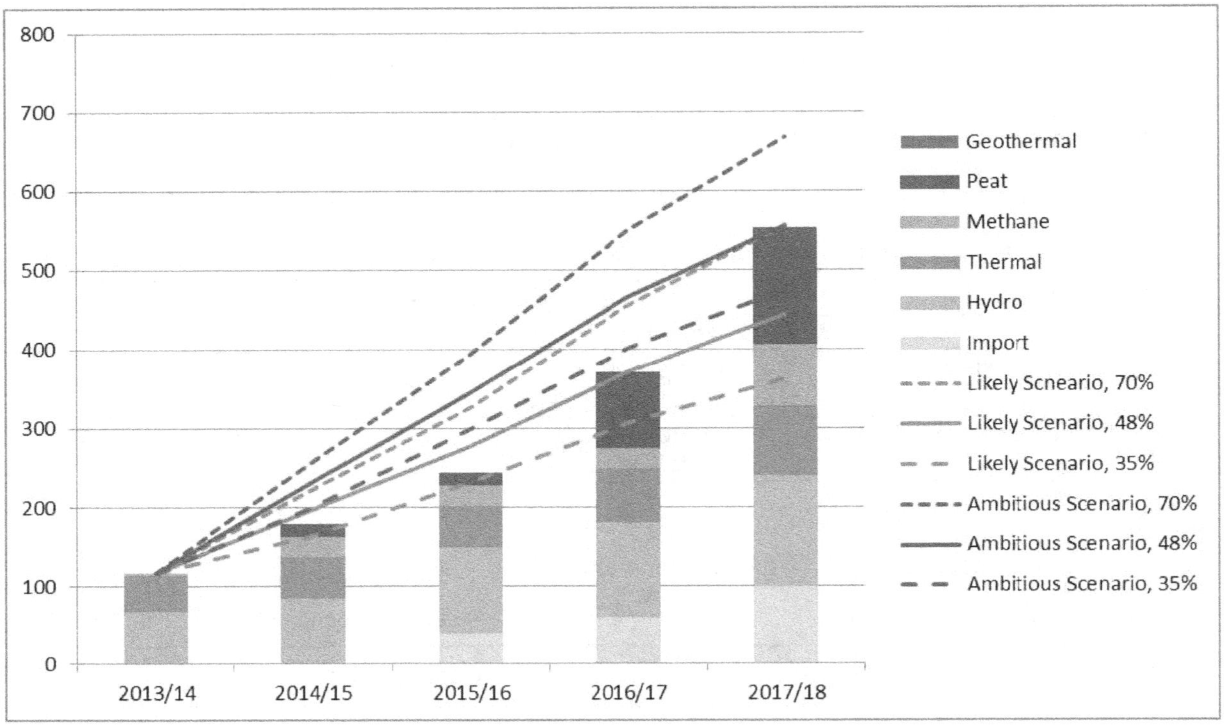

(2) OPTIMIZING THE POWER MIX

According to the EP, the National Power Master Plan and generation road map shall reflect a strategic balancing act to ensure an optimized power mix which reduces the long-run cost of service while simultaneously achieving other policy objectives. Among these include:

* Ensuring security of supply: Adequate supply will be provided to meet expected domestic demand by developing sufficient generation projects and energy import supply agreements. An appropriate reserve margin shall be maintained (dependent upon the make-up of the generation mix, in terms of technology and unit size, and as determined by REG). In line with security of supply considerations, Rwanda will also diversify its energy mix wherever possible, and limit excessive dependency on any one source of power generation (e.g., hydropower). Net imports will be limited to up to a maximum of 20-30% of expected demand.30

* Maximizing exploitation of indigenous energy resources: This will be carried out

where rationale and cost effective, and taking into account the alternative of imports. In the short-term, priority is given to domestic resources such as methane gas resources, geothermal, and peat for base load applications over hydro-based imports and petroleum-based generation sources. The development of other indigenous energy resources such as biomass and solar power will be pursued as long as it will lead to energy sources that are sustainable, affordable, and reliable compared to imports.

* Refocusing and reducing reliance on petroleum-based generation: Utility owned plants based on petroleum-based fuels could be maintained to either cover peak demand or used as reserve to hedge against short term unavailability of generation capacity or imports. This would result in phasing out expensive rental capacity and achieve the policy aim to refocus petroleum-based generation to serve peak load and back-up power demands only by 2020.

* Accelerating regionally-integration: Economically advantageous trading agreements will be concluded with regional power houses (net exporters), in line with technical constraints and energy security guidelines. Regional integration readiness extends far beyond merely building interconnection lines. Among the necessary steps include: negotiating equitable commercial arrangements, establishing guidelines to synchronize systems and harmonize national grid codes, creating new institutional and regulatory arrangements, and developing the capacity necessary to manage the system or power pool. An action plan is under preparation to define all the activities necessary to operationalize energy import opportunities. To ensure Rwanda's interests are advanced internationally, representatives of the Government and the Utility participate regularly in EAC/EAPP technical meetings as active promoters of regional integration.

* Achieving environmental and social considerations, including reductions to the current level of carbon intensity. Only projects that are environmentally and socially sustainable will be implemented. The Master Plan will, as far as possible, integrate the results of a Strategic Environmental Assessment for the Energy Sector and other guidelines. These include macro-level climate risk and sustainability studies, including an assessment of hydropower vulnerability, and future guidelines on power generation ESIAs elaborated by REMA. To advance Rwanda's GHG global contribution to mitigate climate change, the Government targets a 10% reduction in carbon intensity (i. e. the average amount of carbon dioxide produced per unit of electricity generated in the system) by 2018, and a 25% reduction in carbon intensity by 2025.31 A strategy to access

climate finance and incorporate this into planning and budgeting processes will be undertaken32 to further incentivise realization of this HLTO.

Table 9 Carbon intensity targets33

Year	Carbon intensity Reduction Target	Value (tons of CO2/MWh)
Baseline	-	0.504
2018	10%	0.454
2025	25%	0.378

ELECTRICITY GENERATION AND TRANSMISSION ROADMAP

The EDCL will play a key role in pursuing investments in new generation capacity as well as transmission and distribution systems in areas still un-electrified, while at the same time conducting rehabilitation programmes for existing assets and extending transmission and distribution networks. Loss-reduction activities are discussed in chapter 2.3.

The level of investment required in electricity infrastructure is significant. Roughly $3.2 Billion will be required if we are to achieve our target of providing access to electricity (on-grid or off-grid) to 70% of households. Table 10 outlines the full list of projects through which 593 MW can be generated by 2017/18, along with when they could be delivered and at what projected investment cost. Delivery of 563 MW by 2017/18 will cost around $1.6 Billion. If all projects in the current pipeline are successfully implemented at projected scale, then total installed capacity would be closer to 590 MW by 2017/18, a bit higher than required (563 MW). The justification for this margin is to cushion against supply shortfalls due to projects being delayed as a result of technological or financing barriers.

Since the demand profile is uneven, different sources of energy will have a different role in matching demand. Geothermal, hydro and methane based power plants have very low operating costs and can run almost constantly, and thus could provide base-load power. Peat can be operated slightly more flexibly and adjust to meet evening peak demand, whilst solar can only operate during the day. To cover evening peak demand only, it will be more economical to utilize power plants running on HFO or diesel. As these will operate a few hours a day, they are characterized by low investment and high operating costs.

Table 10 Generation roadmap to achieve required supply

Table 11 Projected capital costs

The following are key points to note from the above analysis:

* Even if in the worst-case scenario geothermal power cannot be generated by 2017/18 on commercial terms, Rwanda will be able to meet its most optimistic power demand requirements.

* The large amount of power generation coming online in 2017/18, principally from peat, will allow Rwanda to meet its generation requirements. Of more concern is the short term: 2015/16. For this reason, more emphasis on developing flexible generation such as small hydro, and HFO peaking plants is warranted.

* Based on the existing project pipeline, load-shedding would be the norm if a 70% on-gird connection target was pursued as shown in Figure 7.

(I) FEASIBILITY OF ENERGY RESOURCES

Most proposed generation projects rely on indigenous resources that, in most cases, are yet to be fully proven. Proving these resources will require time and finance (roughly $120m), and attempts to shortcut this step are likely to bear negative economic consequences. Government intends to use its limited resources wisely to demonstrate Rwanda's energy resource potential by undertaking feasibility activities that the private sector is unlikely to bear to reduce perceived investment risks.

Table 12 Status on feasibility and exploration activities of various energy resources

Hydro A large number of local and regional hydro projects have already been identified; however, further funding is required to:

i. complete feasibility work on large regional projects ;

ii. refine the feasibility of domestic hydro resources and undertake a hydropower master plan to be completed in 2015/2016.

Peat REG is procuring a detailed resource assessment of all bogs and creating a national resource database. It will prove the feasibility and drain peat bogs in preparation for private investment. This will allow REG to either develop its own plant or to attract a private investment once the risk associated with bog development is removed.

A peat energy strategy and action plan will be developed by MININFRA, including economic and social-environmental impacts, to ascertain the optimal use of different peat applications. For example it will ascertain the optimal use of peat across a range of applications: power generation, direct industrial heat, steam applications and domestic charcoal substitute. Environmental and social impacts will be studied and appropriate risk mitigation and private sector participation guidelines developed. RSB and REMA to develop technology guidelines.

Government proposes to fund the following:

-Peat development capability

-Detailed feasibility studies for 4 bogs:

-Site drainage in advance of peat harvesting

Geothermal Government will continue to carry out exploration to de-risk the resource, continue developing the necessary institutional arrangements to operationalize a Geothermal Development Program to coordinate activities, and upgrade the existing legal and regulatory framework as required. Geo-scientific surface studies in Gisenyi and Bugarama will continue. Further uses of geothermal energy may be considered to support economic growth actions (ex: industrial heating, drying).

Methane A wide ranging pre-feasibility study will be conducted to identify the range of opportunities available for investors, assessing projects of differing sizes and based on different technology types. Action plan will analyse investor options including different sizes, technologies and possibly splitting the extraction and power generation components for IPP purposes. Lastly, prioritization will be given to technologies which maximise extraction sustainably, subject to value for money.

RSB will support the process by developing relevant technology standards. REMA shall also play a role in developing and/or revising relevant environmental guidelines. REMA, RURA, and NICA, will be responsible to enforce compliance as required by their respective mandates. Investment procedures relevant to the energy sector will be reviewed. This includes the investment code and modalities of engagement.

(II) REFIT

The existing REFIT tariff schedule, with regard to the hydropower, will be adjusted subject to fixed price per output, to ensure only economically viable projects are procured.34 The revised REFIT will be reviewed after a period of three years to see the impact on the utility. Furthermore the review will determine whether the REFIT tariff schedule should remain the same or be revised downwards. In order to reduce risks in projects covered by REFIT mechanism, a standardized PPA approved by MININFRA, RURA, and the Utility shall be included in the overall regulation. Standardized PPAs provide a stable environment for private sector participants intending to invest in those technologies, so that the rules and the price for the off-take of electricity are known in advance and committed to. Competitive processes such as REFIT shall be followed exclusively to identify private sector partners for hydropower projects.

In addition to hydropower, bio-energy and potentially grid-connected solar shall also be considered under REFIT as they are more sustainable and less technologically complex than large-scale methane-to-power projects and geothermal projects. Wind power and peat-to-power projects shall not be included, as they are not fit for purpose to the objectives of the policy instrument.35 Inclusion under REFIT will create a clear incentive for private investors to conduct feasibility studies where preliminary analysis show potential viability.

A "catch-all" bio-energy category shall be included in the REFIT under an "avoided cost approach" rather than a fixed tariff linked to output. Inclusion under REFIT will create a clear incentive for private investors to conduct feasibility studies where preliminary analysis show potential viability. The tariff for these projects would be set equivalent to the long-run marginal cost of REG's current power output as determined before the beginning of each fiscal year in conjunction with annual tariff reviews conducted by RURA. This would effectively place a price cap on new capacity additions.36

(III) AUTONOMOUS GENERATION

Mining and mineral processing is an example of an industry rapidly expanding in Rwanda37 and requires increased energy. However, connecting operations to the grid can be very expensive as mining locations are often relatively remote. As well as this, given the challenges in developing generation projects to keep up with the demand growth, the government will encourage the development of dedicated power plants through simplified regulations and approaches for autonomous generation and wheeling through the grid system. Ambiguity in the law for this type of type of installations will be removed, and the scope of simplified licensing regulations targeting rural electrification activities will be made clear and extended to autonomous generation. In parallel to improving the legal environment, research will be undertaken to investigate the optimal systems integration of solar energy and solar-diesel hybrid energy. The impact of a major scale-up in autonomous generation activities and their integration into the grid will need to be studied further. As building-integrated photovoltaic power may become an important contribution to the energy portfolio in the next years, it will be necessary before undertaking any action to promote this type of solution to run some pilot projects to test the costs, benefits, and systems impact of introducing net metering arrangements.

TRANSMISSION INVESTMENT

Significant reinforcements will be needed to the existing transmission system in order to accommodate the increased generation and demand over the coming years. These extension, rehabilitation and reinforcement projects are outlined in Table 13.

Table 13 Transmission projects

DEVELOPMENTS IN REGIONAL TRADE

The long-term vision is for Rwanda to become an active electricity trading partner and potential exporter of electricity to the regional grid network. In the short term, a push for greater regional economic integration and access to cheaper supplies of power will involve increased imports. These will be secured from sources like large hydro plants in the Lower Kafue Gorge of Zambia (to be imported via Tanzania), and hydro plants in Ethiopia (to be imported via Kenya and Uganda). The cost of power generation in Ethiopia for current and projected projects is below $0.09/KWh, for example, offering a possibility of Rwanda's importing relatively inexpensive power. However, at the same time this must be balanced with security of supply, and so initially a limit of 20% of the energy mix coming from imports has been set, based on consultations and technical considerations.

The Eastern Africa Power Pool (EAPP) was formally established in February 2005. There are currently 9 members including Rwanda, Kenya, Uganda, Tanzania, Burundi and the DRC. EAPP fosters coordinated power development by promoting synergies among the region's electricity utilities and therefore optimizing investments and resource allocation. Presently, EAPP is in the process of building its technical and regulatory capacity. A number of development partners are providing support in the design of the power system and control centre, harmonization of standards, preparation of grid codes and market rules.

Rwanda is a member of the Nile Basin Initiative (NBI) and the EAPP. However, apart from using its share of regional hydro plants – SNEL and SINELAC (Rusizi I and Rusizi II), Rwanda is not connected to any regional transmission network; however, it is pursuing cross-border interconnections with Uganda and Kenya to enable imports from Uganda and Kenya (by 2016) and from Ethiopia (beginning of 2018) in the context of the Nile Equatorial Lakes Subsidiary Action Plan (NELSAP).

International experience has shown that the establishment of wholesale trading arrangements to facilitate full cross-border trade can take a considerable amount of time. The countries also need to develop the necessary technical standards, operational procedures, commercial agreements (both PPA and wheeling agreements), tariffs, regulatory environment and human capacity to manage the interconnected systems. It is estimated that the wheeling and PPA agreements for imports from Kenya and Uganda will be ready by the end of 2015. An action plan is also currently being developed, detailing all the necessary activities to enable a successful power connection to Ethiopia in time when the transmission infrastructure is completed. Rwanda is monitoring the progress of regional activities to capture the synergies with other on-going market integration activities. A revised Rwanda power tariff is expected to contain a unique transmission-related component to help facilitate regional trade. Furthermore, the role and economic impact of various import sources will be assessed in the context of the LCPDP.

In the short to medium term, trade is likely to take place utility-to-utility. Rwanda, Kenya and Uganda signed a MoU to foster coordination in infrastructure development and trade arrangements. Rwanda and Ethiopia also signed another MoU for the supply of power from Ethiopia to Rwanda. Other bilateral arrangements with DRC, Burundi and Tanzania in expanding existing shared power supplies and pursuing bilateral energy development opportunities and joint investments are also under discussion. For the time being net imports will be restricted to 30% of expected demand for security of supply reasons.

The capacity available for import will increase dramatically, from 30 MW at the end of 2015, to about 100 MW at the end of 2017/18. Limitations on import growth are however driven by grid bottlenecks on the Rwandan and Ugandan side and technical power quality and security of supply considerations (i.e., to avoid black-outs in case of faults in other countries). A large number of ongoing projects are underway to strengthen grid interconnectivities and to connect

Rwanda to its East African partners so as to facilitate energy trade are underway. There are also a number of other power interconnection projects between EAPP countries at different stages of implementation. Key transmission projects being developed are:

Table 14 Key regional transmission line projects

Transmission Line Project	Voltage Type	Construction Status	Expected Completion Date
Gilgel Gibe III (Ethiopia) - Suswa (Kenya)	High Voltage Direct Current	Financing completed	December 2017
Lessos (Kenya) – Tororo (Uganda)	400 kV	Under construction	December 2016
Masaka – Mbarara (Uganda)	designed for 400 kV but to be initially operated at 220 kV	Under discussion	December 2016
Mbarara – Mirama	220 kV double circuit	Under construction	April 2015
Mirama – Shango	220 kV double circuit	Under construction	June 2015

ELECTRICITY SUB-SECTOR IMPLEMENTATION PLAN

Table 15 Electricity Sub-sector Implementation Plan

Strategic Action	2013/14	2014/15	2015/16	2016/17	2017/18	Responsible Institution
Demand/ Supply Balance	Annual review.	Dedicated planning unit established; demand survey and forecast undertaken	-Integrate all studies and plans into a National Power Master Plan. -Annual reviews undertaken. -Align with EAPP Master Plan	REG, MININFRA		
Feasibility Studies	Further geothermal studies	Develop Peat strategy action plan	Additional studies as and when required e.g. regional hydro, wide ranging	REG		

			Methane study			
LCPDP	Review Interim Report	Prepare and implement LCPDP	Annual update of LCPDP as part of overall planning exercise	REG		
Reduce carbon intensity	Annual Grid Emission Calculation exercise and update and extend forecasts	REMA with MININFRA				
Timely maintenance and servicing		Full plan of power plant maintenance and grid network developed		EUCL		
Cost-reflective tariff	-'Ability to pay' assessment New methodology calculated	Annual reviews as with previous years. Targeted industries approved	RURA, MININFRA, EUCL, MINECOFIN			
Key Generation Activities	-Develop peat strategy and action plan and implement -Detailed peat resource assessment complete -Methane Action Plan to be undertaken in 2015/16		MININFRA, REG			
Regional Integration	Development of Action Plan to operationalize import opportunities	Implementation of Action Plan	MININFRA			
REFIT	Finalize REFIT revision	Draft standardized PPAs for REFIT	Expand REFIT coverage of clean energy	RURA with MININFRA		

			resources			
Autonomous Generation		Research on optimal system integration and simplified regulation developed. Conduct study on systems impact.	Pilot projects to test impact of net metering	MININFRA		

ELECTRICITY ACCESS

OBJECTIVES

The EP commits the sector to: prioritize of end-users for electricity connections; achieve universal access to electricity in all schools and health clinics by 2018; increase rural energy access through piloting innovative partnerships; introduce greater competition and flexibility in off-grid service provision;; and improve service delivery through institutional reforms.

Over the EDPRS II period, the strategy targets at least 70% of households to have access to electricity. This would be reached from a combination of both on-grid and off-grid solutions:

On-grid access to 48% of households &

Off-grid access to 22% of households by 2018

This represents a big incremental leap from the baseline. As of June 2014, only 20% of Rwandan households were estimated to have access to electricity. Rwanda is also participating in a regional program sponsored by the Global Sustainable Electricity Partnership (GSEP), Eskom, and Duke Energy to develop an electrification roadmap to ensure 500 million people at global level have access to energy by 2025.

Given limited government resources, the targeting of end-users, or consumer groups, for electricity access has also been reprioritized under the EP: large and productive end-users shall be the top priority, followed by schools and hospitals, small and medium enterprises (SMEs) and lastly households. Large and productive energy end-users, and in particular, industries, are key drivers of economic growth in providing employment, marketable goods and services. Many industries require reliable and consistent grid electricity in order to produce efficiently so as to be profitable and regionally competitive. For example, flour millers on average loose three days of production a month due to unreliable electricity.38 Such losses in productivity can be addressed through reliable grid electricity. Therefore:

Up to 230MW of power supply to be provided for productive end-users

This is a current estimate of what is needed by 2018 for productive end-users in industry, manufacturing, mining, industry, coffee and tea producers, and for special economic zones and irrigation programs.39 To meet this, direct access to electricity will be provided to these end-users through dedicated connections and by supplying reliable power to the grid.40

In addition to large and productive users:

100% of schools and hospitals will be provided with access to electricity by 2018 through a mixture of off-grid and on-grid solutions

In total roughly $1.1 billion of financing is estimated to be required to the end of the EDPRS-II period to meet the targets set. There is an urgent need to build both institutional and individual capacities to effectively deliver on access targets.41 This will be addressed in both the SE4ALL Country Action Plan and the Energy Sector Capacity Building strategy.

CHALLENGES IN RURAL/ELECTRICITY ACCESS SUB-SECTOR

Challenge 1: Ensuring the financial sustainability of network investments

The average annual cost of each connected consumer is around $50 (around $45 in financing the loan required for the connection and $5 for operations and maintenance). Under the current tariff structure, a consumer would need to use approximately 130KWh per month in order to fund the cost of their own connection, and despite annual customer growth of 30-40% in recent years, peak electricity demand and sales grew by only 5% in 2012/13. The table below illustrates the current consumption patterns across all of REG's consumers. Currently around half of consumers are using less than 20KWh per month. Thus, even if average household consumption per connection remained at current levels, this would pose a significant challenge to the financial sustainability of network investments, as more and more households who are unable to afford access get connected.

Table 16 Current Electricity consumption patterns

Consumption per month (KWh)	
0 to 5	18.4%
6 to 20	31.2%
21 to 50	26.1%
51 to 150	17.3%
151 and greater	7.0%

Source: EWSA (2013)

Challenge 2: Poor coordination between power distribution and generation plans.

Due to the different determining factors underlying the two plans, there has been poor coordination in the past. Though difficult to integrate, in order to efficiently meet the sub-sector access targets, there is an urgent need to harmonize the distribution planning with changing generation plans.

Challenge 3: Sustainability of off-grid solutions

Preventive maintenance and proper technical support is fundamental to the sustainability of off-grid electrification projects, such as those involving solar PV. In the past, this has not been adequate, even though minimal maintenance is required for off-grid solar systems to maintain on-going functionality. As a result, many projects have had to be rehabilitated at a high cost. There is a need to establish suitable maintenance and support procedures for all projects, incorporating sustainability into the design of programs and strategy.

Challenge 4: Terrain and Settlement Patterns

A significant driver of the cost of any electrification programme is the density of the properties that are to be connected: the more scattered the settlements, the higher the cost of extending the network. Rwanda also has an extremely unique terrain to manoeuvre in terms of extending the power grid. Challenges associated with engineering and

construction show an increasing marginal cost, as rates of existing electrification access rise. As a result, energy access targets may become progressively harder to achieve within a certain budget.

Challenge 5: Access to finance

Achieving a large scale-up in electricity access hinges upon greater household access to finance. Due to their low purchasing power, consumer finance and credit mechanisms are pivotal to assist rural households to switch to solar lighting over kerosene, or to pay off new electricity connections over time. For example, even under the EARP, which is largely financed by international donors, households are still required to put up 10% of the cost of getting electricity. While microfinance and mobile money operators are growing significantly, government and SACCOs may also need to play a strong role to ensure that appropriate financing mechanisms are in place in tandem with new access programs and strategies. Moreover, the private market for off-grid electricity services and technological solutions is still in its infancy. In order to grow, financial inclusion programs targeting these products and services need to be expanded to cover financial organs in rural areas.

SOLUTIONS

The ESSP adopts a several strategies to address the above mentioned challenges, including:

* Realizing better coordination and integrated planning over investments and implementation strategies for energy access and electrification, and informing planning through an LCPDP;

* Reprioritizing target groups for on-grid electrification through a clear policy and planning mechanisms, with productive end-users being of first priority to offset the short-term negative financial impacts to EUCL from new connections;

* Developing and mandating the publishing of a transparent (on-grid) National Electrification Plan by REG valid for 3-years to incentivise industrial and private investment in off-grid solutions;

* Developing an off-grid strategy and action plan in conjunction with an SE4ALL Country Action Plan;

* Placing the private sector and PPPs at the core of implementation and procurement approaches for off-grid access strategies;

* Promoting and monitoring urban densification as a matter of national policy. This falls under MININFRA's direct control but can also be promoted by local communities themselves in its outreach and communication strategies;

* Developing new partnerships between MININFRA, the REG, and local financial institutions to establish new lending products that give customers greater access to credit for grid connections whilst reducing financial risk to the utility.

ELECTRIFICATION STRATEGY & THE ELECTRICITY ACCESS ROLLOUT PROGRAM (EARP)

The first phase of the EARP (2009-2012) aimed at increasing grid connections from a baseline of 6% to 16% of households. It exceeded this target by 1%. The second phase of EARP began in 2012/13 and will finish by the end of 2017/18, with the aim of reaching the consumer groups prioritized above. Government is determined to build on the success of the first phase and where appropriate apply lessons that can help deliver on the 70% electricity access target over the coming 4-years.

The cost per on-grid new connection is high, at roughly $1000; however, donor support has been leveraged and to an extent the socio-economic aspects justify the cost. At the same time it is currently not economical to connect all of these households to the grid irrespective of the location and level of income. For households located far away from the grid network and/or without capacity to afford the grid connection fee, it is more economical to access electricity through off-grid energy solutions or isolated mini-grids. Therefore, the EARP on-grid electrification plan will focus on connecting households, administration offices, schools and hospitals, taking into consideration resettlement plans and other factors.

Currently, customers wishing to be connected pay an amount towards the capital cost of the connection that is dependent on their income. Those well off pay 100%, or 56,000 RWF, while middle income earners pay 50%, and the poor pay a 20% deposit which is paid over 12 months and amounts to 10% of the total costs. The remaining cost is publicly funded through a combination of grants by development partners (80%) and government contributions and loans (10%), ultimately repaid by REG from its operational revenues.

Public Services: As of June 2014, roughly 63% of health facilities, 41% of primary schools, 66% of secondary schools and 64% of administration centres had access to electricity. This was met through a mixture of on-grid connections and off-grid distributions based on basic analysis. EARP will examine the feasibility of reaching the remaining institutions through on or off-grid solutions, whichever is more economical. EARP will also explore the costs and benefits of extending to other public services; ensuring value-for-money.

On-grid Households: Through photographic imaging, EARP has developed a detailed view of household locations, and a strategic perspective on where the network could be extended. Based on the latest household survey data, it will be necessary to connect 669,000 additional households between July 2014 and the end of 2017/18 to reach a target of 48% household on-grid connections. This presents a considerable technical and financial challenge. EARP will continue to continue to bulk buy equipment, encourage local and regional companies to participate, and use Engineering, Procurement and Construction (EPC) contractors for a large share of delivery responsibilities. The EARP program consists of two categories of electricity connection:

* Direct connections: Roughly 362,000 *direct connections* would be needed to reach the 48% target over the entire EARP II program.

* Relocation and Fill-ins: Based on an assessment of relocation plans, around 396,000 *additional fill-in connections are anticipated.* Once the network has been extended to an area, and 75% of households are assumed to be within immediate reach of the network, a significant number of additional network connection requests are anticipated to come from this category.42 Given that the network will already exist, the cost of these connections will likely be less than for the direct connections.43 Achieving this target, however, will depend to a significant degree on the timely availability of all necessary funds to cover the investments, and on the success of urbanisation policies.

Prioritization of end-user connections: The on-grid electrification plan was revised in April 2014 to prioritize productive users, among other changes. This means that areas with higher concentrations of productive users will be connected first. Furthermore, productive user fill-in connections have been prioritized according to their distance from the grid. . The revision included revised industrial demand estimations from MININCOM, which is mandated to work with MININFRA to provide information. The development of industrial parks, SEZs, and development of secondary cities have all been included in plans. The plan will also take into account resettlement policies which MININFRA is monitoring.44 EARP will develop guidelines for the allocation of resources to different end-users to make prioritization clearer. These will balance the need for industrial connections that provide economic growth and increase sustainability of the utility, and household connections that have strong social and energy poverty alleviation considerations. Chapter 3.3 Risk Analysis contains detailed discussion on how the monitoring and promotion of urban resettlement is being dealt with by MININFRA. A summary of the EARP household and industrial connection policy is given in Annex 3.

Off-grid Households: Government intends to dramatically scale up rural electricity access to households through off-grid solutions. Households not expected to be covered under the National Electrification Plan in the medium term and with low ability to afford connection fees will be facilitated with access to off-grid solutions. These include stand-alone solar PV systems, solar lamp kits, biogas digesters and micro-grids powered by small hydro, efficient diesel or solar-wind, and solar-diesel hybrid systems. These solutions will significantly reduce capital costs and the need for government subsidisation. This will also increase the financial sustainability of the EUCL. To facilitate these systems, a sound enabling environment for off-grid energy services is required such as solar home systems and lamps or solar mini-grids. Financial mechanisms will also be developed for use in the short-term to

help the off-grid market develop and become sustainable. These will fall under the Renewable Energy Development Fund (REDF), discussed in more detail in Chapter 2.6. To reach the off-grid household access target of 22%, MININFRA will develop a detailed off-grid strategy. Given that this area has not been measured before, clear monitoring frameworks will need to be developed as part of the strategy.

SOLUTIONS BEYOND CURRENT EARP ACTIVITIES

Off-grid strategy: A Rural Electrification Strategy is currently being developed in collaboration with MININFRA, including separate on-grid and off-grid action plans, as per the EARP Mid-Term Review recommendations. In parallel, several *ad hoc* activities are underway, and will continue to be rolled out to pilot areas that are clearly off-grid. In tandem, innovative PPPs will be developed to test and scale-up off-grid pilots.

The strategy shall prioritize private sector engagement to deliver off-grid solutions, and the most suitable role of Government. The strategy will include market assessments and sharing of information on energy use patterns and market demand with investors, issuing new technology standards to build market confidence, and testing innovative solutions and business models on a pilot basis that can be scaled-up if successful.

Increase competition and flexibility in off-grid provision through measures to simplify licensing: Since the private sector will be expected to deliver the majority of off-grid energy services to end-consumers, in parallel to the development of an off-grid strategy, a conducive and legal and regulatory environment must be developed to support the private sector and avoid direct subsidisation as much as possible. MININFRA will collaborate with RURA to sensibly simplify the existing licensing framework to facilitate off-grid electricity provision through a clearer, more enabling regulatory environment. These efforts are thrust at stimulating more nimble, small-scale power distributors (SPDs). Lessons shall be drawn from pilot projects already under way in Rwanda, and in other similar countries. The advantages and disadvantages of eventual inclusion of SPDs under REFIT frameworks as the grid expands shall be further and more carefully examined.

Beyond simplified licensing, EARP will publish electrification plans in the public domain which will be valid for a period of 3 years. This will make it clearer to both consumers and private developers where potential for off-grid activities exists and incentivise investment in these areas. Two results-based-finance programs are starting in September 2014 and are targeting to reach 18,750 people with the mini-grid program, and the distribution of 330,000 solar lighting systems with the second program.

Pilot innovative partnerships to increase rural access: MININFRA shall develop innovative PPPs to better understand the costs and benefits of grid electricity connections and the most cost effective means to scale up rural access.45 Rigorous evaluation will be a vital part of determining what works. PPPs shall offer rural end-users turnkey solutions that can be delivered by the private sector and generate employment and skills development opportunity for youth in rural areas. Operations and maintenance costs shall be factored into anticipated or permitted investment returns through PPPs, while being the primary responsibility of the operators. Government shall support such programs through in-kind assistance among other means. Capitalising support from FONERWA and other climate and renewable energy financing will be a key contributor to success. Such pilots will be accompanied by awareness campaigns in collaboration with CSOs and Energy Associations, led by MINALOC, to support off-grid market development.

Fiscal reform for peri-urban and urban households to reduce consumption of kerosene and increase alternative solar technology: MININFRA will carry out a study in collaboration with MINECOFIN to assess the impacts of potentially phasing out the exemption from excise duty of kerosene. Tax reform and other demand-pull strategies to increase the relative attractiveness of renewable off-grid technologies compared to traditional biomass or petroleum-based fuels could have a strong complementary impact to other measures. They could strongly incentivize fuel switching or leap frogging directly from traditional biomass energy to solar lighting solutions.

Improve and develop institutions to increase coordination, effectiveness and accountability: In the short-term, all major off-grid programs implemented by the REG shall be consolidated under the EARP. Off-grid electrification strategies will be harmonised with existing EARP Phase II plans. This will clearly identify and earmark which areas are most suitable to be developed for off-grid

Cross-border electrification: Rural villages shall be identified that are located close to Rwanda's borders where services could potentially be provided more cost effectively from other distributors, such as the Uganda Electricity Distribution Company. Following the results of a study carried out by RURA, the regulatory framework for allowing low-voltage cross-border electrification among neighbouring utilities could be developed for this kind of arrangement, subject to there being adequate scope and clear economic benefits.

Various technology solutions will be examined in the Action Plan. Their deployment will be context-specific but could include:

Solar Installations: Small solar PV kits are available for an initial cost of between $50-200, depending on their capacity factors and the typical end-uses they are required to power, with no need to pay further energy costs.

Off-grid hydro projects: Past experience has shown that off-grid hydro projects could represent a cost-effective solution, and represent good value for money when used to provide power to mini-grids at $5200/kW. However, other experiences have shown that irregular plant maintenance incentives and raising capital can be a strong challenge. Micro hydro projects will be encouraged through micro-grids where economically feasible and representing the least-cost option. This will be done through:

* Establishing enabling regulatory frameworks and licensing
* Education of people on off-grid energy solutions
* Provide training and financial incentives to rural communities to operate micro hydro, which is already underway.

Hybrid systems: Solar-diesel hybrid systems may be appropriate in areas that have inconsistent solar radiation or where an anchor end-user such as a mobile phone operating tower needs reliable power. Similarly, solar-wind hybrid systems could be viable in areas with high commercial viability for wind power in order to optimize availability factors. The feasibility of such systems will be analyzed and piloted to access their commercial viability in comparison to mini-grids operating on 100% thermal or renewable energy sources. Beyond hybrid systems efficient diesel generators for independent generation are common in African countries, and therefore their affordability will need to be tested.

Biogas: Micro-scale biogas power plants are possible on a stand-alone and mini-grid basis. Small-scale biogas digester can be used for lighting as well as for cooking or heating. Biogas is further elaborated in chapter 2.4.

ELECTRICITY ACCESS SUB-SECTOR IMPLEMENTATION PLAN

Table 17 Electricity Access Sub-sector Implementation Plan

Strategic Action	2013/14	2014/15	2015/16	2016/17	2017/18	Responsible Institution
On and off-grid harmonization		-Update of on-grid electrification plan -Publish 3 year grid development plan	Harmonization of off-grid plans with EARP Phase II	Publish 3-year plan	REG, eSWAP Secretariat	
Off-grid strategy	Concept proposed	Development and approval of strategy	Implementation and develop national off-grid database	MININFRA		
Regulatory Environment		Develop legal and regulatory environment alongside and informed by the off-grid	RURA, MININFRA			

		strategy				
Productive User prioritization	Propose concept	Electrification Plan developed to reflect	Close monitoring and annual reviews of productive user prioritization	EARP, MINICOM		
Public services connections	Implementation of school and hospital electricity access projects	Analysis of EARP expansion	Development of rigorous feasibility studies for schools and hospitals	REG with MININFRA		
Innovative PPPs for off-grid		Develop PPP pilot concept	Undertake pilot PPP projects. Apply for climate finance, carry out awareness campaigns and evaluate projects	MININFRA		
Small-scale off-grid distributors	Revision of simplified licensing framework	-Analyse eventual inclusion under REFIT with grid expansion -Hybrid system comparative analysis	RURA with MININFRA			
Financial partnerships	Collaboration with local financial institutions to set-up support	Implementation on support via local financial institutions	MININFRA, REG			

ENERGY EFFICIENCY AND DEMAND-SIDE MANAGEMENT

Energy efficiency (EE), energy conservation, and demand-side management (DSM) activities46 are of strong importance in the Rwanda context because the country's natural resources are limited; the population is growing rapidly, a Green Economy vision is in place, and there is a pronounced peak demand load that requires extra power reserve margin and is a key driver for additional generation capacity. It is cheaper to use energy intelligently and efficiently than to unnecessarily expand energy production. Effective DSM measures will have an immediately positive impact on reducing supply requirements and contribute to reducing the long-run cost of power. Therefore, the EP adopts the following objectives:

* Adopt new laws, regulations and codes that mandate energy efficiency measures in public institutions, households, and commercial businesses;

* Restructure the electricity tariff methodology to incentivize efficiency;

* Establish a demand-side management program within REG;

* Encourage and incentivize energy audits among commercial and industrial end-users;

* Promote and remove barriers to implementing priority efficient lighting initiatives;

* Develop and adopt an EAC-wide energy standards and labelling scheme for common household appliances;

* Institutionalize "green" public procurement guidelines and strategies focused on equipment with a high energy footprint.

To meet the policy objectives, an overarching energy efficiency HLTO47 has been set under the ESSP, by which various programs and actions can be commonly measured.

Increase energy efficiency by 10% through Demand-Side measures & an

additional 8% through grid-loss reduction (from a 2013 baseline) by 2018

CHALLENGES TO ENERGY EFFICIENCY AND DEMAND-SIDE MANAGEMENT

Challenge 1: Limited institutional experience

While of growing importance, EE/DSM is a newer policy priority area. As such, no specific strategy yet exists to guide the development and implementation of national-level activities in the sub-sector. Apart from a large-scale CFL replacement program implemented by the utility, only a few *ad hoc* initiatives that squarely address energy efficiency have ever been undertaken in Rwanda. Thus, there is a strong need to build more institutional capacity and technical skills in a sustainable manner in this area. Ambiguous institutional mandates and the lack of a strong leadership role in implementing EE/DSM activities has also led to poor information sharing, slow progress on regulatory development, and ineffective or inadequately enforced codes and standards.

Challenge 2: High degree of system losses

Energy losses that occur between generation and consumption cannot be totally eradicated and are an inherent feature of any electricity networks. Through better network planning and maintenance, however, they can be reduced. The majority of Rwanda's system losses occurs through heat losses in the distribution network.

Challenge 3: Barriers to uptake including high up-front cost

Whilst the high cost of electricity can make returns on EE measures appealing, and good financial savings for customers can be generated, inability to cover up-front investment costs to implement them is a major barrier. Even if the potential pay-back period is not especially long, disposable income in Rwanda is very low. High up-front costs similarly pose a major barrier to clean technology diffusion, even though for many households, despite the fact that satisfaction among early adopters is high. Currently there are few dedicated financial mechanisms to support end-users with the up-front cost of implementing efficiency measures. Another key barrier is often lack of consumer awareness or education to make energy-wise choices. Finally, EE/DSM initiatives are often stymied by split incentives. Examples of this include: difficulties getting household tenants to switch to solar water heaters, because they rent, and the systems are not very portable.

SOLUTIONS TO ENERGY EFFICIENCY AND DEMAND-SIDE MANAGEMENT

NEW LAWS, REGULATIONS AND CODES

MININFRA will develop an Energy Efficiency Strategy48 and Law to serve as underlying implementation framework to support a series of new regulations by RURA, RHA, and other agencies that can mandate energy efficiency measures in public institutions, households, and commercial businesses. MININFRA will be responsible for integrating the promotion of energy smart building technologies into monitoring and implementation of new government asset management policy. Together with RHA, it is also responsible for introducing energy-smart and energy-efficient technologies and practices into Rwandan building codes. RURA is already developing a solar water heater regulation. Considering building codes specifically: EE measures will be implemented in the form of improved building design and use of building materials that increase EE over the entire lifetime of facilities help to reduce lighting, mechanical ventilation and air conditioning energy consumption. Mandatory installation of solar water heaters for all large water consumers (e.g., hotels, integrated developments) will take effect, in parallel to extending subsidy to end-users to incentivize switching. In addition, a training program on how to comply with the new EE building code should be established for architects, engineers and builders. Fostering green building through climate oriented urban planning principles and green architecture will have a strong long-term impact on reducing the need for electricity, and to reach this orientation of house and settlement should follow urban planning. Pilot efforts to promote energy smart building codes, particularly for green field construction projects, are being promoted in the six secondary cities of Huye, Nyagatare, Rusizi, Musanze, Rubavu and Muhanga, in conjunction with the National Urbanization and Rural Settlement Sector Strategy.

GRID LOSS REDUCTION

A grid system loss reduction plan was developed in 2013, encompassing priority proposals and measures identified through an earlier study.49 An investment of $60m over 3 years will result in over $180m of potential energy savings. This will reduce losses from 23% to 15%, capacity savings equivalent to constructing a 15MW power plant. The proposed measures will need to be carefully analysed and prioritized in order to generate the greatest savings in operational cost for a given level of capital expenditure. The plan will be implemented as soon as feasibly possible to reduce forecasted generation capacity requirements.

DEDICATED DEMAND-SIDE MANAGEMENT UNIT IN THE UTILITY

REG will establish a dedicated EE/DSM unit to oversee the design and implementation of relevant efficiency programs to clip electrical peak demand. REG shall develop a staffing and business plan as soon as possible as part of its restructuring/institutional reforms. The unit shall collaborate with MININFRA on improving electricity end-use data collection, so as to better understand trends and patterns and to design appropriate strategies for structuring and target energy efficiency programs. Key metrics include: per capita and total consumption by service and consumer group; breakdown of daily peak demand; and electricity end-use by region. Regular surveys shall be taken to obtain this information, targeting households, industries (e.g., motor drives, boilers, and furnaces), and public utilities (e.g., water and wastewater pumping).

The new unit shall prioritize quick-win energy savings opportunities that reduce demand load and operational costs within public utilities, with priority being given to water and sanitation service provision. Almost half of the required expenditures associated with electricity for water service provision come from pumping stations formerly operated by EWSA. A more detailed audit will examine the payback period for undertaking infrastructure upgrades, including installing variable speed drives and remote sensors, to various plants.

The new unit shall also collaborate with MININFRA and RURA on regulatory development to facilitate related priority measures and actions on the part of electricity end-users. An assessment of the viability of other incentives for LV customers on pre-paid-meters (e.g., rebates) shall be performed to further incentivize shifting demand patterns and smooth demand load during the day. Finally, the unit will be responsible for the promotion and removal of barriers to implementing household and commercial efficient lighting initiatives. It is envisioned, for example, that the unit outsources the implementation of a comprehensive behavioural change marketing campaign focused on priority end-users and actions identified in the strategy. The unit would also support translating existing guidelines into educational curricula and public awareness programs to encourage youth participation.

ENERGY AUDITS

Major users of energy, such as industrial and commercial consumers, shall be encouraged and incentivized to carry out regular energy audits. MININFRA will develop a strategy and business model for an energy efficiency finance facility to bankroll audits (50/50 cost split) and retrofits for industry, which would be initially capitalized by MINECOFIN through a reallocation of the subsidy of the power tariff and DP contributions. The facility would be replenished on the basis of savings achieved. It would also undertake establishing energy performance benchmarks whereby Industries shall be encouraged and required to meet or exceed these benchmarks. This will provide a financial incentive to implement EE/DSM programs. RSB and MININFRA are responsible for developing and adopting minimum energy performance standards (MEPS) for motors and promoting the use of high efficiency motor-drives such as variable speed drives (VSDs) in the industries.

EAC-WIDE ENERGY STANDARDS AND LABELLING SCHEME

RSB is responsible for the development and adoption of an EAC-wide energy standards and labelling scheme for common household appliances and to establish a working group to align regional standards with EAC under existing regional integration processes. A baseline for Rwanda will be established through a market assessment of current conditions.

SOLAR WATER HEATERS

MININFRA is responsible for the promotion and rollout of Solar Water Heater (SWH) programme. This involves carrying out awareness campaigns by engaging with all stakeholders. In addition, MININFRA will work closely with RHA to revise the buildings codes so that SWH are included in new builds. The specific modalities and financing of SWH inclusion in the building code will be determined by a study to be carried out by MININFRA.

EFFICIENT LIGHTING

For household lighting, EE/DSM Unit will investigate expanding and managing bulk procurement and distribution of CFLs for residential customers (based on current consumption and end-user affordability) with targeted subsidies for retrofits. The existing CFL program has already distributed 800,000 heavily subsidised units, resulting in an estimated annual saving of 36GWh. Therefore the CFL program will continue under the EP. As well as this an EE code for street lighting shall be developed. Payments and maintenance for street lighting shall be shifted to local authorities to incentivise them to use them efficiently. An assessment study is also underway to replace the sodium HPS street lamps with LEDs. The EE/DSM unit will provide technical support to conduct economically viable energy-efficient street lighting retrofits and in public institutions.

GREEN PROCUREMENT GUIDELINES (PUBLIC SECTOR)

MININFRA is responsible for promoting efficient use of energy in the public sector. The main electricity consuming facilities in the public sector are government buildings, water and waste water pumping stations and street lighting. RPPA and REMA shall be responsible to

institutionalize "green" public procurement guidelines and strategies focused on equipment with a high energy footprint and to develop clear criteria, guidelines for integrating energy and resource efficiency into existing procurement policy and processes. Policies must be adhered to under certain conditions, as determined by RPPA.

ENERGY EFFICIENCY & DEMAND-SIDE MANAGEMENT SUB-SECTOR IMPLEMENTATION PLAN

Table 18 Energy Efficiency & Demand-Side Management Sub-sector Implementation Plan

Strategic Action	2013/14	2014/15	2015/16	2016/17	2017/18	Responsible Institution
Grid Loss Reduction Plan	Final report	Raising funds for implementation	Implement Phase I	Implement Phase II	REG	
Establish Dedicated EE/DSM Unit		Develop staffing and business plan and establish EE/ DSM Unit Conduct detailed energy end-use surveys	-Undertake demand surveys -Behavioural change campaigns, investigate bulk procurement and distribution of CFLs, assess viability of incentives (retrofit subsidies)	Project Expansion subject to savings made. Provide TA.	REG & MININFRA	
Industry Energy Audits		Develop strategy, business model for EE facility	Develop performance benchmarks	Develop and adopt minimum energy performance standards	MININFRA with RSB	
Green procurement		Develop new guidelines	Approval by RPPA and legislation	Pilot and mainstream	RPPA & REMA	
EAC–Wide Standards and Labelling	EAC Scheme	Standards Development; Raise Funds for Implementation	Pilot implementation of new standards	RSB		

EE Strategy and Law		Develop Strategy. Develop and submit Energy Efficiency Law for approval	Streamline	MININFRA		
Buildings	Adopt new SWH regulations with two-year phased compliance timeline	Close monitoring, evaluate as needed	RHA, RURA and MININFRA			

BIOMASS

OBJECTIVES

The overarching sub-sector policy objective is to promote environmentally sustainable use of biomass fuels, thereby mitigating negative environmental, social and health impacts. Rwandan households will not eliminate the use of traditional biomass fuels in the short run. Indeed, it is the most affordable option to most households, and measures to increase the efficiency of harvesting and consumption through cleaner cooking technologies can render biomass energy a truly sustainable solution. However, as the economy develops, the

strategy aims for alternative clean cooking carriers and technologies, such as biogas, LPG, and peat briquettes, to displace unsustainable, traditional biomass fuels over time. These strategies will be implemented as and where it makes sense. The main HLTO for this sub-sector is the following:

80% of all households to employ cleaner cooking technologies by 2018

In addition to the HLTO, there are several subordinate targets, including: increasing the penetration of ICS to up to 50% of all rural households, distributing 3,500 domestic biogas digesters and 15 institutional biogas digesters annually, and increasing average charcoal yields by 30% from a 2009 baseline.50 These measures will contribute dramatically to reducing traditional biomass energy consumption by the end of EDPRS II period.51

It should be recalled that the EP also calls for:

* Consolidating institutional mandates and strengthening decentralized implementation;

* Improving regulatory oversight over the charcoal sector and mainstreaming more efficient charcoal harvesting and carbonization techniques;

* Increasing access to cleaner cooking technologies by promoting new technology standards, piloting new market transformation activities, and introducing possible fiscal reforms, and;

* Developing a harmonized, regionally-integrated policy and market for sustainable liquid bio-fuels.

CHALLENGES WITHIN THE BIOMASS SUB-SECTOR

Challenge 1: Wood fuel deficit

The current trend towards increased urbanization and the declining state of forest resources points to the need to design effective policies to address some of the pressing challenges in the biomass subsector and the entire energy sector. In 2009, demand for conventional fuel wood and charcoal was 4.2 million tonnes, resulting in a deficit of 870,000 tonnes per year. While less than expected due to government plantation programs, it still represents a 21% deficit in relation to current demand.52

Challenge 2: Lack of a clear ownership

Effective national management of biomass resources and related consumption is a cross cutting-issue that touches upon energy, health, agricultural growth, natural resources management, and local government. Effecting a transition toward clean cooking and modern biomass will bring a number of economic benefits to the country and prevent many

deaths from household pollutants: some 5,680 Rwandan deaths a year are related to household air pollutants, 94% of which are children53. Lack of clearly consolidated institutional accountability, has led to coordination failures, overlaps, and a duplication of effort. For example, ambiguous intuitional mandates and the lack of a more decentralized institutional framework to manage investments under the NDBP has rendered its impact less than optimally effective. In addition, the Energy Balance survey of 2008 is out of date and it is unknown what the share of biomass is in the energy mix today.

Challenge 3: Limited economically competitive, culturally acceptable alternatives: Alternatives to traditional biomass energy for cooking such as LPG are expensive and rare. Many rural households have a low incentive to switch away from traditional biomass fuels as they pay little to nothing for them or simply cannot afford cleaner alternatives. In addition, changing predominant cooking fuel use is a behaviour adjustment that is deeply culturally conditioned. As a result, programs focusing solely on disseminating new technologies without accompanying behavioural change or social marketing campaigns are likely to fall short of being fully successful.

SOLUTIONS FOR THE BIOMASS SUB-SECTOR

To achieve the targets set out for the biomass sub-sector, a new strategy will identify appropriate technologies for households at different income levels while considering resource and market realities in relative geographies. More market-based PPP approaches to scaling up clean cooking programs will be developed and evaluated through various pilots. These could potentially be combined with off-grid electricity access initiatives, where economically and technically feasible. Further solutions are elaborated below.

CONSOLIDATING INSTITUTIONAL MANDATES

The implementation of sustainable biomass energy programs focused on cleaner cooking technologies shall be decentralized in order to accelerate delivery and improve impact. MININFRA will develop the necessary strategies, action plans, be responsible for technology development, and will continue to provide technical assistance through REG to the districts. With support and guidance of MINALOC, district authorities will be required to incorporate delivery of sustainable biomass energy technologies into their annual performance contracts and budget programmes into their plans. Districts will play a pivotal role in education and awareness-raising, and the extension of government subsidy mechanisms and micro-finance schemes. MINALOC shall monitor district development plans more closely for meeting clean cooking and biogas targets. RSB shall elaborate updated national ICS standards with the support of REMA,

MININFRA, and the private sector and other stakeholders. MINIRENA is responsible for developing biomass supply i.e. forestry.

FORMALIZE CHARCOAL PRODUCTION AND SUPPLY

Charcoal regulations: To maintain the right balance of trees harvested for charcoal, RNRA shall closely enforce current regulations, including the licensing regime, to stop illegal wood harvesting. RNRA shall ensure that existing regulations for tree harvesting and replacement are published in the public domain at local levels to improve awareness and compliance.

Better supply chain management and more formalized sector: MININFRA shall undertake efforts to formalize the charcoal sector, including conducting a supply chain analysis, reorganizing charcoal supply centres of Rwanda, and promoting better-organized and trained charcoal producer cooperatives and associations. This will help to streamline efforts to put in place improved carbonization techniques. Local authorities will be used to identify local cooperatives involved in charcoaling who will also train other charcoalers through a 'train-the-trainers' approach. MINALOC will promote the use of improved charcoaling techniques that ensure high yield (Kgs wood/Kgs of charcoal) through training programs and sensitization workshops at the local level.

Government will promote energy conservation measures such as more carbonised charcoal, hydraulic charcoal and other improved technologies among large, non-domestic users of wood and charcoal, such as brick manufacturers.

ACCESS TO CLEANER COOKING ENERGY CARRIERS

Promotion of improved charcoal and wood stoves: Government will place a much stronger emphasis on social marketing/behavioral change communication strategies to promote clean cooking technology alternatives. This can be done through 'Umuganda' meetings as well as training and sensitization workshops on the economic benefits of ICS. These include: a reduction in biomass required, household budget savings, time savings for productive use, and a reduction in deaths and disease from reduced air pollutants. Government aims to ensure that up to 50% of households in rural areas can access an ICS. Ultimately, the target is to reach 63% of rural households having access to improved cook stoves by 2020.

Biogas: The National Domestic Biogas Program (NDBP) targets to disseminate at least 3,500 bio-digesters to households per year, leading to at least 18,000 additional bio-digesters in households by 2018, and 15 bio-gas digesters in institutions such as prisons and schools per year54. To fast-track the program, a national taskforce has been instituted. Through the Institutional Biogas Program (IBP), government is promoting the use of biogas for cooking and heating in schools, hospitals and prisons.

The NDBP will be restructured pending a business evaluation to accelerate dissemination.55

Little success has been had under the current program. Therefore, subsidies will be reformed, pending a more detailed economic analysis, to become more means-tested and in-line with system capacity and market demand. Based on a preliminary analysis, a tentative proposal for altering the subsidy mechanism is provided in Annex 4. Additionally, MININFRA will develop strategies and action plans on end-user financing, fund mobilization, capacity building, and enhancing market transformation.

A feasibility study evaluating the relative merits of new and improved biogas technologies will be undertaken as part of the biomass strategy and action plan.56 At the same time, the Bio-energy Energy Standards Committee under the RSB shall define and publish new standards for biogas digester technologies, including those suitable for institutional plants, which currently do not yet exist. This will examine fiberglass and flexi-biogas versus existing technologies on the basis of reliability, affordability, environmental impact, and job creation. Development of new standards shall take into account new and emerging technologies57 that can make biogas more affordable and reliable.

For the Institutional Biogas Program, MINEDUC, MINISANTE and MININTER (RCS) shall take the lead on implementation and provide budget for routine maintenance and operations of biogas digesters in schools, health centres, and prisons. REG will continue to give technical assistance where necessary.

Liquefied Petroleum Gas (LPG): Measures to promote LPG fuel-switching among urban and peri-urban customers will be implemented. Rwanda is expected to join the Global LPG Partnership as a member. An LPG market assessment and action plan shall be under taken to identify measures to increase the uptake of LPG that increase affordability and distribution efficiency. The action plan shall consider the merits of eliminating non-economic LPG cylinders (20Kgs) by regulation. It shall also evaluate the benefits of extending incentives to retailers to invest in LPG infrastructure and measured by MINICOM and MININFRA to facilitate bulk purchase and storage facilities. A temporary VAT exemption for LPG is already in place to promote its use as a biomass cooking alternative. Further detail is given in the chapter on petroleum sub-sector.

REGIONALLY INTEGRATED MARKET FOR LIQUID BIO-FUELS

Liquid bio-fuels such as biodiesel and bio-ethanol provide alternative sources of fuel for vehicles reducing diesel imports.58 A variety of crops are suitable to produce bio-fuels in East Africa, including Jatropha, maize, and various varieties of sorghum. Since some bio-crops require extensive land, thus competing with policies to scale-up agricultural development, it

is important to take stock of existing marginal lands that can be used to grow bio-crops, and to run test trials on crops to see whether this is a viable solution: one private developer in Rwanda is already doing so. Additionally, given the fact that Rwanda's arable land area is highly constrained in comparison to its neighbours, its policy toward bio-fuels shall be to promote regional approaches, whereby feed stocks are imported duty free from other EAC countries. MINICOM and MININFRA shall promote and harmonize policies and market opportunities for regional biofuel industry development.

Finally, small-scale commercial biogas projects, including those involving the gasification of crop residues or effluents linked to human or agricultural wastes will be promoted through inclusion in the REFIT regime.

BIOMASS SUB-SECTOR IMPLEMENTATION PLAN

Table 19 Biomass Sub-sector Implementation Plan

Strategic Action	2013/14	2014/15	2015/16	2016/17	2017/18	Responsible Institution
Biomass Strategy			Update strategy	Implement strategy	MININFRA	
Charcoal Efficiency	Sensitization workshops and training seminars including the latest	REG, Local Gov.				

	technology					
Technical Support for cook stoves	ICS program	Large awareness campaign	On-going ICS program	Review of appropriate ICS technology	Local Gov. with MININFRA	
Biogas	NDBP on-going	Detailed analysis on subsidies for reform	Subsequent strategy and action-plan development on end-user finance/market. Develop new technology standards.	MININFRA; RSB		
Train charcoal professionals		Design training program	Local level training programs and sensitization workshops	Local Gov. with MININFRA		
Database/ Survey		-Develop National clean cooking database -Carry out Energy Balance survey for Rwanda	Gather data	Monitor	MININFRA with REG	

PETROLEUM

OBJECTIVES

THE EP AND ESSP AIM TO ENSURE THE SAFE, SUFFICIENT, RELIABLE, SUSTAINABLE AND AFFORDABLE SUPPLY OF PETROLEUM AND LPG. THIS WILL ENTAIL EXPANDING DOMESTIC EXPLORATION AND PRODUCTION, BOOSTING INVESTMENTS IN SUPPLY AND STORAGE INFRASTRUCTURE, AND PROMOTING SOUND MANAGEMENT OF DOWNSTREAM PETROLEUM RESOURCES. THE EP OUTLINES THE FOLLOWING POLICY OBJECTIVES FOR THE SUB-SECTOR:

* Accelerate regional cooperation and strategic infrastructure development including new refining, pipeline transportation, and railway infrastructure

* Institute a more effective public-private hybrid model for maintaining strategic petroleum product reserves.

* Enhance the attractiveness of Rwanda as investment destination for upstream oil and gas exploration and development.

* Enhance the effectiveness of price stabilization mechanisms.

* Improve data collection and enforce fuel quality standards through greater checks

* Define clear institutional mandates.

* Implement market transformation activities for LPG

AS A HIGH LEVEL TARGET, THE ESSP COMMITS GOVERNMENT TO THE FOLLOWING: ENSURE THE NECESSARY INFRASTRUCTURE IS IN PLACE TO MEET CURRENT STRATEGIC RESERVE REQUIREMENTS (CURRENTLY 3 MONTHS' SUPPLY).59

CHALLENGES WITH THE PETROLEUM SUB-SECTOR

Challenge 1: Price Volatility. Rwanda has very low security over petroleum-based energy products and the global market for petroleum products can be volatile. Although world prices have been remarkably stable in recent years compared to other periods of time, price volatility and shocks are a cause of concern due to Rwanda's extremely high vulnerability.

Challenge 2: High cost of petroleum products and uncertain product quality. Uneven product quality results from a lack of clear standards, quality control mechanisms, and capacities to carry out adequate quality control.

Challenge 3: Insufficient infrastructure. Currently, MINICOM develops and implements regulations for downstream petroleum activities, while MININFRA is responsible for the management of petroleum infrastructure. In order to meet national policy objectives, additional investment in infrastructure development, which has been lagging over recent years, is required. The storage capacity for petroleum imports is insufficient to cope with rising demand and existing infrastructure does not comply with international EHS risk management standards. Large sums of money are required to upgrade existing infrastructure. Infrastructure development strategies must be closely aligned to anticipated market demand and appropriate reserve levels.

SOLUTIONS FOR THE PETROLEUM SUB-SECTOR

The government approach to address each of the main challenges are summarised on the following page, and then discussed in more detail.

Figure 8Government approach to address Petroleum sub-sector challenges

UPSTREAM PETROLEUM

Upstream relates to the exploration and production of petroleum, along with the supporting infrastructure to undertake these activities, and is the responsibility of MINIRENA. The National Petroleum Exploration and Production Policy, which was developed and adopted by Cabinet in 2013, will be fully implemented. It addresses key issues of exploration and development, licensing, institutional and regulatory frameworks. According to MINIRENA, the upstream policy is expected to provide Rwanda long-term policy clarity and proper regulatory and institutional set-up, along with proper incentives for investors.

Additionally, it is proposed that the issuance of exploration licenses be liberalized. To mitigate energy insecurity that emanates from excessive energy import dependence in the oil and gas sub-sector, Rwanda would have to accelerate exploration of domestic oil and gas resources. The degree to which exploration and potential discovery can be accelerated depends on upstream exploration and development policies, their inherent investor incentives and the expediency of the licensing and regulatory process. Therefore, based on past experience, a license shall be valid for 2 years and extended for another 5 years subject to satisfactory progress on upstream prospecting. Once a resource is discovered one of three contractual arrangements with the government can be arranged: a profit-sharing agreement, a concession agreement, or an equity participation stake.

MIDSTREAM PETROLEUM

Midstream refers to the transportation, storage and wholesale marketing of petroleum. MININFRA is responsible for infrastructure, technology and energy efficiency development of petroleum products. However, MINICOM is responsible for the wholesale marketing and setting strategic reserve requirements. Key interventions here include:

* Develop transportation infrastructure inter-connections for faster, more reliable supplies of petroleum and LPG. Introduce incentives to incentivize retailers and wholesale fuel distributers to increase investments in gas (LPG) storage facilities. Strategic joint investment in Hoima regional refinery project and target participation in other multi-national investments, including bio-diesel blending facilities;

* Encourage and incentivize private investors to undertake bulk purchasing arrangements;

* Assist local importers with storage and distribution infrastructure investments and to undertake bulk purchasing arrangements in order to reduce the price of LPG.

DOWNSTREAM PETROLEUM SUBSECTOR

Downstream petroleum refers to the refining, processing, marketing and distribution of petroleum products, including LPG, which is the responsibility of MINICOM. Key interventions here include:

* MINICOM to update the National Downstream Petroleum Policy to reflect current market situation;

* MINICOM to conclude bulk purchasing agreements for petroleum products with Uganda and Tanzania;

* Regulator to adopt an appropriate domestic fuel pricing methodology;

* Regulator to set and enforce standards for all downstream petroleum products and large fuel consumers to enter into fuel hedging arrangements;

* Regulator to adopt regulation for mandatory submission of data related to petroleum products' trade, sales, and strategic stores;

* MINICOM to closely track market growth and penetration rates for LPG through market surveys, etc;

* MININFRA to carry out promotion campaign to increase uptake of LPG targeting urban, upper and middle-class households;

* MININFRA to promote TVETs to provide training in the production/assembly of LPG low cost stoves to march increasing demand.

* Commence full feasibility studies for a petroleum products pipeline between Hoima, Uganda and Kigali, Rwanda. This will establish a supply route to Rwanda from a new oil refinery expected to be operational in Uganda by 2018.

In view of the ongoing harmonisation of best regulatory practices within the EAC region, all energy components including downstream petroleum should be regulated under one umbrella as common practice in the region.

2.5.4 PETROLEUM SUB-SECTOR IMPLEMENTATION PLAN

Table 20 petroleum subsector implementation plan

Strategic Action	2013/14	2014/15	2015/16	2016/17	2017/18	Responsible Institution
Upstream Policy	Finalize and adopt	Implement policy	MINIRENA			
Exploration Licenses	Analysis	Develop liberalized licensing scheme	Adopt and enforce	RURA		
Regional Investments	Oil pipeline study	Extend pipeline study	Identify other opportunities	Engage in projects and perform feasibility studies	MININFRA	
Fuel pricing	Develop appropriate domestic fuel methodology	Adopt and implement	MINICOM, RURA			
LPG	Market assessment	Develop awareness and uptake campaign. Develop TVET capacity for LPG stove assembly	MINICOM, MININFRA			

2.6 PRIVATE SECTOR ENGAGEMENT

An unprecedented degree of investment will be needed from the private sector in order to better align energy supply with demand growth. The private sector will play a pivotal role in delivering many of the areas described in the ESSP, particularly in the electricity supply and off-grid energy access sub-sectors. The private sector has the potential for generating inclusive and sustainable growth in Rwanda, by responding to the challenges both through the provision of capital and through human and managerial capacity. This major shift requires strategies to leverage private capital and facilitate private sector engagement and partnership in a manner that best exploits the advantages of each actor.

One lesson from EDPRS-I reflected in the principles of the EP is that clear policies and strategies are needed to attract private investors and streamline investment processes. By creating an enabling environment and enacting conducive policies, the public sector can facilitate the private sector to invest in energy-relevant activities. The private sector is adroit at identifying and exploiting market opportunities, managing risks, and scaling-up clean technologies that have already been demonstrated or piloted.

CHALLENGES WITH PRIVATE SECTOR ENGAGEMENT

Past challenges in this area include: passive reactions to expressions of interest, conducting unplanned negotiations without having prior technical or financial feasibility studies including resource assessments, and carefully evaluating the impact of a particular investment against optimization of the energy portfolio.

2.6.1 SOLUTIONS FOR PRIVATE SECTOR ENGAGEMENT

In order to create a more favourable environment for private investors in the sector, Government will develop a coordinated plan to streamline investment procedures, guarantee stable and positive returns, and reduce perceived and real risks to energy infrastructure investment. Among these measures include updating the investment code and clarifying the rules and modalities of engagement for PPPs.

De-risk investments through financing risky upstream resource assessments and pre-feasibility studies: A pipeline of projects will be developed that are investor ready. To facilitate this, preparatory project development work is essential. An Investment Unit already exists to streamline investment, and the government undertakes almost all pre-feasibility and resource assessment work.

The Establishment of a Rwandan Energy Development Fund (REDF): While a number of development partners fund elements of feasibility work, the timescales and governance required often results in funds not being released quickly enough. A Rwandan Energy Development Fund (REDF) could channel this funding through a single, dedicated strategic funding mechanism.

REF would act to streamline access to funding that would focus on early-stage project finance in renewable generation and off-grid solutions. This would be in the form of early-stage seed capital, equity and concessional loans. Other more complex and innovative instruments would be developed over time. The purpose of REDF would be to bring projects to commercial viability thereby leveraging in more private capital into the sector, and help meet government targets. The REDF concept shall be elaborated and established under the auspices of MINECOFIN as the primary means to co-finance strategic domestic energy projects with public resources. Some related initiatives already exist funded by development partners, however these are scattered, and the governance required often results in under-disbursement or funds being released too slowly to meet commercial deadlines. In general, REDF funds would help to bridge any perceived feasibility gap for projects that are not quite commercially viable unless a small or risky up-front part of the project is funded. The REDF could de-risk investment by funding feasibility studies, technology studies, legal due diligence, or additional service infrastructure to that already pledged by Government.

The illustration below indicates: 1) the relative costs and risk of the feasibility and delivery stages of the project; 2) the usual balance of debt to equity funding; and 3) the target role of REDF participation.

Initial capitalization by the GoR of the REDF is proposed at $30m, with development partners expected to provide additional finance. Climate funds have already been approached to provide seed co-financing. Through this application, funding guidelines and a concept note for the REDF are to be developed by MININFRA in collaboration with MINECOFIN and RDB that will outline the rationale, feasibility and optimal governance and institutional arrangements. The aim would be for the REDF to be operational by the end of 2015/16.

Streamline investment promotion processes for IPPs. In partnership with RDB, REG, RURA, and other stakeholders, MININFRA shall work to develop clear, simple and harmonised Investment processes for IPP energy projects. In 2014, a new investment process for unsolicited hydropower projects below 5 MW will be finalized that is expected to shorten the timeframes from project concept to financial closure. On the basis of this experience, streamlined processes will be developed for other categories of projects. A dedicated IPP Technical Working Group or Task Force for this area may also be set up, as part of restructuring of sector governance frameworks.

Empower local enterprises to engage in energy sector deals and introduce more competitive, transparent approaches to service provision where appropriate: Under the 2014 National Energy Policy, competitive bidding and procurement of all energy-related projects, including IPP generation activities, shall be the default option to ensure market transparency as well as value-for-money.60 On the basis of past lessons learned by the EWSA Investment Unit and MININFRA, new procurement guidelines for energy projects solicited by MININFRA, will be developed and aligned with RPPA. These will be developed with a view to ensure that tenders and other competitive bidding processes are fair and unbiased. Wherever feasible, standardized legal documentation will also be used to reduce delays in negotiations. New guidelines shall include templates and manuals for:

1) Pre-bid technical specification documents to ensure that project designs align to strategic priorities and local content guidelines or requirements;

2) Determining bid evaluation committees to ensure highly relevant technical evaluation competencies are included. Award evaluation reports to be used when confirming the selection of winning bidders;

3) Any final negotiated agreements with selected bidder.

Extend and expand investment incentives to private investors: A process shall be instituted with agreement from all parties for which transmission connections could be forward paid by energy developers or operators and recouped through agreed fees or tariffs incorporated in Power Purchase Agreements (PPAs). Government shall facilitate the development of IPP projects through the provision of various incentives, including funding access roads and other facilitating infrastructure for projects that meet certain criteria and for which have a concession from MININFRA has already been awarded. The revised Investment Code treats energy as a strategic sector and extends other fiscal and non-fiscal investment incentives to various projects.

Additionally, MININFRA shall elaborate specific operational guidelines for the provision of access roads, including mechanisms for private sector procurement and reimbursement of access road costs as a way to streamline IPP investments in the energy sector. Lastly, a review of the EAC customs exemption schedule shall also be undertaken to ensure the current list fully encompasses all aspects of electric power facilities and that the formulation can be easily understood by customs inspection officers.

IMPLEMENTATION OF THE ESSP

BACKGROUND AND IMPLEMENTATION PLAN

Implementation of this energy sector plan will be done prudently to a void significant disruption to the entire economy. Further, this will be a joint effort of all key players from policy makers, investors and financiers. Some of the challenges to the implementation of the energy sector strategy include issues of coordination given the complexity of the sector (from petroleum to biomass), financing requirements, exogenous forces (resettlement rates) and others. The basis for this strategy though is to create an elaborate approach of remedying these current and future anticipated challenges. An energy Sector Wide Approach Secretariat (SWAP) was created to that respect to ensure coherence and synergy, ensure cross-sectorial collaboration, bridge all key sector players in consultations on strategic actions required for the sector to grow.

The process of developing the ESSP was highly consultative from its initial conception in 2012 to the updated form here alongside the EP consultation process. All key stakeholders from both government and the private sector were exhaustively consulted, and their ideas form the basis of the strategy. Key stakeholders will be kept in the loop through the implementation process with the SWAP secretariat in the lead and the SWG playing an oversight role. Participatory approaches to ESSP implementation will be maintained through a strengthened SWG and technical working groups.

SEQUENCING OF INTERVENTIONS

For a full description of the sequencing of interventions from each of the sub-sectors over the EDPRS II period please refer to Annex 5.

GOVERNANCE

A full list of the roles and responsibilities of sector stakeholders, and co-ordination and information sharing mechanisms can be found in the EP. For matters of clarity, some of the institutional members of the SWG are: The Lead Ministry (MININFRA), The Lead Donor, Prime Minister's Office, MINECOFIN, Provincial and Kigali City representatives, Development Partners (DPs), Civil Society Organizations, and private sector institutions.

COMMUNICATION PLAN

So as to improve the implementation of the ESSP issues arising from the evaluation process which requires redress will immediately be dealt with inside MININFRA and/or communicated to relevant parties outside the Ministry through the Sector Working Group. REG, given its leading role in projects and programs implementation follow-up will be particularly resourceful in this respect. MININFRA will be responsible for regular

communication of progress and reporting on the status of implementation of energy projects, to the sector stakeholders. Specifically, this will be done through:

* Regular meetings will be held with the Energy SWG, which will participate in joint sector review meetings to assess the performance of the sector

* MININFRA website will be updated quarterly, with significant information about the Strategy and key sector achievements, opportunities as well as plans in pipeline, accessible to the public.

* Local media (newspapers, radio and television) will be used to communicate about the Strategy and state of the sector. This will be partly meant to raise mass awareness on new sector initiatives such as energy efficiency technologies.

* Through MINALOC, the OGS and MINAFFET, MININFRA shall arrange and organise UMUGANDA purposely to address the citizens on both strategy and policy both within the country and outside through our Embassies.

DATA SHARING

The ESSP calls for the development of intricate databases in the form of more detailed planning and new databases in the areas of biomass, off-grid, and EE/DSM. This data needs to also be shared effectively between MININFRA and REG, across government and the NIS in particular, and other stakeholders as well. The SWG, technical working groups, Energy Steering Committee, and IT software upgrades going on at REG and MININFRA will facilitate internal data sharing and sharing of information across government. REG has developed a public data portal on their website which is in its infancy and requires updating. REG will champion this portal for sharing data with MININFRA to assist so data is available to all stakeholders. MININFRA will also develop the capacity to carry out regular reporting, bulletins and policy briefs with the support of the energy SWAP. Additionally, RSB will place standards online for purchase to make it easier for customers to access them.

RISK ANALYSIS

The Rwandan energy sector is exposed to significant risks. There is therefore a need to integrate risk screening into planning, particularly at the sectorial level. Some especially critical risks worth highlighting include:

Import Dependency: Diversifying the portfolio of energy sources both domestically and also externally through regional integration to import from multiple countries (e.g., geothermal from Kenya and hydropower from Ethiopia) is a main strategy to increase energy security. Short and long term supply gaps is a risk factor, driven by the fact that our partners also face strong growth in petroleum-based products and electricity consumption; therefore, they might renege on supply and export commitments in order to meet domestic demand. To mitigate this risk, MININFRA is looking at alternative routes for the import of electricity from a broader set of countries, within the context of the EAPP. The legal framework of partner countries regarding private investments in generation will be examined to ensure that only

projects with a very high probability of success are included in MoUs and plans from countries Rwanda imports power from.

Environmental and climatic shocks: These pose a significant challenge. Extraordinary events such as volcanic eruptions could destroy energy investments and disrupt service provision. Oils spills or methane gas explosions can be catastrophic to humanity and the surroundings. The long-term impact of climate change on rainfall and available hydropower generation capacity could also be detrimental to meeting the country's long-term energy plans. A Disaster Recovery Plan therefore needs to be integrated into energy sector planning.

Insufficient and un-integrated planning and exploratory work: All government stakeholders have an obligation to contribute to electricity planning processes in an accurate and timely manner. This is especially true for the areas of agriculture, mining and industry. The Industrial Policy and other relevant policies shall be integrated into plans to reflect this. In addition, failure to develop a full feasibility study for a project in advance of its development is likely to result in inefficient allocation of resources. The high risk premium attached to an unknown resource or project raises financing costs, and ultimately hinders the country's power generation potential. The ESSP includes a number of measures to increase attention to integrated planning and improve planning capacity more generally.

Urbanisation rates: Under the previous auspices of MINALOC a slower than anticipated rates of urbanisation has occurred. This is a key risk factor to the successful achievement of the electricity access targets. Reducing the marginal cost of new grid connections can be achieved indirectly through greater densification and growth of settlements. To reduce this risk factor and to promote resettlement, an inter-ministerial Human Settlement National Steering Committee was established in late 2014 with MININFRA as chair. The steering committee is responsible for coordinating on and the monitoring of urbanisation rates, and reports quarterly to Cabinet. MININFRA is also establishing an inter-agency taskforce to coordinate infrastructure projects related to urbanisation and will report to the national steering committee. The Energy Unit in MININFRA will play an active role on the taskforce.

Annex 5 covers a full list of risks facing the sector and associated mitigation responses. Some solutions to highlight include:

* Conduct vulnerability and risk assessments for all energy-related investments specifically on the exploitation of Methane Gas and fuel storage facilities.

* Institutional reforms to improve planning capacities and reliable service delivery such as the EWSA Reform

* promoting alternative energy technologies (e.g., biogas) as a means to diversify energy supplies as well as for environmental protection and disaster risk reduction

* Develop domestic resources to increase energy security, and at the same time regional interconnections to reduce load-shedding risks.

MONITORING AND EVALUATION

The importance of evaluation cannot be overstated. Effective M&E contributes to a variety of core principles outlined in the EP, including: increased accountability and transparency to the Treasury and DPs on the use of public funds; enabling a timely resolution of implementation issues that can build investor confidence, and uncovering lessons on the effectiveness of activities so as to justify scaling-up and alternative procurement mechanisms or market-based approaches. . This section provides an overview of areas that need to be monitored as a result of the ESSP, existing systems already in place, and further institutional capacity needs and requirements to carry out M&E more effectively.

One of MININFRA's core mandates is to carry out monitoring and evaluation (M&E) of strategic projects, programs, and strategies in the energy sector that reflect national policies and that are required to achieve the targets set out in the ESSP. High level monitoring of energy sector performance in line with EDPRS II targets will be jointly done by MININFRA and MINECOFIN. The government energy agent, currently REG, is herein mandated with the provision of accurate and up-to-date information and reports, to enable MININFRA to meet its M&E role. Procedurally, the Ministry will monitor and evaluate performance utilising results based management frameworks, i.e., comparing outcomes to pre-defined targets.

TARGETED AREAS

Key indicators to be measured under the ESSP are: generation capacity, grid access to electricity, fuel storage capacity and promotion of biomass. Based on the Energy Policy this strategy goes beyond these indicators, to target by 2018: 563MW generation capacity, 10% reduction in grid carbon intensity, 48% on-grid access to electricity access, 22% off-grid access to electricity, 10% increase in energy efficiency through Demand-Side measures and 8% grid-loss reduction, increasing penetration of improved cooking technologies to 80% and increasing fuel storage to 150 million litres61. These changes in priorities in the energy sector will require the development of monitoring systems in new areas and updates/significant improvements to the existing systems as summarised in Annex 4. In short, these include: improving generation databases, including new indicators such as imports, solar and grid carbon intensity; inclusion of productive users, and monitoring their growth; an off-grid meta-database; a clean cooking meta-database; a complete new energy efficiency database with associated indicators and others.

MONITORING AND REPORTING SYSTEMS

CURRENT SITUATION

Structure: The Sector Working Group acts as the main coordination forum for the sector; providing information and evaluating progress against targets set during the bi-annual joint sector reviews. Below this, technical working groups/taskforces exist to deal with specific sub-sectors/issues. Relevant stakeholders are present at all levels. Information is fed to these coordination groups through a Sector-Wide Approach (SWAP). The SWAP secretariat is housed in MININFRA and mandated to coordinate and provide information on the sector from REG's Management Information System.

Systems: Currently REG is equipped with a Management Information System (MIS) and database to support planning and M&E of the sector. It covers:

* Development of an energy sector baseline database, annually updated

* Maintenance of a comprehensive set of statistics on energy which will be useful for researchers and policy makers

* Designing and implementing a system of planning, monitoring and evaluation of the financial status and physical progress of energy projects

* Creating a system to give regular, comprehensive reports on the execution of the Energy Sector Strategic Plan (ESSP) for 2013/2017

The MIS acts as the main monitoring tool, and evaluation practices such as readiness assessments, baselines estimations, indicator matrices, and reports are developed utilising the MIS tool. The REG will collaborate with the National Institute of Statistics to ensure compatibility and synergies between National data collection surveys and the web based MIS. These systems then inform the coordination groups mentioned above.

Capacity: Each project has a project manager and teams exist for GIS, MIS and the M&E of EARP. However, current systems are neither well-integrated nor modern, and information flows between the utility and ministry are disjointed. Furthermore the focus at the ministry is on monitoring and training and expansion are needed to set up a dedicated M&E Unit and seek external support.

SOLUTIONS

In the face of new demands on the monitoring system as given in the table in Annex 4, and the inadequate existing systems, the following solutions are proposed:

1) Expansion of the MIS in the Energy Utility Co to cope with the new datasets required

2) Full endorsement and integration of the MIS in the utility at all levels of its functionality

3) MININFRA is mandated to ensure its IT system can cope with centralized sharing and also host a light version of the utility's MIS to better exchange information

4) REG shall continue to send updates and project information to the SWAP Secretariat

5) The Secretariat will be empowered as a portal of information and for coordination

6) New databases and associated training are to occur as per Annex 4. For example: the holistic off-grid database, and the investment tracking system to be housed at RDB.

7) Management training is to be given on how to manage monitoring teams and systems

EVALUATION

EVALUATION OF THE ENERGY SECTOR

Beyond project tracking, all activities will need to be evaluated. It must be clarified that two distinct styles of evaluation exist, with the first considered the norm at the moment:

1) On-going and final assessments against targets set;

2) Assessments of the impact of activities on beneficiaries and the economy at large

Both these types of assessment will permit lessons to be learnt to improve strategy formation and project delivery, and also increase the accountability of MININFRA. Led by MININFRA, standard evaluation and reporting formats will be drawn up and agreed upon between Districts and central government. Regular sector reviews will be organized internally and with other partners, particularly in the EDPRS thematic working groups to evaluate sector performance in line with commitments reflected herein. The expansion of the M&E unit in the Ministry will receive the required external expertise and training in various evaluation methodologies to be able to carry out internal evaluation projects. Additionally the ministry will explore how best to engage with external evaluators, when final evaluations are not part of project packages, and seek support to do so.

EVALUATION OF THE ESSP

In terms of monitoring the ESSP, this will be carried out on a quarterly basis in addition to regular monitoring activities. This will result in quarterly briefs to highlight successes, and makes suggestions to improve any areas where little progress is being made. Mid-year evaluation exercises will be carried out to better inform the Sector Working Group Joint Sector Reviews. An interim report and final report will be made internally, rather than externally, given the Draft ESSP has already been followed since 2012/13. The M&E Unit within the Ministry will assist in this exercise. Finally a full assessment of the ESSP will be carried out by an independent evaluation consultancy for accountability and transparency.

COST AND FINANCING

1 COSTING

Total financing: Total financing requirement for remaining 4 years (2014-2018) of the energy sector plan is estimated at roughly US$4 bn. This includes electricity generation and transmission, electricity access, as well as EE and DSM, petroleum and biomass energy as summarized in Table 21 below. The total financing requirements are split between: public (US$ 2 bn or 48%), private sector (US$ 1.5bn or 30%), development partners (US$ 771 m or 19%) and district contributions to EARP ($87 m or 2%).

Expenditure on electricity: Total expenditure on electricity investments is estimated to be 81% of the overall energy sector financing requirements. Roughly two-thirds of this is required for generation and transmission activities to deliver 563MW projected. The remaining one-third is earmarked for electricity access which includes the current EARP program and off-grid electrification, to reach the combined 70% electricity access target.

The remaining 19% is mainly consumed by petroleum activities at 18%, and the rest is required for biomass and EE and DSM activities. For biomass energy, resources will mainly be directed to meet the cost of subsidy62 for the installation of biogas digesters as well as awareness and sensitisation programs.

Petroleum: Government plans to have storage facilities capable of storing three63 months of petroleum consumption equivalent as reserve for commercial and strategic purposes. In addition, a regional project to develop an oil pipeline is underway, which represents 89% of required expenditure in the petroleum sub-sector. The pipeline will greatly reduce the cost of transporting petroleum and increase energy security in Rwanda.

Table 21 SSP costs and financing requirement (2014/15-2017/18)

2 FINANCING STRATEGY

In general, wherever possible, finance secured from development partners, government, and other sources such as climate finance64 will be used to crowd-in private investment. The private sector will also be encouraged through the various incentives to de-risk investment mentioned in chapter 2.6, including establishing the REDF. The REDF will support both off-grid and renewable energy projects. Sector specific financing strategies are described below, and provide a guideline to the approach to the investment needs for each sector. *Ref. Annex 6 for the overview of the Financing strategy.*

Generation: The preferred approach to implementing new generation projects is to initially reduce their risk profile in the resource assessment phase through feasibility studies undertaken mostly with Government support. Following this initial phase, the EDCL will tender each project to independent power producers (IPP), therefore the capital investment requirements will be covered by the private sector. Following the conclusion of the tender, the private operator will perform further detailed feasibility studies to enable specific projects. Under IPP schemes, projects are contained within dedicated special purpose vehicles owned by private investors (typically foreign private equity funds or large operators of generation projects) and financed under non-recourse project finance. Lenders will provide loans to the special purpose vehicles in amounts equal to 60-80% of total project costs depending on the level of the project risk and on the prevailing conditions of the international capital markets. Project owners will provide in the form of equity the balance of the funds required.

In IPP schemes, the generated electricity is sold by the project to the EUCL under a long term PPA (term of 20 to 25 years). As the EUCL does not have a track record of financial sustainability and creditworthiness, such non-recourse project finance arrangements may require some form of sovereign risk guarantee, as long as this is allowed by the financing capacity of the government, and/or the involvement of multilaterals or export credit agencies, including the World Bank, the African Development Bank, etc. In all cases, including the REFIT, the tariff paid by the EUCL for the electricity will be recovered through the electricity tariff paid by its customers.

The Government will continue to grant subsidies and tax exemption to certain equipment necessary to facilitate IPPs as an incentive to boost investment in this sector and also as a means to mitigate the potential business risks. Additionally, in renewable investments, particularly micro-hydro, REDF will be used to reduce the upfront cost of engaging in projects through financial instruments such as soft loans. Development partners are also working in this area to build local capacity both in banks and with private developers to

further reduce barriers and costs to doing business. Private developers will also be encouraged to engage in climate finance through the National Climate Fund; FONERWA.

In the few situations whereby, due to strategic or emergency considerations, it will not be possible or not recommendable to build a project under an IPP scheme (one example is a thermal peaking plant, which is a strategic generation reserve for the country), the approach will be to implement the schemes using government funds allocated in the budgeting process. The EUCL and the Government will recover the investments through the regulatory asset base depreciation component in the energy tariff.

Finally, Development Partners are financing through loans the construction of the international hydro power plants in Rusumo and Rusizi, which will not be implemented in the period covered by this SSP.

Further details for the implementation of the generation projects are provided in the table below.

Table 22 Summary of Generation Pipeline

Technology	Project	Capacity	Expected Commissioning	Financing Scheme
Hydro	Mushishito HPP (RukararaV)	5	2014/2016	IPP
Hydro	Nyabarongo I	28	2014/15	GoR
Solar	Rwamagana Solar	8.5	2014/15	IPP
Methane	Kivu Watt I Methane	25	2014/15	IPP
Peat	Gishoma Peat	15	2014/15	GoR
Hydro	Micro Hydro (IPPS)	20	2015/18	IPP
Solar	RwinkWavu solar	10	2015/16	IPP
Hydro	Micro Hydro (REFIT)	15	2016/18	IPP
Thermal	KSEZ HFO	50	2016/18	GoR
Peat	Hakan Peat	80	2016/17	IPP
Solar	Nyagatare	10	2016/17	IPP
Hydro	Ntaruka B HPP	5	2017/18	IPP

Solar + Bioenergy	Solar + Bioenergy (REFIT)	12	2017/18	IPP
Thermal	Additional HFO Unit	10	2017/18	GoR
Methane	Additional PPA	50	2017/18	IPP
Peat	Akanyaru Peat	50	2017/18	IPP

Domestic transmission and distribution: With regard to the transmission and distribution power lines, necessary to transport the electricity from the generation centres to the users, the Government will invest its own funds through the REG. The investment will be recovered through components in the tariff, so that part of the future capital needs will be

financed through the utility revenues. In alternative, Development Partners might provide grants or soft loans to finance these assets.

Electricity Access Roll-out Programme: The EARP is financed through a basket of funds from both the Government, District contributions and a variety of donors. Most of the non-government funds are supplied in the form of grants or soft loans from donors with minimal interest. Private contractors will be used to roll-out the grid.

Interconnection lines with neighbouring countries: Given the strategic importance for regional trade and energy security, multilateral and development banks are keen to finance interconnection lines with neighbouring countries. Financing is provided in the form of soft loans with low interest rates. Private contractors will carry out the implementation.

Off-grid electrification: The off-grid electrification is very suitable for the participation of the private sector. For individual solar systems, private operators will be invited to supply their products to individual households with the government either providing various modalities of financial support in the initial phase or some form of guarantees to reduce the business risk. Also microfinance institutions are good candidates to provide to individual customers the sources of finance needed to purchase the equipment and will be part of the overall solution. In case of mini-grid solutions, the EDCL will likely issue tenders to allow private operators develop, build and operate the assets, following the payment of a tariff.

As these are new types of business model for Rwanda, and for now perceived to have low return on investment the Government is undertaking measures to encourage private sector participation. As mentioned previously REDF will be established and provide subsidies, soft loans or other types of financial instruments to encourage private sector developers. In this case of mini-grid solutions, the Government is partnering with research institutions to develop demonstration projects. Some of the Donors are keen to support programmes in this area also by introducing innovative schemes, as results based financing, whereby donors will provide financial rewards on the basis of the achievement of certain results (example: number of installed devices), rather than upfront grants during the programme set up. It is still unclear whether sovereign guarantees may also be required in the case of mini-grids, and developing the regulatory environment will be another key factor to reduce private sector risk.

Energy Efficiency, Demand Side Management: In the near future the Government will provide the necessary funds to support the studies, investment and subsidies required for this sector. Once the commitment of the Government to the sector is established, possibly after the successful rollout of major pilot projects, it is envisaged that Donors will provide support for some of the programmes. At the same time, some programmes will become sustainable business initiatives on their own due to potential energy savings; such as

Industrial Audits which are proposed to be funded 50/50 by the Government and industries themselves. The electricity tariff structure will also play an important role in creating incentives to undertake projects in this area.

Biomass: In the near future the Government will provide the necessary funds to support the studies and investment and subsidies required for this sector. There is also interest from Donors in supporting the various programmes within the biomass sub-sector (e.g. biogas, ICS).

Petroleum: For the construction of the storage tanks for petroleum products, the approach will be to involve the private sector to build the infrastructures under government responsibility through lease contracts, whereby private investors will build and operate the storage facilities and receive an annual payment in exchange for the services. It is also envisaged that a portion of the storage facilities will be financed and built directly by the private sector.

With regard to the Eldoret – Kampala – Kigali, the Governments of Kenya, Uganda and Rwanda are currently working on the assumption of financing the portion of the infrastructure in each country's territory. In the future, various schemes are under consideration, including borrowing part of the financial needs from commercial banks or give the project in concession to a private operator for a period of 20/25 years.

CROWDING IN FURTHER FINANCE

Other sources of finance will be used to crowd-in private investment, and free up Donor and Government resources to be more effectively utilised. For example, the private sector shall be encouraged through the various incentives to de-risk investment mentioned in chapter 2.6, including establishing the REDF. Furthermore climate finance sources shall be mainstreamed as an alternative source of capital, in particular for the construction or implementation of clean energy projects or programmes. MININFRA is currently investigating possibilities in this area and will launch a climate finance strategy within the next 12 months65.

In the event of a continued major financing gap for the energy sector, projects will be reprioritized and balanced according to demand and supply objectives, and further support asked of central government during the annual budget cycle.

EDPRS II & CROSS-CUTTING THEMES

1 CONTRIBUTION TO EDPRS 2 THEMATIC AREAS/PRIORITIES

Rwanda's economy has been growing at an annual average rate of 8.3% and government is targeting to achieve an annual average growth rate of 11.5% over the EDPRS period (2017/2018). The third generation of Rwanda's development strategy (EDPRS II) aims at achieving rapid economic growth, rural development, productivity and youth employment, and accountable governance. Ensuring access to affordable and modern sources of energy is essential if these objectives are to be achieved. In order to meet our macro-level objectives, respective targets have been set within the energy sector as highlighted in the figure below:

Figure 10 Summary of EDPRS Vision, Objectives, Targets and approach.

As a productive sector, the energy sector is one that enables other sectors to grow, and serves as a catalyst to facilitate socio-economic transformation and improved livelihoods. The provision of cost effective, appropriate energy solutions supports poverty alleviation, particularly in rural areas where energy services are currently scarce or expensive. The table and discussion below illustrates how the ESSP contributes to EDPRS II priority areas.

Table 23 Impact of ESSP on EDPRS II thematic areas and priorities

Economic transformation for rapid growth	Diversifying the economic base for exports	Energy must be available and cost effective to drive economic growth; this requires minimising the tariff through efficient investment. Petroleum products as a form of energy drives the transport sector and petroleum price movements impact on macroeconomic balances. The price of petroleum and electricity is one factor driving the cost of other goods and services produced, that bears on levels of inflation and Rwanda's competitiveness.
	Private sector development, competitiveness and service delivery	
	Unlocking infrastructure requirements	
	Urbanization	Availability of energy services will accelerate urbanisation and human settlements. There is a tendency for the exodus of households from un-electrified to areas with electricity. This comes with emerging rural socio-economic amenities that are engines of rural growth.
Rural Development		
	Human settlements	
	Agriculture modernization	The availability of sufficient, affordable energy solutions will drive agricultural mechanisation. Through irrigation in rural areas that will lead to higher agricultural productivity.
	Environment and natural resource management	Improved biomass solutions, such as biogas and ICS, preserves the environment and promotes clean growth.
Productivity and youth employment	Education and skills development	Access to electricity is essential to facilitate education on use of modern technologies. Youth training centres such as TVETs require affordable electricity.
	Ensuring a healthy workforce	Transitioning away from traditional biomass to cleaner energy forms will promote a healthier workforce.

	Job creation	Significant employment will be generated in the installation of modern energy infrastructure. Additionally cost effective energy solutions open the door to increased job opportunities through improved business productivity thus being able to create sufficient off jobs annually.
Accountable Governance	Judiciary reform; rule of law	Energy products are less appropriate here. However, providing affordable electricity is a form of government accountability to the electorate.
	Citizen-centered approach and public accountability	
	Development communication	

ECONOMIC TRANSFORMATION FOR RAPID GROWTH

Economic growth is inextricably linked to energy. As energy is tied to our economy, our required economic growth is dependent upon equitable access to energy, and sufficient supply at affordable rates. Energy and private sector development are the leading sectors under EDPRS II, accounting for over half the total cost of financing. Most of this comes from exploring and developing power project that promote Rwanda's self-reliance in power supply. Key benefits include:

Boost on business development: The cost of power impacts greatly on the overall cost of production in Rwanda. Power systems optimization and increasing imports will promote

more affordable and sufficient power supply. This will also boost local investment, increase income generating activities positively impacting on the state of people's welfare.

Promoting agricultural transformation: Agriculture constitutes the backbone of Rwanda's economy employing over 80% of the population, contributing approximately 35% to Rwanda's GDP. Under Vision 2020 it is planned to grow from the current annual average growth rate of 5.8% to 8.5% by 2020. The planned structural shift from conventional farming methods to agro processing, and increasing use of irrigation will require affordable and sufficient energy supply in powering machines and pumping water. The ESSP is therefore targeting 70% electricity access to communities and in turn agro-businesses.

Promotion of mining and mineral value addition: The mining and minerals sector is a key focal point for export-driven growth in the country. Increasing access to affordable and sufficient power supply will render mining and minerals beneficiation investments more viable and regionally competitive. Currently some mining companies lack sufficient electricity and their operations are constrained by the high cost of electricity.

Energy efficiency: EE measures will reduce power consumption without negative consequences on output. These savings will reduce the energy bill to the households, businesses, as well as government, which can then be used for other productive activities.

Boosting industrialisation plans. For Rwanda's economy to be transformed, we need a structural shift from traditional agriculture to industry and service sectors. The switch to focus on productive users, ensuring 100% sufficient access at economically affordable tariffs over the next 5 years, will be a formidable tool for economic transformation.

Reduce declining trade Balance. By fast tracking oil exploration, and developing appropriate supply routes and bulk purchasing, the trade balance burden will be reduced.

Demand stimulation: Increased energy prices reduce demand by reducing use of energy services and motivating selection of higher conversion efficiency equipment. Reducing this cost will stimulate demand and business growth.

RURAL DEVELOPMENT

There are visible disparities between rural and urban areas in terms of access to electricity and income levels. EARP will mainly target rural areas and a great deal of rural households and business units are set to benefit from this program. This effort will bridge the rural-urban disparity in access to electricity, thereby improving on businesses start-ups, enable long working hours and promote rural based employment.

EDPRS-II aims to create Special Economic Zones (SEZs) in other regions on top of the existing Kigali-based one. Rural electrification will support initiatives to construct better schools, hospitals and other social amenities; removing the need for rural-urban migration in search of better quality of life. In the last five years, the proportion of the migrant population opting for the capital city increased from 19% to 27% (see Figure 13). Providing energy services to secondary cities will help stem this potentially unsustainable flow.

Figure 11 Rwanda's internal migrations

Source: National Institute of statistics: Integrated Household Survey (EICV3, 2012/2011)

PRODUCTIVITY AND YOUTH EMPLOYMENT

According to the last integrated households living conditions (EICV 3) survey, youth makes up 39% of the population (i.e. 4,159,000 people between age 14 and 35). This population group could be a formidable tool to Rwanda's future prosperity. However, this requires skills development in order for youth to meet labour market demands. The ESSP will ensure TVETs equip youths with skills in a variety of areas related to sector needs.

ACCOUNTABLE GOVERNANCE

It is the responsibility of any pro-people government to provide socio-economic necessities. Given that a large part of public resources comes from tax revenue paid by residents, these receipts ought to be spent strategically. This is applied to fulfilling commitments related to electricity and other energy services. Government plans to ensure more local participation in the development of energy resources and solutions. This reflects a deliberate effort to empower citizens as part of governance reforms, though direct or indirect ownership of their development process.

MAINSTREAMING CROSS CUTTING ISSUES

CAPACITY BUILDING

Current levels of human and institutional capacity are insufficient to deliver on sector commitments. To implement energy sector projects on time and scale up delivery, an enabling institutional framework and skilled personnel is a pre-requisite. The ESSP puts in place measures to improve energy sector organization and management and a capacity building plan will be developed to cover skills gaps.

Human resource development: Capacity gaps identified among energy sector staff include procurement, project management, and contract management skills. In response to this, capacity will be enhanced through knowledge transfer from long term experts to local counterparts through the support of the Strategic Capacity Building Initiative (SCBI), and through short training courses. There will also be recruitment of external expertise for major transactions in order to ensure that government is getting beneficial deals.

Institutional capacity development: Institutional reforms are underway in both EWSA Ltd and MININFRA to ensure capacity to deliver on the EDPRS II objectives. Detailed proposals on institutional and human skills development are highlighted in the Implementation Plan in Annex 5. Additional guidelines to support capacity building and skills development include:

* Each institution in the energy sector shall have a clear responsible focal point with the mandate to deliver on specific objectives and targets related to capacity building.

* Senior management and administrative personnel of all energy-related agencies shall develop clear policies on training needs and priorities to address key bottlenecks and capacity gaps by the end of FY 2014. Attendance at these training courses shall be incorporated into performance contracts and annual reviews.

* Opportunities for peering and short-term staff exchanges or rotations should be developed as a way to rapidly build capacities.

* Senior management and administrative personnel of all energy-related agencies shall develop clear guidelines and policies for internships reflecting selection criteria and expected outputs so that they are effectively utilised.

ENVIRONMENTAL CONSERVATION, RISK MITIGATION AND GREEN GROWTH

Rwanda is embarking on a low-carbon development pathway as reflected in its recent National Strategy on Climate Change and Green Growth. The ESSP concentrates on developing domestic, cleaner energy resources in the power mix such as geothermal, methane and solar to replace petroleum-based power generation and reduce the environmental impact of electricity consumption.

Rwanda's energy sector is heavily dependent on environmental resources with around half of its electricity coming from hydropower and more than 80% of the population depending on fuel wood for their energy needs. This combined with the country's high climate change and natural disaster vulnerability (as shown by the impact on hydro power in 2005), mean that efforts to adapt and mitigate against the impacts of climate change and preserve the environment will be required. These include, among others:

Reduce reliance on traditional biomass energy: Government is working on a campaign to reduce reliance on traditional forms of biomass from 85% to 50% by 2018. This is being

planned through the use of improved cooking technologies that reduce demand for wood fuel and emit less GHG to the environment. Other initiatives related include the biogas program that is proposed to replace wood fuels for cooking as well as improved charcoal carbonization techniques, reducing charcoal yield and demand for wood fuel.

Increasing energy efficiency: This will be done through appliances and technologies such as CFLs and Solar Water Heaters. Solar water heating systems shall be mandatory for large water consumers to reduce use of electricity for boiling water. In line with the above, regulations requiring new buildings to incorporate green design and use of efficient energy solutions shall be enacted. These include provisions for solar water heating systems, natural lighting, ventilation and open office design among others to reduce energy demand.

Mandatory Environment Impact Assessment (EIA): All power projects are presupposed to have environmental clearance and the Impact certification before project implementation. This is even compounded in the RDB's requirements before issuing an investment certificate to any investments into energy resource development. Where plants are operational before environmental clearance, a mandatory Environmental audit is proposed by REMA.

Disaster Mitigation Activities: These include: the development of a Disaster Recovery Plan over the next 5 years, conducting vulnerability and risk assessment in all energy related investments specifically on the exploitation of Methane Gas and fuel storage facilities, developing contingency and evacuation plans in case of methane explosion in Lake Kivu, and promoting alternative energy sources for environmental protection.

Safety: MININFRA is responsible for mainstreaming disaster prevention guidelines into its operational policies as well as environment, health, and safety (EHS) guidelines to be followed by its implementation agents. International EHS standards shall be applied in all energy infrastructures both public and private owned so as to ensure the safety of both personnel and equipment as well as the conservation of the environment. This shall be especially applicable in tendering of PPPs and IPPs and in the activities of REG.

Elaboration of these plans shall involve all relevant stakeholders and peer review by disaster management experts. Plans including clear protocols to be followed in the event of a “catastrophic” event or “system failure”, such as a total power grid blackout, will delegate clear responsibility for alerting and providing emergency response measures. Fire outbreaks and oil spills, which are the main EHS risks in the petroleum industry, can be mitigated by ensuring strict compliance and enforcement of regulations and the adoption of international best practices in handling safety concerns. Other concerns associated with hazardous materials will be addressed through use of high standard equipment and use of personal protective equipment. In the medium-term all power plants shall also be equipped with emission control systems to reduce exhaust.

REGIONAL INTEGRATION

Rwanda fully supports the deepening of regional cooperation and integration in the energy sector and the sector vision foresees a fully integrated regional exchange of power resources in the long-term. In particular, Rwanda is committed to participating actively in the formulation of the Regional Energy Master plans being coordinated by the EAC, and similar regional energy planning with COMESA and its subsidiary the Communauté Economique des Pays des Grands Lacs (CEPGL), and other regional initiatives such as:

* Regional strategies for efficient procurement, transportation and storage of petroleum products;
* Regional electrical power projects promoted under the auspices of EAPP;
* NELSAP, which falls under the NBI;
* Joint development with the DRC of Lake Kivu methane gas and petroleum exploration.

Existing challenges: The sector is in its infancy, and this is reflected in high transmission losses reaching above 15%, eroding some of the cost advantages at generation stage. There are country specific risks and challenges to be considered. For example, Ethiopia is vulnerable to climate change given its reliance on hydropower, even if it does have a diverse watershed system to mitigate some of the risk, and energy demand is currently growing at 20% a year on average. Such internal conditions will need to be considered in regional trade supply guarantees. Nevertheless regional integration represents an attractive option for Rwanda given its location and small amount of natural resources.

Energy related initiatives to promote regional integration include:

Regional Strategy on scaling up access to Modern Energy Services in EAC: The strategy has 4 main targets, approved by EAC Energy Ministers in August 2005, to be fulfilled by 2015, in line with MDG framework in Scaling-up Access to Modern Energy Services. These are:

a. Provide access to modern cooking practices for 50% of the population that currently uses traditional cooking fuel;

b. Provide access to reliable electricity for all urban and peri-urban poor;

c. Provide access to modern energy services for all schools, clinics, hospitals and community centres; and

d. Provide access to mechanical power for heating and productive uses for all communities.

The Strategy has four service areas that include:

* Policy harmonization at regional and national level;
* Capacity building of both public and private sectors to implement the strategy;
* Formulation and implementation of investment programs; and
* Strategic coordination and Programme management at regional and national level.

The EAC Regional Cross-Border Electrification66 Policy and Model Power Supply Agreement: Cross-Border Electrification (CBE) allows consumers to benefit from resources across the border that are nearer than domestic alternatives, and can allow marginal projects to become feasible when aggregating loads at both sides of the border.

EAPP and EAC: Under the EAPP-EAC initiative, power generation and interconnection projects are identified at Master Plan level, to interconnect the power systems of EAPP and EAC countries.67 A common Transmission Interconnection Code exists to facilitate the integrated development and operations of the regional power systems. The initiative also contains institutional capacity building for members through the training of counterpart staff to enable the implementation of subsequent activities. Additionally, trade in electricity and ancillary services will be available and coordinated at the soon to be established Coordination Centre for the EAPP.

STRATEGIC MATERIALS

ELECTRICITY GENERATION INVESTMENT ROADMAP

Peat-to-Power Generation

A Peat master plan was developed in 1993 indicating Rwanda's potential to develop around 700MW of generation from indigenous peat resources. This study however was undertaken at a high level based primarily on a small number of samples and desk based research. The study does not constitute a basis on which to undertake multi-million dollar investments in generation and significant time and finance must be dedicated to developing a full understanding of Rwanda's peat resources if we are to avoid the pitfalls outlined in Section 2. Time and finance to undertake such studies have been factored into our planning. Peat assessments in the bogs in the North and in Akanyaru have been carried out. These studies estimate the resources and areas to prioritize for mining. These are prerequisites to proceed to detailed feasibility studies.

The table below outlines peat projects planned to be implemented over the EDPRS II period to deliver the demand driven roadmap.

* Gishoma Peat to Power (15MW) expected to deliver in fiscal year 2015/16
* Hakan (80 MW) expected to deliver in 2017/18.

Gishoma is currently under construction and COD is expected by 2015; however, full scale operations will be reached only in fiscal year 2015/16. Implementation is already underway for Hakan with detailed work on hydrology and peat testing on-going. The project has the option for a 40 MW extension to be exercised at a later stage. The option protects the government from an excessive exposure to the same supplier.

Furthermore, GoR will prepare a peat energy strategy action plan to further explore the resource, assess its economic potential, the environmental and social impacts and develop private sector participation. The action plan will ascertain also the optimal use of peat across a range of applications: power generation, direct industrial heat, steam applications, or use as domestic charcoal substitute. As part of the activities, the REG will undertake a detailed resource assessment of remaining existing bogs and create a national resource database. A series of small (10 – 15 MW) projects in the Northern bog could be developed after EDPRS-II period.

Hill top and hill side peat bogs are the quickest to develop as the topography of the land provides natural drainage. It should be possible to prepare such sites within 2-years of

completing a full feasibility study. Once prepared, it is necessary to harvest the site for around 6-months to build up sufficient stock pile of peat for generation. Harvesting/peat mining should ideally be undertaken by the private sector and if possible by the same party that will develop and own the power station. There are clear benefits to keeping the supply chain intact, as each interface between companies poses additional risk.

Following the conclusion of the PPA with Hakan, there is considerable private sector interest in developing generation from our peat reserves. Based on the expressed interest, we propose to initiate a competitive tender for a private sector developer to develop and operate mining and generation infrastructure to provide an additional 100 MW to the grid. We have a number of potential sites including the Akanyaru and around Akagera. As a priority, government must conclude feasibility studies in these areas before progressing to competitive selection of a private partner.

Hydropower Generation

Where correctly sited, hydropower can deliver an economic supply of base load power. We plan to complete the 28 MW Nyabarongo power plant, and develop around 55 MW of domestic hydro projects between now and 2017/18, as illustrated in the roadmap at the start of this chapter. As with peat, the individual nature of each Hydro site necessitates a feasibility study to be carried out in advance of development or contracting with the private sector. The table below outlines the projects we are undertaking during the EDPRS II period:

* 28 MW from Nyabarongo I: to be commissioned early in 2014/15.
* 5 MW of generation from Mushishito HPP (Rukarara V) in 2015/2016
* 20 MW from small scale Micro-hydro (IPPs) for the majority of which feasibility studies are on-going and whose commissioning is expected over the period 2015/16 to 2017/18.
* 15 MW of micro hydro to be developed under the REFIT mechanism over the period 2016/2017 to 2017/2018
* 15MW from Akanyaru MHPP in 2017/2018

Projects under implementation/contracted: Nyabarongo, the Micro-hydros, and Rukarara V are all either under implementation or we have already signed a PPA.

Potential projects for competitive tendering: Feasibility studies are currently underway on a number of projects identified through a Hydro Atlas which was complete in 2008. Upon their completion we will undertake a competitive process to identify a private sector partner, as outlined in chapter 2.6.

Possible addition of Nyabarongo II Multipurpose Dam: A feasibility study was undertaken in 2007 which proposed the placement of a dam along the Nyabarongo River approximately 30km North East of Kigali. The projected cost of the project was significantly above the

benchmark for a hydro project purely for electricity generation. The development of the site is however likely to generate other benefits such as irrigating local land to increase the agricultural yield and supplying drinking water. A full feasibility study is currently underway which will be reported this year. Based on this feasibility study we will take a decision on whether the project should go ahead and how the costs can best be shared between the water and electricity consumers and the beneficiaries of the newly irrigated land.

Methane gas-to-power Generation

The reserves of methane held in suspension in the depths of Lake Kivu represent a significant natural resource which can be used for the generation of electricity. As KivuWatt is the first of a kind for this type of plants the project has had some delays: we expect commissioning to take place within 2014/15 and that by 2015/16 the plant will be operational at least at 15 MW (it's wise maintaining a conservative approach in the first year of operation) and to reach full generation capacity by 2015/16. In addition to providing much needed additional generation, this will prove the technical feasibility of extraction and generation at this scale. The table below outlines the projects which we will need to achieve over the following 5-years:

* 25 MW from KivuWatt I in 2014/15
* 50 MW of additional Methane in 2017/18.
* 3.6 MW from the rehabilitation of REC generation plant in 2014.

Feasibility work: Whilst we expect the commissioning of the KivuWatt plant in 2014/15 we will define an action plan to further assess the resource in Lake Kivu while considering alternative scenarios for resource extraction. The plan will include a study to assess the feasibility of the overall methane gas resource, and thereafter it will be necessary to assess the range of opportunities available for investors, including projects of differing sizes and based on different technology types, and even the separation of gas extraction from the activity of power production. The GoR will prioritize technologies which allow the maximum sustainable extraction of supply subject to be being value for money.

REC: REC is currently looking for technology providers and investors to partner on rehabilitating KP1.

Geothermal power development

Geothermal energy is a clean and reliable source of energy, which is not affected by short-term fluctuations in the weather or international oil prices. When installed, most geothermal plants have relatively very low maintenance costs and high availability. Geothermal energy is not dependent on the time of the day (as solar) or on fluctuations of the weather (as hydropower or wind).

As geothermal exploration is at an early stage across most of the prospects (Ethiopia started the first geo-scientific studies in in 1969 but geothermal exploration is only part of recent history) and the resource potential is characterized by a high level of uncertainty, the Government is undertaking an approach of resource de-risking by exploring the prospective geothermal areas until proven resources are available, including carrying out step-wise exploration and ranking of all prospects. The activities expected to be undertaken are:

* Surface exploration;
* Exploration drilling and
* Develop a pilot plant as proof of concept.

However, the exact scope of work undertaken by the Government will depend on the resource estimation and on funds available.

In spring 2014, MININFRA developed a programmatic approach to geothermal exploration comprising two areas of activities:

* Setting up the necessary institutional arrangements to govern the geothermal sector and improving the strategy and regulations that govern it: and
* Feasibility through exploration of the key prospects, starting from executing more accurate surface studies in Kinigi, Gisenyi and Bugarama and drawing a lesson learnt from the drilling in Karisimbi.

Institutional arrangements and exploration and commercial strategy: international experience shows that countries with consolidated geothermal exploration programmes have set up the necessary institutional, policy and legal environment to allow the sector to prosper.

The following step will be an upgrade of the legal and regulatory framework to address the unique needs of geothermal energy activities. This will include also a close coordination of the mining and energy concessions between relevant Ministries. In the end, a detailed Geothermal Strategy will be developed which will be formally approved. A Geothermal Law has already been drafted and is pending approval once the policy and strategy are refined.

Feasibility of Rwanda's geothermal Resource: Based on surface studies conducted in the past four sites with geothermal potential have been identified: Karisimbi, Kinigi, Gisenyi and Bugarama. In Karisimbi, a drilling campaign was concluded in March 2014, leading to no conclusive, positive results. In the other prospects, on-going or planned geo-scientific surface surveys are being performed using best available technical information and methods. As lessons are being analysed from Karisimbi drilling activities, a geothermal master plan is being developed, based on a refined estimation of the resource potential. As part of resource feasibility assessments, a broad range of applications of geothermal energy, beyond power (including: industrial heating/cooling), shall be considered.

SUB-SECTOR ADDITIONAL TABLES

Table 24 Electricity Access: The EARP Connection Policy

Service offered	Time taken to process	Cost requirements
Connection to electricity	1 working days	56.000 RWF
Industries in Economic zone	15 calendar days	Free of charge
Industries between 1 and 5.3Km to the national grid	15 calendar days, after completion of the line	20.000.000 RWF. The transformer substation for the industry (factory) is not included in the price
Industries falling beyond 5.3Km to the national grid	15 calendar days, after completion of the line	20,000,000 RWF, for 1 to 5.3Km and 20,500,000 RWF per Km beyond 5.3Km, excl. transformer substation for the industry
Supplementary meter three phase	1 working day	86.000 RWF(VAT included)
Supplementary single phase	1 working day	53.300 RWF (VAT included)
Supplementary water meter	1 working day	47.436 RWF (VAT included)
Alteration to metering equipment	10 working days	Free
Meter reading	From 15th - 30th of each month	Free
Billing: Bank payment contract service-Payment on EUCL account previous to consumption from 6 months onwards	From 6 months onwards	Free
Correction of errors if any	Immediate	Free
Changing address	Immediate	Free
Ending contract	Immediate	Free
Outsourcing of prepayment cash power	Through SMS MEDIA, etc.	Domestic Company Registration; Non fiscal taxes of local government.
Reconnection	Immediate	1,000 RWF

Planned power or water interruptions	2 days advance notice via national media	Free
Change of pipe or change of ferrule size	5 working days	Quotation fee
Change of cable size or additional supply phase	5 working days	Quotation fee
Services and products put out to tender	30 days until opening date of the offers	Fee to purchase the tender document
Disconnection notice	5 days advance notice	Free

Major reforms are suggested to improve the effectiveness of the biogas subsidy and NDBP. The minimum technical requirements for a family to qualify for a capital subsidy for installing a biogas plant shall include the following: (i) own at least 2 cows that are home fed (zero grazed); (ii) have adequate space for biogas construction; (iii) have a permanent settlement; (iv) have easy access to water for mixing with cow dung; (v) able to financially co-contribute a reasonable share of total cost, after the government subsidy top-up is taken into consideration. In order to better target the effectiveness of the subsidy, the following categorization is tentatively proposed:

Table 25 Proposed Biogas Subsidy Amount Scaled to Income

Ubudehe Income Category	Subsidy amount	Justification
Category 1	Full coverage, less unskilled Labour costs (RWF 495,000)	These are the poorest households in Rwanda and hence affordability is very low. By definition, they may own no livestock and therefore may lack the minimum required feed-stock which is a criterion for obtaining the subsidy. Very careful scrutiny thus needs to be placed on customers in this category applying for a capital subsidy.
Category 2	Increase from RWF 300,000 to RWF 400,000	These households comprise the majority of potential target customers for the program (over 60% of total). By increasing the subsidy afforded to this category, an increase in market uptake is likely.
Category 3	Reduce from RWF 300,000 to RWF 200,000	These households are among the self-sustaining household categories. They can afford top up or access credit from lenders.
Category 4	No subsidy	These households have the capacity to raise their own revenues and have the required collateral to secure credit from lenders.

ENERGY SECTOR PERFORMANCE INDICATOR MATRIX

Table 26 Energy sector performance indicator matrix

Sector Outcome	Indicator	Baseline	High Level Targets			
		2013/14	2014/15	2015/16	2016/17	2017/18
563 MW of electric power installed capacity	MW of electricity system equivalent installed capacity (domestic generation + imports)	119.6	188	255	332	563
70% of households have access to electricity: - 48% on-grid - 22% off-grid	% of all households with electricity access	20.6%	25.5	35%	50%	70%
	% households with access to on-gird electricity	21%	23%	30%	38%	48%
	% households with access to off-gird electricity	0.5%	2.5%	7%	12%	22%
80% of all households employ cleaner cooking energy technologies	% of households using cleaner cooking energy technologies	60%	62%	68%	74%	80%
10% electricity output saved from efficiency measures	Total MWh saved from Demand-Side EE Measures calculated as % equivalent of total system output	8.3%	8.3%	8.5%	9%	10%
Realization of EAC Regional Integration Policy Priorities for the Energy Sector	Number of Fully Implemented EAC Regional Integration Priorities	-	-	2	4	5
150 million litres of strategic fuel reserves/ storage capacity	Million Litres of Fuel in Strategic Reserve	50	70	85	115	150

REPUBLIC OF RWANDA RURAL ELECTRIFICATION STRATEGY

The Government of Rwanda recognises the vital role that electricity access plays in accelerating economic development through improving health and standards of living. Energy and particularly access to electricity is the Government's key priority. This is why significant investments have been made and progress registered led to over 24% of households getting access to electricity. More efforts need to be made for the Government to achieve the set targets of 70% by 2017/18 and 100% by 2020.

For the above targets to be met, a combination of solutions that focus on the location, income and consumption level is required instead of the traditional connection to the grid that may not be suitable for all households. The most cost effective means for increasing access to electricity is through the use of off grid solutions that have wide range of technologies such as a basic solar lantern that can charge a phone or radio to a solar home system that can light an entire house and power appliances such as a television and Mini-grids that can provide higher levels of electricity to both households and small and medium businesses.

The Government developed this strategy with the objective of ensuring that Rwanda's households have access to electricity through the most cost effective means by developing programmes that will facilitate both the end users to access less costly technologies and increase private sector participation in the provision of these solutions.

The four distinct programmes in the strategy include; the provision of basic solar systems as a basic necessity to the less privileged population under *Ubudehe* 1, the establishment of a risk mitigation facility that will support the private sector, mechanisms that will increase, the development of mini-grids in suitable locations and the continued rollout of the Electricity Access Rollout Programme (EARP).

ACRONYMS AND ABBREVIATIONS

ACRONYM	DESCRIPTION
EARP	Electricity Access Roll-out Programme
EDCL	Electricity Development Corporation Limited
EDF	Rwanda Energy Development fund
EDPRS	Economic Development and Poverty Reduction Strategy
EU	European Union
EUCL	Electricity Utility Corporation Limited
FONERWA	National Fund for Environment in Rwanda
KWh	Kilowatt-hour (Unit of electricity)
MINALOC	Ministry of Local Government
MINECOFIN	Ministry of Finance and Economic Planning
MININFRA	Ministry of Infrastructure
REG	Rwanda Energy Group

RPPA Rwanda Public Procurement Agency

RURA Rwanda Utilities Regulation Authority

SACCOs Savings and Credit Cooperatives

SE4ALL Sustainable Energy For All

TWG Technical Working Group

1 INTRODUCTION

1.1 BACKGROUND

The strategic framework for Rwanda's energy sector is established in the Energy Sector Strategic Plan (ESSP) and the National Energy Policy (NEP), which set targets up to 2017/18. These documents recognize the essential role of electricity access in accelerating economic development, as well as improving health outcomes and standards of living for people in Rwanda. The target for electricity access is for 70% of households to have access by 2017/18, to be met through a combination of on-grid and off-grid supply. 100% access to electricity is targeted by 2020.

Advancing technology means that there is an ever-expanding range of ways for households to access electricity: a solar lantern that can also charge a phone or radio; a larger solar home system that can light an entire house and power appliances such as a television; and a grid connection that can power large-scale commercial and industrial use. In recognition of this, a key principle of this Strategy is to provide the most appropriate form of electricity access to households. A pathway will be established such that as households' energy requirements increase in line with the country's economic growth they can graduate to costlier, higher-powered forms of electricity.

The financing and implementation of this Strategy will be undertaken in partnership with the private sector, where competition will help drive down costs and improve customer choice. This builds upon the significant private sector interest in both solar home systems and mini-grids in Rwanda and across Africa. In order to maximize impact, Government resources will be used in a targeted fashion to: i) help provide a basic level of electricity access to those with the lowest income; ii) reduce the risks perceived by the private sector in providing systems on finance through the establishment of a risk mitigation facility; and iii) provide social goods such as education, information dissemination and standards to support the private sector and protect consumers.

The Rural Electrification Strategy can be considered as four distinct programmes:

1. Government will establish a mechanism to allow low-income households to access modern energy services through a basic solar system as a basic necessity.

2. Government will establish a risk-mitigation facility targeting the private sector such that solar products will be made available on financial terms that the population can afford.

3. Mini-grids will be developed by the private sector with Government playing a key role in identifying sites and establishing a framework through which these can become financially viable investments.

4. Government will continue to roll out the electricity network via EARP, focusing on connecting high consumption users and driving economic growth.

The implementation of the Strategy is expected to channel hundreds of millions of dollars of investment by the end of 2017/18 in both the on-grid and off-grid sectors, providing access to upwards of a million households.

1.2 PROGRESS OF EARP AND ALIGNING ACCESS TECHNOLOGIES TO CONSUMER NEEDS

PROGRESS OF EARP

The access priority over the last seven years has been on extending the national distribution system across the country and providing consumers with access to grid electricity, as indicated in Figure 1, below.

Figure 1. Percentage of the population with grid access (source: EARP)

These efforts have been led by the *Electricity Access Roll-out Programme (EARP)*, under which access has increased from 364,000 households in June 2012 to 590,000 households (24% of the total) by June 2016.

As illustrated in Figure 2, below, EARP has extended the national grid into every district in the country. This will continue to act as the power backbone, providing power to large users and driving economic growth.

Figure 2. National grid access provision (source: EARP)

ALIGNING ACCESS TECHNOLOGIES TO CONSUMER NEEDS

Figure 3, below, indicates the percentage of consumers connected under EARP by consumption level. The relatively low rates of consumption (almost half of consumers are currently using less than 20 kWh per month) means that, in addition to the need to source large amounts of finance up front, these consumers will require continuous subsidies as the revenue they produce for EUCL is insufficient to cover the financing and maintenance costs of their connection. The ESSP estimated that a consumer would need to use approximately 130 kWh per month in order to fund the cost of their own connection.

In order to meet consumer needs, a more holistic approach to energy access is required. This is the focus of this Rural Electrification Strategy.

Figure 3. Levels of household consumption (Source EDPRS 2)

1.3 THE EMERGENCE OF ALTERNATIVE APPROACHES TO ACCESS PROVISION

Two emerging technologies, standalone solar systems and mini-grids, have recently started to be delivered at large scale across Africa, and there is significant scope for these technologies to be used in Rwanda to rapidly scale up electricity access. A brief description of the technologies, the status of emerging industries in Rwanda and the problems that are being encountered is outlined below.

Stand-alone solar systems

These systems consist of solar panels that harvest the energy of the sun, storing it in a battery so that it can be used both during daytime and in the evening. A range of products are available at sizes and prices to suit different budgets and consumption patterns:

- High-quality solar lantern with a port to charge a mobile phone
- Basic solar home system consisting of multiple light fixtures throughout a house and the ability to power a radio or energy-efficient TV
- Advanced solar home system able to provide power more in line with a grid connection, powering devices such as a refrigerator

The observed consumption rates of consumers connected through EARP, and significant improvements in the technology and cost of off-grid solutions, make it clear that off-grid solutions should play a more important role in expanding electricity access.

A growing market for these systems is developing in Rwanda. However, given the high capital costs for these systems compared to average earnings, the vast majority of prospective consumers cannot afford to pay for the systems outright. This has led to suppliers of systems acting as sources of finance.

The key challenges faced by the stand-alone solar market are:

- affordability of the systems for consumers;
- consumer access to finance to pay for the systems;
- repayment risks related to credit facilities that the private sector provides while selling products;
- lack of standards in the market place, which has led to substandard products being sold, reducing consumer confidence; and
- awareness of consumers on the range of products and financing options available and the perception that solar home systems are a “second class” of energy.

This Strategy outlines initiatives to address each of these issues.

Mini-grids

A mini-grid is a standalone distribution network that is not connected to the national grid. Mini-grids require at least one source of generation or a hybrid combination, which is connected to businesses and households.

These mini-grids can be based on a range of technologies. Solar and hydro have the advantage of very low operating costs, but have high upfront costs and the availability of power is intermittent. Diesel generators can produce power when it is needed, but have significant operational costs and complexities associated with the purchase of diesel.

Mini-grids are expensive, costing around $1000 - $1500 for each connected consumer, around 50% higher than connecting consumers to the national network under EARP. As a consequence, mini-grids should only be used in specific circumstances, where: i) given the distance or other geographical constraints they are cheaper than connecting to the national network; and ii) there is sufficient demand to justify the investment.

Figure 4, below, indicates areas that are considerably far from the national grid and could be suitable sites for mini-grid development. Assessments will be made to determine sites with potential generation sources such as hydro and the related demand available to make mini-grids a viable option.

Figure 4. Potential mini-grid installation areas; source EARP

In scaling up the availability of mini-grids, two key challenges exist:

1. Identifying relevant sites: The cost of mini-grids means that they are only viable in very specific circumstances. Given that these are long-term investments, an understanding of both demand and the likely proximity of EARP is required.

2. Sharing of the risks with the developer and operator: Where mini-grids are developed and operated by the private sector, a number of risks are presented. As well as general finance and construction risk, mini-grids present a number of demand and generation risks which need to be allocated between Government and the private developer, such as: What if the projected demand doesn't materialise? What if the Rwandan franc depreciates? What if the river a small hydro was based on stops flowing? A clear framework is required on the allocation of these risks.

A REVISED APPROACH TO THE MEASUREMENT OF ENERGY ACCESS

There is a requirement to align targets with the revised approach to measuring access. Historically, energy access has been measured as the percentage of households connected to the grid. In recognition of the fact that a grid connection will not be the most efficient form of access for many households, and the emergence of alternative technologies, this Strategy proposes the use of the SE4ALL Multi-Tier Framework to define five levels of access, as illustrated in Table 1, below (a more detailed presentation of the framework can be found in Annex 2).

Table 1. Energy usage tier levels

Level	Tier 1	Tier 2	Tier 3	Tier 4	Tier 5
Energy usage	Household lighting, radio and phone charging	Household lighting, radio, phone charging and basic appliances (TV or fan)	Tier 2 plus medium appliances such as low power refrigeration	Tier 3 plus high power appliances such as pumping	24/7 high power suited to commercial and industrial uses

Under the ESSP, 48% of households were targeted for on-grid connection by 2017/18. Under the revised targets, access from larger solar home systems and mini-grid connections will also be taken to satisfy this element of the target, since they can also provide appropriate high-quality electricity access. The 48% target is therefore reframed as including both on-grid and any other system providing Tier 2 or higher access levels.

To achieve the targets highlighted in the ESSP, 22% of households will gain access to at least Tier 1 energy service. Government will facilitate distribution of a range of standalone solar systems that will provide this basic level of access to those on the lowest income (through Programme 1 of this strategy). These systems will be Lighting Global quality-verified and, alone or in combination, will be able to provide Tier 1 access to households. In doing so, they will not only offer high-quality light in homes, but they will also allow for the charging of basic electronic devices such as mobiles phones or small radios.

The revised targets for electricity access are presented in Table 2, below.

Table 2. Revised breakdown of the 70% access target

	Revised Target proposal - 2017/18	Original Targets (EDPRS 2 & SSP) 2017/18	2020 Targets
Tier 0 (no access)	30%	30%	0%
Tier 1	22%	(off-grid) 22%	100% Access
Tier 2	48% (of which approx. 31-35% grid)		
Tier 3			
Tier 4-5		(grid) 48%	
Total Access	70%	70%	

In addition to providing energy access, a key target of Programme 1 is the eradication of kerosene, which would deliver significant expected health, economic and educational benefits for households.

2 OBJECTIVES, PROGRAMMES, PRINCIPLES AND THEMES

2.1 Objectives

Advances in technologies, along with reductions in cost, mean that off-grid solutions can be the most cost-effective way of providing essential energy services for a significant proportion of households. Because off-grid systems can be scaled to meet demand requirements, they can provide an affordable and flexible way for households to start progressing up the energy ladder, particularly for those on low incomes. It is in this context that MININFRA has developed this Rural Electrification Strategy. The overarching objectives of the Strategy are outlined below:

Primary objectives of the Rural Electrification Strategy

1. Ensure that by 2018, 70% of Rwandans have access to electricity and that by 2020, 100% of Rwandans have access to electricity. A range of options from standalone solar systems through to isolated mini-grids and grid connection will be available.

2. Government will encourage households to access the most appropriate form of electricity based on their income levels and usage patterns, and ensure that as households' energy needs increase in line with economic growth they are able to access technologies aligned with these increased needs.

3. Consumers will continue to be connected to the national power system through EARP

and the task of wiring up the country will continue. Government resources will be channeled to driving economic growth.

2.2 Programmes

In order to ensure that "each household will be able to access the most appropriate form of electricity based on their income levels and usage patterns", this Strategy is broken out into four discrete programmes based on the consumer and technology, as below.

Programmes under the Rural Electrification Strategy

1. Government will establish a mechanism to allow low-income households to access modern energy services through a basic solar system as a basic necessity.

2. Government will establish a risk-mitigation facility targeting the private sector such that solar products will be made available on financial terms that the population can afford.

3. Mini-grids will be developed by the private sector with Government playing a key role in identifying sites and establishing a framework through which these can become financially viable investments.

4. Government will continue to roll out the electricity network via EARP, focusing on connecting high consumption users and driving economic growth.

2.3 Driving principles

This Strategy has been developed in line with the following driving principles:

• Rural electrification must be driven by economic efficiency: Implementing policies and practices for extending service should take into account the aim of offering electricity service to all rural consumers at the lowest possible cost. This will enable the efficient use of scarce financial resources and minimise the need for subsidies to bridge the gap between supply cost and affordable tariffs for low-income rural consumers.

• The private sector will take a lead role in financing and delivering off grid energy access: There is significant private sector interest in the delivery of rural electrification technologies such as solar home systems and mini-grids, and this interest will be harnessed as much as possible, leading to a number of advantages:

- The strain on government resources will be minimised.

- The power of competition will be leveraged to deliver better consumer choice, value and service.

• Government financial support will only be used to address affordability gaps and market failures: Government finance will be used where it is required to enable the private sector to operate or to bridge affordability issues for the lowest earning households of the population. In general, Government support will only be used to:

- enable the lowest earning house-holds entry level energy access as a basic necessity;

- establish a risk mitigation facility for the private sector to provide finance to the remainder of the population; and

- supply social goods to support the program such as education/promotion and support in the supply chain, and work to establish an enabling framework within which the private sector could operate.

• Finance will be targeted at ensuring consumers have the most appropriate, cost effective technology for their needs: Given the range of new standalone technologies on the market and the variety of consumption requirements of different households and businesses, there is an opportunity to better align Government's electricity access interventions with customer needs. This Strategy is intended to ensure that Government financial support is well targeted, giving people the power they need while making the best use of limited Government resources.

• The project is intended to be financially sustainable: Whilst these programmes will initially require funding from Government and its development partners, they are expected to catalyse a sustainable private-sector-led market for off-grid energy provision. Once these companies have proven the market's viability, they will be able to take on a greater share of the investment risk. This will allow for more limited Government interventions going forward, alleviating the fiscal burden.

2.4 Cross-cutting themes

There are five cross-cutting themes that will be addressed in each of the programmes:

1. Consumers will be encouraged to gain access through the most efficient option: The introduction of standalone solar systems and, in some areas, mini-grids, means that many consumers will now have more than one option through which they can receive access to electricity. It is important that consumers select an option that will service their needs and represents an efficient use of both their and Government's resources. By way of example, if a household only requires access to power a small number of lights and charge a mobile phone, it is not an effective use of Government money to subsidise a grid connection (the subsidy cost could range between $500 and $900). Instead, it would be more efficient for the household to purchase a solar home system, and in the future graduate to a grid connection. The levels of Government support to each of the connection options will be calibrated to ensure that the selection that is most financially prudent for a household is also most economically sensible for the country.

2. The private sector and competition will be used: The delivery of solar home systems will be led by the private sector to help to reduce the financial and delivery burden placed upon Government and stimulate economic activity in the private sector, including job creation and the establishment of a set of Rwandan entrepreneurs. Additionally, a competitive market will be established to:

- help drive costs down;

- increase customer choice and encourage innovative approaches to be developed that may better fit the Rwandan market; and

- diversify the risk associated with relying on one vendor to roll out the systems.

These benefits will be realised by establishing a "level playing field" for all qualifying companies and transparent and standard processes for accessing the support provided by Government and development partners. In addition, the effectiveness of the market will be continually monitored to ensure it is working effectively and delivering on these benefits.

3. Standards and Consumer protection will be put in place: Whilst this Strategy seeks to attract a wide range of private companies and a multitude of different products there is a need for certain service levels and standards to be enforced to both protect consumers and mitigate against the risk of inferior products or suppliers. To do so, standards will be set and enforced in two key areas:

I. Minimum technical standards of equipment:

- For standalone solar systems these standards will be aligned with the "Lighting Global" accreditation to ensure that only accredited products can be sold and qualify for Government support.

- Where mini-grids are installed the distribution network must confirm to standards agreed with EUCL to "future proof" these grids, such that they can subsequently be connected to the national electricity network.

II. Quality of Service Standards:

- Suppliers of solar home systems who wish to be eligible for Government support identified in this Strategy must confirm to certain standards around maintenance and repair of the system and system replacement in the event that it is faulty. These standards will be developed as part of the implementation of this Strategy.

- Mini-grid operators will similarly be required to commit to "quality of service" standards such as maximum levels of outages.

4. Recycling and Environmental protection will be established: The increased penetration of modern electricity access will make a number of products such as kerosene lamps redundant. There is some residual value in the materials that make up these products and a private sector led approach to recycling these redundant objects will be developed in parallel with entering into agreements with private suppliers.

5. Local capacity and enterprise will be developed: Recycling and Environmental protection will be established: The need for a nationwide supply chain and the opportunities in retailing and installing solar home systems represent an excellent opportunity to develop local enterprise and employ Rwandan nationals. Equally, after installation, there will be a need for technicians to maintain the units and a secondary market is likely to develop in the future for spare parts such as batteries. To ensure the programmes outlined in this Strategy deliver as much economic benefit as possible, Government will encourage training and capacity development of local staff. Additionally, ways of attracting Rwandan capital into the programmes will be investigated as it would also help to retain some of the profits from the programmes in the country.

3 DETAILED DESCRIPTION OF PROGRAMMES

3.1 Policy statements for programmes

Programme 1: Government will establish a mechanism to allow low-income households to access modern energy services through a basic solar system as a basic necessity.

Households with the lowest income that would not be able to purchase a solar system present a significant repayment risk to the private sector. In recognition of the economic, social, and health benefits that basic access to electricity provides, Government of Rwanda, with the support of development partners, will establish a mechanism to allow low-income households to access modern energy services through a basic solar system.

Government will take the lead in the identification of key beneficiaries of the proposed mechanisms.

Key policy statement 1

- Government will establish a mechanism to allow low-income households to access modern energy services through a basic solar system as a basic necessity.
- Households will be able to choose from a range of products and systems from a number of accredited suppliers. This market-led approach will help to drive down costs, allow for innovation and increase customer choice.

PROGRAMME 2: GOVERNMENT WILL ESTABLISH A RISK-MITIGATION FACILITY TARGETING THE PRIVATE SECTOR SUCH THAT SOLAR PRODUCTS WILL BE MADE AVAILABLE ON FINANCIAL TERMS THAT THE POPULATION CAN AFFORD.

For households in Rwanda that are not connected to the grid, a standalone solar system would be of significant benefit, both in terms of well-being (through transitioning away from the negative health effects of primary fuels), and financially (through savings in the costs of primary fuels and purchasing very high cost electricity such as batteries or paying for phone charging).

Unfortunately, the uptake of solar home systems by these households is extremely low. The discussions with the private sector have indicated that it has proven difficult for them to provide systems on financial terms these consumers can afford (such as monthly repayment plans). This is because the risks inherent in providing systems to these consumers drives up the cost of capital for the suppliers and results in them either being unable to provide the systems or having to sell them at such a high price only the wealthy can afford them.

To address these challenges, a risk-mitigation facility will be established to encourage the private sector to expand coverage in the market and provide products on financing terms that are affordable. In developing this risk-mitigation facility, MININFRA will engage with both the private sector and development partners.

Key policy statement 2

Government will establish a risk-mitigation facility to encourage the private sector to increase sales of solar products and services, the risk-mitigation facility will:

- be targeted such that finance is used as effectively as possible to deliver the maximum number of households connected for the least support;
- ensure that the level of support a company receives is directly correlated with its delivery on Government targets;
- encourage companies to make solar products, solar home systems, or services available on repayment plans; and
- be granted in return for a commitment from the company to meet certain criteria, such as sales targets and quality and scope of service.

PROGRAMME 3: MINI-GRIDS WILL BE DEVELOPED BY THE PRIVATE SECTOR WITH GOVERNMENT PLAYING A KEY ROLE IN IDENTIFYING SITES AND ESTABLISHING A FRAMEWORK THROUGH WHICH THESE BECOME FINANCIALLY VIABLE INVESTMENTS.

Mini-grids are small distribution systems isolated from the national power system which includes a source of power generation. This generation is usually provided by hydro or solar, often in conjunction with either battery storage or diesel generation to handle the intermittency of power output presented by renewables. It is likely that they could play a role in energy provision in Rwanda but, given the large investment costs (an EU study for Rwanda estimates around $1500 per connection – more than grid access), there are a number of pre-conditions that need to be met to make them viable. These include:

1. Distance from the grid: Where a connection is available to the national electricity network a mini-grid is unlikely to be financially viable, since the costs of power generation in a mini-grid are usually much higher. In deciding where to locate a mini-grid it must be determined whether this is the least-cost option for providing Tier 3 power to households and businesses. This will, in a large part, be determined by the proximity of the grid.

2. Demand: Given the large fixed costs of a mini-grid in both the network and the generation technology, there needs to be a demand that is both high, and spread across the day for it to be viable. Most households consume power during the evening but for a mini-grid based on solar or hydro to be viable it is likely that there would need to be a large demand during the day too.

Given the constraints above, the relatively small size of the country and the planned extent of EARP, it is suspected that mini-grids are likely to be financially viable in a limited number of cases. The identification of sites eligible for the development of mini-grids will be led by REG. As a first step a number of candidate sites will be identified. This will be informed by the sites of potential mini-hydro projects, geographically isolated centers of demand such as mobile phone towers or water pumping stations and the rural settlement plans. A detailed feasibility study will be undertaken on these candidate sites and those where a mini-grid represents the least-cost option for power provision will be tendered out to the private sector.

Key policy statement 3

- In order to reduce costs and de-risk investment for prospective mini-grid developers, Government will first identify eligible sites and undertake a financial and technical feasibility study. Where the provision of access through a mini-grid represents the least cost option, Government will undertake measures to stimulate demand, through either policy or investment. These sites will then be tendered out to private developers.

PROGRAMME 4: GOVERNMENT WILL CONTINUE TO ROLL-OUT THE ELECTRICITY NETWORK VIA EARP, FOCUSING ON CONNECTING HIGH-CONSUMPTION USERS AND DRIVING ECONOMIC GROWTH.

Unlike the other programmes detailed in the Strategy, EARP is not new. However the programme need to be modified so that there is a coherent and holistic approach to rural access. One of the key objectives of this Rural Electrification Strategy is to ensure that *"each household will be able to access the most appropriate form of electricity based on their income levels and usage patterns"*. This means that a number of the consumers who were initially targeted to receive an "on-grid" connection will now be better served through access to a solar home system or mini-grid connection. This approach would allow the financial resources available for EARP to be channeled to high consumption areas such productive use centers that will drive economic growth and specific households that are capable of paying for the connection costs

Achieving this requires:

1. Planning: The On grid plan is under review to ensure that the financial resources targeted for connecting productive areas (agro processing industries, mining areas and others) that will drive economic growth are being prioritized.

2. Policy: A Tier 2 solar home system is cheaper for a consumer than to connect to the grid, the connection policy needs to be revised and so that the financial and social incentives provided by government are aligned and take into considerations sources of electricity that are suitable to different categories of households.

4 DETAILED IMPLEMENTATION PLAN

4.1 Institutional Framework

Before presenting the roles and responsibilities of Government institutions, it is worth clarifying the separation of roles between the private and public sector, presented in Table 3, below:

Table 3. Roles and responsibilities of Government and the private sector

Roles and responsibilities of Government	Roles and responsibilities of the Private Sector
Government will: - provide Tier 1 access to those households with the lowest incomes; - de-risk investment by the private sector through the provision of a risk-mitigation facility; - establish the enablers for the market to expand including the development of an institutional and regulatory framework and increased consumer awareness; - disseminate information; - enforce quality standards; - provide fiscal incentives to transition, as well as disincentives to remain on primitive fuels; and - establish a policy and regulatory framework to incentivize the private sector to recycle redundant items such as kerosene lamps and used batteries.	In order for the private sector to benefit from the Government programmes developed during the implementation of this Strategy, they must: - for standalone solar systems, provide only products certified by Lighting Global (or another appropriate and agreed internationally recognized standard where Lighting Global not available); - for mini-grids, conform to standards set by the Rwanda Standards Board - commit to a minimum service and warranty period for units (details to be agreed); - offer solutions to Government for the recycling of old kerosene lamps; and - report to EDCL quarterly, providing sales and other relevant information (details to be agreed).

Within Government, the successful implementation of this Strategy will require clear institutional arrangements to be developed to cover coordination, implementation, financial intermediation, and monitoring and evaluation.

A summary of potential institutional roles and responsibilities is illustrated in Table 4, overleaf:

Table 4. Potential institutional roles and responsibilities for the EDF

Function	Institution	Roles & Responsibilities
Coordination Hub	MININFRA	- Key decisions on strategy and implementation - Ownership and responsibility for delivering targets
	Technical Working Group	- Sector coordination and communication

	(TWG) on Access (Chaired by MININFRA)	- Delegated responsibility for implementation decisions - Manage monitoring and reporting - Supported by Panel of Experts and Private Sector
	Private-Sector Body (e.g., PSF sub-group on energy)	- Private sector body to provide coordinated partnership with government through the TWG and other sector coordination activities - Engage with government in developing the enabling environment and market growth activities
Technical Hub	EDCL	Manage the technical aspects of the program including: - Monitoring vendor performance (including sales volumes) - Leading the dissemination of information - Zoning areas as "priority off-grid" to expand the market for private companies
	Rwanda Standards Board	- Setting product quality standards - Certifying vendors - Enforcing product quality standards
	RURA	- Monitoring prices and the level of competition in the market - Setting regulations for the off-grid and mini-grid sectors
Financial Hub	MINECOFIN	- Provision of finance for social goods, energy access for the Vulnerable and a contribution towards guarantees and other risk mitigation instruments.
	FONERWA	- Coordination and mobilization of donor funds - Accessing international climate finance - Channeling funds to appropriate windows
	Institution TBD	- Provide loans to the private companies - Manage risk-mitigation facility
Local implementation	MINALOC	- Support in identifying mini-grid locations - Set and monitor dissemination targets at a district level
	DISTRICTS / SACCOs	- Support in the dissemination of information - Support in monitoring vendor performance and product quality standards - Help to enforce payment - Coordination and tracking Ubudehe scheme and implementation Management of possible theft insurance

4.2 FINANCING THE PROGRAMMES

Public and Private sources of finance are expected to support the investments necessary to achieve the goals of this strategy. Some of the sources of public finance available includes; the Scaling up Renewable Energy Program (SREP), from the Climate Investment Funds which approved a total of up to USD $50 Million the that will be used in developing private sector-led off-grid and mini-grid markets in Rwanda. In addition, the private sector which is expected to play a lead role in implementing this strategy will provide the commercial equity and debt to support their investments in the sector.

4.3 Communication Plan

Communicating this Strategy with key partners is critical to ensuring smooth implementation. Stakeholders such as Government institutions, civil society, development partners, and the public at large must be aware of the Strategy and its benefits, and the challenges that may be met during its implementation. The Communication Plan is expected to be implemented by MININFRA and will involve conducting regular meetings with energy-sector stakeholders as well as holding press conferences and talk shows at different media houses and road shows. The Communication Plan is tailored to specific stakeholders as summarized in Table 5, below.

Table 5. Summary of Communication Plan

Stakeholder	Messages to be communicated	Channel
Government institutions and Development partners	- New roles and responsibilities of the different government institutions - Expected outputs for the different quarters - Impacts on rural electrification	- Meetings - Sharing of annual Reports
Private sector	- Market changes to promote greater cooperation - New developments, including the formation of a procurement cycle and development of new processes for procurement - The focus on fair and competitive procurement and a contestable market	- Meetings - Conferences
General public	- Information on the programmes and products available - The impacts of the Strategy on their health, the livelihood of the community, and the economy	- Media houses, print and electronic (newspapers, radio and television stations) - Road shows

The details on the specific dates on when these activities above will be carried out are in the detailed Implementation Roadmap (Annex 1).

THE SE4ALL MULTI-TIER FRAMEWORK

Attributes Indicator	Tier 0	Tier 1	Tier 2	Tier 3	Tier 4	Tier 5	
	No Access	Basic	Advanced				
Capacity	Power		V. Low Power Min 3 W	Low Power Min 50 W	Medium Power Min 200 W	High Power Min 800 W	Very High Power Min 2 kW
	AND Daily Capacity		Min 12 Wh	Min 200 Wh	Min 1 kWh	Min 3.4 kWh	Min 8.2 kWh

	OR Services		Lighting of 1,000 lmhrs/day + phone charging	Lighting, fan, TV, + phone charging possible			
Duration	Hours per day		Min 4 hrs	Min 4 hrs	Min 8 hrs	Min 16 hrs	Min 23 hrs
	Hours per evening		Min 1 hrs	Min 2 hrs	Min 3 hrs	Min 4 hrs	Min 4 hrs
Reliability					Max 14 distruptions per week	Max 3 disruptions per week of total duration < 2 hours	
Indicated Minimum Technology				Mini-grid			
					Main grid		

STRATEGIC ECONOMIC AND LEGAL INFORMATION

ECONOMIC ENVIRONMENT

MAJOR FEATURES OF THE ECONOMY

Rwanda's economic performance in the near future depends very much on the strategic investment programmes to improve its infrastructure, the global demand for its exports, and the improved business climate and its effects on promoting private investment. In order for Rwanda to overcome infrastructure bottlenecks and other supply-side constraints, investment is needed in, *inter alia*, broadening access to electricity by increasing household grid-connectivity; the railway line to facilitate Rwanda's import/export trade; the construction of an international airport in Bugesera; and in irrigation systems to promote agricultural productivity.

Growth in Rwanda has also become increasingly dependent on growth in its key trading partners. [13] Its concentrated export base and heavy dependency on foreign aid leaves the country vulnerable to sharp global downturns and/or sharp increases in commodity prices, which could affect Rwanda's economy through the following channels: slowdown in global demand for exports; reduction in FDI; slowdown in tourism receipts and inward remittances; and contraction of the foreign-aid envelope. Similarly, rising fuel prices are a threat. Export diversification and lower dependence on aid would reduce Rwanda's vulnerability over the medium to long-term.

The Republic of Rwanda, with an area of 26,300 km^2 and a population of approximately 11.7 million, is the most densely populated country in Africa. It is located in central and eastern Africa, bordering Burundi, the Democratic Republic of Congo, Tanzania, and Uganda. With a per capita GDP of US$595 in 2011, Rwanda remains a least developed country.

Rwanda is still a rural economy: only 19% of the population live in urban areas. [1] The agriculture sector employs about 80% of the population, and constitutes about one third of Rwanda's GDP. Agricultural activities are mainly subsistence farming, and agricultural output is predominantly in the informal sector, with one third still produced in the non-monetary economy. [2]

3. The mining sector's contribution to GDP is still negligible, but its share in total exports has been significant (Table AI.1) . The share of manufacturing to GDP remains low, at 6.6% in 2011, while the share of services increased to 46% over the review period (Table I.1) .

4. As a landlocked country, trading costs are high (Chapter III) . In addition, the economy is highly vulnerable to external shocks, because of its narrow export base, its heavy dependency on foreign aid, and the rapid rise of international fuel prices. Its exports have been concentrated in a few products/minerals, and to a few markets, although recently there have been some diversification efforts and progress (see section (3)) . The authorities consider that supply-side constraints include: poor infrastructure, in particular rural transport links; high energy costs; lack of access to credit and weak organization of the rural sector; lack of good farming practices and export-related standards to enable diversification into agri-processed industries; lack of product diversification; and low competitiveness of manufacturers.

5. The national currency, the Rwanda franc (RF), appreciated slightly against the U.S. dollar between 2005 and 2008, before depreciating again in 2009-11 (Table I.1) . Rwanda accepted the obligations under Article VIII of the IMF Articles of Agreement in 1998, and maintains a system free of restrictions on payments and transfers for current international transactions.

RECENT ECONOMIC DEVELOPMENTS

Rwanda's economy developed relatively rapidly during the period under review, with real GDP growth averaging 8.5% annually from 2005-11 (Table I.1) . Per capita GDP more than doubled in the same period, from US$289 to US$595. The poor benefited from Rwanda's fast economic growth, as the poverty rate fell from 56.7% in 2006 to 44.9% in 2011 [3] , while Rwanda's UNDP Human Development Index improved from 0.390 to 0.429. [4]

Rwanda's economic growth has been facilitated by prudent macroeconomic policies, both fiscal and monetary. Foreign aid, which accounts for around half of total government revenue, has been managed well. Total revenue has increased, mainly driven by higher taxes and grants. At the same time, total expenditure and net lending also increased, probably due to increased expenditure on infrastructure. The overall fiscal balance (including grants) changed from a small surplus (2.2%) in 2005 to a small deficit (-1.6%) in 2010.

Monetary policy has been somewhat "proactive". After the onset of the global economic crisis, the Central Bank (the National Bank of Rwanda, NBR) cut its policy rate (the key repo rate or KRR) three times (since November 2009), to encourage economic activities. The KRR remained unchanged between November 2010 and October 2011, during which the Central Bank was reluctant to increase interest rates to contain inflationary pressures. The KRR was only increased again in October 2011 (it was increased three times between October 2011 and May 2012) . [5] In 2011, inflation rose rapidly, mainly due to higher global food and fuel prices, and core inflation was up from 2.3% in 2010 to 5.7%. Nevertheless, inflation was contained at a single-digit rate, while it was in double-digits in Rwanda's neighbouring countries. [6] It appears that inflation was contained mainly due to improved food production and a reduction in fuel taxes (in July 2011 and January 2012, respectively), and the final increase in the KRR.

The authorities considered the "sustained stability" of the exchange rate also limited the pass-through of imported inflation to the domestic market. [7] According to the IMF, Rwanda's exchange rates have been slow to move in line with macroeconomic fundamentals, owing to the dominant role of the NBR in the market, which discourages banks from trading among themselves. [8] As from 27 December 2010, the official exchange rate is the weighted average computed from a previous foreign-exchange interbank market transaction and an intervention transaction by the NBR. The NBR applies a margin of +/-0.8% to the official rate to derive a customer rate. From 1 May 2011, the *de facto* exchange-rate arrangement has been reclassified to a stabilized arrangement, from a crawl-like arrangement, although the *de jure* exchange rate arrangement is classified as floating. [9] According to the authorities, the NBR has been implementing a market-driven managed float exchange rate regime, under which the Central Bank intervenes only to smooth the exchange rate volatility depending on the volume of available official foreign exchange reserves.

During the period under review, the lending rates remained high, and the interest rate spread was wide, partly reflecting a lack of competition in Rwanda's banking sector (Table I.1) . Despite the high lending rates, total new authorized loans by commercial banks and the Development Bank of Rwanda (BRD) have been increasing. Loans distributed to commerce, restaurants, and hotels account for the highest share (36.7%), followed by public works and buildings (24.7%) . Loans to the agriculture sector, and insurance and other non-financial services, more than doubled from 2010 to 2011.

Vision 2020, which contains Rwanda's long-term development goals, aims to transform Rwanda from a low-income agriculture-based economy to a knowledge-based, service-oriented economy by 2020. The Government intends to achieve this through, *inter alia*, trade policies, in particular export diversification and promotion policies (Chapter II) . Against this background, the Government has undertaken a number of reforms to, *inter alia*, overcome bottlenecks; lower business costs and improve the investment environment; and reduce the effects of external shocks to economic development. Rwanda was among the top global reformers from 2009 to 2011

Rwanda's economic (including trade) and structural policy reforms have paved the way for its relatively fast economic growth, driven mainly by improved productivity in agriculture and industry, increased exports, strong domestic demand [11], and improved investment climate. Partly reflecting the improved business environment and lower business costs, investment increased during the period under review (Table I.1) .

Agriculture production has benefited from a number of programmes to address soil fertility, soil erosion, and in particular the crop intensification programme (CIP) focusing on facilitating access to fertilizers and selected seeds, land-use consolidation, and improved irrigation (Chapter IV) . Productivity in agriculture has improved, and agricultural exports have been increasing since 2007 (Table AI.1) .

The non-agriculture sectors have recovered from the global demand decline and the tight credit conditions in the domestic banking sector. Strong performance in the mining sector was stimulated mainly by higher prices for minerals on international markets. Despite its small share of GDP, manufacturing has been growing. Performance was driven by beverages and tobacco, and food processing. Construction was boosted by infrastructure projects, as well as commercial, administrative, and residential building.

The services sector remained the largest contributor to GDP during the period under review, accounting for close to half of GDP. Services growth was robust as financial services continued to grow significantly, followed by health, education, and public administration, reflecting continued high public expenditure to stimulate the economy (Chapter IV) . On the other hand, transport suffered due to high oil prices.

TRADE PERFORMANCE

The share of goods and services exports to GDP fell from 11.5% in 2005 to 10.9% in 2010, before rebounding to 13% in 2011. During the same period, the share of imports was up from 25.2% to 32% (Table I.1) . The current account deficit widened, from 2.2% of GDP in 2005 to 7.4% in 2011, while the overall balance remained in surplus, thanks in part to inflows to finance large public and private investment projects (Table I.2) . International reserve coverage stayed above five months of prospective imports.

Imports increased faster than exports during the review period, in part reflecting the increasing international food and fuel prices. Fuelled by imports and partly financed by substantial donor inflows, total final consumption expenditure accounted for 98% of GDP (Table I.1) . As a consequence, the trade deficit increased over the period.

Rwanda chiefly exports agricultural products, in particular coffee and tea, and mining products. In 2011, primary products accounted for 85.5% of total exports, down from 88.7% in 2005 (Chart I.1 and Table AI.1) . During the same period, the share of manufactures to total merchandise exports rose from 11.3% to 14.1%, reflecting Rwanda's efforts to shift its exports from raw materials and commodity products to processed goods. Other consumer goods (5.6%), and machinery and transport equipment (5.4%) are the major manufactured exports (Table AI.1) .

Rwanda's Balance of Payments, 2005-11

(US$ Million)

	2005	2006	2007	2008	2009	2010	2011
Current account	-58	-134	-83	-230	-373	-421	-462
Trade balance	-229	-299	-404	-613	-762	-787	-1,100
Exports, fob	125	147	177	268	235	297	464
Imports, fob	-354	-446	-581	-881	-997	-1,084	-1,564
Services and income (net)	-194	-161	-140	-136	-215	-292	-244
Services (net)	-167	-132	-123	-101	-178	-246	-189
Income (net)	-27	-29	-17	-35	-37	-46	-55
Trade and services and income balance	-422	-460	-545	-749	-977	-1,079	-1,342
Current transfers (net)	365	326	461	519	604	657	881
Private	47	77	99	73	80	91	133
Public	318	248	363	446	524	567	747
Capital and financial account	165	216	197	316	427	499	683
Capital account	94	1,400	92	210	200	286	197
Capital transfers	94	1,400	92	210	200	286	197
Debt forgiveness	0	1,227	0	0	0	0	0
Other capital transfers	94	174	92	210	200	286	197
Financial transactions account	72	-1,184	105	106	227	214	486
Public sector capital (LT) (net)	54	-1,105	80	105	81	52	207
Private sector capital (LT) (net)	-5	25	81	90	154	181	231
Lt. debt			3	10	43	129	149
Amortization			-4	-4	-8	-12	-55
Direct investment	11	31	82	85	119	64	138
Other capital	23	-105	-57	-89	-9	-19	48
Errors & omissions	12	0	-3	-28	3	-6	14

Overall balance	119	82	111	58	57	72	235
Indicators (%)							
Balance of goods/GDP	-8.9	-9.6	-10.8	-14.0	-16.7	-14.0	-17.6
Current account balance/GDP	-2.2	-4.3	-2.2	-5.2	-8.2	-7.5	-7.4
Gross official reserves (months of prospective imports of goods and services)	7.6	6.8	7.0	5.1	6.2	5.9	5.8

Source: Information provided by the Rwandan authorities.

After a drop in 2010 due to lower global demand, the value of Rwanda's exports increased significantly in 2011, partly because of increased international prices of coffee, tea, and mineral products (Chart I.2 and Table AI.2) . Europe remains the main destination, although the EU's share fell by almost half between 2005 and 2011, while Switzerland's share more than doubled. The second biggest destination is Africa: however, the share of Rwanda's exports to other EAC countries fell from 24.8% to 17.7%, as Kenya's share dropped from 22% to 13.9%. The shares of other African countries increased. As Rwanda only joined the EAC in 2009, it may be some years before the effects of membership on its export performance become noticeable.

5. Rwanda has preferential market access to a number of international markets including the EU and the United States, as well as other EAC members and the COMESA market (Chapter II) . Despite eligibility for a wide variety of preferential trade schemes, Rwanda's goods are still exported mainly to a few traditional trading partners, and utilization of these preferential market access opportunities remains low.

Rwanda's imports remain dominated by capital goods and consumer goods (Chart I.1 and Table AI.3) . Capital goods imports include machinery, to build domestic industrial capacities and promote the manufacturing sector. Processed goods are also imported for consumption, since the domestic manufacturing sector is still small.

7. Between 2005 and 2011, the value of Rwanda's imports more than tripled (Table AI.4) . Rwanda is a net importer from the EAC region (nearly one third of imports) (Chart I.2) . The shares of Uganda, Tanzania, and Burundi rose while Kenya's share fell. The share of imports from European countries declined, as did the share of the Middle East, although the UAE accounted for 5% of total imports in 2011. The increase in the share of Asian countries mainly reflects increases in imports from, *inter alia*, China and India.

Rwanda remains a net services importer (Table I.2) . Although tourism is rebounding strongly and becoming one of Rwanda's largest foreign exchange earners, trade in services remains in deficit, and the deficit has been increasing in recent years, reflecting the faster increase in services imports over exports. Imports of transportation services increased particularly rapidly as well as government services. [12]

INVESTMENT PERFORMANCE

Foreign direct investment (FDI) flows increased significantly between 2005 and 2009, from US$14 million to US$119 million, probably reflecting the improved business environment, including lower business costs (Table I.3) . However, FDI inflows contracted sharply in 2010 as a consequence of the global economic crisis. Data were not available on the sectoral breakdown of FDI, the major sources or whether FDI increased significantly after Rwanda joined the EAC.

Nevertheless, FDI flows into Rwanda are still much lower than into the other EAC countries (except Burundi) . Although the increase in FDI reflects partly economies of scale in the EAC member states, its low level in Rwanda also reflects its still-high business costs. Further reforms are needed to lower business costs, and to transform the improved investment climate into increased economic activity by the private sector.

TRADE AND INVESTMENT REGIMES

GENERAL FRAMEWORK

Since Rwanda's previous Trade Policy Review, its institutional framework has remained generally unchanged. The new Constitution of the Republic of Rwanda was published in the *Official Gazette* on 4 June 2003, and has been amended three times. The first Amendment, on 2 December 2003, was about the term of office of the President and Vice President of the Supreme Court, and the organization of the National Public Prosecution Authority; the second, on 8 December 2005, covered the administrative organization of national boundaries; and the third on 13 August 2008, mainly dealt with organization of the election of the members of the Chamber of Deputies.

Executive authority in Rwanda is vested in the President and Cabinet. The President is elected for a seven-year term, renewable only once. The Parliament is composed of the Senate and Chamber of Deputies. It is in charge of passing laws, legislating, and overseeing executive action in accordance with procedures determined by the Constitution. The Supreme Court and other courts exercise judicial power. In particular, the Commercial High Court and three commercial courts (Nyarugenge, Huye, and Musanze) handle trade disputes. The executive, legislative, and judiciary bodies are independent and separate. Each Ministry formulates policies relating to its field of activities by drafting bills.

The Ministry of Trade and Industry has the main responsibility for formulating and implementing trade policy. Other ministries and agencies with primary and shared responsibility for trade policy development include: the Ministry of Finance and Economic Planning, Ministry of Foreign Affairs, Ministry of Agriculture, and the Ministry of East African Affairs. Government institutions, such as the Rwanda Development Board, Rwanda Revenue Authority, National Bank of Rwanda, and Rwanda Bureau of Standards also play a key role in trade policy formulation and implementation.

Coordination of trade policy is under the Ministry of Trade and Industry through the National Development and Trade Policy Forum (NDTPF) which is made up of representatives from the public sector, private sector, academia, and civil society. The NDTPF was originally established as the forum for stakeholder consultations on the Economic Partnership Agreement (EPA) negotiations. Under the Rwanda Trade Policy of 2010 [16], it was proposed to replace the NDTPF with a broader technical and consultative committee, the National Trade Policy Forum, with sub-committees to deal with specific trade issues. A senior-level policy-making committee was also proposed, comprising permanent secretaries and heads of institutions, to be responsible for overall supervision of trade policy formulation and implementation. The Department of Trade would serve as the secretariat for the National Trade Policy Forum.

Another important forum for consultation on trade policy making is the Private Sector Development Cluster, which brings together government, private sector, and development partners. Private sector representation has been mainly through the Rwanda Private Sector Federation (PSF), the umbrella organization for the business community. The PSF has ten sector-specific chambers and its secretariat has five departments, including a trade and policy advocacy department, which participates in national consultations on trade policy development.

Rwandan legislation establishes the primacy of international legal instruments, including WTO Agreements. Ratified or approved treaties or international agreements rank above domestic legislation once they have been published in the *Official Gazette*, subject to their implementation by the other parties.

Recent changes in Rwanda's trade-related legislation have been driven mainly by the need to promote trade and improve the business environment. The main changes include new laws on intellectual property and special economic zones, and laws relating to companies, and on arbitration and conciliation in commercial matters (Table II.1) .

Selected trade and trade-related legislation, December 2011

Law and number
Law modifying and complementing Law No. 10/2009 of 14/05/2009 on mortgages, No. 13/2010 of 07/05/2010
Law modifying and complementing Law No. 07/2010 of 27/04/2009 relating to companies No. 14/2010 of 07/05/2010
Law creating and organizing condominiums and setting up procedures for their registration No. 15/2010 of 07/05/2010
Law governing credit information system in Rwanda, No.°16/2010 of 07/05/2010
Law governing negotiable instruments, No. 32/2009 of 18/11/2009
Law determining the organisation, functioning and responsibilities of Rwanda Revenue Authority, No. 08/2009 of 27/04/2009
Law on mortgages, No. 10/2009 of 14/05/2009
Law on security interests in movable property, No. 11/2009 of 14/05/2009
Law establishing the National Law Reform Commission, No. 01/2010/OL of 09/6/2010
Law on the organization of the craft sector, No. 19/2010 of 09/06/2010
Law on the protection of intellectual property, No. 31/2009 of 26/10/2009
Law relating to commercial recovery and settling of issues arising from insolvency, No. 12/2009 of 26/05/2009
Law relating to companies, No. 07/2009 of 27/04/2009
Law relating to electronic messages, electronic signatures and electronic transactions, No. 18/2010 of 12/05/2010
Law establishing the commercial courts and determining their organization, functioning and

jurisdiction, No. 59/2007 of 16/12/2007
Law regulating capital market in Rwanda, No. 01/2011 of 10/02/2011
Law regulating Kigali International Arbitration Centre, No. 51/2010 of 10/01/2010
Law regulating special economic zone, No. 05/2011 of 21/03/2011
Ministerial Order determining fees for registration of companies' business activities, No. 03/09/MINICOM of 08/05/2009
Law determining the establishment, organization and functioning of Cooperative Organizations in Rwanda; No. 50/2007 of 18/09/2007

Source: Information provided by the Rwandan authorities and various online sources.

TRADE POLICY OBJECTIVES

Rwanda's plans for economic and social development are set out in the Government's Vision 2020 and the Economic Development and Poverty Reduction Strategy (EDPRS) . [17] Vision 2020 seeks to fundamentally transform Rwanda for it to become a middle-income country by 2020. Its main objectives are: in the short term, promotion of macroeconomic stability and wealth creation to reduce aid dependency; in the medium term, transformation from an agrarian to a knowledge-based economy; and, in the long term, creation of a productive middle class fostering entrepreneurship. In order to achieve these objectives, six main pillars were identified: good governance and a capable state; human resource development and a knowledge-based economy; a private-sector-led economy; infrastructure development; productive and market-oriented agriculture; and regional and international economic integration.

The EDPRS is a medium-term strategy towards attainment of the long-term Rwanda Vision 2020 objectives. The priority areas identified under the EDPRS were: poverty and vulnerability reduction; institutional capacity-building and social capital formation; sustainable management of the natural environment; good governance, and enhanced efficiency and accountability of the public sector; enhanced performance of the private sector, focusing on ICT; economic infrastructure development (transport, energy, water, and ICT); and rural development and agricultural transformation.

The 2010 Rwanda Trade Policy document set out five objectives: increased productivity and diversified sustainable productive capacities for trading nationally, regionally, and internationally; enhanced participation of importers and exporters of goods and services in regional and international trade, taking advantage of trade opportunities; increasing investment, including foreign direct investment, in production of competitive goods and services for the export market; increased human resources skills in trade and development through training and retraining in private and public institutions; and strengthened science, technology, and innovation policies, strategies, and institutions, including intellectual property laws, in support of industrial development and creative knowledge-based industries.

The Ministry of Trade and Industry's strategic plan includes five components [18] : (i) to increase the value of existing exports; (ii) to diversify the export base, particularly in manufacturing and services; (iii) to promote and facilitate all Rwandan traders; (iv) to increase investment which drives growth and job creation; and (v) to provide an environment for the private sector that facilitates its growth.

It is important to note that Rwanda has also tried to integrate in its trade policy other key trade-related issues and strategies developed by other ministries (Table II.2) with a view to ensuring coherence in trade policy.

Key sector policies and strategies, December 2011

Policies and strategies	Ministry
Industrial Policy (2011)	Ministry of Trade and Industry
Science, Technology and Innovation Policy (2006)	Ministry of Youth and ICT
National Energy Policy and Strategy 2008-2012	Ministry of Infrastructure
Rwanda Transport Master Plan (2008)	Ministry of Infrastructure
National Export Strategy (2011)	Ministry of Trade and Industry
Competition and Consumer Protection Policy and Act (2009)	Ministry of Trade and Industry
Intellectual Property Policy and Act (2009)	Ministry of Trade and Industry
Companies Act (2009)	Ministry of Trade and Industry
Law Regulating Labour in Rwanda (2009)	Ministry of Public Service and Labour
Small and Medium Enterprises Policy (2010)	Ministry of Trade and Industry
Special Economic Zone Policy (2010)	Ministry of Trade and Industry
Tourism Policy and Master Plan (2009)	Ministry of Trade and Industry
Hides and Skins Policy (2009)	Ministry of Trade and Industry
Rwanda Extractive Industry Strategy (2006)	Ministry of Natural Resources
Rwanda Tea Strategy (2008)	Ministry of Agriculture
Rwanda Coffee Strategy (2008)	Ministry of Agriculture
Rwanda Horticulture Strategy (2006)	Ministry of Agriculture
Rwanda Craft Industry Strategic Plan 2009-2013	Ministry of Trade and Industry
National Information and Communication Technology Strategic Plan (2012)	Ministry of Youth and ICT

Source: Information provided by the Rwandan authorities.

TRADE AGREEMENTS

World Trade Organization (WTO)

1. Rwanda has been active in the negotiations under the Doha Development Agenda, where it shares the position of the African Group, of which it was coordinator in 2005, as well as sharing common positions with the ACP Group and the LDC Group. In the negotiations on trade facilitation, it is one of the proponents of the proposals on freedom of transit (TN/TF/W/133 and TN/TF/W/39) . Rwanda has also been coordinator of the African Group in the negotiations on trade facilitation. On TRIPS and public health, Rwanda submitted a proposal (IP/C/W/445) on behalf of the African Group on the implementation of Paragraph 6 of the Doha Declaration. In the agriculture negotiations, Rwanda is seeking improved market access and the reduction of trade-distorting subsidies and tariff peaks, and elimination of tariff escalation. It has also called for duty-free-quota-free treatment for all exports from LDCs. In the NAMA negotiations, it is looking for the reduction of non-tariff barriers. In services negotiations, it supports the LDCs' Services waiver. Rwanda has also called for technical assistance and capacity building through the Enhanced Integrated Framework and Aid for Trade (Common Report, Chapter V) .

2. Rwanda has made some notifications to the WTO (Table II.3); however, a large number remain outstanding. Rwanda has not been involved in any dispute, in any capacity, in the WTO.

Status of WTO notifications, 2005-11

WTO Agreement	Description of requirement	Date	Symbol of latest notification
GATS Article III:4 and/or IV:2	Contact and enquiry points	25/05/2004	S/ENQ/78/Rev.6
GATT 1994 Article VI Art. 16.5	Anti-dumping	26/02/2010	G/ADP/N/193/RWA
TBT Annex 3C	Acceptance of/withdrawal from a code	07/03/2005	G/TBT/CS/N/159
Committee on Import Licensing (Article 7.3)	Import licensing procedures	18/10/2011	G/LIC/N/3/RWA/2
TBT (Article 15.2)	Administrative arrangements laws/regulations	24/02/2005	G/TBT/2/Add.85
TBT (Article 2.9)	Technical regulations	21/02/2007	G/TBT/N/RWA/8
TRIPS and Public Health, paragraph 2 (a)	Intellectual property	19/07/2007	IP/N/9/RWA/1

Source: WTO documents.

Regional and bilateral trade agreements

Rwanda acceded to the EAC Treaty on 18 June 2007 and became a full member of the Community on 1 July 2007. Rwanda began implementing the EAC Customs Union in July 2009 and the Common Market in July 2010. It is also a member of the Common Market for Eastern and Southern Africa (COMESA), and initialled an interim Economic Partnership Agreement with the

EU under the East African Community in November 2007 (Common Report, Chapter II) . Rwanda is also a member of the Economic Community of the Great Lakes Countries (CEPGL) .

INVESTMENT REGIME

Rwanda's policies for economic development strongly emphasize foreign direct investment and private-sector-led growth. The Government recognizes that creating an enabling environment for investment requires a sound legal framework, application of the rule of law, and elimination of institutional and practical barriers, such as corruption. The investment regime is governed by Law No. 26/2005 on Investment and Export Promotion and Facilitation.[19] The ten priority sectors for investment are: information, communication, and technology; tourism; energy; agriculture and agri-based industries, fishing, and forestry; industry; re-export trade; mining; research; infrastructure; and waste recycling.

Law No. 26/2005 fixes the minimum initial capital investment requirement for foreign investors at US$250,000 to qualify for tax and other investment incentives. Land is owned by the State, but both foreign and local investors may acquire land through leasehold agreements of up to 99 years.

To register a local enterprise or a foreign subsidiary, the Rwanda Development Board provides a quick and efficient registration service allowing companies to have their business incorporated within 24 hours. This process involves simultaneously obtaining the certificate of incorporation (business registration), tax identification number (tax registration) and the social security registration for employee pension submission. The fee to register a local or a branch of a foreign company in Rwanda is RF 25,000, while the fee for registering additional activities or requesting a duplicate of a lost registration certificate is RF 10,000; the fee for cessation of trading activities is RF 5,000.

Businesses are subject to a range of taxes, including corporate income tax, VAT, excise duty, and withholding tax levied by the Rwanda Revenue Authority (RRA), as well as decentralized taxes levied by provinces and districts. Collection of property tax (on houses and land), rental income, and trading licensing has been transferred to local authorities.

Income tax in Rwanda is regulated under Law No. 16/2005 on Direct Taxes on Income. An individual who earns income from domestic and foreign sources, and a non-resident person who has income from a source in Rwanda, is subject to personal income tax on annual income above RF 360,000 (Table II.4) .

Personal income tax

Annual income	Tax rate
0 – 360,000	0%
360,000 – 1,200,000	20%
1,200,001 and above	30%

Source: RDB (2010), *Investor Info Pack 2010.*

6. Intermediate business owners pay a lump sum tax of 4% on annual turnover not exceeding RF 20 million. Businesses with an annual turnover above RF 20 million must be registered.

A withholding tax of 15% is levied on dividends, interest payments; royalties; service fees, including management and technical service fees; and performance payments to artists, musicians, and others made by resident individuals or entities including tax-exempted entities.

8. Corporate income tax is levied on business profits at a rate of 30% (lowered from 35% in January 2006), while public and not-for-profit organizations are exempted. Resident entities are liable for corporate income tax on business profits whether from domestic or foreign operations. Non-resident entities are liable for tax on business profits derived through a permanent establishment in Rwanda. Regarding cross-border economic activities, Article 6 of the Law provides for avoidance of double taxation.

Income from agricultural activities is exempt from income tax, if the proceeds do not exceed RF 12 million in the tax period. Rwanda has no specific legislation dealing with capital gains tax, thus any gains from sale or disposal of assets is taxed as part of business profits.

Rwanda improved its business regulatory environment significantly during the period under Review. A number of reforms relating to investment were undertaken, and significant steps were made to improve the legal framework. New commercial legislation was developed. The main laws include: a company law, a secured transaction law, an insolvency law, a labour law, a law establishing commercial courts, and a law on the protection of intellectual property.

The Rwanda Development Board (RDB) was established to facilitate new investment and fast tracking economic development by enabling private-sector growth. The RDB was set up by bringing together under one roof all government agencies involved in promoting investment, such as: the Rwanda Investment and Export Promotion Agency (RIEPA), the Rwanda Commercial Registration Service Agency (RCRSA), the Human Resource and Institutional Capacity Development Agency (HIDA), the Rwanda Information and Technology Agency (RITA) and the Rwanda Office of Tourism and National Parks (ORTPN), CAPMER, Privatisation Secretariat and the Environmental Impact Assessment Unit of the Rwanda Environmental Management Authority. The RDB reports directly to the President and is guided by a Board that includes all the key Ministers (e.g. Finance, Trade, Infrastructure, Agriculture) .

The RDB provides investors with a "one-stop" service centre for guidance on laws, policies, incentives, investment climate and trends, investment opportunities, costs of setting up business, process for finding land, work permits and visas, tax payment, construction permit, utilities and notary services, and sector-specific information. In addition, the centre provides environment clearance and investment certificates and through the Office of the Registrar General, issues company registration certificates, registration of secured transactions, security interests in movable property, and registration of intellectual property rights.

As a result of its reforms, Rwanda emerged among the top global performers; according to the World Bank Doing Business Report, out of 183 countries, Rwanda's "ease of doing business" ranking changed from 158th in 2007 to 58th in 2011 (Table II.5) and 45th in 2012. Rwanda was the top reformer in the EAC. Its reforms included reducing the time and number of procedures needed to start a business, improving regulations to ease access to credit, and reducing the time required to register property.[20] In addition, Rwanda introduced single border posts with neighbouring countries and automated customs clearance to facilitate trade. Since February 2012, Rwanda has established an electronic single window (AsycudaWorld), which helps businesses to clear goods online.

Despite improvements in business environment, local and foreign private investment remains low because, *inter alia,* high transportation costs and poor IT performance. In addition, there have been complaints that the rapid regulatory changes were carried out without sufficient consultation.

Infrastructure bottlenecks, high taxes, and tax administration issues remain major challenges for the private sector as it competes in global and regional markets.

In June 2010, the Ministry of Trade and Industry issued the Small and Medium Enterprises (SMEs) Development Policy, where the definition of SMEs includes micros as well as small and medium enterprises (Table II.6) . The 2011 census enumerated 123,526 establishments; the private sector accounts for 96.5% of the total. Some 87.5% of SMEs operating in Rwanda were formally registered, and 24% of these pay tax on a regular basis. SMEs account for 98% of all businesses in Rwanda and 41% of private-sector employment (small and micro businesses account for 36% of private-sector employment and medium-sized enterprises account for 5%. SMEs concentrate mainly in commerce and services sectors (93%) .

Doing business

	2007	2008	2009	2010	2011
Ease of doing business (rank)	158	150	139	67	58
Starting a business	58	63	60	11	9
Dealing with licences/dealing with construction permits	133	124	90	89	82
Employing workers	106	95	93	30	..
Registering property	134	137	60	38	41
Getting credit	159	158	145	61	32
Protecting investors	162	165	170	27	28
Paying taxes	83	50	56	60	43
Trading across borders	175	166	168	170	159
Enforcing contracts	69	44	48	40	39
Closing a business	151	178	181	183	183

.. Not available.
Note: From 2009, the ranking of "dealing with licences" changed to "dealing with construction permits".
Source: World Bank *Doing Business Reports,* various years.

SMEs

Size of enterprise	Net capital investment (RF million)	Annual turnover (RF million)	Number of employees
Micro	Less than 0.5	Less than 0.3	1-3
Small	0.5-15	0.3-12	4-30
Medium	15-75	12-50	31-100

Source: MINICOM (2010), *Small and Medium Enterprises (SMEs) Development Policy,* Kigali.

SMEs are hindered by: limited transport and energy, lack of a strong insurance industry, limited capital and access to finance; difficulties in enforcing contracts; and limited business development skills. In addition, their tax burden is relatively high: at least seven separate tax regimes are in force, and the World Bank estimated 3% of Rwanda's GDP is spent on compliance issues, including taxation, environmental regulations, EAC and international quality and safety standards required for export, and the Government's health protocols.[21]

In 2009, the *Centre d'Appui aux Petites et Moyennes Enterprises* (CAPMER), a public/private institution mandated to provide training, advice, and technical support to SMEs, was integrated into the Rwanda Development Board (RDB), to combine its mandate with export and investment promotion and general private-sector development services. Institutions offering services to SMEs include the MINICOM, RDB, Rwanda Enterprise Investment Company (REIC), and the Private Sector Federation (PSF) . The Ministry of trade and Industry, is in charge of SME development through the Department for SME development.

It appears that the Government wishes to simplify the tax system and reduce tax rates. A move towards a flat tax regime is being discussed. As external grants and borrowing contribute 48% of government revenue, if more SMEs are encouraged to register and pay taxes, the Government could increase internal tax revenue and reduce its dependency on foreign aid and debt.

Rwanda has bilateral investment treaties with Belgium, Germany, Luxembourg, Mauritius, South Africa, South Korea, Switzerland, and the United States, and double taxation treaties with Belgium and Mauritius.[22]Rwanda is a member of the Multilateral Investment Guarantee Agency (MIGA) and the International Centre for the Settlement of Investment Disputes (ICSID) .

INTERNATIONAL ASSISTANCE TO RWANDA

ECONOMIC ASSISTNANCE STRATEGY

The Government of Rwanda is interested in ensuring proper donor co-ordination to enhance the several reforms it is undertaking. The best way to coordinate aid is through the budget reform where Government spending is reflected through a comprehensive, prioritized, programme and output oriented budget. Currently, the Government intends to move away from focusing on inputs and towards the delivery of goods and services and the outcomes of those services.
Accordingly, the budget process will concentrate on ensuring:

TRANSPARENCY

By having clearly defined sector objectives, outputs and activities; allowing participation of civic society in the budget process, and improving the management of the budget.

COMPREHENSIVENESS

By creating a consistent, predictable National Policy and Budget Framework and including all Government expenditure in an integrated (recurrent and development) budget.

PRIORITIZATION

By defining the role of Government and ensuring priority programmes and activities are allocated the required resources to execute that role.

RELIABILITY

Through proper estimation of all resources, both domestic and external.

In order to achieve these objectives, the donor community has to assist the effort at each of these stages:

TRANSPARENCY

By clarifying **all the activities they are undertaking in Rwanda.**

COMPREHENSIVENESS

By providing **full information on all the expenditure they are supporting** either within the Government budget or outside the budget.

PRIORITIZATION

Through ensuring that their **funding only goes to the Government determined priority sector/ programme/ project activities, and through the Government budget.**

RELIABILITY

By providing information on the **amounts that will actually be disbursed** towards the activities of the Government of Rwanda **by specific time frames.** This will enable Government to make reliable resources forecasts over the years.

THE ROLE OF THE GOVERNMENT

Over the next three years, the Government will create a consistent, predictable National Policy and Budget Framework through which ministries are provided with reliable ceilings within which to achieve agreed upon outcomes (see MTEF Action Plan 2000-2002). This will entail developing a clear and concise national policy with a medium term (three-year) fiscal strategy. To move away from input oriented budgeting, the Government will also introduce missions, objectives and outputs for each ministry, which will be the basis for the ministries to design measurable output oriented budgets. Financial management will be improved by using a more computerized budget accounting and monitoring system, and provision of flash reports to donors. The coming into being of the Office of the Auditor General is also one aspect of improving accountability. The budget will be comprehensive by including all resources and all expenditures, using standard programme classification. Therefore projects financed outside the Government budget will have to be brought in.

The budget calendar, which reflects the specific activities to be undertaken, is given in Annual Buget Calendar, with highlights of some activities related to donor participation.

With regard to fiscal transparency, the Government of Rwanda has made a start in certain areas.The role of Government has been defined and will continue to be better defined in the exercise of developing specific ministry missions, objectives and outputs. Fiscal law is in preparation to govern the management of the budget. National Accounts will be published annually reflecting the outturn of the Government operations in any previous year, and accessible to the general public. With improved preparation and presentation of the budget, it will be possible to indicate the major/ priority activities that the Government is undertaking, in the Budget statements. A statement on the macroeconomic framework, through which the budget is framed, will be made. The macroeconomic framework is being developed using a multidisciplinary team of experts/ officials. A more computerized accounting and reporting system is being developed, and it is intended to include none financial data on achievements planned and accomplished. In all this, a timetable of activities will be produced.

THE ROLE OF DONORS

The Current Situation

In Rwanda, where externally financed budget support provides an important part ofrecurrent financing, the predictability of the budget is highly influenced by the nature of the financial agreements for this budget support. At present, most of these arrangements are annual rather than multi-year and typically subject to complex and often inter-locking conditions. In this context, it is very difficult, if not impossible, for approved budget allocations to be fully honoured by MINECOFIN on timely basis.

The management of external resources, which form a large proportion of the budget, is not harmonised.Also, a significant amount of external financial support to public sector activities is provided off budget and often with little, if any, information on disbursements remitted to MINECOFIN.

Consequences

As a consequence, off-budget funding reduces the comprehensiveness of the budget and, in the process undermines the ability of MINECOFIN (and indeed of Cabinet) to impose a hard-budget constraint on spending ministries. The "MTEF Contract" relies on a guaranteed firm budget ceiling being imposed on line ministries in exchange for the achievement of a pre-agreed set of output targets.

What Needs to be Done

If this situation is to change, it will be necessary:

To simplify the conditions for accessing budget support and ensure their mutual consistency;

To introduce multi-year rather than annual arrangements; and ideally

To introduce arrangements with an appropriate aid agency which might provide some sort of "funding of last resort" role to give "insurance" to budget allocations in the event of slippages in the disbursement of budget support or major external shocks to tax and customs revenues.

The long-term objective of the budget reform which has taken the form of a Medium Term Expenditure Framework (MTEF) is to develop integrated three-year estimates. This will be based on the planned outputs by each ministry, reflecting the predetermined objectives. Projects are one means of achieving objectives. Other activities carried out by ministries are also a means of achieving specific objectives. It is therefore essential to look at all the activities of a ministry and agree on the overall outputs to be produced and the objectives to be achieved.

The implementation of the budget depends on the availability of funds at the right time. The estimates of resources therefore need to be accurate and with a clear flow over the three-year period, as well as within each financial year. This can be achieved if donors provide the Government with reliable information on what levels of assistance they will provide over the three-year period and the possible flow during each year.As the budget process provides better information, with improved accountability and transparency, the need for specific project financing will fall away and be replaced by programme financing. The ultimate goal will be budget support. With clear objectives and specific outputs elaborated in the budget, monitoring will focus on the outputs and thus reporting will be standardised.

Currently, the Government is seeking from its development partners the following:

Off budget resources to be brought into the budget. The actual accounting for these resources may initially be different from the Government accounting system, but the aim is to bring these into the Government system.

If the inclusion of the off budget is seen as difficult to adopt immediately, information on the activities should at least be properly recorded and monitored. In this way, it can be factored into the definition of ceilings and corresponding output targets, even if the actual flow of funds is distinct from the normal budget.

As ministries develop objective and output based budgets, with clear **programmes** for the achievement of the objectives, projects will be a part of the overall activities within the programmes, and donors may consider shifting to programme financing rather than project financing.

Budget support is the ultimate goal in a working MTEF, and donors should start considering this. The Government will meanwhile be improving the preparation and presentation of the budget to ensure it is transparent enough for donor confidence to provide overall support.

US ASSISTANCE

The United States officially renewed its commitment to the Rwandan people by providing over $108 million of development assistance in late December 2014 to fund ongoing and new development projects. These funds, implemented through the United States Agency for International Development (USAID), will continue the United States' work to accelerate Rwanda's progress to middle income status and a better quality of life for its people.

USAID's development projects in Rwanda, implemented in partnership with the Government of Rwanda, focus on several priority areas, including economic growth and agriculture, food security and nutrition, democracy and governance, basic education, youth employment, and health. The $108 million in funds constitutes the majority of funds provided by the United States through USAID for 2015 development projects in Rwanda.

Over the last ten years, USAID has contributed over $1 billion to support the Rwandan people, and has contributed significantly to major development successes in that time period, including:

- Support for prevention, care and treatment of HIV/AIDS including contributing to the provision of anti-retroviral treatment to 82,500 adults and children through the President's Emergency Plan for AIDS Relief;

- Training and equipping dairy farmers and dairy-sector businesses with skills to improve their products and markets, efforts which have created over 6,000 new jobs in the industry in the last two years;

- Creation and distribution of innovative and interactive literacy materials for P1 and P2 students and teachers in all of Rwanda's public primary schools that is giving students a solid foundation for their future learning; and

- Strengthening civil society by building their management capacity, ability to produce evidence-based research, and expanding opportunities for civic participation.

INVESTMENT AND BUSINESS AND LEGAL CLIMATE - STRATEGIC INFORMATION AND CONTACTS FOR STARTING BUSINESS

Rwanda enjoys strong economic growth, high rankings in the World Bank's Ease of Doing Business Index, and a reputation for low corruption. The Government of Rwanda has undertaken a series of pro-investment policy reforms intended to improve Rwanda's investment climate and increase foreign direct investment (FDI). The country presents a number of opportunities for U.S. and foreign direct investment, including in renewable energy, infrastructure, agriculture, mining, tourism, and information and communications technology (ICT).

Yet, despite its business-friendly reputation, FDI in Rwanda lags well behind some of its neighbors in the East African Community (EAC), making up a mere 1.5 percent of GDP in 2013. Potential and current investors cite a number of hurdles and constraints, including high transport costs, a small domestic market, limited access to affordable financing, inadequate infrastructure, ambiguous tax rules, and an under-skilled workforce ill-suited to the needs of foreign investors.

General labor is available, but Rwanda suffers from a shortage of skilled workers, including accountants, lawyers, and technicians. Higher institutes of technology, private universities, and vocational institutes are improving and producing more and better-trained graduates each year. The change in 2009 from French to English as the language of instruction, from grade four onward, was abrupt, and deficits among some graduates remain a significant issue.

There is no difficulty obtaining foreign exchange in Rwanda or transferring funds associated with an investment into a usable currency and at a legal market-clearing rate. In 1995, the government abandoned the dollar peg and established a floating exchange rate regime, under which all lending and deposit interest rates were liberalized.

The government maintains a high-profile anti-corruption effort and senior leaders articulate a consistent message emphasizing that fighting corruption is a key national goal. The government investigates corruption allegations and generally prosecutes and punishes those found guilty.

There are neither statutory limits on foreign ownership or control, nor any official economic or industrial strategy that discriminates against foreign investors.

Rwanda benefits from low violent crime rates; its strong police and military provide a security umbrella that minimizes potential criminal activity and political disturbances. On multiple occasions between 2008 and 2014, however, unknown assailants detonated grenades in Kigali and other areas of the country.

Rwanda is a member of the EAC, and participates in a customs union that helps facilitate the movement of goods produced in the region and allows EAC citizens with certain skills to work in any member state.

Rwanda has also established a free trade zone outside the capital, Kigali, which includes current and planned future communications infrastructure. Bonded warehouse facilities are now available both in and outside of Kigali for use by businesses importing duty-free materials.

1. OPENNESS TO, AND RESTRICTIONS UPON, FOREIGN INVESTMENT

Attitude toward Foreign Direct Investment

The Government of Rwanda (GoR) understands that private sector development is critical if Rwanda is to achieve its aim of reaching middle-income status by 2020, and reducing the country's reliance on foreign aid. Over the past decade, the GoR has undertaken a series of pro-investment policy reforms intended to improve the investment climate, expand trade in products and services, and increase levels of foreign direct investment.

Rwanda enjoys strong economic growth–which averaged 7 percent annually from 2010 to 2014–high rankings in the World Bank's Doing Business report (#46 out of 189 countries in 2015, third best in Africa behind Mauritius and South Africa), and a reputation for low corruption. The country presents a number of opportunities for U.S. and foreign direct investment, including in clean and renewable energy, infrastructure, agriculture, tourism, mining, and information and communications technology.

Despite its business-friendly reputation, FDI inflows into Rwanda lag well behind some of its peers in the EAC–a mere 1.5 percent of GDP in 2013. Potential and current investors cite a number of hurdles and constraints, including Rwanda's landlocked geography and resulting high freight transport costs, a small domestic market, limited access to affordable financing, and frequently arbitrary tax, investment, and immigration rules.

In 2006, the GoR consolidated multiple investment-related government agencies – including the Office of Tourism and National Parks and the Rwanda Investment and Export Promotion Agency – to establish the Rwanda Development Board (RDB), which today serves as the country's chief investment promotion agency.

The RDB offers one of the fastest business registration processes in Africa. New investors can register online at the RDB's website and receive approval to operate in less than 24 hours, and the agency's "one-stop shop" helps foreign investors secure required approvals, certificates, and work permits.

Despite the RDB's investment facilitation role, however, some foreign investors say they face difficulty in obtaining or renewing work visas due to the GoR's demonstrated preference for hiring local or EAC residents over third country nationals.

Investors have also cited the inconsistent application of tax incentives and import duties as a significant challenge to doing business in Rwanda. Under Rwandan law, foreign firms should receive equal treatment with regard to taxes, as well as access to licenses, approvals, and procurement.

Rwanda's judicial system suffers from a lack of resources and capacity, including well-functioning courts. The Heritage Foundation's Economic Freedom Index has cited the judiciary's lack of independence from the executive. Investors occasionally cite the GoR's casual approach to contract sanctity and say the government fails to enforce court judgments in a timely fashion. The neutral arbitration clause of the U.S.-Rwanda Bilateral Investment Treaty, which entered into force on January 1, 2012, may mitigate some of these concerns for U.S. investors, but has yet to be tested. The host government has honored international arbitration clauses in contracts when invoked, though sometimes reluctantly.

In 2008, the GoR implemented business reform legislation, which included new bankruptcy regulations and arbitration laws. In 2009, it enacted a new intellectual property law and a law to strengthen investor protections by requiring greater corporate disclosure, increasing the liability of directors, and improving shareholders' access to information.

In 2011, the GoR reformed tax payment processes and enacted additional laws on insolvency and arbitration. Under the 2012 penal code, the government may compel a firm to disclose proprietary information to government authorities under the auspices of a criminal investigation of fraudulent bankruptcy or other alleged criminal offense. These laws were designed to facilitate international business and further improve the investment climate.

Historically, the government has encouraged foreign investment through outreach and tax incentives. The only difference in treatment between foreign and domestic companies is the initial capital requirement for official registration, which the GoR sets at USD 250,000 for foreign investors, and USD 100,000 for domestic investors. There are no reports of foreign investors declining to invest due to these differing treatments.

Foreign investors can acquire real estate, though there is a general limit on land ownership, and both foreign and local investors can acquire land through leasehold agreements that extend to a maximum of 99 years.

In 2007, the GoR established the Rwanda Public Procurement Agency to ensure transparency in government tenders and divestment of state-owned enterprises. Rwanda's ranking in Transparency International's Corruption Perception Index has improved significantly, falling from 102 in 2008 to 49 in 2013, which is the third best in Africa after Botswana and Cape Verde. A 2014 report by Rwanda's Office of the Auditor General cited continuing problems with inappropriate procurement methods, but said violations had fallen significantly from years past.

There are no laws requiring private firms to adopt articles of incorporation or association that limit or prohibit foreign investment, participation, or control.

Other Investment Policy Reviews

In 2012, the WTO conducted a Trade Policy Review of the East African Community (EAC), which includes Rwanda:**https://www.wto.org/english/tratop_e/tpr_e/tp371_e.htm**

In 2006, UNCTAD conducted an Investment Policy Review (IPR) of Rwanda:**http://unctad.org/en/pages/PublicationArchive.aspx?publicationid=508**

Laws/Regulations of Foreign Direct Investment

The Rwanda Development Board serves as Rwanda's chief investment promotion agency

Limits on Foreign Control

Rwanda has neither statutory limits on foreign ownership or control, nor any official economic or industrial strategy that discriminates against foreign investors.

Screening of FDI

There is no mandatory screening of foreign investment. However, the RDB does evaluate the business plans of investors who seek tax incentives in order to record incoming foreign investment and better allocate incentives to qualified foreign investors.

Competition Law

Rwanda's Ministry of Trade and Industry published a Competition and Consumer Protection Policy in July 2010.

Investment Trends

Rwanda's new investment code, which will be published in 2015, offers new incentives to investors in the energy, ICT, logistics, and light manufacturing sectors. In particular, the government has identified energy investments as critical to allow the country to reach middle-income status by 2020. Rwanda is also working to position itself as a services hub, including as a regional center for logistics and air cargo transport.

Table 1

Measure	Year	Index or Rank	Website Address
TI Corruption Perceptions index	2014	55 of 175	transparency.org/cpi2014/results
World Bank's Doing Business Report "Ease of Doing Business"	2015	46 of 189	doingbusiness.org/rankings
Global Innovation Index	2014	102 of 143	globalinnovationindex.org/content.aspx?page=data-analysis
World Bank GNI per capita	2013	USD 630	data.worldbank.org/indicator/NY.GNP.PCAP.CD

Millennium Challenge Corporation Country Scorecard

The Millennium Challenge Corporation, a U.S. Government entity charged with delivering development grants to countries that have demonstrated a commitment to reform, produced scorecards for countries with a per capita gross national income (GNI) or USD 4,125 or less. A list of countries/economies with MCC scorecards and links to those scorecards is available here: **http://www.mcc.gov/pages/selection/scorecards**. Details on each of the MCC's indicators and a guide to reading the scorecards are available here: **http://www.mcc.gov/pages/docs/doc/report-guide-to-the-indicators-and-the-selection-process-fy-2015**.

2. CONVERSION AND TRANSFER POLICIES

Foreign Exchange

There is no difficulty obtaining foreign exchange or transferring funds associated with an investment into a usable currency and at a legal market-clearing rate. In 1995, the government abandoned the dollar peg and established a floating exchange rate regime, under which all lending and deposit interest rates were liberalized. The central bank holds daily foreign exchange sales freely accessed by commercial banks.

Since January 2007, the Rwandan franc (RWF) has been convertible for essentially all business transactions. Rwanda has a liberal monetary system and complies with International Monetary Fund (IMF) Article VIII and all Organization for Economic Cooperation and Development (OECD) convertibility requirements.

Remittance Policies

Investors can remit payments only through authorized commercial banks. There is no limit on the inflow of funds, although local banks are required to notify the central bank of all transfers over USD 10,000 to mitigate the risk of potential money laundering. Additionally, there are some restrictions on the outflow of export earnings. Companies generally must repatriate export earnings within three months after the goods cross the border. Tea exporters must deposit sales proceeds shortly after auction in Mombasa, Kenya. Repatriated export earnings deposited in commercial banks must match the exact declaration the exporter used crossing the border.

Rwandans working overseas can make remittances to their home country without impediment. It usually takes two to three days to transfer money using SWIFT financial services. Other financial services companies such as Western Union and Money Gram are also available to investors seeking to transfer funds.

3. EXPROPRIATION AND COMPENSATION

The government reserves the right to expropriate property "in the public interest" and "for qualified private investment" under the expropriation law of 2007. The government and landowner negotiate compensation directly depending on the importance of the investment and the size of the expropriated property. Valuation of expropriated property is often opaque and controversial.

In the past several years, a number of property owners have protested expropriation of their property by the City of Kigali and claimed that the compensation offered was below market value and not in accordance with the expropriation law.

Implementation of the Kigali City Master Plan has at times created additional threats of expropriation, as property owners in selected areas have been compelled to construct multi-story commercial developments or face potential eviction from their property.

Rwanda's 2007 Law Relating to Expropriation in the Public Interest requires the government to pay compensation to property owners prior to relocation or expropriation. Similarly, the 2015 Law Relating to Investment Promotion and Facilitation (hereafter noted as the 2015 investment code) forbids the expropriation of investors' property in the public interest unless the investor is fairly compensated. In practice, however, these procedures have not always been followed.

4. DISPUTE SETTLEMENT

Legal System, Specialized Courts, Judicial Independence, Judgments of Foreign Courts

Under the U.S.-Rwanda Bilateral Investment Treaty, U.S. investors have the right to bring investment disputes before neutral, international arbitration panels. Disputes between U.S. investors and the GoR in recent years have been resolved through international arbitration, court judgments, or out of court settlements.

Rwanda is signatory to the International Center for Settlement of Investment Disputes (ICSID) and African Trade Insurance Agency (ATI). ICSID seeks to remove impediments to private investment posed by non-commercial risks, while ATI covers risk against restrictions on import and export activities, inconvertibility, expropriation, war, and civil disturbances.

Rwanda is a member of the East African Court of Justice for the settlement of disputes arising from or pertaining to the East African Community (EAC). Rwanda has also acceded to the 1958 New York Arbitration Convention.

In 2012, the GoR launched the Kigali International Arbitration Center (KIAC), an alternative business settlement venue that aims to reduce the costs of contract settlement and enforcement for investors. Rwanda's Private Sector Federation has estimated that for investors pursuing claims via commercial courts, court fees can typically total up to 68 percent of the value of court awards.

Rwanda's commercial courts address commercial disputes and facilitate enforcement of property and contract rights. National laws governing commercial establishments, investments, privatization and public investments, land, and the protection and conservation of the environment are currently the primary directives governing investments in Rwanda.

Judgments by foreign courts and contract clauses that abide by foreign law are accepted and enforced by local courts, though local courts lack capacity and experience to adjudicate cases governed by non-Rwandan law. There have been a number of private investment disputes in Rwanda, though the GoR has yet to stand as complainant or respondent in a World Trade Organization (WTO) dispute settlement.

Rwanda signed and ratified the Multilateral Investment Guarantee Agency (MIGA) convention on October 27, 1989. MIGA issues guarantees against non-commercial risks to enterprises that invest in member countries.

Rwanda has maintained good relations with the U.S. Overseas Private Investment Corporation (OPIC) since the 1960s. Although OPIC's portfolio of investments and insurance policies in Rwanda is small, the corporation is seeking to expand investments in the country.

Bankruptcy

In 2008, the GoR implemented business reform legislation, which included new bankruptcy regulations and arbitration laws. In 2009, it enacted a new intellectual property law and a law to strengthen investor protections by requiring greater corporate disclosure, increasing the liability of directors, and improving shareholders' access to information.

In 2011, the GoR reformed tax payment processes and enacted additional laws on insolvency and arbitration. Under the 2012 penal code, the government may compel a firm to disclose proprietary information to government authorities under the auspices of a criminal investigation of fraudulent bankruptcy or other alleged criminal offense. These laws were designed to facilitate international business and further improve the investment climate.

Investment Disputes

There have been a number of private investment disputes in Rwanda, though the GoR has yet to stand as complainant or respondent in a World Trade Organization (WTO) dispute settlement.

In 2013, one dispute with a foreign investor in Rwanda was settled through international arbitration.

Rwanda signed and ratified the Multilateral Investment Guarantee Agency (MIGA) convention on October 27, 1989. MIGA issues guarantees against non-commercial risks to enterprises that invest in member countries.

Rwanda has maintained good relations with the U.S. Overseas Private Investment Corporation (OPIC) since the 1960s. Although OPIC's portfolio of investments and insurance policies in Rwanda is small, the corporation is seeking to expand investments in the country.

International Arbitration

In 2015, one U.S. investor notified the Rwandan government of its intent to file a claim under the U.S.-Rwanda Bilateral Investment Treaty if the two sides' dispute could not be resolved during the negotiation and consultation period.

In 2012, the GoR launched the Kigali International Arbitration Center (KIAC), an alternative business settlement venue that aims to reduce the costs of contract settlement and enforcement for investors. Rwanda's Private Sector Federation has estimated that investors are forced to spend around 68 percent of the value of court awards pursuing claims via commercial courts.

Rwanda's commercial courts address commercial disputes and facilitate enforcement of property and contract rights. National laws governing commercial establishments, investments, privatization and public investments, land, and the protection and conservation of the environment are currently the primary directives governing investments in Rwanda.

ICSID Convention and New York Convention

Rwanda is a member of the International Center for Settlement of Investment Disputes (ICSID) and a signatory to the African Trade Insurance Agency (ATI). ICSID seeks to remove impediments to private investment posed by non-commercial risks, while ATI covers risk against restrictions on import and export activities, inconvertibility, expropriation, war, and civil disturbances.

Rwanda is a member of the East African Court of Justice for the settlement of disputes arising from or pertaining to the East African Community (EAC). Rwanda has also acceded to the 1958 New York Arbitration Convention.

5. PERFORMANCE REQUIREMENTS AND INVESTMENT INCENTIVES

WTO/TRIMS

The Government maintains measures that may violate the WTO's TRIMs (Trade Related Investment Measures) by allowing parallel imports of goods from countries where patents and original trademarks are not registered and recognized.

Investment Incentives

Rwanda offers tax and other incentives to investors in priority sectors such as export, manufacturing, energy, ICT, financial services, and construction.

Performance Requirements

Unless stipulated in a memorandum of understanding characterizing the purchase of privatized enterprises, performance requirements are not imposed as a condition for establishing, maintaining, or expanding other investments. Such requirements are imposed chiefly as a condition to tax and investment incentives. Rwanda's 2015 investment code eliminates VAT exemptions in favor of corporate income tax reductions available to investors in priority sectors, which include export, manufacturing, energy, ICT, financial services, and construction.

Under the 2015 investment code, international companies that base their headquarters or regional offices in Kigali and invest a minimum of USD 10 million in Rwanda, in addition to fulfilling a number of other requirements, are exempt from corporate income tax.

The 2015 investment code also offers a corporate income tax rate of 15 percent, down from 30 percent, to investors who export at least 50 percent of the goods (excluding coffee, tea, and minerals) and services that they produce in Rwanda, or who invest in the energy, transport, ICT, or financial services sectors. Finally, the 2015 investment code offers tax holidays of up to seven years to investors who invest at least USD 50 million in Rwanda.

Some investors have cited the GoR's unwillingness to support visas for expatriate staff as one of the most significant limitations on doing business on Rwanda. Under the 2015 investment code, the government allows registered investors who invest a minimum of USD 250,000 to hire up to three expatriate employees, without the need to conduct a labor market test in Rwanda. Investors who wish to hire more than three expatriate employees must conduct a labor market test, unless the available position is listed on Rwanda's "Occupations in Demand" list.

Some current investors have complained that coordination between the RDB and the Rwanda Revenue Authority (RRA) is limited, resulting in assessment by the RRA on duties or taxes on registered investments despite the RDB's assurance that such investments qualified for tax-exempt or tax-incentivized status. The GoR has recently prioritized expanding Rwanda's tax base and increasing revenue. Consequently, the RDB's ability to issue tax incentives to new foreign investors has been constrained, and is limited somewhat further by the 2015 investment code.

There is no legal obligation for nationals to own shares in foreign investments or requirement that shares of foreign equity be reduced over time. However, the government strongly encourages local participation in foreign investments.

While the government does not impose conditions on the transfer of technology, it does encourage foreign investors, without legal obligation, to transfer technology and expertise to local staff to help develop Rwanda's human capital. There is no legal requirement that investors must purchase from local sources or export a certain percentage of their output, though the government offers tax incentives for the latter.

The government is not involved in assessing the type and source of raw materials for performance, but the National Bureau of Standards determines quality standards.

Effective November 1, 2014, Rwanda requires that all U.S. citizens possess a visa to enter Rwanda. A visa valid for 30 days for the purpose of tourism can be purchased for USD 30 upon arrival at Kigali International Airport or at Rwanda's land borders. Accepted forms of payment include U.S. dollars printed after 2006 and credit cards issued by Visa.

U.S. citizens planning to remain in Rwanda for more than 30 days must apply for a permit within 15 days of their arrival at the Directorate General of Immigration and Emigration in Kigali. The government generally processes visa applications for U.S. citizen investors in a timely manner. However, some investors have complained that the application process for work permits and extended stay visas has become onerous. Immigration authorities frequently request extra documentation detailing applicants' qualifications and, at times, have taken several months to adjudicate cases. Applicants may facilitate the process by ensuring that they travel with original police clearances, preferably stamped or notarized. Educational documents should be on original letterhead. Applicants should also obtain a certified copy of diplomas, if the original is not carried.

Investors should be aware that East African Community (EAC) applicants are given hiring preference and the Immigration Office may refuse work permits for non-EAC citizens when it is deemed that an EAC citizen can undertake the job in question.

Data Storage

The Rwandan government has not implemented forced localization policies. It does not require IT providers to turn over source code, or that data be stored in Rwanda.

6. RIGHT TO PRIVATE OWNERSHIP AND ESTABLISHMENT

Local and foreign investors have the right to own and establish business enterprises in all forms of remunerative activity. The Rwandan constitution stipulates that every person has the right to private property, whether personal or in association with others. The government cannot violate the right to private ownership except in the public interest and only then after following procedures that are determined by law and subject to fair compensation.

The law also allows private entities to acquire and dispose of interests in business enterprises. Foreign nationals may hold shares in locally incorporated companies. The government has continued to privatize state holdings, including formerly state-owned Cimerwa cement, though the government, ruling party, and military continue to play a dominant role in Rwanda's private sector.

7. PROTECTION OF PROPERTY RIGHTS

Real Property

The law protects and facilitates acquisition and disposition of all property rights. Investors involved in commercial agriculture have leasehold titles and are able to secure property titles, if necessary. A property registration and land titling effort, the result of a 2005 land law, was completed in 2013. The 2015 investment code states that investors shall have the right to own private property, whether individually or in association with others.

Intellectual Property Rights

The 2015 investment code also guarantees protection of investors' intellectual property rights, and legitimate rights related to technology transfer.

As a Common Market for Eastern and Southern Africa (COMESA) member state, Rwanda is automatically a member of African Regional Intellectual Property Organization (ARIPO). It is also a member of the World Intellectual Property Organization (WIPO) and is working towards harmonizing its legislation with WTO trade-related aspects of intellectual property. The Ministry of Commerce (MINICOM), the Rwandan Revenue Authority (RRA), and the Rwandan Bureau of Standards (RBS) work together to address issues involving counterfeit products on the Rwandan market. Through the RBS and the RRA, Rwanda has worked to increase protection of intellectual property rights, but many goods that violate patents, especially pharmaceutical products, make it to market nonetheless.

Rwanda has yet to ratify WIPO internet treaties, though the government has taken steps to implement and enforce the WTO TRIPS agreements. Intellectual property legislation covering patents, trademarks, and copyrights was approved in October 2009. A Registration Service Agency, which is part of the RDB, was established in 2008, and has improved intellectual property right protection by registering all commercial entities and facilitating business identification and branding.

For additional information about treaty obligations and points of contact at local IP offices, please see WIPO's country profiles at **http://www.wipo.int/directory/en/**

Resources for Rights Holders

Point of Contact at Embassy: Jeffrey D. Bowan
BowanJD@state.gov

The Rwanda Development Board (RDB) and the Rwandan Bureau of Standards (RBS) are the main regulatory bodies for Rwanda's intellectual property rights law. The RDB registers intellectual property rights, providing a certificate and ownership title. The RBS inspects imported products to ensure compliance with standards.

8. TRANSPARENCY OF THE REGULATORY SYSTEM

The government generally employs transparent policies and effective laws to foster clear rules consistent with international norms. Institutions such as the Rwanda Revenue Authority, the Ombudsman's office, Rwanda Bureau of Standards (RBS), the National Public Prosecutions Authority (NPPA), the Rwanda Utilities Regulatory Agency, the Public Procurement Agency, and the Privatization Secretariat all have clear rules and procedures. However, some investors claim that the RRA unfairly targets foreign investors for audits.

There is no formal mechanism to publish draft laws for public comment, although civil society sometimes has the opportunity to review proposed laws. There is no government effort to restrict foreign participation in industry standards-setting consortia or organizations.

Some investors complain that the strict enforcement of tax, labor, and environmental laws impede investment. In 2009, the government updated the labor code to simplify labor recruitment and facilitate the hiring, firing, and retention of competent staff.

In 2003, Rwanda established an ombudsman's office that monitors transparency and regulatory compliance in all governmental sectors. The Rwanda Utility Regulation Agency, the Office of the Auditor General (OAG), the Anticorruption Division of the RRA, the RBS, and the National Tender Board also enforce regulations. Since 2010, the press has reported many cases of alleged malfeasance involving private citizens and Rwandan officials that have led to investigations and arrests of high-ranking officials, as well as a number of resignations.

There is no informal regulatory process managed by nongovernmental organizations. Existing legal, regulatory, and accounting systems are generally transparent and consistent with international norms, but are not always enforced.

A key component of the government's regulatory system is the Office of the Auditor General, which was established in 1999 to audit government adherence to fiscal controls. In recent years, the OAG's annual reports to parliament have prompted wide-ranging criminal investigations of alleged misconduct and corruption.

Consumer protection associations exist, but are largely ineffective. The business community has been able to lobby the government and provide feedback on government policy and execution through the Private Sector Federation, a business association with strong ties to the government.

Rwanda is a member of the United Nations Conference on Trade and Development's (UNCTAD) international network of transparent investment procedures, **http://rwanda.eregulations.org/**. Foreign and national investors can find detailed information on administrative procedures applicable to investment and income generating operations including the number of steps, name and contact details of the entities and persons in charge of procedures, required documents and conditions, costs, processing time and legal bases justifying the procedures.

9. EFFICIENT CAPITAL MARKETS AND PORTFOLIO INVESTMENT

Access to affordable credit is a serious challenge in Rwanda. Interest rates are high, banks offer short-term loans only, and Rwandan commercial banks are unable to issue significant loan values. Investors who seek to borrow more than USD one million must often engage in multi-party loan transactions, usually leveraging support from larger regional banks. Credit terms generally reflect market rates and foreign investors are able to negotiate credit facilities from local lending institutions if they have collateral and "bankable" projects.

The private sector has limited access to credit instruments. Most Rwandan banks are conservative, risk-averse, and trade in a limited range of commercial products, though additional products are becoming available as the industry matures and competition increases. Credit cards are not used extensively, except in major hotels, grocery stores, and larger restaurants that cater to tourists. Debit cards have been introduced on a limited basis. In December 2011, Visa International opened an office in Rwanda and announced a partnership with the central bank through which the company is working to expand electronic payment services throughout Rwanda. While the use of credit cards is becoming more popular, outside of Kigali, Rwanda remains primarily a cash-based economy. An over-the-counter (OTC) market was established in 2008, with the assistance of the U.S. Department of the Treasury. Trading volume is limited and confined to the sale of government treasury bills and a few corporate bonds and shares.

In December 2010, Heineken launched the country's first initial public offering (IPO) for 30 percent of the shares in its Rwandan subsidiary, Bralirwa. Subsequently, Bank of Kigali (BOK) became the second listed Rwandan firm, with its shares officially trading on the Rwanda Stock Exchange from September 1, 2011. Kenya Commercial Bank (KCB), Kenya's National Media Group (NMG), Kenyan supermarket chain Uchumi (USL), and Equity Bank also cross-list their shares, bringing the total number of companies traded on the Rwanda Stock Exchange to six.

In June 2010, Rwanda became the seventh country in the world to adopt the IMF's Policy Support Instrument (PSI), a program designed for countries that have achieved macroeconomic stability and no longer require financial support from the IMF. In December 2014, the Executive Board of the IMF completed the second review of Rwanda's economic performance under IMF Policy Support Instrument, and concluded the 2014 Article IV consultation with Rwanda.

Rwanda is one of just a few sub-Saharan Africa countries to have issued sovereign bonds. In April 2013, Rwanda launched a USD 400 million, 10-year Eurobond priced to yield 6.875 percent. Orders eventually reached more than 9 times the bond's issue size. The GoR earmarked the proceeds to fund a new convention center, build a 28-MW hydropower station, and expand RwandAir, the state-run carrier.

Money and Banking System, Hostile Takeovers

The private sector has limited access to credit instruments. Most Rwandan banks are conservative, risk-averse, and trade in a limited range of commercial products, though additional products are becoming available as the industry matures and competition increases.

Meanwhile, Rwanda's financial sector remains highly concentrated. Around 50 percent of all bank assets in Rwanda are held by four to five of the largest commercial banks, while just one bank – state-owned Bank of Kigali (BoK) – holds 30 percent of all assets.

The IMF gives the National Bank of Rwanda (BNR), Rwanda's central bank, high marks for its effective monetary policy.

10. COMPETITION FROM STATE-OWNED ENTERPRISES

Rwandan law allows private enterprises to compete with public enterprises under the same terms and conditions with respect to access to markets, credit, and other business operations. Since 2006, the government has made an effort to privatize SOEs, to reduce the government's non-controlling shares in private enterprises, and attract FDI, especially in the information and communications (ICT), tourism, banking, and agriculture sectors.

Rwandan investors and investor groups have acquired minority and majority stakes in former SOEs. Government shareholders, including the Rwandan Social Security Board and other government savings schemes, back a number of these investor groups. Individuals with close ties to the government and/or ruling party lead other firms. Current SOEs include water and electricity utilities, as well as companies in construction, ICT, aviation, mining, insurance, finance, and other investments. The government continues to own significant and sometimes controlling interests in telecommunications, insurance, hotels, food production, and other sectors.

Some private firms assert that SOEs and private enterprises in which the government owns shares, or that have close ties to government officials, receive preferential treatment with regard to access to credit and tax compliance enforcement.

SOEs generally have boards of directors that function independently. However, GoR officials and their representatives sit on SOE boards and exercise considerable influence. Most SOEs are required to publish audited annual reports, but some are not readily available.

Sovereign Wealth Funds

In 2012, the Rwandan government launched the Agaciro Development Fund, a sovereign wealth fund that includes investments from Rwandan citizens and the international diaspora.

11. CORPORATE SOCIAL RESPONSIBILITY

There is a growing awareness of corporate social responsibility (CSR), but only a few companies–chiefly foreign-owned–have implemented sustainable programs. In recognition of the firm's strong commitment to CSR, the U.S. Department of State awarded Sorwathe, a U.S.-owned tea producer in Kinihira, Rwanda, the Secretary of State's 2012 Award for Corporate Excellence for Small and Medium Enterprises.

12. POLITICAL VIOLENCE

Rwanda is a stable country with relatively little violence. A strong police and military provide a security umbrella that minimizes potential criminal activity and political disturbances.

In 2012 and 2013, there was fighting in the eastern Democratic Republic of Congo (DRC) between Congolese armed forces (FARDC) and the M23, an armed group comprised mostly of soldiers who defected from the FARDC. While M23 was defeated militarily in November 2013, the FARDC and United Nations (UN) peacekeepers continued to engage in combat operations against other armed groups in the DRC state of North Kivu, which borders Rwanda.

In late August 2013, cross-border fire landed within the borders of Rwanda in Rubavu district, including within the city of Gisenyi. The GoR blamed these incidents on the FARDC. In early December 2012, a small element of armed individuals crossed the border from eastern DRC and attacked a ranger camp northwest of Kinigi. The attack, which occurred just south of Volcanoes National Park, left one ranger dead. The Democratic Forces for the Liberation of Rwanda (FDLR) claimed responsibility for this incursion. The FDLR is an armed group that includes former soldiers and supporters of the regime that orchestrated the 1994 genocide and that continues to operate in eastern DRC, near the border with Rwanda.

FARDC carried out military operations against the FDLR in eastern DRC in early 2015. The U.S. Department of State recommends that U.S. citizens exercise caution when traveling near the

Rwanda-DRC border, given the possibility of fighting and cross-border shelling involving the FDLR and other armed groups in the region.

Grenade attacks aimed at the local populace occurred on a recurring basis between 2008 and early 2014 in Rwanda. Four attacks occurred in Kigali in 2013 and early 2014, killing five and injuring 48 persons.

Despite occasional violence along Rwanda's border with eastern DRC, there have been no incidents involving politically motivated damage to investment projects or installations since the late 1990s.

13. CORRUPTION

The government maintains a high-profile anti-corruption effort and senior leaders articulate a consistent message emphasizing that combating corruption is a key national goal. The government investigates corruption allegations and generally prosecutes and punishes those found guilty. Enforcement is the same for both foreign and local investors. High-ranking officials accused of corruption often resign during the investigation period and many have been prosecuted. Senior government officials take pride in Rwanda's reputation for being tough on corruption, and numerous governmental institutions play an active role in investigating public officials accused of such.

Rwanda has signed and ratified the UN Anticorruption Convention. It is a signatory to the OECD Convention on Combating Bribery. It is also a signatory to the African Union Anticorruption Convention. Giving and accepting a bribe is a criminal act, and penalties depend on circumstances surrounding the specific case. U.S. firms have identified the perceived lack of government corruption in Rwanda as a key incentive to investing in the country.

Some firms have reported occurrences of petty corruption in the customs clearing process, but there are few or no reports of corruption in transfers, dispute settlement, regulatory system, taxation, or investment performance requirements. A local company cannot deduct a bribe to a foreign official from taxes. A bribe by a local company to a foreign official is a crime in Rwanda.

The Office of the Auditor General has pursued many corruption cases in recent years, most of which involved misuse of public funds. The Rwanda Governance Board monitored governance more broadly and promoted mechanisms to control corruption. The Rwanda Revenue Authority's Anticorruption Unit had a code of conduct and an active mechanism for internal discipline. The Office of the Ombudsman, the National Tender Board, the Rwanda Utilities Regulatory Agency, and the National Bureau of Standards also enforced regulations.

UN Anticorruption Convention, OECD Convention on Combatting Bribery

Rwanda has signed and ratified the UN Anticorruption Convention. It is a signatory to the OECD Convention on Combating Bribery. It is also a signatory to the African Union Anticorruption Convention

Resources to Report Corruption

Mrs. Aloysie CYANZAYIRE
Chief Ombudsman
Ombudsman (Umuvunyi)
P.O Box 6269, Kigali, Rwanda
+250 252587308
omb1@ombudsman.gov.rw / sec.permanent@ombudsman.gov.rw

Mrs. Pauline Jeanne Gashumba
Director of Preventing and Fighting Corruption
Ombudsman (Umuvunyi)
P.O Box 6269, Kigali, Rwanda
+250 252587308
gashumba.pauline@ombudsman.gov.rw

Mr. Felicien Mwumvaneza
Commissioner for Quality Assurance Department (Anti-Corruption Unit)
Rwanda Revenue Authority
Avenue du Lac Muhazi, P.O. Box 3987, Kigali, Rwanda
+250 788309563
felicien.mwumvaneza@rra.gov.rw / commissioner.quality@rra.gov.rw

Mr. Obadiah BIRARO
Auditor General
Office of the Auditor General
Avenue du Lac Muhazi, P.O. Box 1020, Kigali, Rwanda
+250 78818980
oag@oag.gov.rw

Contacts at NGOs operating in Rwanda:

Mr. Apollinaire Mupiganyi
Executive Director
Transparency International Rwanda
P.O: Box 6252 Kigali, Rwanda
+250 788309563
amupiganyi@transparencyrwanda.org / mupiganyi@yahoo.fr

Mr. Lewis Mudge
Country Representative
Human Rights Watch
Kigali, Rwanda
+250 788502870
mudgel@hrw.org

14. BILATERAL INVESTMENT AGREEMENTS

Rwanda is eligible for trade preferences under the African Growth and Opportunity Act (AGOA), which the United States enacted to extend duty-free and quota-free access to the U.S. market for nearly all textile and handicraft goods produced in eligible beneficiary countries. The United States and Rwanda signed a Trade and Investment Framework Agreement (TIFA) in 2006, and a Bilateral Investment Treaty (BIT) in 2008. Rwanda has also signed bilateral investment treaties with Switzerland (1963), Germany (1967), and Belgium (1985). Rwanda signed bilateral investment treaties with the Republic of Korea, Mauritius, and South Africa, but those treaties have yet to enter force.

Bilateral Taxation Treaties

Rwanda does not have a bilateral taxation treaty with the United States.

15. OPIC AND OTHER INVESTMENT INSURANCE PROGRAMS

The Overseas Private Investment Corporation (OPIC) has provided financing and political risk insurance to eleven U.S. projects in Rwanda since 1975, including Sorwathe Tea Ltd., Forestry and Agricultural Investment Management, Gigawatt Global, and Westrock Coffee Holdings, LLC. Given Rwanda's political, economic, and currency stability, OPIC officials have expressed interest in expanding the corporation's portfolio in Rwanda and are currently evaluating potential projects.

The Export-Import Bank (EXIM) continues its program to insure short-term export credit transactions involving various payment terms, including open accounts that cover the exports of consumer goods, services, commodities, and certain capital goods. Rwanda is a member of the Multilateral Investment Guarantee Agency (MIGA) and the African Trade Insurance Agency (ATI).

16. LABOR

General labor is available, but Rwanda suffers from a shortage of skilled labor, including accountants, lawyers, and technicians. Higher institutes of technology, private universities, and vocational institutes are improving and producing more and better-trained graduates each year. Carnegie Mellon University has opened a campus in Kigali–its first in sub-Saharan Africa–and currently offers masters-level courses in information and communication technologies. In 2012, the government extended basic compulsory education from nine to twelve years. In 2009, the government designated English, rather than French, as the language of instruction for students from grade four onwards. The Rwandan education system is struggling with the transition, given a shortage of teachers qualified to teach in English.

Rwanda has ratified all the International Labor Organization (ILO) eight core conventions and attempts to adhere to these conventions protecting worker rights. Policies to protect workers in special labor conditions exist, but enforcement remains inconsistent. The government encourages, but does not require, on-the-job training and technology transfer to local employees.

In 2000, the government revised the national labor code to eliminate gender discrimination, restrictions on the mobility of labor, and wage controls. In 2009, parliament passed a new labor code, which sets the minimum age for formal employment at 16 and for hazardous work at 18, and strengthened prohibitions on the use of child labor and hazardous or forced work. Approximately 16 percent of children in Rwanda are engaged in child labor, particularly in agriculture and in domestic service. Tea is included on the U.S. government's List of Goods Produced by Child Labor or Forced Labor.

Companies find skill deficits in many sectors when hiring, though such deficits will continue to shrink as literacy rates increase and Rwandan institutions of higher learning produce additional, qualified graduates. Rwanda's literacy rate was 71 percent in 2013, up from 58 percent in 1991.

17. FOREIGN TRADE ZONES/FREE PORTS/TRADE FACILITATION

Rwanda is a member of the East African Community (EAC), and participates in a customs union that helps facilitate the movement of goods produced in the region and allows EAC citizens with certain skills to work in any member state. Rwanda is also a member of the Economic Community of the Great Lakes (CEPGL), along with the DRC and Burundi; and of COMESA, which includes Rwanda, Burundi, Comoros, DRC, Djibouti, Egypt, Ethiopia, Kenya, Libya, Madagascar, Malawi, Mauritius, Seychelles, Sudan, Swaziland, Uganda, and Zimbabwe. COMESA countries have a free trade agreement that permits goods originating in member states and that comply with certain rules of origin to enter other member markets duty free. Value addition on imported raw materials must reach three percent to qualify for duty free entry.

Rwanda has established a free trade zone outside the capital, Kigali, which includes current and planned future communications infrastructure. Bonded warehouse facilities are now available both in and outside of Kigali for use by businesses importing duty free materials.

18. FOREIGN DIRECT INVESTMENT AND FOREIGN PORTFOLIO INVESTMENT STATISTICS

Table 2: Key Macroeconomic Data, U.S. FDI in Host Country/Economy

	Host Country Statistical source*		USG or international statistical source		USG or International Source of Data: BEA; IMF; Eurostat; UNCTAD, Other
Economic Data	Year	Amount	Year	Amount	
Host Country Gross Domestic Product (GDP) ($M USD)	2013	6,951	2013	7,521	www.worldbank.org/en/country
Foreign Direct Investment	Host Country Statistical source*		USG or international statistical source		USG or international Source of data: BEA; IMF; Eurostat; UNCTAD, Other
U.S. FDI in partner country ($M USD, stock positions)	N/A	N/A	N/A	N/A	
Host country's FDI in the United States ($M USD, stock positions)	N/A	N/A	N/A	N/A	
Total inbound stock of FDI as % host GDP	2012	17.4	2013	1.5	World Bank

*National Bank of Rwanda

Table 3: Sources and Destination of FDI

A significant share of foreign direct investment in Rwanda is made through holding companies based in Mauritius, which serves as a regional tax haven.

Direct Investment from/in Counterpart Economy Data					
From Top Five Sources/To Top Five Destinations (US Dollars, Millions)					
Inward Direct Investment			Outward Direct Investment		
Total Inward	495	100%	Total Outward	N/A	100%

South Africa	110	22%			
Libya	58	12%			
Mauritius	55	11%			
Kenya	54	11%			
Netherlands	36	7%			
"0" reflects amounts rounded to +/- USD 500,000.					

Source: IMF Coordinated Direct Investment Survey

Table 4: Sources of Portfolio Investment

Portfolio investment data are not available for Rwanda.

IMPORTANT CONTACTS

CONTACT FOR MORE INFORMATION

Jeffrey D. Bowan
Economic and Commercial Officer
United States Embassy
2657 Avenue de la Gendarmerie, P.O. Box 28 Kigali, Rwanda
+250-252-596-538
BowanJD@state.gov

BEST LAW FIRMS

GASARABWE & ASSOCIATES

11 Avenue Bigogwe-Kiyovu
gasarabwe-associates.com
Gasarabwe & Associates was founded in 1996 by Ms Claudine Gasarabwe. It has continued to grow in size and business, and is now one of the Leading Law Firms in Rwanda. Gasarabwe & Associates has a team of five committed Advocates: The firm is also in proc ...
Telephone:(+250)788302169

R & PARTNERS LAW FIRM

23, Rue Akagera Kiyovu-Kigali
r-partnerslawfirm.com
R & Partners Law Firm has a team of three advocates. The firm is in process to expand its human resources to accommodate more lawyers. It is however one of the leading bilingual law firms in Rwanda specialized in corporate. The firm brings together a rang ...
Fax:(+250)7 88 51 62 86 / (+250)7 88 52 82 64 / (+250)7 88 53 07 81/

TRUST LAW CHAMBERS

1680 Umuganda Boulevard, Kacyiru
www.trustchambers.com

Trust Law Chambers is a leading law firm in Rwanda and prides itself in providing world-class advice on all areas corporate and commercial law. Our client base is broad ranging from foreign investors, banks and International Financial organisations, t ...
Telephone:+250 252 503075

MAITRE JEAN CLAUDE BATWARE

Kigali, Rwanda, B.P. 6700 Kigali
Maitre Jean Claude Batware is a professional lawyer with a bachelor degree in Law from the National University of Rwanda. He was born in Gafunzo, Cyangugu, Rwanda, 1967. He worked as Chief Associate of Judicial Society of the National Society of Insurance ...
Telephone:250-252 501336 / 0788302250

MAITRE RICHARD RWIHANDAGAZA

10, Ave. de la Justice, 2nd Floor, BP 2894
Maitre Richard RWIHANDAGAZA who is the Managing of the law firm R & Partners founded in February 2006. He is practicing Law as an Advocate since 2001. He holds a Law degree from the National University of Rwanda and a Certificate in Arbitration and Altern ...
Telephone:250 (0)78851 6286
Fax:250-252 510-514
E-mail: rwirich@yahoo.fr

MAITRE ARSÈNE RUTIYOMBA

B.P. 6202, Kacyiru
Maitre Arsène Rutiyomba was born in Nyamugali, Rwanda, in 1963. He graduated from Rwanda National University, Bachelor's Degree in Law in 1992. He then worked as legal consultant at Institut des Sciences Agronomiques 1993-1997 and as attorney from 1998-pr ...
Telephone:250-0788502965
Fax:252 51514
E-mail: rarsene@yahoo.com

MAITRE GATERA GASHABANA

Avenue de la Paix, Immeuble Printerset second floor
Maitre Gatera Gashabana was born in Kalehe, DRC, 1957 and studied law at University of Kinshasa and got Bachelor's Degree in Law, 1985. He worked as attorney at Court of Appeals, Kinshasa, until 1986. Today Gatera is consultant to several Kigali organiza ...
Telephone:250-0788303744, 252 510393
Fax:252 510393

MAITRE MOSES GATAMA KIIZA

2nd Floor, Concord Building, Boulevard de l'Umuganda, Kacyiru, Kigali, P.O.Box: 6381 Kigali
www.equityjurischambers.com
Maitre Gatama Kiiza works for Equity Juris Chambers. He holds a Master's Degree in International Law from McGill University, Montreal, Canada and a Bachelor of Laws Degree from National University of Rwanda specialised in practices inter-alia, civil, bus ...
Telephone:+250 0722203877/ 0788303877/ 0728300981/ 0788300981
Fax:admin@equityjurischambers.com

MAITRE PROJECT KABUREGE

Kigali, Rwanda, B.P. 2623, Kigali

Born in Nyamabuye Gitarama, Rwanda in 1941, Maitre Kaburege holds a law degree from the Belgian university of ULB (Université Libre de Bruxelles). He worked as legal consultant to the Ministry of the Interior, 1983-1992 and as attorney from 1992-present ...
Telephone:250 252 571121 / 0788302328

MAITRE THÉOPHILE KAZENEZA

12, Avenue de la Justice, Kigali, Rwanda
Maitre Théophile Kazeneza was born in Taba, Gitarama, Rwanda in 1965. Graduated from Rwanda National University, Bachelor's Degree in Law, 1993 went on work as legal consultant, 1992-1995; professional representative, 1995-1997 and attorney, 1997-present ...
Telephone:250-0788513203
E-mail: kazetho@yahoo.com

MAITRE CALVIN MITALI

2nd Floor, Concord Building, Boulevard de l'Umuganda, Kacyiru, Kigali, Rwanda, P.O.Box: 6381
www.equityjurischambers.com
Graduate from University of Warwick, United Kingdom, he hold a Master's Degree in International Business Law and a Bachelor of Laws Degree from National University of Rwanda, practicing Corporate, Civil and Labour Law. Languages: English, Kinyarwanda and ...
Telephone:+250 0722203877/ 0788303877/ 0728300981/ 0788300981
E-mail: calvin.mitali@equityjurischambers.com

MAITRE ISAIE MUHAYIMANA

Rue des Cooperatives, N0. 4, SOCOBICO Building, Kigali, Rwanda
Born in Mubuga, Gikongoro, Rwanda, 1951. Maitre Isaie Muhayimana graduated from Rwanda National University with a bachelor's Degree in law in 1977. he worked as magistrate to the Supreme Court, 1977-1981; private practice, 1981-present; practices contract ...
Telephone:250-252 572564 / 0788300698
Fax:252 572919
E-mail: mhayis731@hotmail.com

MAITRE DONATIEN MUCYO

Maitre Donatien Mucyo works at Cabinet MPAYIMANA Isaie, in front of MANUMETAL, Kigali. He was born in born in Minembwe, DRC in 1964. Graduated from University of Lubumbashi, DRC he holds a bachelor's Degree in Law, 1997. Internship in law office since Mar ...
Telephone:0788524528

MAITRE JEAN MARIE VIANNEY MUGEMANA

Kigali, Rwanda, B.P. 2369, Kigali
Maitre Jean Marie Vianney Mugemana was born in Byumba, Rwanda, 1951. Graduated from Catholic University Louvain, Belgium he holds a bachelor's degree in Law, 1976; Special License in Economic Law, 1993. Prosecutor General, 1982-1984, Ministry of Justice, ...
Telephone:00252582343 / 00250 0788300325
Fax:00252 571444

MAITRE LÉOPOLD MUNDERERE

Kigali, Rwanda, B.P. 2264, Kigali
Born in Kivu, Gikongoro, Rwanda, 1966. He graduated from Rwanda National University with a Bachelor's Degree in Law, 1992. Legal consultant to the Ministry of Environment and Tourism; attorney for SORAS and SONARWA; private practices, 1997-present: practi ...
Telephone:250-252 574394 / 002500788503481

E-mail: munderereleopold@yahoo.fr

MAITRE BÉATRICE MUTALIKANWA

B.P. 277, Kigali
Born in Kibungo, Rwanda, 1959. Graduated from Rwanda national University, Bachelor's Degree in Law, 1982. Teacher at Lycée Notre Dame des Citeaux., 1982-1990; training of magistrates, 1994-present; private practice with husband Felicien Mutalikanwa, 1994- **...**
Telephone:00-252 574078 / 00250 0788303135
Fax:00252 571308

MAITRE FÉLICIEN MUTALIKANWA

Kigali, Rwanda, B.P. 277, Kigali
Born in Butare, Rwanda, 1958. Graduated from Rwanda National University, Bachelor's Degree in Law, 1982. Private practices and consulting attorney for commercial enterprises, 1982-present. Languages: French, excellent; English, fair.
Telephone:250-252 574078 / 250 0788300240
Fax:252 571308
E-mail: fmutalikanwa@yahoo.fr

MAITRE CHRISTIAN-JOSEPH NDONDERA

Kigali, Rwanda
Maitre Christian-Joseph Ndondera works at Cabinet d'Avocats, Haguma Associés, Kigali. Born in Bujumbura, Burundi, 1968. Graduated from Rwanda National University, Bachelor's Degree in Law, 1997. Practices general law. Languages: French, excellent; Engl **...**
Telephone:250-252 574591 / 250 0788517266
Fax:252 510514
E-mail: Ndochris@hotmail.com

MAITRE JEAN CHRYSOSTOME NKURUNZIZA

Kigali, Rwanda, B.P. 769, Kigali
Born in Rwanda, 1962. Graduated from Rwanda National University, Bachelor's Degree in Law, 1986. Secretary General of interprofessional union of workers, 1992-1994; attorney, 1993-present: practices civil, criminal, commercial, and administrative law. L **...**
Telephone:250-252 572030 / 252 570610

MAITRE JEAN BOSCO RUSANGANWA

Kigali, Rwanda, B.P. 1890, Kigali
Born in Mudasomwa, Gikongoro, Rwanda, 1967. Graduated from Rwanda National University, Master's Degree in Law, 1993. Attorney and visiting professor, UNR, ULK, and UNILAK: practices general law. Languages: French, excellent; English, fair.
Telephone:250-252 574087 / 252 516758
E-mail: ibrusan@yahoo.fr

MAITRE ATHANASE RUTABINGWA

Avenue Akagera, Kiyovu, P.O. Box 6886
Maitre Athanase Rutabingwa was born in Kampala in 1972. He graduated from the National University of Rwanda with bachelor's Degree in law in 1999. Private Practice from 1999 to date. Specializing in Commercial and Business Law, civil and international la **...**
Telephone:250-0788305784

MAITRE ARSÈNE RUTIYOMBA

Kigali, Rwanda, B.P. 6202
Maitre Arsène Rutiyomba was born in Nyamugali, Rwanda, 1963. Graduated from Rwanda National University, Bachelor's Degree in Law, 1992. Legal consultant, Institut des Sciences Agronomiques 1993-1997; attorney, 1998-present: practices civil and criminal la **...**
Telephone:250-0788502965
Fax:252 51514
E-mail: rarsene@yahoo.com

MAITRE CLAUDINE GASARABWE

11 Rue Bigogwe Kiyovu, Kigali, B.P. 4144
Claudine Gasarabwe was born in Bukavu in 1963. She studied law at University of Burundi, Bachelor's Degree in Law, 1990. Legal consultant in Burundi, 1990-1995; private practice, 1996-present; practices business, banking, labor, and criminal law. Langua **...**
Telephone:250-0788302169 / 252 571098
Fax:252 517383
E-mail: gasarabwe@yahoo.fr

MAITRE THADDEE BARISEBYA

Rubavu, BP: 243 Gisenyi
Maitre Thaddée Barisebya was born in Rubavu in 1965. He holds a bachelor in law from ULK, Gisenyi Campus, 2008. After an intensive training offered by the Danish centre for Human Rights (DCHR) now DIHR, Thaddee worked as a judicial defender (2001 - 2008) **...**
Telephone:+250788527880
E-mail: batayo500@yahoo.fr

TRAVELING TO RWANDA

US STATE DEPARTMENT SUGGESTIONS

COUNTRY DESCRIPTION: Rwanda is a landlocked country in central/east Africa. It is recovering from a civil war and genocide in which as many as one million Tutsis and moderate Hutus were killed. Hotels and guesthouses are adequate in Kigali, the capital, and in major towns, but limited in remote areas.

ENTRY REQUIREMENTS: A passport and evidence of yellow fever immunization are required. Visas are not required for American citizens entering Rwanda for less than 90 days. U.S. citizens planning on working in Rwanda should apply for a work permit at the Department of Immigration as soon as possible after arrival in Rwanda. Detailed entry information may be obtained from the Embassy of the Republic of Rwanda, 1714 New Hampshire Avenue, N.W., Washington D.C. 20009, telephone 202-232-2882, fax 202-232-4544, Internet site: http://www.rwandaemb.org/rwanda/. Overseas inquiries may be made at the nearest Rwandan Embassy or Consulate.

Travelers who wish to travel to the neighboring Democratic Republic of the Congo (DROC) with visas and/or entry/exit stamps from Burundi, Rwanda, Uganda or Zimbabwe may experience difficulties at the DROC airport or other ports of entry. Some travelers with those visas or exit/entry stamps have been detained for questioning in DROC.

AREAS OF INSTABILITY: Most of Rwanda has been calm since the war and genocide ended in July 1994. Insurgents opposed to the current government launched attacks against Rwanda from bases in the DROC beginning in early 1997. While the government has largely brought the insurgency under control, sporadic attacks continue to occur in the northwest. U.S. citizens should avoid travel to the following communes (zones) in the northwest: Ndusu, Gatonde, Giciye, Kinigi, Mutura, Kidaho, Nyamyunba and Kayove. Unexploded ordnance still remains a danger off well-traveled roads in the northwest.

The Government of Rwanda has recently reopened the Parc National des Volcans (translation: Viruga National Park) and will be providing military escorts for those individuals with official passes to track gorillas. Visitors to the park risk being the target of extremist attacks. U.S. citizens are advised not to stay overnight in the park.

U.S. citizens are urged to avoid travel to the border areas between Rwanda and Burundi because of the unstable security situation in Burundi.

REGIONAL TERRORISM: One of the many Hutu rebel factions in the Great Lakes region has committed, and continues to threaten, violence against American citizens and interests. This faction was responsible for the March 1999 kidnapping and murder of several Western tourists, including U.S. citizens, in neighboring Uganda. A Hutu rebel faction was responsible for the kidnapping of four foreign nationals in August 1998 in a region of the DROC which borders Rwanda. Hutu rebel factions are known to operate in northeastern DROC and surrounding areas, including sections of Rwanda, Uganda, Tanzania and Burundi.

CRIME INFORMATION: Pick-pocketing in crowded public places is common, as is petty theft from cars and hotel rooms. The loss or theft of a U.S. passport should be reported immediately to local police and to the nearest U.S. Embassy or Consulate. The pamphlets A Safe Trip Abroad and Tips for Travelers to

Sub-Saharan Africa provide useful information on personal security while traveling abroad and on travel in the region in general. Both are available from the Superintendent of Documents, U.S. Government Printing Office,
Washington D.C. 20402, via the Internet http://www.access.gpo.gov/su_docs or http://travel.state.gov.

MEDICAL FACILITIES: Medical facilities are limited. Some medicines are in short supply or unavailable. Travelers generally bring their own supplies of prescription drugs and preventive medicines. A missionary hospital run by Americans is located in Kibogora, in the southwest of Rwanda, and has some surgical facilities.

MEDICAL INSURANCE: Doctors and hospitals expect cash payment for services. The Medicare/Medicaid program does not provide for payment of medical services outside the United States. Check with your own insurance company to confirm whether your policy applies overseas, including provision for medical evacuation. Ascertain whether payment will be made to the overseas hospital or doctor or whether you will be reimbursed later for expenses you incur. Some insurance policies also include coverage for psychiatric treatment and for disposition of remains in the event of death. Useful information on medical emergencies abroad, including overseas insurance programs, is provided in the Department of State, Bureau of Consular Affairs brochure Medical Information for Americans Traveling Abroad, available via its home page and automated fax service at (202) 647-3000.

OTHER MEDICAL INFORMATION: Malaria is prevalent in Rwanda and there are periodic outbreaks of meningitis. Information on vaccinations and other health precautions may be obtained from the Centers for Disease Control and Prevention hotline for international travelers at 1-877-FYI-TRIP (1-877-394-8747); fax, 1-888-CDC-FAXX (1-888-232-3299); or by visiting the CDC Internet home page at http://www.cdc.gov.

TRAFFIC SAFETY AND ROAD CONDITIONS: While in a foreign country, U.S. citizens may encounter road conditions that differ significantly from those in the United States. The information below concerning Rwanda is provided for general reference only and may not be totally accurate in a particular location or circumstance.

Safety of Public Transportation: Poor
Urban Road Conditions/Maintenance: Fair
Rural Road Conditions/Maintenance: Poor
Availability of Roadside Assistance: Poor

Excessive speed, careless driving and the lack of basic safety equipment on many vehicles are a hazard. Drivers frequently have unexpected encounters with cyclists, pedestrians and livestock. Nighttime driving is particularly hazardous and discouraged. Roadways are often not marked and lack streetlights and shoulders. While the main roads in Rwanda are in relatively good condition, during the rainy season many side roads are passable only with four-wheel drive vehicles. Travelers may be stopped at police roadblocks throughout the country, where their vehicles and luggage may be searched. Service stations are available along main roads. Public transportation can be dangerous due to overloading, inadequate maintenance and careless drivers.

CIVIL AVIATION OVERSIGHT: As there is no direct commercial air service at present, or economic authority to operate such service, between the U.S. and Rwanda, the U.S. Federal Aviation Administration (FAA) has not assessed the Rwandan Civil Aviation Authority for compliance with international aviation safety standards. For further information, travelers may contact the Department of Transportation within the U.S. at 1-800-322-7873. The U.S. Department of Defense (DOD) separately assesses some foreign air carriers for suitability as official providers of air services. For information regarding the DOD policy on specific carriers, travelers may contact DOD at 618-256-4801.

COMMUNICATIONS: Telephone communication to and from Rwanda can be unreliable. Cellular phones and Internet connections are available in Kigali and are generally reliable.

CURRENCY REGULATIONS: The Rwandan franc is freely exchangeable for hard currencies in banks and Bureaux de Change. Several Kigali banks can handle wire transfers from U.S. banks including Western Union. Credit cards are accepted at only a few hotels in Kigali and only to settle hotel bills. Travelers should expect to handle most expenses, including air tickets, in cash.

CRIMINAL PENALTIES: While in a foreign country, a U.S. citizen is subject to that country's laws and regulations, which sometimes differ significantly from those in the United States and may not afford the protections available to the individual under U.S. law. Penalties for breaking the law can be more severe than in the United States for similar offenses. Persons violating Rwandan law, even unknowingly, may be expelled, arrested or imprisoned. Penalties for possession, use, or trafficking in illegal drugs in Rwanda are strict and
convicted offenders can expect jail sentences and heavy fines.

CHILDREN'S ISSUES: For information on international adoption of children, international parental child abduction, and international child support enforcement issues, please refer to our Internet site at http://travel.state.gov/children's_issues.html or telephone 202-736-7000.

REGISTRATION/EMBASSY LOCATION: U.S. citizens who plan to travel to Rwanda are urged to register with the U.S. Embassy and to obtain updated information on travel and security in Rwanda. The U.S. Embassy
is located at Boulevard de la Revolution; the mailing address is B.P. 28, Kigali, Rwanda, telephone 250-75601/75602, fax 250-72128.

PRACTICAL INFORMATRION FOR TRAVELERS

REQUIREMENTS FOR U.S. CITIZENS TO ENTER RWANDA

TOURIST TRAVEL

- U.S. Passport must be valid 3 months beyond intended stay
- Tickets and Documents for return or onward travel
- Visa not required for stay up to 3 months. Eff. Aug 1 1999
- Vaccination: International Certificate of Vaccination for Yellow Fever required.

BUSINESS TRAVEL

- U.S. Passport must be Valid 3 months Beyond Intended Stay
- Tickets and Documents for Return or Onward Travel

- Visa not required for stay up to 3 months. Eff. Aug 1 1999
- Vaccinations - International Certificate of Vaccination required for Yellow Fever.

EMPLOYMENT OR STUDY TRAVEL

Contact the nearest Embassy or Consulate

REQUIREMENTS FOR NON U.S. CITIZENS TO OBTAIN VISA TO ENTER RWANDA

TOURIST VISA

- 1. Your valid, signed, Passport
- 2. 2 Application forms, fully completed and signed
- 3. 2 Passport-type photographs required
- 4. International Certificate of Vaccination for Yellow Fever
- 5. Copy of round trip airline tickets or itinerary, or letter from travel agent

BUSINESS VISA

- 1-4. As Above
- 5. A business letter of responsibility is required, to be typewritten on your company letterhead and addressed to:
- **Embassy of Rwanda, Visa Section, Washington DC**
- **The letter must explain all of the following**
- Nature of business to be performed
- Name and address of reference to be visited
- Guarantee of return transportation and sufficient funds for the visit.
- The letter should be signed by an officer of the company other than the applicant.

PROCESSING INSTRUCTIONS

- Please forward the completed requirements detailed above to:

TRAVEL DOCUMENT SYSTEMS, INC. 734 FIFTEENTH ST N.W. SUITE 400 WASHINGTON D.C. 20005

- Your application will be checked and hand carried to the Embassy, and is usually processed in 72 hours (4 business days).

FEES

- Include one (1) check or money order payable to "TDS Inc." for the TDS service Fee per visa, Embassy Consular Fee per visa, and return postage or Federal Express.
- Tds handling fee: $30.00 per visa
- Consular fee: $30.00 per visa

RETURN POSTAGE

- U.S. Registered Mail: $ 6.50 (Up to 3 passports)
- Federal Express: $15.50 (Up to 3 passports) /Saturday Delivery $10 extra

VISA INFORMATION

- The RWANDA tourist or business visa is usually valid for three months from date issued, for a stay according to the dates specified on your application, not to exceed 90 days.

Information and Fees are Subject to Change. Revised 8/99

GETTING THERE

Diplomatic ties have been restored between the United States and Rwanda. Passport and visa are required. Multiple-entry visa (extendable) for a stay of up to 1 month requires a US$30 fee (cash, check or money order), two application forms, two photos and immunization for yellow fever. Exact date of entry into Rwanda is required with application. Include prepaid envelope or $1.50 postage for return of passport by certified mail.

At the height of the hostilities, when DP asked about entry permission, a spokesperson replied, "We know nothing." Later, after things had calmed down, it seemed the embassy staff had developed a sense of bureaucratic humor. When we asked if there were any Americans in jail in Rwanda, we were told, "We have none; they have been behaving so far." You should know the first of the 12 conditions for entry and stay in Rwanda is that "proper attire and conduct are required of persons staying in Rwanda." The embassy maintains that it is safe to travel in Rwanda.

EMBASSY LOCATIONS

U.S. Embassy in Rwanda
Boulevard de la Revolution
BP 28, Kigali
Tel [250] (7) 5601/2/3
FAX [250] (7) 2128

Embassy of the Republic of Rwanda

1714 New Hampshire Avenue, N.W.
Washington, D.C. 20009
Tel (202) 232-2882

Canadian Embassy in Rwanda

Rue Akagera, BP 1177
Kigali
Tel 73210, FAX: 72719

Rwandan Embassy in Canada

121 Sherwood Drive
Ottawa, Ontario, Canada K1Y 3V1
Tel (613) 722-5835/722-7921
FAX (613) 729-3291

Permanent Mission of Rwanda to the U.N.

124 East 39th Street
New York, NY 10016
Tel (212) 696-0644/46

Consulate General in Chicago

Tel (708) 205-1188
Consulate General in Denver
Tel (303) 321-2400

GETTING AROUND

Rwanda has a total road length of 3036 miles; a mere 286 of them are paved. There are neither railways nor ports. There are eight airfields in the country, three of them with a permanent surface.

Air Rwanda flies internally from Kigali to Gisenyi and Kamembe. Occasionally, you can fly between Gisenyi and Kamembe. Due to the amount of foreign aid into the country, Rwanda's road system isn't too bad. As in neighboring Burundi, the roadways are served by a fleet of relatively late-model Japanese minibuses. The buses leave most towns when they are full. Larger government buses also traverse Rwanda's roads, although they are fewer and farther between. They cost less than the minibuses, but take longer to get to their destinations.

ACCOMMODATION

Hotels: Found mostly in Kigali; they are expensive. Missions with dormitory accommodation are recommended, particularly in remote districts and smaller towns. Ruhengeri and Gisenye mission station hotels are excellent.

Guest-Houses: Outside the main towns there are guest-houses, which are generally cheaper than hotels. There is a guest-house at the edge of the Kagera National Park at Biumba in the northeast of the country.

Camping: This is now forbidden. Rest huts are available on the expedition route in the Virunga Volcanoes.

RWANDA- LARGEST HOTELS

DES MILLE COLLINES HOTEL

PO Box 1322
Kigali
Kigali
Rwanda

Tel No: 76 530/36
Fax No: 76 541
Number of Rooms: 112
Single Room Prices From: 159.85 US Dollars

Pleasant 1970 downtown hotel situated in the business centre of the city. All rooms come with bath, minibar, cable TV and phone; some with balcony. Suites. Bar, snack bar, restaurant, nightclub. Disabled access. Outdoor swimming pool. Free parking. Renovations took place in 1994.

FACILITIES

Car Parking
Conference Facilities
Disabled Facilities
Swimming Pool

LOCATION INFORMATION

Airports: Kigali 100 kms, Gregoire Kayibanda Int'l 11 kms

MERIDIEN UMUBANO HOTEL

Po Box 874
Kigali
Rwanda

Tel No: 82176
Fax No: 83361
Number of Rooms: 92
Single Room Prices From: 133.4 US Dollars

1979 hotel located 5km from city centre. 12 suites, comfortable rooms. 2 restaurants, coffee shop, bar, meetings to 200, safaris arranged. Telex: 22561 HOMER RW ATT: MERIDIEN UMUBANO.

FACILITIES

Conference Facilities
Golf
Swimming Pool
Tennis

LOCATION INFORMATION

Airport: Kigali 8 kms

MONEY

Currency: Rwanda Franc (FRw) = 100 centimes. Notes are in denominations of FRw5000, 1000, 500 and 100. Coins are in denominations of FRw50, 20, 10, 5 and 1.

Credit cards: Accepted at only a few hotels in Kigali. MasterCard is most widely accepted, with more limited use of Diners Club. Check with your credit card company for details of merchant acceptability and other services that may be available.

Traveler's checks: Generally not recommended.

Exchange rate indicators against Sterling and the US Dollar: The following figures are included as a guide to the movements of the Rwanda Franc against Sterling and the US Dollar:

	May'97	Aug'97	Mar'98	Oct'98
£1.00=	496.52	490.10	575.93	525.78
$1.00=	303.22	304.24	348.48	311.03

Currency restrictions: The import and export of local currency is limited to FRw5000. The import and export of foreign currency is limited to the amount declared on arrival.

HOLIDAYS

Jan 1New Year's Day.
Jan 9 Eid al-Fitr (End of Ramadan).
Jan 28 Democracy Day.
Apr 24 Easter Monday.
May 1 Labour Day.
Jul 1 National Holiday.
Jul 4 Independence Day.
Aug 15 Assumption.
Sep 25 Kamarampaka Day.
Oct 26 Armed Forces' Day.
Nov 1 All Saints' Day.
Dec 25 Christmas.

DANGEROUS PLACES

The entire country of Rwanda can be considered unsafe. Travelers are regularly the victims of theft, petty crime and murder. Sporadic violence is a problem in Kigali as well as in the interior. Fighting caused thousands of refugees to flee into neighboring Burundi as well as other countries in the region. In 1996, Paul Kagame ensured the safety of returning refugees and a trickle began returning to Rwanda, many to find their land and dwellings seized by squatters. The northwest has recently swelled with extremist Hutus, many returning from refugee camps in Zaire. This area is becoming a hotbed for insurgent activity. Travelers should use extreme caution everywhere in Rwanda. Do not travel into the troubled areas of Kigali or anywhere in or near Gisenyi. Do not travel after dark.

HEALTH INFORMATION FOR TRAVELERS TO EAST AFRICA

Burundi, Comoros, Djibouti, Eritrea, Ethiopia, Kenya, Madagascar, Malawi, Mauritius, Mayotte, Mozambique, Reunion, Rwanda, Seychelles, Somalia, Tanzania, Uganda

NOTE: Please check the Outbreaks section for important updates on this region, including information on the Epidemic of Meningococcal Disease in Addis Ababa, Ethiopia.

Several cases of African trypanosomiasis (African sleeping sickness) have been reported from this region recently, including cases among tourists visiting game parks. For more information and recommendations on trypanosomiasis, see Travelers' Health Information on African Trypanosomiasis.

Food and waterborne diseases are the number one cause of illness in travelers. **Travelers' diarrhea** can be caused by viruses, bacteria, or parasites, which are found throughout the region and can contaminate food or water. Infections may cause diarrhea and vomiting (E. coli, Salmonella, cholera, and parasites), fever (typhoid fever and toxoplasmosis), or liver damage (hepatitis). Make sure your food and drinking water are safe. (See below.)

Malaria is a preventable infection that can be fatal if left untreated. Prevent infection by taking prescription antimalarial drugs and protecting yourself against mosquito bites (see below). Most travelers to malaria risk areas in this region should take mefloquine to prevent malaria. You can be infected with malaria in all areas of this region except the cities of Addis Ababa, Ismara, and Nairobi, the islands of Reunion and Seychelles, and in highland areas above 2,500 meters. For more detailed information about the risk in specific locations, see **Malaria in East Africa**.

A certificate of yellow fever vaccine may be **required** for entry into certain of these countries. For detailed information, see Comprehensive Yellow Fever Vaccination Requirements.

Dengue, filariasis, leishmaniasis, onchocerciasis, trypanosomiasis (sleeping sickness), and Rift Valley fever are diseases carried by insects that also occur in this region. Protecting yourself against insect bites will help to prevent these diseases.

Schistosomiasis, a parasitic infection, is found in fresh water in the region, including Lake Malawi. Do not swim in fresh water (except in well-chlorinated swimming pools) in these countries. (For more information, please see the Swimming Precautions on the Making Travel Safe page.)

Because motor vehicle crashes are a leading cause of injury among travelers, walk and drive defensively. Avoid nighttime travel if possible and always use seat belts.

CDC Recommends the Following Vaccines (as Appropriate for Age):

See your doctor at least 4–6 weeks before your trip to allow time for shots to take effect.

- Hepatitis A or immune globulin (IG).
- Hepatitis B, if you might be exposed to blood (for example, health-care workers), have sexual contact with the local population, stay longer than 6 months, or be exposed through medical treatment.
- Meningococcal (meningitis) vaccine, if you plan to visit the western half of Ethiopia (see meningitis map) from December through June.
- Rabies, if you might be exposed to wild or domestic animals through your work or recreation.
- Typhoid, particularly if you are visiting developing countries in this region.
- Yellow fever, if you travel anywhere outside urban areas.

- As needed, booster doses for tetanus-diphtheria, measles, and a one-time dose of polio vaccine for adults. Hepatitis B vaccine is now recommended for all infants and for children ages 11–12 years who did not receive the series as infants.

To Stay Healthy, Do:

- Wash hands often with soap and water.
- Drink only bottled or boiled water, or carbonated (bubbly) drinks in cans or bottles. Avoid tap water, fountain drinks, and ice cubes. If this is not possible, make water safer by BOTH filtering through an "absolute 1-micron or less" filter AND adding iodine tablets to the filtered water. "Absolute 1-micron filter" are found in camping/outdoor supply stores.
- Eat only thoroughly cooked food or fruits and vegetables you have peeled yourself. Remember: **boil it, cook it, peel it, or forget it.**
- If you travel to an area where there is risk for malaria, take your malaria prevention medication before, during, and after travel, as directed. (See your doctor for a prescription.)
- Protect yourself from insects by remaining in well-screened areas, using repellents (applied sparingly at 4-hour intervals) and permethrin-impregnated mosquito nets, and wearing long-sleeved shirts and long pants from dusk through dawn.
- To prevent fungal and parasitic infections, keep feet clean and dry, and do not go barefoot.
- Always use latex condoms to reduce the risk of HIV and other sexually transmitted diseases.

To Avoid Getting Sick:

- Don't eat food purchased from street vendors.
- Don't drink beverages with ice.
- Don't eat dairy products unless you know they have been pasteurized.
- Don't share needles with anyone.
- Don't handle animals (especially monkeys, dogs, and cats), to avoid bites and serious diseases (including rabies and plague). (For more information, please see the Animal-Associated Hazards on the Making Travel Safe page.)
- Don't swim in fresh water, including Lake Malawi. Salt water is usually safer. (For more information, please see the Swimming Precautions on the Making Travel Safe page.)

What You Need To Bring with You:

- Long-sleeved shirt and long pants to wear while outside whenever possible, to prevent illnesses carried by insects (e.g., malaria, dengue, filariasis, leishmaniasis, and onchocerciasis).
- Insect repellent containing DEET (diethylmethyltoluamide), in 30%–35% strength for adults and 6%–10% for children. Unless you are staying in air-conditioned or well-screened housing, purchase a bed net impregnated with the insecticide permethrin. (Bed nets can be purchased in camping or military supply stores.)

- Over-the-counter antidiarrheal medicine to take if you have diarrhea.
- Iodine tablets and water filters to purify water if bottled water is not available. See Do's above for more detailed information about water filters.
- Sunblock, sunglasses, hat.
- Prescription medications: make sure you have enough to last during your trip, as well as a copy of the prescription(s).

After You Return Home:

If you have visited an area where there is risk for malaria, continue taking your malaria medication weekly for 4 weeks after you leave the area. If you become ill after your trip—even as long as a year after you return—tell your doctor where you have traveled.

SUPPLEMENT

POWER STATIONS IN RWANDA

HYDROELECTRIC

OPERATIONAL

Hydroelectric station	Community	Coordinates	Type	Capacity (MW)	Year completed	Name of reservoir	River
Ntaruka Power Station	Ntaruka		Run of river	11.5 MW	1959[7]	N/A	Nyabarongo River
Mukungwa Power Station	Mukungwa		Run of river	12 MW	1982	N/A	Nyabarongo River
Mukungwa II Power Station	Mukungwa		Run of river	2.5 MW[8]	2010	N/A	Nyabarongo River
Nyabarongo I Power Station	Nyabarongo		Run of river	28 MW[9]	2014[2]	N/A	Nyabarongo River
Rukarara Hydroelectric Power Station	Rukarara		Run of river	9.5 MW	2010[10]	N/A	River Rukarara
Rusizi I Hydroelectric Power Station	Rusizi		Run of river	30 MW	1958	N/A	Ruzizi River
Rusizi II Hydroelectric Power Station	Rusizi		Run of river	44 MW	1989	N/A	Ruzizi River

PROPOSED

Hydroelectric station	Community	Coordinates	Type	Capacity (MW)	Year completed	Name of reservoir	River
Rusumo Power Station	Rusumo		Run of river	80 MW[1][11]	2018	N/A	Kagera River
Nyabarongo II Power Station	Nyabarongo		Run of river	120 MW[1]	2020	N/A	Nyabarongo River
Rusizi III Power Station	Rusizi		Run of river	147 MW[12]	2020	N/A	Ruzizi River
Rusizi IV Power Station	Rusizi		Run of river	200 MW	2025	N/A	Ruzizi River

THERMAL

OPERATIONAL

Thermal power station	Community	Coordinates	Fuel type	Capacity	Year completed	Name of Owner	Notes
KivuWatt Power Station	Kibuye, Karongi District		Methane	25 MW	2015	Contour Global	Under expansion to 100MW[4]
Kibuye Power Plant 1	Kibuye, Karongi District		Methane	3.5MW	2012	Government of Rwanda	
Gishoma Thermal Power Station	Rusizi District, Western Rwanda		Peat	15 MW	2016	Shengli Energy Group and Punj Lloyd	

PROPOSED

Thermal power station	Community	Coordinates	Fuel type	Capacity	Year completed	Name of Owner	Notes
Gisagara Thermal Power Station	Gisagara District, Southern Rwanda		Peat	80 MW	2020 (expected)	Hakan	
Symbion Thermal Power Station	Nyamyumba, Gisenyi, Rubavu District		Methane	50 MW	2018 (expected)	Symbion Power Inc.	Can be expanded to 100MW

SOLAR

OPERATIONAL

Solar power station	Community	Coordinates	Fuel type	Capacity	Year completed	Name of Owner	Notes
Ngoma Solar Power Station	Kibungo, Ngoma District		Solar	2.4 MW	2011	Government of Rwanda	Operational
Rwamagana Solar Power Station	Agahozo, Rwamagana District		Solar	8.5 MW	2015	Scatec Solar Company & Gigawatt Global Cooperatief[11]	Online

PROPOSED

Solar power station	Community	Coordinates	Fuel type	Capacity	Year completed	Name of Owner	Notes
Kayonza Solar Power Station	Rwinkwavu Kayonza District		Solar	10 MW	2020	Government of Rwanda	Under development

RWANDA DIPLOMATIC MISSIONS

Belgium

Ambassade de la République Rwandaise
1, Avenue des Fleurs
1150 Bruxelles
Phone: (32) 2 7630 738
Fax: (32) 2 7630 753

Burundi

Ambassade de la République Rwandaise
24, Avenue du Zaire
B.P. 400 Bujumbura
Phone: (257) 228 755
Fax: (257) 223 254

Canada

Embassy of the Republic of Rwanda /
Ambassade de la République Rwandaise
121 Cherwood Drive
Ottawa, Ontario
K1 J3 V1
Phone: (613) 722 8350
Fax: (613) 722 4052

China

Embassy of the Republic of Rwanda
30, Xiushui Beijie
100600 Beijing
Phone: (861) 65321820
Fax: (861) 22104

Ethiopia

Embassy of the Republic of Rwanda
Africa Avenue, H-17K-20
No. 001
B.P. 5618 Addis Ababa
Phone: (251) 1 610300 / 610357 / 610987
Fax: (251) 1 610411

France

Ambassade de la République Rwandaise
12, Rue Jadin
75017 Paris
Phone: (33) 1 47 66 54 20
Fax: (33) 1 42 27 74 69

Germany

Botschaft der Ruandischen Republik
Beethovenallee 72
53173 Bonn
Phone: (49) 228 355 228
Fax: (49) 228 351 922

Israel

Embassy of the Republic of Rwanda
30, Heh-B?l-lyor Street
P.O. Box 21572
Tel Aviv
Phone: (972) 3691 2319
Fax: (972) 3696 3408

South Africa

Embassy of the Republic of Rwanda
Suite 113, Infotech Building
1090 Arcadia Street, Hatfield
Pretoria
Phone: (27) 12 342 1741 / 342 1742
Fax: (27) 12 342 1743

Switzerland

Botschaft der Ruandischen Republik /
Ambassade de la République Rwandaise
60 Eigerstrasse
3007 Bern
Phone: (41) 31 301 0611/301 8610
Fax: (41) 31 371 4475

Tanzania

Embassy of the Republic of Rwanda
32, Upanga Road
P.O. Box 2918
Dar es Salaam
Phone: (255) 30119
Fax: (255) 46917

Uganda

Embassy of the Republic of Rwanda
Nakaima Road, Plot No. 2 (near National Museum)
P.O. Box 2468
Kampala
Phone: (256) 41 343 662
Fax: (256) 41 258 547

United Kingdom

Embassy of the Republic of Rwanda
42 AV Lumer Road, No. 2
OBX London
Phone: (44) 171 9302 570
Fax: (44) 171 9302 572

United Nations

Permanent Mission of Rwanda to the United Nations
124 East 39th Street
New York, NY 10016
United States
Phone: (212) 679 9010 / 9023 / 9024
Fax: (212) 679 9133

United States

San Francisco
Scott Heldford
Consulate General of Rwanda
120 Montgomery St.
Suite 950
San Francisco, CA 94104
Phone: (415) 772 9181
Fax: (415) 772-9830

Washington, DC
Embassy of the Republic of Rwanda
1714 New Hampshire Avenue, NW
Washington, DC 20009
Phone: (202) 232-2882
Fax: (202) 232-4544

IMPORTANT ADDRESSES

IMPORTANT ADDRESSES

Office of Tourism and National Parks
Office Rwandais du Tourisme et des Parcs Nationaux (ORTPN)
B.P. 905
Kigali RWANDA

Phone: (250) 76515/7 or (250) 76514
Fax: (205) 76512

Chamber of Commerce and Industry
B.P. 319
Kigali RWANDA

Phone: (250) 83538 or (250) 83541
Fax: 250 83532

HOTELS

Kigali

Baobab Hotel
B.P. 1406
Kigali RWANDA
Phone: (250) 75633, 73281

Guest House Ituze
Kacyiru
B.P. 2797
Kigali RWANDA
Phone: (250) 84289
Fax: (250) 84289

Hotel Chez Lando
Remera
B.P. 1519
Kigali RWANDA
Phone: (250) 82050, 84328
Fax: (250) 84380

Hotel des Diplomates
B.P. 269
Kigali RWANDA
Phone: (250) 75111, 7511
Fax: (250) 75365

Hotel des Mille Collines
B.P. 1322
Kigali RWANDA
Phone: (250) 76530
Fax: (250) 76541

Hotel Isimbi
B.P. 1163
Kigali RWANDA
Phone: (250) 72578, 72581, 75109, 72795
Fax: (250) 75109

Hotel Umubano
B.P. 874
Kigali RWANDA
Phone: (250) 82176, 82177
Fax: (250) 82178

Butare

Hotel Faucon
Butare
B.P. 366 Butare
Butare RWANDA
Phone: (25) 30138 Butare

Hotel Ibis
Butare
B.P. 103 Butare
Butare RWANDA
Phone: (250) 30335 Butare
Fax: (250) 30335 Butare

Ruhengeri

Hotel Muhabura
Kigombe, Ruhengeri
B.P. 118 Ruhengeri
Phone: (250) 46296 Ruhengeri

Hotel Urumuli
Kigombe, Ruhengeri
B.P. 89 Ruhengeri
Phone: (250) 46702 Ruhengeri

TRAVEL AGENTS AND TOUR OPERATORS

Air Master Travel Rwanda
B.P. 10
Kigali RWANDA
Phone: (250) 74931, 73852
Fax: (250) 73853

B.P. 5649
Kampala UGANDA
Phone: (041) 250267

Changa Travel Agency
Avenue de la Justice
B.P. 3246
Kigali RWANDA
Phone: (250) 77564, 77103
Fax: (250) 77669
Represents Air Burundi

Flight Services
B.P. 865
Kigali RWANDA

GTS Gatera Travel Service
B.P. 2520
Kigali RWANDA
Phone: (250) 83866, 82177
Fax: (250) 83867

ITT
(International Tours and Travel Ltd.)
Immeuble SORAS
B.P. 924
Kigali RWANDA
Phone: (250) 74057
Fax: (250) 75582

Nord Sud International Travel and Tours Agency
Avenue de la Paix
B.P. 183
Kigali RWANDA
Phone: (250) 75310
Fax: (250) 75349

Rwanda Tours
B.P. 449
Kigali RWANDA
Phone: (250) 75037
Fax: (250) 85693

Rwanda Travel Bureau
B.P. 1395
Kigali RWANDA
Phone: (250) 77777, 78560
Fax: (250) 78565

Satguru Travel and Tours Service
B.P. 2111
Kigali RWANDA
Phone: (250) 73079
Fax: (250) 72231

SOMACO
B.P. 1108
Kigali RWANDA
Phone: (250) 82847, 77690

Transworld Tours and Travel
10 Avenue de la Paix
B.P. 1003
Kigali RWANDA
Phone: (250) 77472, 77070
Fax: (250) 77473

TRASER
(Travel Agency Services)
Bat. BRD
B.P. 3859
Kigali RWANDA
Phone: (250) 74990
Fax: (250) 73126

Travel Agency Services
B.P. 977
Kigali RWANDA
Phone: (250) 73124

CAR HIRE

Air Master Travel Rwanda
See Travel Agents and Tour Operators

Auto World Company
B.P. 1305
Kigali RWANDA
Phone: (250) 73138, 74390 Kigali
(250) 62652 Gitarama
Fax: (250) 74147

B.P. 12001
Kampala UGANDA
Phone: (041) 533450

EUROPCAR
B.P. 394
Kigali RWANDA
Phone: (250) 72983

GTS Gatera Travel Service
See Travel Agents and Tour Operators

ITT (International Tours and Travel Ltd.)
See Travel Agents and Tour Operators

Nord Sud International Travel and Tours Agency
See Travel Agents and Tour Operators

Orange Line
B.P. 1315
Kigali RWANDA

SOCOR s.a.r.l.
Boulevard de la Revolution
B.P. 10
Kigali RWANDA
Phone: (250) 78646
Fax: (250) 73853

Taxi Service du Rond Point
Hotel des Mille Collines
Phone: (250) 76586

Taxi Service Mille Collines
Hotel des Mille Collines
Phone: (250) 76530
Fax: (250) 76541

TRANSAFRICA
B.P. 2248
Kigali RWANDA
Phone: (250) 74543, 82347
Fax: (250) 72385, 82347

TRASER (Travel Agency Services)
See Travel Agents and Tour Operators

BASIC TITLES ON RWANDA

IMPORTANT!
All publications are updated annually!
Please contact IBP, Inc. at ibpusa3@gmail.com for the latest ISBNs and additional information

TITLE
Rwanda A "Spy" Guide - Strategic Information and Developments
Rwanda A Spy" Guide"
Rwanda Banking & Financial Market Handbook
Rwanda Business and Investment Opportunities Yearbook
Rwanda Business and Investment Opportunities Yearbook
Rwanda Business and Investment Opportunities Yearbook Volume 1 Strategic Information and Opportunities
Rwanda Business in Rwanda for Everyone: Practical Information and Contacts for Success
Rwanda Business Intelligence Report - Practical Information, Opportunities, Contacts
Rwanda Business Intelligence Report - Practical Information, Opportunities, Contacts
Rwanda Business Law Handbook - Strategic Information and Basic Laws
Rwanda Business Law Handbook - Strategic Information and Basic Laws
Rwanda Business Law Handbook - Strategic Information and Basic Laws
Rwanda Business Law Handbook - Strategic Information and Basic Laws
Rwanda Constitution and Citizenship Laws Handbook - Strategic Information and Basic Laws
Rwanda Country Study Guide - Strategic Information and Developments
Rwanda Country Study Guide - Strategic Information and Developments
Rwanda Country Study Guide - Strategic Information and Developments Volume 1 Strategic Information and Developments
Rwanda Diplomatic Handbook - Strategic Information and Developments
Rwanda Diplomatic Handbook - Strategic Information and Developments
Rwanda Ecology & Nature Protection Handbook
Rwanda Ecology & Nature Protection Handbook
Rwanda Ecology & Nature Protection Laws and Regulation Handbook
Rwanda Economic & Development Strategy Handbook
Rwanda Economic & Development Strategy Handbook
Rwanda Energy Policy, Laws and Regulation Handbook
Rwanda Foreign Policy and Government Guide
Rwanda Foreign Policy and Government Guide
Rwanda Immigration Laws and Regulations Handbook - Strategic Information and Basic Laws
Rwanda Investment and Business Guide - Strategic and Practical Information
Rwanda Investment and Business Guide - Strategic and Practical Information
Rwanda Investment and Business Guide - Strategic and Practical Information
Rwanda Investment and Business Guide - Strategic and Practical Information
Rwanda Labor Laws and Regulations Handbook - Strategic Information and Basic Laws
Rwanda Land Ownership and Agriculture Laws Handbook
Rwanda Mineral & Mining Sector Investment and Business Guide - Strategic and Practical Information

TITLE
Rwanda Mineral & Mining Sector Investment and Business Guide - Strategic and Practical Information
Rwanda Mining Laws and Regulations Handbook
Rwanda Privatization Programs and Regulations Handbook
Rwanda Privatization Programs and Regulations Handbook
Rwanda Recent Economic and Political Developments Yearbook
Rwanda Recent Economic and Political Developments Yearbook
Rwanda Recent Economic and Political Developments Yearbook
Rwanda Taxation Laws and Regulations Handbook
Rwanda: Doing Business and Investing in Rwanda Guide
Rwanda: Doing Business and Investing in Rwanda Guide
Rwanda: How to Invest, Start and Run Profitable Business in Rwanda Guide - Practical Information, Opportunities, Contacts

Title
Kuwait Energy Policy, Laws and Regulations Handbook
Libya Energy Policy, Laws and Regulations Handbook
Malaysia Energy Policy, Laws and Regulations Handbook
Mexico Energy Policy, Laws and Regulations Handbook
Morocco Energy Policy, Laws and Regulations Handbook
Namibia Energy Policy, Laws and Regulations Handbook
New Zealand Energy Policy, Laws and Regulations Handbook
Nigeria Energy Policy, Laws and Regulations Handbook
Norway Energy Policy, Laws and Regulations Handbook
Oman Energy Policy, Laws and Regulations Handbook
Pakistan Energy Policy, Laws and Regulations Handbook
Papua New Guinea Energy Policy, Laws and Regulations Handbook
Papua New Guinea Oil & Gas Sector Energy Policy, Laws and Regulations Handbook
Peru Energy Policy, Laws and Regulations Handbook
Philippines Energy Policy, Laws and Regulations Handbook
Qatar Energy Policy, Laws and Regulations Handbook
Sri Lanka Energy Policy, Laws and Regulations Handbook
Romania Energy Policy, Laws and Regulations Handbook
Russia Energy Policy, Laws and Regulations Handbook
Saudi Arabia Energy Policy, Laws and Regulations Handbook
Sudan Energy Policy, Laws and Regulations Handbook
Suriname Energy Policy, Laws and Regulations Handbook
Syria Energy Policy, Laws and Regulations Handbook
Trinidad and Tobago Oil & Gas Sector Energy Policy, Laws and Regulations Handbook
Tunisia Energy Policy, Laws and Regulations Handbook
Turkey Energy Policy, Laws and Regulations Handbook
Turkmenistan Energy Policy, Laws and Regulations Handbook
Ukraine Oil & Gas Sector Energy Policy, Laws and Regulations Handbook
United Arab Emirates Energy Policy, Laws and Regulations Handbook
United Kingdom Energy Policy, Laws and Regulations Handbook
United Kingdom Oil & Gas Sector Energy Policy, Laws and Regulations Handbook
United States Energy Policy, Laws and Regulations Handbook
Venezuela Energy Policy, Laws and Regulations Handbook
Vietnam Energy Policy, Laws and Regulations Handbook
Vietnam Energy Policy, Laws and Regulations Handbook
Yemen Energy Policy, Laws and Regulations Handbook

www.ingramcontent.com/pod-product-compliance
Lightning Source LLC
LaVergne TN
LVHW080035210926
848481LV00011B/3194
9781433072529